Convict Maids

Studies in Australian History

Series editors:
Alan Gilbert, Patricia Grimshaw and Peter Spearritt

Stephen Nicholas (ed.)   *Convict Workers*
Pamela Statham (ed.)   *The Origins of Australia's Capital Cities*
Jeffrey Grey   *A Military History of Australia*
Alastair Davidson   *The Invisible State*
James A. Gillespie   *The Price of Health*
David Neal   *The Rule of Law in a Penal Colony*
Sharon Morgan   *Land Settlement in Early Tasmania*
Audrey Oldfield   *Woman Suffrage in Australia*
Paula J. Byrne   *Criminal Law and Colonial Subject*
Peggy Brock   *Outback Ghettos*
Raelene Frances   *The Politics of Work*
Luke Trainor   *British Imperialism and Australian Nationalism*
Margaret Maynard   *Fashioned from Penury*
Dawn May   *Aboriginal Labour and the Cattle Industry*
Joy Damousi and Marilyn Lake (eds)   *Gender and War*
Michael Roe   *Australia, Britain, and Migration, 1915–1940*
John F. Williams   *The Quarantined Culture*
Nicholas Brown   *Governing Prosperity*
Jan Todd   *Colonial Technology*
Shurlee Swain with Renate Howe   *Single Mothers and Their Children*
Tom Griffiths   *Hunters and Collectors*

Convict Maids

The forced migration of women to Australia

Deborah Oxley

Department of Economic History, University of New South Wales

CAMBRIDGE
UNIVERSITY PRESS

Published by the Press Syndicate of the University of Cambridge
The Pitt Building, Trumpington Street, Cambridge CB2 1RP, UK
40 West 20th Street, New York, NY 10011–4211, USA
10 Stamford Road, Oakleigh, Melbourne 3166, Australia

National Library of Australia cataloguing-in-publication data

Oxley, Deborah.
Convict maids: the forced migration of women to
Australia.
Bibliography.
Includes index.
1. Women convicts – Australia – History. 2. Women –
Australia – History. 3. Convict labor – Australia –
History. 4. Australia – Social conditions – 1788–1851.
5. Australia – Economic conditions – 1788–1851.
I. Title. (Series: Studies in Australian history (Cambridge,
England)).
994.0082

Library of Congress cataloguing-in-publication data

Oxley, Deborah, 1963–
Convict maids: the forced migration of women to Australia/
Deborah Oxley.
    p.   cm. – (Studies in Australian history)
Revision of the author's thesis (Ph.D.).
Includes bibliographical references and index.
1. Convict labor – Australia – History. 2. Penal colonies –
Australia – History. 3. Women prisoners – Australia – History.
4. Women immigrants – Australia – History. I. Title. II. Series.
HV8950.A8095   1996
364.6'8–dc20   95–36710

ISBN 0521 441315 Hardback
ISBN 0521 446775 Paperback

Transferred to digital printing 2000

Contents

List of Illustrations	vi
Acknowledgements	viii
Contemporary Measures and Standards	x
Introduction: Creative Tensions	1
1 Elizabeth: A Note on Data and Method	17
2 Mercury's Charges: The Crimes of Convict Women	34
3 Piso's Justice: Irish and English Offenders	63
4 Economic Accoutrements: The Skills of Convict Women	98
5 Ireland's Distant Shores: Working Life in Ireland	129
6 England's Castaways: Working Life in England	147
7 Colonial Requirements: Coerced and Free Immigrants	171
8 Misconceptions	198
9 Britain's Loss, Australia's Gain? Concluding Remarks	232
Appendices	244
1 Convict Vessels	244
2 Crime Classification	246
3 Stolen Goods Classification	247
4 Social-skill Classification	248
5 Irish Census Classification	249
6 English Census Classification	250
7 Free Immigrant Classification	251
8 Statistical Appendix (with contents list)	251
Notes	274
Bibliography of Works Cited	314
Index	330

Illustrations

MAPS
Ireland   128
England   146

FIGURES
1.1   Broadsheet ballad, 'The London Convict Maid'   16
1.2   Convict indent from the *Competitor*, showing entry for
      Elizabeth Coltman   18
1.3   Convict indent from the *Elizabeth*   22
1.4   Convict indent from the *Pyramus*   24
1.5   Prison photograph of Margaret Greenwood   30
1.6   Female convicts landed in Sydney, 1788–1840   32
2.1   Proportion of women convicts with prior convictions   42
2.2   Categories of crime for which women convicts were
      transported   43
2.3   Crimes and prior conviction rates of women convicts   44
2.4   Categories of property stolen by women convicts   48
2.5   Crimes and duration of sentence of women convicts   56
2.6   The Daisy   61
3.1   Female crime in Ireland and England   68
3.2   Property stolen by women convicts in Ireland and England   69
3.3   Women's prior convictions by country of trial   71
3.4   Women's sentences by country of trial   72
3.5   Female crime in village and town   73
3.6   Property stolen by women convicts in village and town   74
3.7   Female conviction rates and the London Season   89
3.8   Female crime in London and England   91
3.9   Property stolen by women convicts in London and England   93
4.1   Age distributions of women convicts and Irish and English
      women   110

4.2   Age distributions of women convicts and female prisoners   111
4.3   Female mortality on convict voyages   113
4.4   Literacy of Irish and English women convicts   115
4.5   Female convict age distributions and clustering   117
4.6   Skill levels of Irish and English women convicts   122
4.7   Female convict skill and literacy   123
4.8   Skill acquisition of female convicts   124
4.9   Female convict conjugal status and motherhood   126
5.1   Regional origins of women convicts   130
5.2   Literacy and numeracy among Irish women   137
5.3   Literacy among Irish-born convict women   138
5.4   Skill levels among Irish women   139
5.5   Skill levels among Irish-born convict women   139
5.6   Female occupational structures in Ireland   140
5.7   Literacy rates of Irish emigrant convict women   142
5.8   Skill levels of Irish emigrant convict women   143
6.1   Literacy and skill among English-born convict women   159
6.2   Literacy among English adult female paupers and convict
       women   162
6.3   Female illiteracy in England: workers, paupers, prisoners
       and convicts   163
6.4   Skill levels among English women   165
6.5   Female occupational structures in England   165
6.6   Female occupational spread of workers, paupers, prisoners
       and convicts   168
7.1   Original poster, c. 1883   170
7.2   Broadsheet, 1833   174
7.3   Original poster, 1834   176
7.4   Original poster, 1836   177
7.5   Original poster, c.1884   178
7.6   Free and forced immigration to New South Wales, 1788–1840   183
7.7   Age distributions of free and forced immigrants   185
7.8   Literacy rates for free immigrant women and convict women   186
7.9   Literacy rates between England and Ireland's female
       immigrants and women convicts   187
7.10 Occupational profiles of single immigrant women and
       convict women   188
7.11 Advertisements for colonial women workers, 1837   190
7.12 Convict women arrivals, 1832   191
7.13 Female immigrant arrivals, 1836   192

TABLE

4.1   Female convict occupations   119

Acknowledgements

Invariably, books are indebted to a number of sources. On the financial side I must thank the Commonwealth postgraduate research award scheme for funding my PhD studies and in so doing providing the groundwork for this book. Rewriting the thesis into a somewhat more readable form commenced in 1993 during study leave granted by my then employer, the University of Melbourne, continued during my tenure as the George Johnston Scholar in Australian History at the University of Sydney in the first part of 1994, and has finally come to fruition back where it began, in the Department of Economic History at the University of New South Wales, generously supported by a Vice-Chancellor's postdoctoral research fellowship. My thanks to all concerned. On the technical side, Figures 1.1, 7.2, 7.3, 7.4, 7.11, 7.12 and 7.13 have been reproduced in this book with the kind permission of the Mitchell Library, State Library of New South Wales. Figures 1.2, 1.3, 1.4, 1.5, 7.1 and 7.5 have been reproduced with the kind permission of the Archives Authority of New South Wales.

I would also like to express my deepest gratitude to a number of important people, all of whom are in some way represented in this monograph. To Barrie Dyster for his supervision and unstinting willingness to read and re-read chapters of my thesis. To John Beattie, Beverley Kingston and Lyndall Ryan for similar services rendered. Their comments have been invaluable. So too have been those of Peter Oxley, who read several drafts of this manuscript and throughout the whole process engaged willingly in endless discussions on many of the topics involved. To Patricia Daden for assisting with data entry all those years ago, and Beryl Oxley for tirelessly reading out 13 752 rows of seemingly mean- ingless numbers from a computer printout in order to verify their accuracy. To Phillipa McGuinness at Cambridge University Press for her cheerful disposition and faith in this project. Similarly, to Patricia Grimshaw, Carol Oxley, Jeremy Keens, Stephanie Whitlock, Ann Roberts, Susan Thomas, Belinda Holdsworth, Storely Oxley and those already listed, all of whom proffered their interest and encouragement. They have helped make the writing of *Convict Maids* a most enjoyable engagement. To Steve Nicholas for the fun we had doing other (related) work on this database. To Peter Roberts for providing me with the unexpected, a photograph of a convict woman included in my study. A special thanks to my parents for all they have done for me, which is quite simply too much to list. And finally to my love, David Meredith, for being my sounding board, for many insightful conversations about convicts, and for doing all the graphs in this book!

Deborah Oxley

Contemporary Measures and Standards

CURRENCY

References to sums of money are in the imperial measure:
£   pounds sterling
s   shillings
d   pence
£1 = 20s
1s = 12d
The following figures are for England in 1824–25.

FEMALE WAGE RATES

Occupation	Per Annum £	Per Week
Housemaid	10–16	3s 10d – 6s 2d
Under-housemaid	8–10	3s 1d – 3s 10d
Lady's maid	14–16	5s 5d – 6s 2d
Average female servant	12	4s 7d
Silk worker	13	5s

Note: 1 London money wages tended to be higher.
2 Monetary wages of domestic servants were supplemented through employer provision of food and lodging. Consequently, money wages represented only one-third to one-half of total compensation.
3 Silk, other textile and factory workers were hired on a weekly basis with no security of tenure, so their real annual income was likely to be significantly below £13 when allowing for sickness, non-attendance, and insufficient labour demand. Additionally, they did not typically receive food and lodging, making their money wage approximate their total compensation.

PRICES OF SOME STAPLE FOODS

Staple	Quantity	Price
Bread	4 pound (1.8 kg) loaf	10½d
Wheat		66s 2½d
Barley }	quarter hundredweight (12.7 kg)	38s 2d
Oats		25s 3d

Sources: Primary sources on wages .quoted in T. McBride, *The domestic revolution: The modernisation of household service in England and France, 1820–1920* (London 1976), pp. 62–3; on prices quoted in B. R. Mitchell and P. Deane, *Abstract of British historical statistics* (Cambridge 1962), pp. 488, 498.

For my parents, Beryl and Peter

Introduction: Creative Tensions

White Australia has a very short history. Even so, it is inadequately understood. As with many other histories of settler societies, there are areas of blindness relating to the nature of the invasion and the ongoing process of dispossessing the original inhabitants. Perhaps a certain distaste for such origins accounts for a tendency to view that period as alien, its inhabitants foreign. Aborigines were so different as to be considered incomprehensible, when considered at all. Similarly, Australia's convicts were disregarded as criminal outcasts, yet another blight on Australia's beginnings to be overcome.

Passage of time, altered historical methods, groundswell changes in the foci of historical enquiry, have brought forward a new tale. Slowly our eyes are opening to witness the complexity of factors and interrelationships which formed our society over the last two centuries. At last we no longer exclude these groups entirely from our historical research. Conflict, costs, collaboration, interactions—these are terms we now find in the literature.[1] Recent times have also seen convict history rewritten: convict men built this country.[2] This was the beginning of a flow of immigrants who would fertilise Australia's shores. These men—this human capital—underpinned development. The status of their labour was elevated.

Yet significant gaps remain. Not all convict labour has been thus rewarded. Notably, women are absent from the story of colonial economic development. We know women were there, albeit in fewer numbers than men, but we do not know enough about what women did in the colony. We do not know what work they performed, nor the terms on which they formed relationships, nor the part they played in invasion. Bits of their story are understood, but in the grand narrative of colonial growth, women are strangely missing. Our lack of knowledge is treated as their lack of activity. At best they appear as a misspent resource, at worst as drunken, refractory nuisances draining the colony dry. Can this really be the entire story?

Gendering colonial economic development is no easy task. It involves discerning the parts played by men and women in expanding the

1

economy, and giving each status. Work typically done by women should not be ignored. Reproduction and the household sector need to be placed alongside the paid sector if we are to understand the functioning of the economy as a whole and the multiplicity of roles women played.[3] And if the economy is broken down into non-market and market sectors, the latter further fragmented by sexually segregated labour markets, then we also need to understand how these fragmented parts formed and interacted. For example, how did convict women responsible for unpaid childcare participate in paid work? If they could not partake, how did they survive—dependence on the state, or upon a man, or in some other way? If a man had a wife and child to support, what type of work did he seek, and what type of home was created?

Several stages are involved in building gender into our analysis of Australia's colonial economy. Before we are able to assess the dynamics of the colony, it is necessary to ascertain what its raw materials—its building blocks, the convicts—were like. Firstly, we need to know who the convict women were: dissipated idlers and abandoned whores, or potential workers and mothers. This requires us to investigate the nature of their crimes and assess what type of criminals we are dealing with. Their backgrounds as workers then need considering. What type of skills did female convicts bring to New South Wales? What had been their experiences of working life? Were they a cross-section of British and Irish workers, or perhaps the sweepings of the gaols? Perhaps they differed from workers in other ways. And if it appears that convict women were possessed of a range of working abilities, were these skills redundant or were they suited to colonial requirements? What accounts for the 'bad press' these women have received?

The story of colonial socio-economic development will not be told convincingly until the above questions are answered, and they will not be answered without an extensive quantitative study which pulls together detailed information on the backgrounds of these individual women who were part of Australia's coerced immigration. How many women, what ages, transported from which county in what year—these are important pieces of the jigsaw, but they need assembling to become meaningful. A mere inventory is not enough. This is a history that more than most needs contextualising in its broader international setting, because white Australia was the product of policies written and enforced 12 000 miles away on the other side of the globe, built on the labour of people whose life experiences from birth to transgression were quintessentially Irish and English, with some Scottish and Welsh thrown in. Writing this history means delving into many topics and alighting on others: the nature of crime and punishment in a period of immense change when laws were rewritten, police forces first emerged, and penitentiaries were conceptualised; paths of economic development and disintegration in Ireland as it dealt with absentee landlords and a rapidly growing and powerful close neighbour; the impact of English industrialisation on working-class living standards and the position of women in the economy and society; the value of 'women's work'; the interaction between households and markets; the nature of colonial economic development; and transportation as one stream in the worldwide migrations of the nineteenth century. Once we understand the potential (and limitations) of the female labour supplied to the colonial economy, we can meaningfully evaluate the various roles of convict women in this newly invaded land as workers, lovers, mothers, partners or adversaries with men. It is at this point that we can answer whether convict women were economically irrelevant, or a resource misspent by a wasteful state, or an active group of women hidden from history. We can move away from women's history and men's history, from separate analyses of household and market sectors, to an integrated history which values all contributions irrespective of the accidents of birth, be they ethnicity or sex. *Convict Maids* is a first step, asking, who were the female convicts?

Convict origins

There are compelling grounds for reassessing female convict origins. Decades of historical enterprise have led to certain tensions within the literature, with a fundamental mismatch between convict backgrounds and characters (perceived as negative) and convict achievements (undoubtedly positive). Let us begin by exploring how this literature has evolved.[4]

In answering who the female convicts were, reference needs to be made to the broader enquiry, who were the convicts? Three factors united the 24 960 women and 132 308 men transported to Australia: all were judged guilty of breaking the law, all had been found out, and all were being punished with transportation.[5] While some may have been wrongfully accused and convicted, we must assume that most were justly dealt with by the laws of the time. These common elements have led many commentators to unite convicts in other ways, perceiving them as a homogeneous social entity, as a *class* of people.

Convicts were dealt with compassionately in the early twentieth century. Nineteenth-century disdain for convicts was lessened as time put distance between the colonial society organised hierarchically around convict/free status and the society which succeeded it. The early twentieth century brought forward sympathetic historians writing about multifaceted oppressions in Britain and Ireland which were responsible for creating convicts: these people were not deplorable, aberrant criminals, but admirable political rebels and morally innocent village Hampdens.

The most influential historian in this field was George Arnold Wood.[6] Recently arrived from England to take up the Chair of History at the University of Sydney in 1891, Wood did not suffer any debilitating intellectual inheritance of Australia's 'convict stain'. Instead he was influenced by contemporary British research into village labourers, state welfare and trade unionism undertaken by the likes of the Webbs and the Hammonds.[7] Wood was a traditional historian, and he used traditional historical tools. He read letters, the many volumes of *Historical Records of Australia*, and Molesworth's 1838 report on transportation, and he employed other qualitative evidence. From these he concluded that most convicts were, in essence, the victims of a terribly unjust legal system which disproportionately represented the interests of the aristocracy. Convicts were 'more sinned against than sinning', their sentences imposed by 'blustering ruffians of the Bench' who 'hanged as many of them as their notions of decency permitted, and those who could not, in their opinion, decently be hanged, they branded with the convict brand and shipped to "Botany Bay".'[8] Antagonism between aristocrats and criminals arose, 'not because convicts were more immoral than aristocrats, but because convicts were men who in various ways disturbed the comfort of aristocrats'.[9] Wood effectively negated the convicts' crimes as justifiable acts of social rebellion, or temporary solutions to poverty, manufactured by oppressive and inequitable economic and social systems. He argued that 'the greatest English criminals remained in England' on the court benches and in the House of Lords.[10]

In fact, for Wood, the convicts were more moral than the class who condemned them. In a question which must have generated some ire back in 1921, Wood asked a meeting of the Royal Historical Society, 'did any convict family ever live in New South Wales more disreputable in respect to personal morality than the royal family of England?'[11] Finally, the charge was made. 'We should not condemn the criminal convicts until we have first condemned, and with a far severer condemnation, the criminal lords and bishops who created a condition of society in which criminality was so inevitable that he who understands will forgive and even forget.'[12] Convicts were victims. Primarily they were country-folk: small-time farmers made landless as the Enclosure movement consolidated land holdings, and rural workers made redundant by increasingly efficient agricultural production. Faced with economic hardship, these people had little alternative but to steal to supplement meagre earnings, or no earnings at all. Their acts were political. But not everyone was willing to forgive and forget. This benevolent view did not go unchallenged.

Three decades after Wood's seminal article the ground shifted in the convict origins debate. The major works reinvestigating convict origins were by Manning Clark, Lloyd Robson, A. G. L. Shaw and H. S. Payne.[13]

Using new data and new techniques, Clark, Robson and Shaw overturned Wood's findings. Shaw's methodology was again largely that of the traditional qualitative historian, but he called on the results of the other two researchers to back up different claims. Clark in the early 1950s and Robson in the first half of the 1960s, however, broke new ground by employing hitherto neglected sources in a quantitative manner, and also broke with the reigning orthodoxy on convict class origins. So too did Payne utilise similar methods, but to different ends. Payne's was the dissenting but unheard voice, demonstrating through a quantitative study of female convicts in Tasmania a picture consistent with that of Wood. Yet it is the works of Clark, Robson and Shaw which have underpinned subsequent research and interpretation, and which repeatedly surface even in the most recent books such as *The Fatal Shore* by Robert Hughes.[14]

The new source was the convict indents, and the new method was quantitative. The extent to which Clark's methodology was truly empirical is arguable: his two major articles, published in *Historical Studies* in 1956, do present some figures, but details of the sample are not given. Among the women convicts, he appears to have surveyed just a few hundred. As with much of Clark's work, these articles are largely influenced by subjective assessments formulated on impressionistic readings of qualitative sources and, indeed, when the empirical evidence conflicted with his expectations, it was rejected. Robson, however, was rigorously empirical in his method, although again there are weaknesses with the interpretations. Robson, Clark's postgraduate student, undertook a substantial quantitative study of the transportees to the eastern colonies, based on a systematic sample of 5 per cent of convicts, collecting every twentieth individual listed in the indents, providing a database of more than 7000 cases (1248 of them women) which he handled without the aid of computer. Instead, Robson employed punch cards and a knitting needle. Not surprisingly, the output was basically descriptive statistics, which were then located within a framework of qualitative evidence. What conclusions did these historians reach?

A particular and resilient theme emerged, resurrecting a nineteenth-century notion: convicts belonged to a professional criminal class. Indeed, next to those hanged for their sins, Australia's convicts were considered the very worst members. These were professional criminals or, in the case of women, professional prostitutes, who lived entirely through crime, choosing not to work because legitimate employment was too bothersome or because they had been trained for no other life. More than this, the term 'class' was meant to denote that this professionalism was widespread and organised.

To Shaw the convicts were 'professional and habitual criminals', 'ne'er-do-wells' springing from '"the dregs of society"', commonly trained from the cradle ... All in all they were a disreputable lot'.[15] More conservatively, Robson concluded, 'the convicts were neither simply "village Hampdens" nor merely "ne'er-do-wells from the city slums". But if the Hampdens are placed at one side of a scale, and ne'er-do-wells on the other, the scale must tip towards the ne'er do-wells'.[16] On the other hand, Clark found categorically that 'the evidence ... shows quite clearly that the convicts in the main were recruited from the criminal classes of Great Britain and Ireland', a class to which convicts 'belonged by taste and circumstance'.[17] Clark concurred with Friedrich Engels, finding that 'the town thief was not the handicraftsman reduced to destitution by the introduction of machinery, or the worker affected by the alternate booms and slumps of capitalist society, but a man practising the craft of the lowest rung of the working classes'.[18] What were these? 'Theft and prostitution were the main occupations of those born to filth and wretchedness'.[19]

Allegations of whoredom particularly attracted historical attention, and were used to spice the colonial story. One factor that Clark, Robson and Shaw did share with their *bête noire*, Wood, was a belief in the women's prostitution. Wood, however, was less inclined to damn the women on these grounds. He declared, 'the immorality of the convict women was far less guilty than the immorality of British seamen and British officers'.[20] Other historians held a different opinion. Often on the basis of little more than selective contemporary remarks, a number of significant historians concluded that the women presented what they (moralistically) considered to be a rather revolting picture. Readily historians invoked appearance as their descriptive metaphor. Lloyd Robson's examination led him to believe 'the picture presented of the women convicted and transported to Australia is not an attractive one'.[21] In the eight lines of his book dedicated to females, A. G. L. Shaw, in similar theme, wrote that although 'how many were prostitutes will never be known, almost all contemporaries regarded them as particularly "abandoned"; and even if these contemporaries exaggerated, the picture they presented is a singularly unattractive one'.[22]

In Robson's favour, he did attempt to quantify how many of the women were prostitutes. Relying on reports made by gaolers and surgeon-superintendents (who, Robson failed to recognise, frequently confused promiscuity and cohabitation with prostitution) and occasionally taking the word of the woman herself, Robson estimated that about 20 per cent of the female convicts transported to Van Diemen's Land (the only ones for whom this information was recorded) had been prostitutes.[23] However, overlooking the four-fifths who were not prostitutes by his own estimation, Robson concluded, somewhat surprisingly, that these women were 'a bad lot'.[24] He continued: 'But though primary sources agree on the generally bad character of these females, it would not do to conclude that most were prostitutes. That many were, there is no doubt'.[25] Yet Robson himself demonstrated there was doubt. The feeling left by his analysis is one of some women being found *guilty* of the charge of prostitution. Prostitution was not an indictable offence—it was not tried before a judge or bench of magistrates—and could not be punished with transportation.[26] But why was prostitution of such significance anyway?

. Because prostitution was judged to be evidence of immorality. Prostitution and badness were confused. It was not a measure of illegality, it was not seen as a function of an economy in which women were disadvantaged, or, indeed, as a comment on patriarchal relations, but it was seen as proof of convict women's depravity. These were the 'notorious strumpets and dangerous girls' which peppered nineteenth-century accounts.[27] Convict women were of 'bad character', though not all bad enough to be 'prostitutes': that was the claim. This was the simple equation: prostitution was 'bad'. And, despite Robson's caveat, the equation was read the other way too: women who were 'bad' were classified whores. Demonstrably convict women were bad because they broke the law. The inevitable followed. Time and again the theme rings out, 'convict men were drunken and demoralized professional criminals, and most of the women equally drunken and demoralized prostitutes'.[28] Without explanation or source, 'many were prostitutes'.[29] 'A significant (but unascertainable) number of women transported were prostitutes'.[30] (If the number is not ascertainable, how is it known to be significant?) But we do not know—and perhaps cannot know—how many women sold sex for a living. If we did possess this information, what would we make of it?

Sadly, more attention was devoted to labelling convict women as prostitutes than to exploring any other aspect of their lives. Even the concept of prostitute that was employed was limited and unhelpful, conceptualised as about morality rather than work. Limited, it was also limiting, leaving great areas unprobed, such as the skills convict women brought with them, the work they did in the colony, the relationships they formed, the families they bore, or the homes they made. Even if it was unintentional, these authors have been interpreted as having promoted the notion that there was a criminal class in Britain comprised of habitual and professional criminals, that the convicts belonged to it, and that the women of this class were, above all else, immoral whores.

Such images are dangerous. Subsequent historians accepted Robson *et al.* as demonstrating the criminal-class origins of Australia's convicts 'beyond reasonable doubt'.[31] This has had a deep and profound effect on colonial Australia's historiography with serious ramifications. Belief in a criminal class led Humphrey McQueen to describe Australian society as a 'deformed stratification ... vomited up by the forces delineating class in

Britain', while both Manning Clark and Miriam Dixson depicted it as 'a cold and barren society'.[32] Calculations estimating the net cost-benefit of transportation may be perverted if recidivism rates are misunderstood due to expectations of habitual criminality; 'currency lads and lasses'—the white children born in the colony—might shine more brightly for having their convict parents act as a foil; and cruel practices may be more readily justified if convicts were irredeemably bad.[33] Most significant of all, and so noticeable in the classic texts on Australian economic history, convicts as aberrant and immoral non-workers disappear from the story of colonisation.[34]

Cracks in the looking glass

In the 1970s and 1980s this stereotype of female convict depravity began to crack. Responding to the implicit inequality, and moved by the second wave of feminism that had just swept Australia's shores, came the works of Miriam Dixson and Anne Summers.[35] Dixson and Summers placed women back on the agenda of historical enquiry but worked within the dominant portrayal of female whoredom, seeking to reinterpret what it meant rather than to question its fundamental validity. Prostitution, like marriage, was part of the female condition under patriarchy in which women traded sexual services for economic support. Focusing on sexual exploitation highlighted systemic discriminations, but to an extent robbed convict women of agency. Women in Dixson's colonial story emerged as 'the victims of victims', an outcast group which provided an outlet for male hostilities bred of male servitude. Women's lot was subject to violence, brutality. Summers too portrayed a dismal status for women at the mercy of the 'imperial whoremaster'. Focusing on the Australian end, she asserted 'that many of the women were whores is beyond dispute', but recast prostitution as a female occupation foisted upon women transportees by the denial of official accommodation and support, leaving them with no alternative but to prostitute themselves for survival.[36] Enforced whoredom added a unique dimension to women's punishment not experienced by their male counterparts. However, in Summers' story women did not accept their low status compliantly: their spirits were refractory and their actions rebellious.

Self-consciously returning to the visual imagery of earlier writers, in 1978 Michael Sturma wrote a challenging piece entitled 'Eye of the Beholder: the Stereotype of Women Convicts'.[37] Sturma used the more positive findings made by Robson and Clark relating to the women's crimes and occupations prior to transportation, allowing the women to be located in their economic context. Sturma also highlighted the confusion that existed over the issue of prostitution. Nineteenth-century critics (and twentieth-century historians) had confused cohabitation with promiscuity, and the latter with fee for service. That *de facto* relationships were common among the working classes in Britain had not been recognised by largely middle-class commentators, helping to cement the identity established between female criminals and sexual immorality.

> An almost obsessional interest in 'feminine sin', more than a devised policy of social control, influenced perceptions of the women transported. This is not to imply mere prudery. It was related in part to the growing predominance of middle-class values. Added to this, of course, was a preoccupation with sex which was the concomitant of an emerging cult of respectability.[38]

The following year Portia Robinson reiterated this theme, pointing out the now infamous calculation made by Samuel Marsden. Marsden was concerned with the degree of immorality in the colony, and set about classifying every adult female into the categories 'wives' (including a few widows) or 'concubines', and children as either 'legitimate' or 'illegitimate'. All those not married in the Church of England were deemed concubines. In 1806 this meant in excess of 70 per cent of the female population, some 1035 women out of a total 1430.[39] Also referring to that year, Deirdre Beddoe refuted the extent of prostitution among Welsh convict women prior to their colonial subjection to the 'royal pimp', critically appraising contemporary comments from both British and Australian ends.[40] Uni-dimensional representations of female convicts had arisen from earlier historians' indiscriminate acceptance of biased nineteenth-century opinions that erroneously identified the women as abandoned prostitutes.

The characterisation of *all* convict women as drunken whores was rejected as an outlandish and class-based accusation not bounded by fact.[41] In its place was acknowledgement that before transportation some women engaged in prostitution, but prostitution was considered work (a realisation undoubtedly familiar to women engaged in the trade).[42] It was one economic option. Beddoe argued that destitute women turned to prostitution to ameliorate their poverty before they considered turning to crime.[43] This is not a new claim. Daniel Defoe recognised this in 1711: 'men rob for bread, women whore for bread'.[44] The nineteenth-century social commentators Henry Mayhew and John Binny declared, in almost disparaging tones, that women 'have no necessity to resort to the more daring career of theft to supply their wants, but have only to trade upon their personal charms in order to secure the apparent luxury of an idle life'.[45] That the motive was idleness rather than want was disputed. Women 'on the town' told Mayhew that prostitution was a means of providing food for their families, even if the job was unpalatable.[46] One young woman, a prostitute, was interviewed by another critic as part of the research for a book entitled *My Secret Life*. Critically, the author asked, 'Well, what do you let men fuck you for? Sausage rolls?' Her rebuttal: 'Yes, meat-pies and pastry too.'[47]

Prostitution was one option for survival, ranked lower than other forms of non-sexual work but above crime, for some women although presumably not all. However, these three options were not discrete. Ordinary work melded with prostitution, and both on occasions joined hands with crime. Just as unemployment could create poverty, so too could low pay, and Mayhew found practising hat-binders and pastry-cooks—to name but two professions—numbered among London's prostitutes.[48] Additionally, more recently Robinson has emphasised how whoredom was a structural and complementary aspect of other forms of employment, with house servants expected to 'oblige' the master and his sons, willingly or not.[49] Prostitution, harassment and sexual abuse were part of many women's working lives, but they were not measures of female immorality.

Ending the obsession with 'feminine sin' allowed research to progress in other directions, creating a far more vibrant picture of female convicts than had hitherto been seen. More conscious of the biases embedded in nineteenth-century opinions, historians began both to question these sources and to seek alternative evidence. Robinson's work on the first forty years of settlement indicated that convict women were small-time first offenders suffering from the harsh conditions prevailing in Britain.[50] In her perceptive yet greatly neglected study of Welsh convict women, Beddoe comprehensively examined the circumstances, motives, demographic and occupational features of her chosen women, as well as their experiences voyaging to Australia and those in the colony.[51] In 1983 John Williams similarly suggested that Irish convict women sent to Van Diemen's Land were nowhere near as reprobate as hitherto thought.[52] Transported female felons began to reveal their greater depths. In 1962 Ken Macnab and Russel Ward wrote that the first generation of native-born whites demonstrated an 'extraordinary change for the better in the character, as compared with that of their parents', a change that happened *in spite* of their convict parents and not because of them.[53] In 1985 Portia Robinson overturned this view. From 'weak beginnings' came a more admirable 'hatch and brood of time', but the reforming drive was maternal and therefore convict.[54] New research meant that in Australia convict women had attained value as 'good mothers'. Monica Perrott demonstrated that at least in the early years women had also been active economic agents: for example as publicans, dealers, housemaids and kitchenmaids, cooks, nurses, field workers, textile producers, mantua makers and sempstresses.[55]

Life in the Female Factory at Parramatta was revealed by Hilary Weatherburn and Annette Salt: this was a place of often cruel secondary punishment, but also a lying-in hospital, a point of distribution for assigned convicts, and a house of industry.[56] Less intended by colonial officials, the factory was a female enclave and a site of sisterly insurgence. Katrina Alford highlighted the nexus between production and reproduction that was so crucial in women's lives.[57] Other historians, such as Alan Atkinson, Marian Aveling, Michael Belcher, Paula Jane Byrne, Kay Daniels, Mary Murnane and Martin Sullivan, emphasised the agency and resourcefulness shown by convict women in the courts, the male-dominated marriage market and in the economic arena where servant and master fought their traditional battles, but with different ammunition.[58] Sturma continued his work and witty titles, producing an analysis of what he ironically called *Vice in a Vicious Society*, suggesting New South Wales was not nearly so vile as reputed.[59] Michael Roe and, more recently, John Hirst have stressed how white settlement quickly adopted the features of a free society.[60] Marilyn Lake further questioned the factors influencing female convict imagery with its dichotomies of moral/immoral, contented/discontented, good/bad, and went on to suggest that representations of convict women as victims and as agents need not be mutually exclusive.[61] Robinson's extensive study of convict lives came to fruition in *The Women of Botany Bay*, providing detailed background information on about five thousand women.[62] Around the same time Babette Smith produced *A Cargo of Women*.[63] This book dealt with a smaller number—some ninety-eight women transported with one of Smith's progenitors, Susannah Watson—but also portrayed a rich picture of existence and the negotiations that made life what it was in England and the colony. Most recently, Lyndall Ryan drew attention to the complexity of female convict experience and its variability according to the time and place involved. She identified three crucial phases in female transportation: commencing in 1788 with a focus on exile; moving in 1814 to a system of forced domestic labour administered through assignment to private masters, and punctuated by confinement in the Female Factory for women who transgressed or became pregnant; and finally, in the last ten years of transportation to Van Diemen's Land from 1843, to the probation period based on incarcerating and observing the women and from which freedom was won through hard labour, good conduct and the desire to reform.[64]

Creative tensions

A new image has thus emerged of who female convicts were once they arrived in the colony, but this has led to an unresolved tension in the literature.[65] There is a fundamental mismatch. The legacy of the 1950s and 1960s research was an image in which convict origins lay in an outcast professional criminal class, the women immoral whores, with the obvious corollary that convicts would make poor workers and parents in the colony. Three decades of research later, it appears that in Australia convicts were successful in establishing a socio-economic system which quickly replicated aspects of the Anglo-Celtic culture that spawned the settlement, moving rapidly to the status of a 'free society' in which female convicts laboured as workers, wives, lovers and mothers. How had such a transition been possible if the fundamental building blocks of the society—the convicts—had been the poorly trained and poorly socialised beings that the earlier historiography claimed? Depraved origins sit uncomfortably with colonial success. There are two possible solutions to this bewildering situation: either the colonial economy was extremely reformatory, or the orthodoxy on convict origins is wrong.

Without a resolution to this conundrum, much work takes on a schizophrenic character. Robinson's work demonstrated how in Australia, convict women ran small businesses, employed others, and practised skilled trades.[66] Their 'responses to colonial opportunities and disadvantages were as stridently varied and determinative as were those of the women who came free and unconvicted'.[67] They made good mothers. On the origins of convict women, however, Robinson wrote that the (English) women arrived as 'one class, the damned whores of the criminal haunts of Britain'.[68] Convict women's bad reputation came not from the colonial end, but from Britain.[69] In part this was unjust. Contemporaries damned the women solely because of their status as convicted felons, drawing no distinction between thieves or murderers and classifying all as 'felons of the darkest complexion'.[70] Robinson identified that convict women's lives were hard, marked by poverty, squalor and limited opportunities for improvement.[71] But this translated into a belief that the women came from one level of society, the 'poorest and worst criminal elements in Britain and Ireland', comprised of people who were unemployed, unskilled and unenterprising.[72] Tainted class origins from 'the lowest order of society' meant that convict women

> did not, therefore, bring with them to New South Wales a familiarity with, or expectation of, those standards, values, customs, obligations and privileges which were an intrinsic part of the British hierarchical social system. Instead, they brought with them the memories of experiences which had resulted directly from their economic and social background as members of the lowest order of British society.[73]

Robinson recognised this 'apparent dichotomy between the feckless nature of the convicts in Britain, transported because they thieved and stole rather than worked, and the respectability they gained in the penal colony as a direct result of their own labour and economic achievements', but identified its resolution as the dynamic leading to the development of Australian society.[74]

Herein lies the central contradiction, the unresolved tension in the literature: how could women unfamiliar with ordinary working and family life adapt so well to Australian conditions? How could women of 'no trade' practise skilled work? Perhaps, given the opportunity, women reformed. Robinson found 'the land itself a major determinative in influencing and shaping the society'.[75] But sunshine cannot impart skills where none hitherto existed, and who was there to teach these female skills in a colony populated with convicts, with so few free working-class women? Nor is it explained why criminals who chose not to work in England would want to change their minds in New South Wales. If the answer is not reform (and I am not discounting the possibility entirely), is it perhaps that the old characterisation of convict origins is wrong? It is precisely this 'apparent dichotomy' which throws doubt on the original characterisation of convict women as belonging to a professional criminal class, and demands that we reassess convict origins.

Agenda

Anticipating the shifting story of colonial Australia, several historians had already commenced a re-evaluation of convict backgrounds with preliminary investigations suggesting that Welsh women, some Irish women in Van Diemen's Land, a shipload here, a boatload there, were not the reprobates some thought.[76] Responding to this tension on a broader front was the 1988 publication *Convict Workers: Reinterpreting Australia's Past*.[77] This provided the largest and most comprehensive analysis of some 20 000 transportees sent to New South Wales. In a series of conclusions, this book found that 'the convicts transported to Australia were ordinary British and Irish working-class men and women. They were not professional and habitual criminals, recruited from a distinct class and trained to crime from the cradle'; that the immigration of male convicts was 'effective', that the convict men brought useful skills to Australia and that these were efficiently allocated through a labour market manipulated by the government.[78] Such findings represent a significant maturing of recent attitudes towards convicts and convict Australia which have, over the last three decades, fitted increasingly uneasily with the dominant explanation of convict origins which claimed that ancestry lay within a 'criminal class'. But these findings are mostly about convict *men*. Was the same true for convict women?

The image presented of female convicts as damned whores originating from a professional criminal class, unskilled in all but vice and unfit to contribute anything positive to colonial development—or simply that they were criminals and prostitutes from the 'lowest orders' of British society with few useful skills—still needs challenging. The issue remains unresolved for that large group of women landing in New South Wales in the peak period of transportation. *Convict Maids* attempts a resolution, reassessing convict women as criminals and as workers.

Chapter One briefly introduces the cast, data and method employed in examining these issues. Criminality is the theme explored in Chapters Two and Three. The first of these begins with a brief discussion of Britain's changing criminal code and then launches into the question of what sort of criminals the convict women were: professional members of a criminal class, or workers who occasionally stole. Answers are sought through an analysis of past criminal records, the nature of their offences, their victims, and the treatment convict women received from the courts. Chapter Three considers a number of key issues arising out of the literature that claims some women were more 'criminal' than others. Differences between country and town women are considered, along with comparisons between crime in three different areas: Ireland, England and the most urban of all centres, the great metropolis of London.

The book then moves on to look at these women as workers. Chapter Four canvasses some opinions regarding female convict workers and their impact on colonial economic development. An inventory is made of the economic assets that convict women acquired and brought with them to the colony in order to assess if convict women were likely to be maling-erers draining the nation's wealth dry—as suggested by some—or poten-tially useful members of the community. Age, health, literacy, numeracy and occupational training are some of the key features examined, all of which were important determinants of worker productivity.

Having established what skills convict women brought to New South Wales, in Chapters Five and Six the book considers the gravity of economic changes happening in Ireland and England, giving the broader economic backgrounds from which convict women came. Ireland and England in the late eighteenth to mid-nineteenth centuries are briefly described, outlining the dynamics of each and locating where convicts fitted into these rapidly shifting and diverging economies. A comparison of convict occupations with those of women surveyed in the 1841 Irish and English censuses also allows us to establish whether convict women were similar or dissimilar to working women left behind. Were these criminals from the 'lowest orders' of society, the sweepings of the gaols, the least skilled and least equipped to venture to New South Wales? Or were they more like non-criminal workers, bringing a representative range of skills? Did they perhaps differ from workers left behind in some other less extreme way?

Knowing what skills convict women brought and the type of backgrounds from which they emanated, we need to ask, were these the skills demanded in the colony? Immigration policies highlight who was desirable as an immigrant in the eyes of officialdom. Free immigration into colonial New South Wales is therefore the focus of Chapter Seven, outlining policy as a guide to female skills required in the colony, and investigating a sample of free immigrant women to see who it was the colony actually received. This chapter concludes by comparing those women deliberately attracted to immigrate with convict women forced to New South Wales, assessing the relative merits of these two labour flows.

Chapter Eight attempts to understand why historians have viewed transported women in the ways they have, and why economists failed to accurately identify colonial women's economic worth. Values embedded in the nineteenth-century literature on convict women and criminal classes are critically evaluated and consideration given to their impact on historical thinking. How these affected perceptions about the economic value of women in the colonial economy is then teased out. Finally, Chapter Nine argues for a new view of the convict women who, along with convict men, free immigrants and indigenous people, made white Australia a flourishing concern whose success would ultimately free it from the umbilical bonds of Empire.

THE LONDON
CONVICT MAID.

Charlotte W——, the subject of this narrative, is a native of London, born of honest parents, she was early taught the value and importance of honesty and virtue; but unhapily ere her attaining the age of maturity, her youthful affections were placed on a young Tradesman, and to raise money to marry her lover, she yielded to the temptation to rob her master, and his property being found in her possession, she was immediately apprehended, tried at the Old Bailey Sessions, convicted, and sentenced to seven years transportation. On her arrival at Hobart Town, she sent her mother a very affecting and pathetic letter, from which the following verses have been composed, and they are here published by particular desire, in the confident hope that this account of her sufferings will serve as an example to deter other females from similar practices.

YE London maids attend to me,
While I relate my misery,
Thro' London Streets I oft have stray'd,
But now I am a Convict Maid

In innocence I once did live,
In all the joy that peace could give.

But sin my youthful heart betrayed,
And now I am a Convict Maid.

To wed my lover I did try,
To take my master's property,
So all my guilt was soon displayed,
And I became a Convict Maid.

Then I was soon to prison sent,
To wait in fear my punishment,
When at the bar I stood dismayed,
Since doomed to be a Convict Maid.

At length the Judge did me address,
Which filled with pain my aching breast
To Botany Bay you will be conveyed,
For seven years a Convict Maid.

For seven years oh, how I sighed,
While my poor mother loudly cried,
My lover wept, and thus he said,
May God be with my Convict Maid.

To you that hear my mournful tale,
I cannot half my grief reveal,
No sorrow yet has been pourtrayed,
Like that of the poor Convict Maid

Far from my friends and home so dear,
My punishment is most severe,
My woe is great and I'm afraid,
That I shall die a Convict Maid.

I toil each day in grief and pain,
And sleepless through the night remain,
My constant toils are unrepaid,
And wretched is the Convict Maid.

Oh could I but once more be free,
I'd ne'er again a captive be,
But I would seek some honest trade,
And ne'er become a Convict Maid.

BIRT, Printer, 39, Great St. Andrew Street Seven Dials.

Figure 1.1 Broadsheet ballad, 'The London Convict Maid'. Ref. D366/15 no. 10: CY1118 f. 1376, Mitchell Library.

CHAPTER ONE

Elizabeth: A Note on Data and Method

Friday, 13 June 1828. Elizabeth Coltman stood there. Dark brown hair tousled, cheeks ruddier than ever, hazel eyes squinting in the wind—summertime in England. Elizabeth was just over five feet tall, by an inch, and her face was dotted with several small dark moles. Salt water wetted her lips. The *Competitor* rocked from side to side at its dock, lulled by the rhythm of the waves. Built fifteen years earlier in Whitby up in Yorkshire, this vessel weighed 425 tons, and today it was preparing for the open seas. Once before, in 1823, it had made the long voyage to Australia, on that occasion visiting Van Diemen's Land with a cargo of 160 male convicts. All but three landed safely. Five years later and it was time for another trip, this time carrying female offenders to their exile. Elizabeth had rarely been outside Warwickshire before, and now she was heading for Sydney Cove. Milling about her were ninety-eight other women, all prisoners awaiting the same fate: transportation 'beyond the seas'. Nearly all were new faces to Elizabeth. She had probably met Caroline Humphries earlier in detention when both were tried in Coventry County Gaol, just two weeks apart, but it seems unlikely that she was acquainted with Hannah Buttledoor, Rachel Bryant, Harriet Wakefield or any of the others. Perhaps Elizabeth felt lonely. Isolated. Apprehensive ... or was it excitement that she felt? Here they all were, together, about to embark on the longest journey of their lives.

No one recorded just how Elizabeth felt as she left her home country of thirty years. We can only guess at the emotional impact of this forced migration. Like Charlotte W——, the London convict maid in Figure 1.1, many women would have experienced enormous distress, being separated from their husbands, lovers, children, parents and friends, from familiar places and recognisable, comfortable social practices. They might have been less disturbed at losing the economic landscape of intermittent employment which ill fitted their constant need for food, clothing and shelter. Such uncertainty might have made some women impervious to their Antipodean adventure. And yet others may have felt a happy anticipation and hope for a better life in all its facets—work, love, family and weather—as they abandoned difficult relationships and unpleasant jobs.

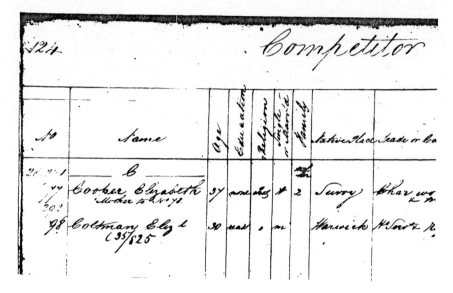

Figure 1.2 Convict indent from the *Competitor*, landed 1828 from London, showing entry for Elizabeth Coltman. *Convict indents of transported prisoners* 4/4003–4019.

But while Elizabeth's feelings remain enigmatic, other details about her are known. Scribes were beavering away in the midst of this throng of heaving humanity. Not interested in emotions, these recording clerks were keenly attentive to other features of Elizabeth's being. Working for British administrators who wanted to know what social and economic assets convict women possessed, these people pried into Elizabeth's luggage—her social, cultural and economic baggage—carefully itemising what was found.

Even before Elizabeth left gaol to proceed to the docks, she was questioned in some detail. Firstly, it was the Home Office. Since 1810, lists had been compiled of offenders awaiting transportation in the prisons and on the hulks. These were the 'hulk lists', also stored as registers by the Admiralty.[1] To begin with, these lists were sketchy, transmitting only basic information on length of sentence and not even specifying the offence being punished with transportation. Over the years, however, colonial Governors had requested that more details be sent, including previous convictions and transportable offence, and in June 1824 the British Transportation Act was passed. It required there to be written

a certificate specifying concisely the Description of his or her Crime, his or her Age, whether married or unmarried, his or her Trade or Profession, and an account of his or her Behaviour in Prison before and after Trial, the Gaoler's observations on his or her temper and Disposition, and such information concerning his or her Connexions and Former Course of Life as may have come to the Gaoler's knowledge.[2]

By the time of Elizabeth's committal on 29 March 1828, careful records were being kept. Court reports were searched, and future transportees were quizzed not only about their criminal profiles but also age, conjugal status and occupation.

Another inquisitive clerk awaited them at the wharf. His name was John Clark. In his account submitted to the government he charged £10 or more (depending on the number of convicts involved) for the following service.

> Perusing and arranging the Documents and Writings transmitted by his Majesty's Secretary of State for the Home Department relating to [the relevant number of] Convicts sentenced to be transported and preparing a list of such Convicts comprising therein the particular Jurisdictions at which they were respectively convicted, the time of their respective convictions, their several sentences &c. to enable me to prepare a contract and bond for the transportation of them at 1s each.[3]

Clark's list was called an 'indent'. The indent bore the Secretary of State's signature and assigned ownership of the convicts' labour, first to the ship's master and then to the colonial Governor. Three copies were made: one for the Secretary of State, one for the shipping contractor, and one for the Governor. In order to construct his indent, Clark collated the relevant documentation, attended the docks several days before the voyage was expected to take place, inspected the convicts and called the roll, and finally questioned them, checking their answers against his paperwork. Most pertinent among his papers were the hulk lists, the documents transmitted by the Home Office. Clark employed the hulk lists in constructing his indent, and then both list and indent journeyed on board ship to New South Wales. As indicated in the above excerpt, Clark was also responsible for drawing up the contract with the shipper. Additionally, he had to procure testimonials of the convicts' landing in New South Wales and report back to the Home Office. His efforts were handsomely rewarded, typically earning him in excess of £15 per ship.

During the voyage the hulk lists were checked again and annotated. Each ship carried a surgeon-superintendent who was responsible for convict health and behaviour. Throughout the voyage, the ship's surgeon kept a journal recording the comings and goings of the sick bay, general levels of well-being and the conduct of the prisoners. Then at some point in the journey, convicts were once again surveyed. The 1837 Select Committee on Transportation was informed of events by George Arthur, Governor of Van Diemen's Land. On arrival in Australia, the surgeon-superintendent presents what I think is called the hulk list; however it is a return of all the prisoners who are on board, drawn up by himself; there are particular instructions in this country given to the surgeon to keep such a return. He minutely marks down every occurrence during the voyage; and nothing is to be passed over without being entered in his journal. The surgeon-superintendent delivers in a return showing the name, the number, the age, the birth-place, the crime, the period of conviction, when and where the sentence, whether married or single, whether he can read or write, or whether he can only read, or whether he can do neither, where taught, his trade, the character he brought from the gaoler, the character from the hulk, the alleged qualifications what he is able to do, and then his behaviour on board the transport. In addition to this return the surgeon-superintendent presents a despatch from the Secretary of State, which includes the *indent* ...[4]

the latter being Clark's list. As we know that the hulk lists were drawn up in Britain and sent on the voyage, this suggests that either the surgeon generated a new set of documents based in part upon the hulk lists and gave them the same name as their progenitors, or more likely that he checked and annotated the original hulk lists.

But this hunger for convict details did not stop there. About three days after the ship docked in Sydney Harbour but before being allowed to disembark, Elizabeth and her colleagues were subjected to a fourth round of bureaucratic data collection. The only person allowed to leave the vessel was the surgeon-superintendent, who delivered to the Colonial Secretary the annotated hulk lists, the indent and any other relevant information. This was then transmitted to the muster-master who prepared two large abstracts of all the material he required before boarding the ship in the company of the principal superintendent of prisoners to perform 'a most minute examination of every prisoner on board'.[5] The completed abstracts provided two copies of the ship's muster roll, one to remain in Sydney, the other to return to Britain. This was the culmination of all the stages of collection, each building on the other, creating a final document which drew together and supplemented what was considered to be all the important knowledge held in the hulk lists, indents, surgeons' annotations and final interrogation by the muster-master. These valuable, information-packed musters provide the foundation for *Convict Maids*. Confusingly, these leather-bound volumes of ships' musters have come to be known as the *convict indents*.[6] For consistency with earlier works and archival practice, the ships' musters shall be referred to as the convict indents throughout this book. Reproduced are the handwritten indent for Elizabeth from 1828 (Figure 1.2); the first page of the indent of an Irish ship, *Elizabeth*, landing in the same year (Figure 1.3); and one of the later printed indents, documenting an Irish voyage in 1836 on board the *Pyramus* (Figure 1.4).

Convict indents functioned as a type of pre-photographic passport, containing detailed information which allowed the unique identification of each individual convict. Thus they recorded intimate details on hair and eye colours, distinguishing physical features, height and age. This is how we know that Elizabeth's hair was dark brown, her eyes hazel, that she had a ruddy complexion marked by several small dark moles, was 5 feet 1 inch tall and thirty years of age. Naturally, sentences were chronicled: it was, after all, necessary to know how long a convict was to remain under judicial authority. And as we have seen, by 1826 the range of other information collected was extensive. Criminal histories were noted. The transportable offence was logged, sometimes noting the victim, along with the sentence passed, the date and place of trial, and the number and length of any previous convictions. Additionally, data were gathered regarding religion, conjugal status, children, place of birth, level of education (write, read, neither) and 'trade or calling'. They recorded up to four of the latter.

Doubts have been raised about the validity of the occupational and educational material that have deterred its rigorous use, and claims about convicts' skills or lack thereof have not always been supported by empirical evidence. The problem arose after Dr Peter Cunningham, surgeon-superintendent on board the convict transport ship the *Recovery* in 1819, was reportedly asked by the ship's convict clerk, 'When I ask what their trades are, all the answers I can get from three-fourths of them is "A thief, a thief". Shall I put these down as *labourers*, sir?'[7] Perhaps prisoners thought they were being asked their crimes. However, this has been interpreted as placing a question mark over whether information was accurately recorded.[8] Others have claimed that the data were corrupted because convicts themselves deliberately lied about their skills. Indeed, there are contemporary protestations that some convicts over-stated their talents in order to get better jobs in the colony, having first been informed of what occupations were in demand by friends on shore shouting out to convict ships anchored in Sydney Harbour. On the other hand, there were coexistent claims that convicts *under*-stated their skill base to avoid being sent where they did not want to venture, or to elude public labour.[9] For every quotation supporting one case, a counter-quotation can nearly always be found refuting it. Reliability is a problem

Following pages:

Figure 1.3 Convict indent from the *Elizabeth*, landed 1828 from Cork. *Convict indents of transported Irish prisoners* 4/7076–7078, AONSW.

Figure 1.4 Convict indent from the *Pyramus*, landed 1836 from Cork. *Convict indents of transported Irish prisoners*, 4/7076–7078, AONSW.

"Elizabeth" 4

Muster Roll of 192 Female Irish Convicts arrived
Watter Cock Commander from Ireland; Joseph H
by the Hon't Alexander Mc Leay Colonial Secretary

No	Name	Age	Education	Religion	Single or Married	Family	Native Place	Trade or Calling	Offence
28.6	A								
6	Atkins Mary Ann	21 Years	reads				Queens Co	Dish & Needlewm	Stealing Nankeen
45									
45	Austin Mary 33/58	30	M.	Protest		children two	Dublin	H. maid Laundy	Stealing Watch
28.13	B								
13	Burke Ellen	26	none	reads	s		Cork	Kitchenmaid	House Robbery
44									
44	Burke Mary	45			married two		Dublin	Serv't all work & plain Cook	Robbing Person
46									
46	Brown Ann 33/335	20			s		Do	Nursegirl	Do a child
66									
67	Blagg Margret	24			s		Kildare	Housemaid Washer	Stealing Blankets
67									
68	Barrington Eleanor	16			s		Queens Co	Housemaid	Robbing Pson
96									
97	Butler Catherine	18	reads				Kilkenny	Straw Plaiter & Nursegirl	Stealing Clothes
108									
109	Bryan Margaret	30	none			two	Limerick	Farm Servant	Do Cloth
117									
118	Buckley Mary	19	none		s		Do	Housemaid & Washer	House Robbery
168									
170	Byrne Judith	20	reads		s		Westmeath	Do	Stealing Money
169									
171	Bollestor Bellasty	25	Do		married mone		Do	House & Dairy Woman	Robbing Pson
175									
177	Byrne Mary	22	Do		s		Wexford	Nursemaid & Kitchen Do	House Robbery
180	Byrne Elizabeth	30	Do	Protest	s		Wicklow	Farm Servt	Robbing Person

from Ireland : Walter Cock Commander

Joseph H Hughes Surgeon Superintendent

in Sydney Cove the 12ᵗʰ January 1828 on board the Elizabeth

Hughes Surgeon Superintendent ; Muster held on board the said Ship

the

16 children

Mustered No 192
Drowned 1
Died 1
194 Total

Where Tried	When Tried	Sentence	Former Conviction	Height		Color of			How Disposed of, and Remarks
				Ft.	In.	Complexion	Hair	Eyes	
	1826								
Armagh	14 July	7	2	5	2¾	Sad freckled Sone Pockpitted	Dk Brown	Brown	
No marks									
Dublin	5 October	7	none	5	0¾	Fresh Pockpitt	Do	Do	Grey	Mr Sorrell
No marks									
	1827								
Cork	2 April	7	none	4	5½	Sad Freckled	Do	Do	Dark Hazel	
Burnt mark on her left arm	Good looking								
Dublin	28 Septr	7	4	5	0¾	Do Pockpitt	Do	Do	Bright Hazel	John Sims
No marks									
Do	6 Do	7	none	4	9	Fresh	Lt Brown	Blue	
No marks									
Do	27 March *1827*	7	2	5	2½	Do Fair	Brown	Lt Grey	David Layton
No marks									
Do	Do	7	none	5	=¾	Freckled	Lt Do	Hazle Grey	
No marks									
Kilkenny	25 Do	7	none	5	5	Do	Do	Do	Hazel	
Left eye seems covered with a film and cast a different colour									
Limerick	10 June	7	none	5	1½	Ruddy	Brown	Grey	
No marks									
Do	16 March	7	none	5	1½	Fresh Do	Dark Do	Slaty Do	
No marks									
Westmeath	13 Do	7	2	5	0	Ruddy	Do	Dk Grey	Thoᵗ Meehan
Vertical scar over right eye brow — Cousin to James McDermott									
Do	13 Do	7	2	5	1½	Do Freckled	Do	Blue	
No marks	Husband in the army 65ᵗʰ Regt								
Wexford	13 Do	7	none	5	3	Do Do	Do	Do	Wm Chelsnor
No marks									
Wicklow	9 Do	7	none	5	1	much Do	Do	Do	
No marks									

LIST of FEMALE CONVICTS by the Ship PYRAMUS (2), George Nathaniel Livesay, Master

Standing No. of Convict	Indent No.	Name	Age	R. Reads W. Writes	Religion	Single, Married or Widow	Male	Female	Native Place	Trade or Calling	Offence	Where	Trie...
549-36	1	Elizabeth Gaffney	19	None	Rom. Cath.	Single			Dublin	House maid, all work	Pledging	Antrim	
550-36	2	Mary Reid	17	R & W	Protestant	Single			Antrim	All work	Stealing linen	Antrim	
551-36	3	Susan Thompson	22	R	Protestant	Single			Down	All work	Stealing tub	Antrim	
552-36	4	Ellen Tally, or Carr	16	R	Protestant	Single			Antrim	House maid	Stealing gowns	Antrim	
553-36	5	Sarah Tally	17	R	Protestant	Single			Antrim	All work	Stealing cotton	Antrim	
554-36	6	Mary Ann Mc Cann	20	None	Rom. Cath.	Single			Armagh	Needle woman, all work	House robbery	Antrim	
555-36	7	Mary Ann Donaldson	23	R & W	Protestant	Single			Edinburgh	Needle woman, house maid, all work	Stealing clothes	Antrim	
556-36	8	Jane Jennings	22	R & W	Protestant	Single	1		Armagh	House maid, all work, plain cook	Stealing coat	Antrim	
557-36	9	Matilda Wilson	26	R	Protestant	Widow	1		Armagh	Laundress, needle woman	Stealing table linen	Armagh	
558-36	10	Elizabeth Lawless	20	None	Rom. Cath.	Married			Westmeath	All work	Stealing clothes	Armagh	
559-36	11	Rose Parks	20	R	Protestant	Single			Newry	Laundress, house maid, needle woman	Stealing clothes	Armagh	
560-36	12	Sarah Hillock	22	R	Protestant	Married			Armagh	Kitchen maid, all work, country	Stealing potatoes	Armagh	
561-36	13	Rachael Alexander	18	R	Rom. Cath.	Single			Armagh	Nurse maid	Stealing potatoes	Armagh	
562-36	14	Jane Mc Clare	12	R & W	Protestant	Single			Armagh	Nurse girl	Stealing glasses	Armagh	
563-36	15	Mary Oakan	30	None	Rom. Cath.	Single			Carlow	Laundress, dairy maid, house maid	Stealing blanket	Carlow	
564-36	16	Mary Ryan	22	R	Protestant	Widow		1	Wexford	House maid, all work	Stealing money	Carlow	
565-36	17	Judith Deering	29	None	Rom. Cath.	Widow			Carlow	All work	Man robbing	Carlow	
566-36	18	Mary Moyles	24	None	Rom. Cath.	Widow			Carlow	Laundress, all work	Man robbing	Carlow	
567-36	19	Catherine Carty	27	None	Rom. Cath.	Married			Carlow	Dealer	Shoplifting	Carlow	
568-36	20	Anne R'Sorcy	19	None	Rom. Cath.	Single			Dublin	House maid, all work	Perjury	Carlow	
569-36	21	Anne Whelan	26	None	Rom. Cath.	Married	1		Westmeath	Kitchen maid, all work	Picking pockets	Cavan	
570-36	22	Jane or Bridget	22	None	Rom. Cath.	Single			Westmeath	Nurse maid, all work	Stealing calico	Cavan	
571-36	23	Mary Donnelly	38	None	Protestant	Widow			Cavan	Laundress, needle woman	Stealing fowls	Cavan	
572-36	24	Ellen Curtis	35	None	Rom. Cath.	Single			Dublin	Kitchen maid	Man robbing	Cavan	
573-36	25	Ellen Gordon, or Mc Lally	40	None	Rom. Cath.	Married	1	1	Monaghan	All work, country	Shoplifting	Cavan	
574-36	26	Catherine Clarke	21	None	Rom. Cath.	Married			Cavan	All work	Picking pockets	Cavan	
575-36	27	Mary Kelly	16	None	Rom. Cath.	Married			Clare	Nurse maid, laundry maid	House burning	Clare	
576-36	28	Mary Linahan	26	None	Rom. Cath.	Widow	1	1	Cork	All work	Stealing linen	Cork	
577-36	29	Mary Lyons	24	None	Rom. Cath.	Single			Cork	House maid	Stealing sheep	Cork	
578-36	30	Catherine Morrisey	20	None	Rom. Cath.	Single			Limerick	Nurse maid, house maid	Stealing money	Cork	
579-36	31	Judith Shea	20	None	Rom. Cath.	Married			Cork	Dairy maid	Stealing money	Cork	
580-36	32	Honora Buckley	22	R & W	Rom. Cath.	Married	1		Cork	Laundress, house maid	Stealing clothes	Cork	
581-36	33	Honora Shea	45	None	Rom. Cath.	Widow	1	2	Cork	All work, country	Stealing fowls	Cork	
582-36	34	Judith or Mary Shea	18	None	Rom. Cath.	Single			Cork	Market woman	Stealing fowls	Cork	
583-36	35	Judith Cashly	45	None	Rom. Cath.	Widow	2	2	Cork	All work, country	Stealing fowls	Cork	
584-36	36	Johanna Mulcahy	50	None	Rom. Cath.	Single			Cork	All work, country	Stealing fowls	Cork	
585-36	37	Margaret Shea	17	None	Rom. Cath.	Single			Cork	Market girl	Stealing fowls	Cork	

O. Pineo, *Surgeon Superintendent, Arrived from IRELAND*, 14th December. 1836.

	Sentence	Former Conviction	Height Feet	Height In.	Complexion	Color of Hair	Color of Eyes	Particular Marks or Scars. Remarks.	Colonial History: Colonial Sentence	Ticket of Exemption / Leave	Pardon Conditional / Absolute / Colonial	Certificate of Freedom	Dead or left the Colony
1	7 Years	8 Days	4	7	Fair ruddy	Light brown	Hazel	Mark of a burn right side of mouth, lost top of third finger of right hand, TEBA indistinct, inside lower left arm.					
2	7 Years	4 Months	5	1½	Fair and freckled	Light brown	Hazel	DHMR indistinct inside lower left arm.				43/1607	
3	7 Years	7 years, served 6 months at Down Patrick.	4	10¾	Ruddy and freckled	Brown	Grey to blue	Lost a front upper tooth, horizontal scar right side of forehead.					
4	7 Years	None	5	1¾	Ruddy	Brown	Grey	Blue horizontal scar over right eyebrow. Sister of No. 36-553.					
5	7 Years	4 Months	5	3	Brown	Dark brown	Hazel	Wart right side of nose, scar right eyebrow, scar left thumb. Sister of No. 36-552.					
6	7 Years	None	4	10	Ruddy and freckled	Brown	Grey	Has an impediment in speech, scar left cheek bone, a mole right cheek, and three on same jaw, scar back of fore finger of right hand, small red natural mark palm of left hand, little finger of same hand contracted, scar under left jaw.		41/253		43/387	
7	7 Years	None	4	9½	Ruddy and freckled	Light brown	Blue	Mark of a burn back of left hand.				43/534	
8	7 Years	None	5	5½	Ruddy and pockpitted	Brown	Bluish	Scar left cheek bone, scar right jaw, scar right side of nose, lost a front upper tooth, scar left ear.		40/1677		44/731	
9	7 Years	None	5	1½	Ruddy	Brown	Light grey	Small scar left jaw, scar ball of left thumb, mole back of lower left arm.		40/2921		44/1872	
10	7 Years	None	5	1	Dark sallow	Brown	Brown	Small scar back of lower right arm.	"	"	"	"	[illegible] Parramatta [illegible]
11	7 Years	None	5	2½	Ruddy and freckled	Light	Bluish	Left arm short.				44/2096	
12	7 Years	None	5	5½	Dark ruddy and freckled	Dark brown	Brown	Small mole left cheek.		41/2370		44/1575	
13	7 Years	None	5	0¾	Ruddy and much freckled	Brown	Grey	Scar over left eyebrow, mark of a burn back of right hand, scar heel of same.		40/1770		43/2196	
14	7 Years	None	4	8½	Ruddy and freckled	Brown	Hazel	Nose a little cocked, slight scar left cheek bone, mole inside lower right arm.				45/187	
15	5 Years	None	5	2	Ruddy and freckled	Brown	Blue	None.		41/181		43/20	
16	7 Years	None	5	1	Sallow, freckled, and little pockpitted	Black	Brown	Lost two front upper teeth, marks of scrofula left side of neck, mark of a bite inside right wrist.					
17	7 Years	None	5	2	Ruddy and pockpitted	Brown	Hazel grey	None.				47/425	
18	7 Years	None	5	4	Ruddy and freckled	Brown	Grey	Small round scar right elbow.				44/1533	
19	3 Years	None	4	9¾	Dark ruddy and freckled	Dark brown	Hazel	Lost a front tooth right side of upper jaw, two scars left side of forehead, scar over right eyebrow, scar on front of chin, small mole inside lower right arm.		40/2526			
20	3 Years	None	5	1	Ruddy	Dark brown	Hazel	Small mole under right eye, small pock pit right cheek, small mole lower part of right side of neck.					
21	7 Years	2 Days	5	2¾	Ruddy and freckled	Brown	Hazel	Little finger of each hand a little crooked. Husband Patrick Byrne, about five years ago, Elizabeth Hanlon, Roslyn Castle, 1836.				C42/1306	
22	7 Years	None	4	2½	Ruddy and freckled	Light brown	Bluish	Scar right side of under lip. Brothers John McManus, 4 years, and Edward McManus 3 years ago.				44/70	
23	7 Years	None	5	1¾	Sallow freckled and little pockpitted	Dark brown	Dark grey	Small pock pit above left elbow, scar inside and outside right wrist, scar back of right hand.		41/957		43/1592	
24	7 Years	None	5	1½	Brown and freckled	Dark brown	Hazel	Nose a little cocked, top of middle finger of left hand disfigured from a cut.				44/531	
25	7 Years	None	5	0¾	Ruddy and freckled	Dark brown	Hazel	Lost two front teeth, right side of upper jaw, eyebrows partially meeting. Husband Roger Gordon or Duffy, per Captain Cook, 1832.		40/169		43/315	
26	7 Years	None	5	0	Dark ruddy and freckled	Dark brown	Hazel	Small scar left cheek, little finger of right hand contracted from a cut, scar under left jaw. Husband Richard Murphy, 1833. Brother Thomas Clarke, 1832.		41/740			
27	Life	None	4	10	Dark ruddy and freckled	Brown	Brown	Small mole upper part of right arm, scar back of right hand, mark of a burn back of left hand, scar back of fore finger of same.		47/623	CP 57/52		
28	7 Years	None	5	2	Dark ruddy and freckled	Brown	Hazel	Raised scar on front of chin, lost a part of a front upper tooth, horizontal scar on forehead, scar on upper lip, another below right side of under lip.				46/809	
29	Life	None	4	9½	Brown and freckled	Dark brown mixed with grey	Grey	Scar left side of forehead, nose cocked, two blue dots back of right hand, two small moles inside lower left arm.		44/343	[illegible]		
30	7 Years	None	5	0	Ruddy and freckled	Brown	Light hazel	Scar outside left elbow.					
31	7 Years	None	5	1	Ruddy & much freckled	Dark brown	Hazel	None.		42/2763		43/1570	
32	7 Years	None	5	2½	Fair ruddy and freckled	Light brown	Grey	Horizontal scar over right eyebrow.				42/1035	
33	7 Years	2 Months 2 Months 2 Months	5	1½	Ruddy and freckled	Brown	Hazel	Lost four upper front teeth. Son Daniel Shea, 1836, Mother of Nos. 36-582 and 36-585.		41/1546		43/1503	
34	7 Years	None	5	0¾	Ruddy and freckled	Sandy	Dark hazel	Cast inward in left eye, nose a little pockpitted. Daughter of No. 36-581.				43/1525	
35	7 Years	2 Months 3 Months 4 Months	4	7¾	Dark sallow and freckled	Dark brown nearly black mixed with grey	Brown	Lost a front upper tooth, angular scar on centre of forehead, scar on centre of upper lip. Sister of No. 36-581. Brother Denis Conkly, 13 years ago.					
36	7 Years	None	4	9	Ruddy and much freckled	Brown mixed with grey	Brown and speckled	Lost several front teeth, two small scars right side of forehead.		41/2711			
37	7 Years	None	5	2	Brown and freckled	Brown	Hazel	Nose a little cocked, small pockpit back of left hand, small scar right side of forehead. Daughter of No. 36-581.					

for both quantitative *and* qualitative data, and historians must constantly challenge the validity of sources, and find ways of testing them and methods of using them which overcome some limitations. For example, using comparable qualitative data *en masse*—quantifying it—can minimise some problems. A biography of an individual convict based on a single convict indent (without corroborative evidence) might well be a fantasy, if that convict lied. The story is less likely to be a fantasy if several thousand indents are used together. For such a mass of information to be wrong would require *systematic* lying on behalf of convicts.

However, there is little evidence that convicts did lie or that records were erroneous. Convict indents appear very reliable sources. According to J. T. Bigge, famed for his enquiry into Governor Macquarie's administration, the muster taken at the end of the voyage was 'of a very detailed nature'.[10] The only doubts he raised about accuracy related to whether convicts were married or not, and he believed that any inexactitude could be ironed out by collecting this material back in Britain.[11] This was the case after 1824, not only for the question of conjugal status, but for occupation and literacy also. These musters, or convict indents, were the end product of information that had been collected systematically and repeatedly verified. At a minimum of four points in Elizabeth's incarceration she had been questioned: in prison, by Clark before departure, by the surgeon on board, and in Australia by the muster-master. No doubt after arrival she was interrogated again. Intuitively, I suspect convicts might have been very wary about lying.[12] When Elizabeth had stolen silk the law had found her out and now she was being shipped half way around the world as punishment for her sin. Living under penal servitude, it seems doubtful that it would have been worth her while to risk being found out a second time for lying to authorities who might impose unpleasant rebukes. Contemporaries thought likewise, and argued for the veracity of the convict records. Governor Arthur continued his evidence to the Select Committee:

> With the information which he [the muster-master] had collected from the surgeon-superintendent and from the hulk list he has already some part of the history of the convict before him, and with that information he generally draws from him many more particulars. The man perceives at once that the officer who is examining him does know something of his history; and not being quite conscious how much of it is known, he reveals, I should think, generally a very fair statement of his past life, apprehensive of being detected in stating what is untrue.[13]

The manner in which the indents were generated suggests they were faithful transcriptions of sound evidence. So too does the detail in which they were recorded. Over one-third of the women listed more than one trade or calling—Elizabeth gave two: she was both a house servant and a ribbon weaver. There was no point in presenting two, three or four lies when one would have sufficed. Additionally, occupations were carefully itemised. There were dairymaids and kitchenhands, needlewomen and tailoresses, pottery packers, straw plaiters, fishing-net makers, glass grinders and polishers and many, many more (discussed in Chapter Four). Certainly they were not all labourers. This meticulous listing suggests that the information was recorded accurately. Authorities would have been unlikely to expend such energies collecting all this information—at length, in great detail and persistently—unless their experiences over the years suggested it was both reliable and useful. Indeed, these records were employed in allocating convicts to jobs in the colonies, with Molesworth's Select Committee on Transportation concluding from their evidence that 'the previous occupation of the convict in this country mainly determines his condition in the penal colonies'.[14]

Intuition and testimony aside, there seems little evidence that convicts did lie systematically. Cross-referencing information internally within the document, and comparing it with other sources external to the indents, are two of the ways in which we can test for the robustness of the data. Occupational aggregates assembled in the *Convict Workers* study of some 20 000 men and women displayed diversity, and generally individuals possessed skills appropriate to their age, gender and geographic place of work. These claimed professions were also consistent with the empirically derived measure of numeracy based upon patterns of age-heaping[15] and with literacy reflecting the finding that 'all local investigations reveal ... a greater tendency for some occupational groups to be literate than others'.[16] Spot checks demonstrate a high correlation between occupations stated in court records (when this information was available) and those listed in the indents.[17] A consistent tale is revealed when comparisons are made with census data.[18] Convict indents appear reliable and robust. Such checks and balances on the reliability of the information were made possible only by computerising the indent data, a technological advantage that we have over researchers of the 1950s and 1960s. Had previous historians possessed the necessary technology to group the diverse occupational information, to cross-tabulate it with other variables, and to generally jump up and down on it, then perhaps they would have been more inclined to employ this valuable source.

Few historical records exist that are so rich, promising to reveal so much, as the convict indents. Workers—and in particular women—evade explicit attention in most extant documents from past centuries, but when workers erred a whole bureaucratic system swung into action. Nineteenth-century criminal registers have been usefully employed in probing the realities of day-to-day life, but even these records pale when compared with the wealth of detail preserved in the convict indents.[19] These offer us a unique insight into the lives of those criminals who went on to colonise New South Wales, people emanating from systems in turmoil as Ireland's economy diversified, England industrialised, modern consumer society was born, new classes emerged while old ones were transformed, gender relations were renegotiated, the first police forces emerged, and Britain's 'bloody' legal code was reformed. Delving into the convict indents holds promise of bountiful rewards: a window into criminal worlds, working lives, personal histories, at a time of immense change, with a view comparatively uncluttered by the biases of contemporary observers.

Such detailed information allows us to piece together bits of individual women's lives. Elizabeth Coltman's story has already been partially revealed. She was in her thirtieth year when transported. Born in Warwick and tried in neighbouring Coventry, she had practised as a house servant and a ribbon weaver, and it seems to be this latter employment which brought her down: seven years' transportation for stealing silk, her first offence. The recording officer noted that she was married, but did not comment on whether Elizabeth was leaving children behind. A Protestant, she had been taught to read as had many of her religion, and perhaps she found some solace on board ship huddled up with a book, probably the Bible (reading matter tended to be limited).

Another of Elizabeth's compatriots on board the *Competitor*, six years her senior, also appears to have come awry at work. Hannah Buttledoor was a laundress. But—like Oscar Wilde—one thing she had been unable to resist was temptation. Stood in the dock, she heard the verdict pronounced. Guilty. Seven years for stealing clothes (that she had laundered?). As far as was known by the court, this was a first offence. She was like Elizabeth in other ways too. Hannah was a Protestant. Reading was numbered among her accomplishments. Hannah's eyes were hazel, her complexion ruddy and freckled, and she stood 4 feet 11½ inches tall. Unlike Elizabeth's, Hannah's hair was a sandy brown. Hannah was from Norwich, where she lived and supported her two children in the absence of her deceased husband. What became of her children left behind in England, I wonder.

The other woman from Coventry—Caroline Humphries—also shared some features with Elizabeth. Caroline could read, was a Protestant, and had worked as a house girl. But there the similarities end. Caroline was only seventeen, and at a diminutive 4 feet 7¾ inches had not yet finished growing. She had been born in Birmingham, Elizabeth in Warwick. Caroline (alias Catherine) already had two convictions when she was tried for stealing gowns, an offence which scored her transportation for fourteen years (ten of which she would serve before being pardoned). Young, childless and single, it is hard to tell how much Caroline and the other two women would have held in common.

Perhaps Caroline could relate more easily to Rachel Bryant and Harriet Wakefield who were also young, single, childless and Protestant. Rachel, twenty-three, had been born in Taunton and was tried in Bridgewater, and in between she worked as a silk weaver, needlewoman and allworker. She stood 4 feet 9¾ inches tall, had a ruddy and freckled complexion with dark brown hair and brown eyes, and was distinguished by a raised mole between her eyes and towards the left side. Harriet was noticeable for the small scar on her nose and another on the outer corner of her left eye. Younger than Rachel, the 17-year-old Harriet was also taller, at 5 feet 4 inches. Her complexion was fair, her hair brown, eyes hazel. She had worked in Nottingham as a needlewoman. Rachel and Harriet were both guilty of more serious crime: robbery from the person. Harriet was awarded fourteen years, Rachel a life sentence. Both were first offenders.

These are but five shipmates. Their brief stories reveal the type of material held in the convict indents, and are interesting in themselves. What their tales do *not* indicate is how representative Elizabeth, Hannah, Caroline, Rachel and Harriet were of the other women on board the *Competitor*, or on the other ships. For example, all of these women were Protestant: surely this was not typical. Far from it, in fact. Most convict women were Catholic, and Irish. In this respect Margaret Shannahan was more representative. Margaret was transported in 1833 on the *Caroline* sailing from Cork. She had been born and subsequently tried in King's County for house robbery, on this occasion scoring seven years' transportation. Already Margaret had served a three-month sentence for an earlier offence. She was only seventeen. Young, single, illiterate, this sallow and freckled girl with brown hair and grey eyes worked as a housemaid before her exile. The indent records that Margaret sported the mark of a burn on the outer corner of her left eye. Some forty years later this scar was still visible. Margaret's photograph is to be found in Figure 1.5. After the gruesome death of her husband William Greenwood in a carting accident, and seemingly abandoned by her eight adult children, Margaret returned to crime, becoming a drunk and a vagrant who was repeatedly incarcerated. Showing her truculent but bewildered, the picture was taken in the 1870s when it had become prison policy to photograph inmates, leaving us a rare and poignant image of a convict woman.[20] How rare were Margaret's experiences, I wonder? However fascinating and important such personal tales are, the point remains that individual stories alone cannot tell us about the whole. Specific cases need contextualising within the broader picture. Otherwise the reader is left unaware whether these examples were picked at random, or

Figure 1.5 Prison photograph of Margaret Greenwood, née Shannahan, transported on the Caroline, landed 1833 from Cork. Index to photographic descriptions book, volume 3 3/6040, AONSW.

deliberately selected to suit some sinister purpose of my own (such as including an incredibly rare photograph!). How we usefully mine this precious vein of indent material is thus an important question.

An extensive range of possibilities is open to researchers of our female convict past.[21] Individual histories may be explored in detail, a shipload surveyed, or a large number investigated together. Deirdre Beddoe has offered a fascinating insight into the Welsh women transported to Australia and, employing indent data, John Williams began to unfold the story of lawbreaking Irish women in Van Diemen's Land.[22] Portia Robinson traced a much larger group of convict women—around 5000—who arrived in New South Wales up until 1827, through court records and other sources in Britain and Ireland.[23] The outcome has been an enriching dose of anecdotal evidence. Other historians have looked at single voyages. Anne Needham and associates investigated the women transported on the *Neptune* in 1790, and Marjorie Tipping has breathed life into the *Calcutta* convicts who founded Hobart in Van Diemen's Land.[24] Particularly impressive has been Babette Smith's venture into the lives of ninety-nine convict women who traversed the globe aboard the *Princess Royal*.[25] This was a delightful blend of overview with individual experience, a successful wedding of the two main approaches.

But the extent of the picture is limited. As with the *Competitor*, we are left to ponder upon how representative the *Princess Royal* was of other English ships, let alone the Irish ones. And this was a specific moment in convictism: did women arriving in 1829 bear any relation to those who came in 1789, 1809 or even 1839? Similarly, the collection of individual experiences falls short of portraying the grand overview. The anecdotal approach fails to capitalise on its major asset—the numbers involved—by refraining from moving beyond individual stories. If these stories were aggregated and synthesised, this would allow the construction of a framework in which works such as Smith's could so usefully be situated.

Convict Maids aims to build such a framework, to draw a bigger picture than afforded by a single boatload. It does not present the whole picture—this has many panels corresponding to the several different stages in the sixty-five years of female transportation to the Australian colonies—but a sketch of a significant phase in this process of colonisation. Only the colonies of New South Wales and Van Diemen's Land received women prisoners (why Western Australia was denied women is another interesting question), but between them they accepted some 24 960 women, split evenly. Focusing on the first colony, this book covers the peak period of transportation to New South Wales when a majority of women arrived, commencing in 1826 when the data are most complete and ending in 1840 with the cessation of transportation to that colony. All the convict vessels surveyed in this study are listed in Appendix 1.

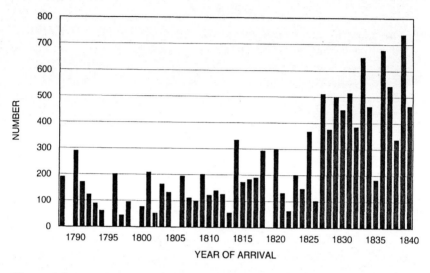

Figure 1.6   Female convicts landed in Sydney, 1788–1840.

Figure 1.6 illustrates the number of convict women arriving in the colony each year and their concentration in this later period. (Further details of this and all other graphs can be found in the Statistical Appendix.) *Convict Maids* includes well over one-half of all women transported to New South Wales, one-quarter of the total who ever sailed to Australia. I want to introduce you to 6876 convict women. But I have not the patience nor the space to greet each Elizabeth and Margaret as individual players on this great stage of history.

Nor would such an approach serve my purpose. While I might feel guilty of losing sight of the specific, an aggregate approach allows me a vision of the bigger picture—a framework of understanding into which individuals may then be placed. Here is one advantage of the quantitative approach. How typical Elizabeth was of the mass of her convicted compatriots *can* be assessed. By looking at all the women, I can tell you that Elizabeth was typical in terms of age and education, but not in terms of religion or country of origin—a majority of convict women came to New South Wales from Ireland, not England. It is only this grand overview which permits questions regarding what type of criminals these transportees were, what skills convict women as a group brought with them to Australia, the type of labour supply they constituted, how they compared with English and Irish working women left behind and with free immigrant women to Australia. Elizabeth shall be grouped with her sisters.

This book is an investigation of the convict indents. Presented is an inventory of the contents of Elizabeth's various pieces of baggage plus the contents of thousands of other similar bags carried by thousands of other similar women shipped out to New South Wales because they transgressed the laws of Britain, and got caught. (Throughout, 'Britain' denotes England, Wales, Scotland and Ireland.) It is also an attempt to relate this catalogue of details to the wider context which links three disparate countries—Ireland, England and Australia—at a time of immense change. But why study female convicts at all? Because historical enterprise has led to a number of unresolved tensions emerging in the story of white settlement; because these women have been misunderstood and misrepresented on too many occasions; and because convict women formed a significant but as yet little understood part of white Australia's colonial heritage. To understand our own development we need to understand our origins. 'Without a knowledge of the origins, the science of history can come to no conclusion'.[26]

CHAPTER TWO

Mercury's Charges: The Crimes of Convict Women

A ustralia was not colonised by adventurers seeking excitement and hopeful of making their fortunes, but by bureaucrats, soldiers, gaolers and most significantly of all, by convicts. Australia was a strategically placed dumping ground for Britain's criminals.[1] One feature clearly distinguished Elizabeth Coltman from traditional colonists: she was a law-breaker. Just this one attribute was responsible for enmeshing the lives of 6876 women sent as forced immigrants to New South Wales shores between 1826 and 1840. All were criminals in the eyes of the law. Each was guilty of either a felony or a serious misdemeanour, and in punishment Mercury's charges were banished to the distant reaches of the world. Theoretically, exile was for a finite number of years; in reality, it meant life. Had Mercury, patron of rogues, vagabonds and thieves, reneged on his duties in allowing those in his care to end up transported against their will to a foreign land, forever?

Contemporaries may not have thought so, if only by comparison with the alternatives. Transportation to Australia should be seen in broader terms of the criminal law and the position it had reached by the nineteenth century, because law and punishment were not set in stone; instead, they were highly fluid, and increasingly so by the eighteenth and nineteenth centuries.[2] From the Middle Ages there was a distinction between felonies and misdemeanours: the latter was a minor offence such as petty larceny (the theft of less than one shilling) that could be punished by whipping or short-term imprisonment in the gaolhouse, while a felony was a more serious crime. Most offences were felonies, the term catching in its net everything from simple grand larceny (theft of one shilling or more) through to the most violent of crimes.[3] All felonies were capital offences with one punishment for those found guilty, death. There was no extensive gaol system and the penitentiary was yet to be born, so there was no place to put criminals for lengthy periods of detention. Offenders faced the gibbet, Albion's fatal tree—the wooden structure whence the noose would hang. This was a harsh code that punished all felons alike, irrespective of the seriousness of their crime, be it theft or murder.

From the fourteenth century the ferocity of the criminal code was tempered through the wider application of what was called 'benefit of clergy'.[4] This originated from churchmen's claims that they were subject only to the authority of ecclesiastical courts, not to civil jurisdiction even when accused of secular offences. While this position was not wholly accepted by the state, a benefit was granted. Tried in the King's court, a guilty but ordained cleric could claim the benefit of his station, exempting him from the death penalty. Instead, punishment was determined and administered by the religious order. Courts accepted as evidence of clerical status the ability to read a verse from the Psalms, and from this test of literacy there emerged an avenue for mitigating the severity of the legal code: those who were literate, and those whom the court chose to consider literate, could be saved from execution. Discretion was thus built into the system as the court decided who was and was not literate on grounds other than reading ability, and in this context a good character witness became a key element in winning judicial favour.[5] Benefit of clergy had become secularised in practice, and this was recognised in law by a statute of 1487 allowing the benefit to be applied on one occasion to men who were not clergy (although adherence to this limit was erratic).[6] Between 1623 and 1693 benefit was gradually extended to female offenders. Before this, a woman would be hanged when a man would go free, unless she could plead for clemency on grounds of pregnancy.[7] Ultimately the abolition of the literacy test in 1706 meant that everyone was eligible, whether the court deemed them literate or not.[8] Granting of the benefit was accompanied by a brand upon the brawn of the thumb with 'M' for murder and 'T' for theft, identifying those freed under its auspices, and for seven years from 1699 branding with the usual marks was done 'on the most visible part of the left cheek nearest the nose', although this practice soon reverted to the thumb before branding was finally stopped in 1779.[9] But, apart from this physical punishment, there was no alternative punitive action and a clergied felon was discharged with his or her freedom.

At the end of the seventeenth century, punishment had become dichotomous: a guilty felon would either hang or go free subject to corporal punishment, greatly reducing the ferocity of the code. Courts had employed the benefit of clergy as a device for exercising their own discretion and leniency, but there was a reaction against this. Many in the government believed the gallows was the only effective deterrent against crime, and others were disturbed that a murderer or rapist could walk free. A contrary development was instigated which enhanced the law's brutality. While eligibility for the benefit extended from the fourteenth century, there was a contraction in the number of offences to which it applied. Initially, all felonies were clergiable, but from the end of the fifteenth century onwards a series of exemptions were made. At first, the process moved slowly. It began with violent crimes such as murder, and others which threatened human well-being such as various forms of robbery and breaking into houses when people were present indoors. The guiding light had been to protect the person, but increasingly it was to protect property and to attack crimes deemed widespread and difficult to prevent. By 1565 picking pockets was exempted from benefit, burglary following suit soon after. Yet near the end of the seventeenth century the only larceny for which benefit could *not* be claimed was horse stealing, presumably due to the value of these animals.[10]

In a flurry of legislation from 1689 a bloodier code emerged. Where once there had been fifty capital statutes, by the end of the eighteenth century there were more than two hundred. Benefit of clergy could not be claimed for those stealing to the value of five shillings, or for goods of similar value gained through breaking into houses, shops, warehouses, stables, or through shoplifting; for the theft of linen or cotton from bleach greens worth ten shillings or more; and if forty shillings' worth of goods were taken from an empty house or outhouse. Private interests had sheep stealing and cattle theft included on this prohibitive list, and in one fell swoop the iniquitous 1723 Black Act targeted dozens of felonies and defined a host of new property crimes not seen before on the statute books. Property was redefined. Things of a 'base nature'—such as dogs, hares and fish—that once could not be stolen because they were no one person's property found they were now possessed.[11] Customary rights of workers to the sweepings and gleanings of harvested fields, gathering small and unused pieces of coal, collecting firewood from forests, trapping rabbits and grazing animals on common lands were turned into property crimes like poaching.[12] A popular ditty declared:

> The law locks up the man or woman
> Who steals the goose from off the common
> But leaves the greater villain loose
> Who steals the common from the goose.[13]

Forms of worker resistance such as penning anonymous letters were outlawed. Conspiring to form a trade union was even a crime, as the Tolpuddle Martyrs found out to their cost. In 1739 domestic servants pilfering from their masters were targeted.[14] Essentially, this process of redefining the law brought about a division between non-capital offences (for which benefit could be claimed) and capital offences (for which it could not).[15] Additionally, it produced more criminals who would be hanged and it highlighted the anomaly of non-capital offenders for whom there was no effective reproof. In 1718 a way was found to lessen the severity of capital sentences and to punish non-capital felons: transportation.[16]

As early as 1597 transportation 'beyond the seas' was countenanced for ridding the community of those who 'will not be reformed of their roguish kind of life', and several schemes were tried.[17] However, the intention was not made effective until the Transportation Act of 1717 that opened America to receive British felons.[18] Punishment was revolutionised. Felons could be disciplined rather than simply freed or executed. Sending criminals offshore became the alternative to capital punishment that had been so badly lacking. Pardoning a capital offender now meant commuting their death sentence to exile for either fourteen years or life.[19] Banishment was also created as a regular punishment for non-capital offences, presenting courts with a new choice and one that judges increasingly preferred over granting benefit of clergy.[20] Indeed, the discretionary powers of judges and juries were increasing in other ways too. Distinctions between felonies and misdemeanours were becoming confused, with the outcome that punishments became interchangeable. Petty larceny and serious assault, both misdemeanours, by the eighteenth century were punishable by transportation, while conversely some non-capital felonies were reprimanded with whipping and imprisonment.[21] Discretionary powers were once again being exerted by judges who chose which offenders to whip or brand and let free, and which to transport. This tendency was further emphasised late in the century when branding of clergied felons was replaced with a system of fines and imprisonment—both eminently variable—which for the first time formally permitted punishment to be adapted to the severity of the offence.[22] Transportation thus emerged as a substitute for hanging, but it was also the alternative to complete freedom for many who, just a few years earlier, could have claimed the benefit of clergy, undergone a brief physical punishment and walked unobstructed from the court. The position of transportation is thus ambiguous, as it acted neither wholly to mitigate the severity of the law, nor to harden it. What it did achieve was an increasing differentiation in punishment which made the legal system more discerning and effective than when it applied the same punishment to all felons irrespective of their crime: death, or freedom.

Banishing sections of the criminal population did, however, have its own set of problems, and one was destination. In 1776, nearly sixty years after the Act was passed, the American avenue was thwarted by the War of Independence, but not before some 50 000 miscreants had been exiled there and sold as servants.[23] Cessation of this profitable trade coincided with an increasingly harsh criminal code that meant more and more criminals needed accommodating, yet Britain possessed no extensive domestic prison system. Consequently, there emerged a severe problem of overcrowding on hulks (prison ships) and the few existing gaols. When American independence was finally won in 1783, that convict route was sealed forever. Soon after, in 1786, the decision was taken to send convicts to New South Wales, and in 1788 the British invaded the Australian continent. On this occasion, there was no selling of convicts (indeed, there was no market); instead, convict labour would be directed by a colonial governor. This method of peopling a new colony continued in New South Wales until 1840, in Van Diemen's Land to 1850, and in Western Australia until the late 1860s.

The severe legal code which had been generated, in part as a back-lash against an increasingly lenient practice of the law, but also by the changing nature of society, dominated the period when convicts were first transported to Australia in 1788. It meant that Australia received from England and Ireland criminals sentenced directly to transportation and those who escaped death. But law and punishment did not then ossify and remain constant over the subsequent fifty years while New South Wales acted as a receptacle for criminal outcasts. Contingent with the massive changes occurring in British society in the first half of the nineteenth century—agricultural and industrial revolutions, urbanisation and the demise of paternal authority, the birth of the railway, union of Ireland and Great Britain, the selective extension of enfranchisement, the abolition of slavery and the replacement of the Speenhamland system of outdoor relief with workhouses, to name but a few—the legal code transmogrified once more. Most significantly, the number of crimes punishable by death diminished sharply. It had taken centuries to build the bloody code; it took less than two decades to dismantle it. In 1820 the Black Act was repealed, and over the next seventeen years Robert Peel and John Russell between them removed almost two hundred capital offences. Price tags were attached to crimes indicating the relative gravity of offences. Theft of one shilling was no longer a transportable offence, unless it was a second or higher conviction. For first offenders, the cost was set at five shillings for theft from a shop or person compared with forty shillings for larceny from a dwelling; this linked punishment with value, at least in theory. By the time transportation to New South Wales ended in 1840, only eight capital statutes remained on the books, the main ones being murder, treason, piracy, burglary, robbery with violence, and arson of dwelling houses with people therein.[24]

Peel's reforms did not end there. New methods of punishment were explored, and the Prison Act that was passed in 1823 commenced a shift towards the penitentiary and incarceration as the chief mode of castigation, promoting religious instruction, reform through hard labour, and uniformity of treatment considered lacking in transportation.[25] Generally Peel pushed away from *ad hoc* and private initiatives in the direction of a more ordered penal system. The nature of detection was enhanced by the establishment of organised and regular police forces in the metropolis from 1829 and in the countryside from 1835, with 3300 Peelers and Bobbies in London in the first instance, ultimately doing away with the need for private associations for the prosecution of felons.[26] These latter organisations were concerned not only with locating crime, but with financing its prosecution. Private prosecution was costly, prohibiting many poorer victims from bringing charges. Consolidating and extending earlier developments, an Act of 1818 made financial allowances to prosecutors and witnesses in cases of felony, and the Criminal Justice Act of 1826 regularised criminal proceedings by extending the system of cost recovery to include expenses related to misdemeanours, covering the costs of witnesses and of parish constables detaining and conveying suspects.[27] The short-term outcome of improvements in detection and prosecution, and the greater leniency of a criminal code not predicated on hanging, was an increase in the reporting rate.[28] Leniency had grown from 1811 when the practice of the law was increasingly to commute capital sentences to transportation, so that by the late 1820s only one in twenty death sentences were carried out.[29] The combined effect of these shifts was that between 1825 and the end of the decade there was a doubling in the number of individuals transported.[30]

Criminal pursuits

Despite the brutality of the legal system which reigned for much of the period of transportation, and the rather inexact methods of detection and prosecution that were only just beginning to be rectified in the late 1820s and 1830s, many influential critics believed that the apparatus of the state efficiently identified those criminals who were of the very worst description and who belonged to a professional criminal class by desire, accident or even genetic predisposition. It was suggested that a 'criminal type' existed and that those belonging to it could be identified from their physical characteristics, before a crime had even been committed it would seem:

> Female thieves, and above all prostitutes, are inferior to moral women in cranial capacity and circumference, and their cranial diameters are less; but, on the other hand, their facial diameters are larger, especially in the jaw. Criminals have the darker hair and eyes, and this holds good also to a certain extent of prostitutes, in whom fair and red hair now surpasses and now approximates to the normal.

(How hair dyes must have confused their research!) Criminal women supposedly possessed receding foreheads, asymmetrical faces, projecting cheekbones and masculine faces that bore a 'hard, cruel look'.[31] Notions of individuals genetically predisposed to crime could emerge only within a discourse which perceived criminal law as unchanging, not as socially constructed but as somehow 'natural', just and imposed by a higher super-human authority. Believing this must have been particularly difficult, given the breadth of change being wrought by Robert Peel and his like, but believe many did. While punishments changed, the sanctity of private property remained paramount and gained in authority. Henry Mayhew, journalist and social commentator, was explicit upon this topic. 'To thieve, however, is to offend, at once socially, morally, and religiously; for not only does the social but the moral and religious law, one and all, enjoin that we should respect the property of others'.[32] This undermined the possibility that legal systems were the product of (unequal) human endeavour while concomitantly allowing the criminal to be vested with values of immorality and depravity, to be viewed with distaste and contempt.

Transportees were thus not held in the highest regard by some critics, who left written records of their offended sensibilities. One nineteenth-century commentator writing in the *British Monthly* described them as 'the most murderous, monstrous, debased, burglarious, brutified, larcenous, felonious and pickpocketous set of scoundrels that ever trod the earth'.[33] Notions of a 'criminal' or 'dangerous' class were gaining greatest currency at the very time when convicts were being shipped out to New South Wales. Conjuring up wild images of criminal depravity, nineteenth-century books documented the sins of the 'predatory classes'. Pages were filled with 'mobsmen' and 'sanctuary men', the infants of such scoundrels springing up 'rank and noxious in a hot bed of vice', generating 'a heterogeneous outcast tribe', a 'moral pestilence'.[34] Crime was nearly the exclusive preserve of 'this dismal substratum, this hideous black band of society'.[35] It was also this group's only pursuit: criminals were professionals at what they did, and they were organised. Within this influential discourse it was not poverty which drove individuals to offend occasionally, but greed for other people's property teamed with a repugnance to honest labour which led some individuals to live exclusively by crime. Nineteenth-century commentators represented four-fifths of offenders as criminals who would stoop to anything other than paid employment to make their living.[36] Immoral individuals choosing to live entirely off the proceeds of crime, eschewing work as a bad and foreign idea, were parasitic and hostile, hence dangerous to other classes. Feeding off society, criminals of this class personified all values antithetical to a respectable working class, and challenged the very sanctity of private property upon which other social classes rested. Criminals were lazy, immoral, dishonest, disrespectful and threatening. Next only to those who danced at the end of the hangman's rope, Australia's convicts were said to be the worst of those apprehended.

Insistently, one question begs to be asked: how well does this image fit convict women? What *sort* of criminals were these women who helped found the new settlement in New South Wales? Despite the rhetoric surrounding convict women regarding whoredom, prostitution is not an issue because it was not a transportable offence. If the image of convicts as professional criminals is correct, then certain characteristics with regard to crimes and occupations would be expected. Professionalism should have equated with recidivism—unless the thieves were very artful, which seems unlikely given their behavioural flaws of 'mental imbecility', 'aversion to continuity' and inability to apply themselves.[37] Further, crime needed to beget substantial income. Were these contract killers and black-mailers? Counterfeiters? (Certainly the most direct way of making money illegally was to make money illegally, literally.) Alternatively, attaining a living through crime might be achieved through the theft of property, if stealing was done effectively. Goods stolen needed to be either of a quality or a quantity sufficiently high to generate wealth by resale, or diverse enough to satisfy criminal consumption directly. As for occupational skills and other forms of human capital investment, a professional and habitual criminal would neither need any nor possess the stamina of character required to attain them; but this is the subject matter of later chapters. Does the evidence sustain these assumptions?

Criminals who lived by crime must by definition have committed offences regularly. It would seem fair to assume that constant criminal activity led, at least on a handful of occasions, to arrest, prosecution and verdicts of guilty. Did Britain transport its repeat offenders? Apparently not. If convict women habitually offended, they certainly were not habitually apprehended and punished. Figure 2.1 illustrates this point. Nearly two-thirds—64 per cent—of Elizabeth's compatriots were transported for their first offence, with a further 28 per cent having only one short-term sentence previously recorded against their name and another 6 per cent with two. Less than 3 per cent of women had already offended on more than two occasions. Typically, those with a criminal record had served sentences of between one and six months' detention for committing the same type of offence which later led to their transportation.[38] Undoubtedly some of these women would have committed other, undetected, crimes, but as historians we have no more evidence of reconviction rates than did nineteenth-century judges and juries who officially passed sentence on these women. There is no way of discerning the 'dark figure' of un-detected crime during this period. What we can descry is that most convict women were not recidivists.

Nor were most women transported for their first offence because it was extremely heinous. While most violent crimes were committed by first offenders, most first offenders were not violent criminals. Offences

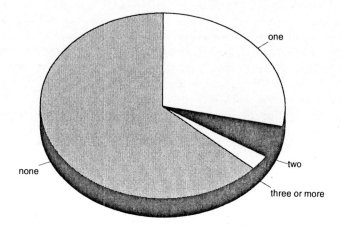

Figure 2.1   Proportion of women convicts with prior convictions.

leading to the women's transportation have been grouped into nine categories with the method of classification given in Appendix 2. Figure 2.2 shows graphically the crimes of convict women. Among the thousands of convict women transported, only 121 were recorded in the indents as guilty of explicitly violent crimes.[39] Thirty-eight had employed violence in the course of committing property offences, while eighty-three women had committed offences where violence was both the means and the ends. These were the felons beloved of storytellers and salacious news reporters. Not all murderers met their end at the gallows; some were sent to Australia. Eighteen convict women had murdered, and a further two had committed infanticide. Five women had attempted murder (including Rachael Atkinson's attempt on her own child),[40] and two were guilty of assault with intent to kill. There were five attempted poisonings, another five guilty of administering poison with the outcome not stated, and a drowning (not a murder?). Concealing murder accounted for another convict, two more were done for conspiring to murder, and one other merely on suspicion. A further twenty-five were guilty of manslaughter, one of their number being guilty of robbery as well. One attempted murderess had teamed her effort with robbery, and another had achieved the double. There were a couple of stabbings, twelve assaults—one aggravated, one malicious, and five violent incidents—and three accessories to rape, in addition to a handful of other acts. Figure 2.3 details how prior conviction rates varied by type of crime. Few violent criminals were permitted a chance to reoffend. An attempted poisoner, one transportee guilty of manslaughter and five sentenced for assault were the only singularly violent offenders known to have committed a previous offence, while those committing violent property crimes—twenty women guilty of

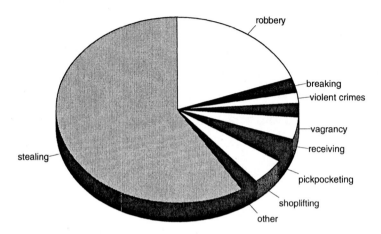

Figure 2.2 Categories of crime for which women convicts were transported.

robbery and assault plus two active women exiled for combining robbery, assault and stealing—were more likely to possess a criminal past, in their cases most likely non-violent attacks on property. Violence, then, was swiftly dealt with by the British legal system. Unpleasant these crimes were, but also aberrant by convict standards.

Violence was but a small sliver of total offences. Most convict women were not murderers, but thieves. They were property offenders. Ninety-four per cent of women were guilty of crimes against property: some shoplifting, picking pockets, receiving and breaking, but more noticeably robbery and primarily stealing. Overwhelmingly, stealing was the convicts' favoured crime, unrivalled by any other. Elizabeth and her compatriots Hannah Buttledoor and Caroline Humphries were thieves, but these three were just the tip of the iceberg. Information was missing for only 235 women. Out of 6641 crimes committed, 3909 were larcenous. Six out of every ten women had been transported for stealing some item or other, or for a related crime like pawning or pledging stolen goods. This also included five women who had been done for embezzlement, three for defrauding and ten for obtaining goods by false pretences.[41] Most convict women were thieves, but not habitually so: 61 per cent of them were first offenders with a further 31 per cent possessing but a single previous conviction. Deciding to steal rather than, say, rob meant that the vast majority of women preferred a victim who was not around to be personally threatened during the act (nor indeed to threaten them in retaliation).

But not all women took this option. While not grave in the way that murder was, not all property crimes can be dismissed as trivial. Some convict women were willing to be ruthless in the pursuit of other people's

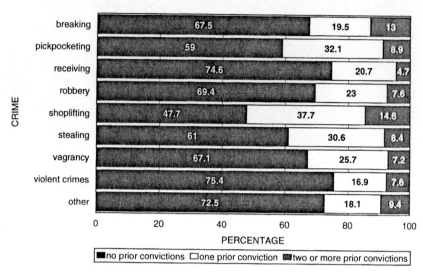

Figure 2.3   Crimes and prior conviction rates of women convicts.

property, and it should be borne in mind that even if poverty was the driving force behind much crime, poverty could be brutalising. Contemporaries regarded severely those offences which at least had the potential to involve direct personal contact, entailing an implicit threat to the victim's safety. Robbery was theft with force or threat, and was excluded from the benefit of clergy along with murder; and rob many convict women did do. Of convict women, 20 per cent were robbers. For this they were promptly transported, 69 per cent first offenders. 'Theft with force'—robbery—was the second most prevalent crime, involving 1300 women plus the further 38 women mentioned earlier for their aggressive behaviour, explicitly teaming robbery with violence—two killing to achieve their goal. Convict women committed robbery of various types: man robbery, person robbery, robbery in the street and from houses. It was this latter offence for which Margaret Shannahan (met in Chapter One) had fallen foul of the law. Robbing a person was the reason why both Rachel Bryant and Harriet Wakefield had found themselves part of the ship's company on the *Competitor*, while Caroline Rose (alias Rowles), Ann Maria Steel and sisters Sara and Maria Jeggings were four of the forty-one women transported on the *Numa* from London for man robbery. This was the offence most typically associated with prostitutes robbing clients. There were three bleach-green robbers (women forcibly stealing fabrics laid out to bleach in the sun) but they paled into insignificance next to those fifty-five women guilty of that most glamorous of offences, highway robbery.

The next most popular crime was once more in impersonal vein, shop-lifting. Numerically, no other crime came anywhere near stealing, with or without force, in the crime stakes. While 80 per cent of women were thieves or robbers, shoplifting in third place scored only 5 per cent. More than 300 convicts had lifted goods from shops or barrows. Shoplifters were those convicts most likely to have a criminal history, with over half already familiar with the justice system. Running shoplifting a close second in the crime stakes (but stealing a very poor fourth) was the pick-ing of pockets, with 271 women thus engaged. Picking pockets brought assailant and victim into closer proximity than did stealing or shoplifting, though rarely with threat of serious mischief. It had been among the first property crimes denied benefit of clergy, but this was because the offence was considered prevalent and difficult to stop rather than a threat to life and limb.[42] Next to shoplifters, the pickers of pockets were most likely to have committed previous offences, with 41 per cent possessing some criminal record. However, this still meant that nearly half the shoplifters were transported for their first offence and for their second in another 38 per cent of cases, while the majority of pickpockets were first offenders.

Ranking in fifth position on the list were receivers. Perhaps the closest to professional criminals were the 258 women done for receiving stolen goods. This operation would have required them to be more organised than most if they were running a business with a distribution network, but again there is little evidence of regularity: three-quarters had no criminal record. Breaking into an occupied house came next, and was a more serious offence in that it implicitly threatened violence. As with robbery, this crime was quickly made non-clergiable, and those sent to New South Wales were often escaping capital punishment.[43] Sarah Oxley, a 17-year-old nursemaid from Yorkshire guilty of housebreaking, was sentenced to death at the Old Bailey in October 1829; upon appeal, her sentence was commuted to life transportation and she arrived in New South Wales on board the *Roslin Castle* in the following year.

Quite at the other extreme from crimes threatening force or promising illegal dividends was vagrancy. This was one rare offence where English and Irish law differed. One hundred and fifty-four vagrants were trans-ported from Ireland, a crime that in the rest of Britain received a short-term custodial sentence of two weeks' hard labour subsequent to the enactment of the 1824 Vagrancy Act.[44] Arguably, two weeks in gaol were preferable to life in the workhouse, but this was not the choice in Ireland.[45] Never was there a clearer example of the class basis and social construction of crime than in the outlawing of 'being without visible means of support'. Either the banishing of vagrants was a very harsh punishment for women so clearly suffering poverty, or else judges saw themselves as bestowing transportation as an escape to a land of greater opportunity. According to the Reverend John West, Irish judges were motivated not by the desire to punish but by 'a vague notion of humanity'.[46] Other authorities feared that crimes were deliberately committed to incur punishment, and that transportation would 'resolve itself in the estimation of the people into merely gratuitous emigration'.[47] I wonder if Betty Boyle and Margaret Fahy, two vagrants sent out together on the *City of Edinburgh* in 1828, and the other women transported for this crime perceived transportation in such a benevolent way.

Transportation caught in its net a hotch-potch of other crimes, but with numbers so small they did not warrant their own slice of pie in Figure 2.2, except as 'other'. Once more, most of these miscellaneous crimes were against property rather than the person. Forgery was one such violation. This was the most direct way of making money through crime and was not excessively difficult in a pre-hologram era when watermarks on, and metal threads through, paper were not commonly used and when coins could be replicated from plaster moulds, as Henry McCave and Julia Smith attempted to demonstrate.[48] Additionally, the government was keen to stamp out crimes against the currency for obvious reasons of protecting the integrity of the nation's means of commerce. And yet only sixty-four such offenders were transported for forgery, coining, passing bad notes and uttering base coin.

Beyond these offences, most others involved just a handful of women. Five were done for breach of trust and sixteen for committing perjury. Seven women (four from Ireland) were guilty of variously cutting, maiming and feloniously killing beasts. Cruelly butchering animals and leaving them to be found was one way to register complaints against landlords; most unfortunately for the poor animals concerned this was not an uncommon form of rural protest, although it was unusual to be transported for it. A few arsonists were sent (twenty), a brothel keeper, and then there were three women guilty of sacrilege, three of bigamy, one of incest (no details given), two of rioting, three conspirators, another of possessing firearms, and three incidences of stripping children exclusively for the value of their garments. One woman was transported for procuring an abortion, while two other women were transported for selling their children, one case appearing very peculiar. Honora McCarthy arrived in the colony in 1839 on board the *Whitby*. A first offender, she had been sentenced to life for 'offering her child for sale to a surgeon'— that is, for supplying the burgeoning trade in bodies for the purpose of dissection.[49] Presumably the child had died of natural causes. This gruesome case looks more bizarre when the description of Honora in the indents is perused. She is described as being seventy years old (either a transcription error or the child she was selling was itself an adult), a widow and, strangely, childless. She was uneducated, a Catholic from

Cork, who stood 5 feet 5 inches in height, had a sallow and freckled complexion, grey hair and brown eyes. She had lost her two front upper teeth, bore a small scar on the palm of her left hand near the forefinger, and her eyebrows met in the middle (the sure sign of a witch!).

Many, many personal stories are embedded in convict history, only hinted at in the indents. Most involve theft, or a robbery. What motivated these women is both fascinating and elusive. Few left written records. Those that did may or may not have written the truth, and yet others might not clearly have understood themselves. But while we cannot go back in time to ask, we can infer much from the nature of their crimes and the conditions of their lives. What can we glean about motive from the objects of their thefts?

Stolen goods

What did women like Elizabeth Coltman steal in their supposed quest for a livelihood derived from crime? Information was frequently recorded regarding the items attained through stealing or, occasionally, through robbery, passing or receiving. In 275 cases the indent merely stated 'goods', in twenty-eight incidents 'forged items'; then there was the odd 'parcel' and 'a bundle'. Dismissing these as rather ambiguous descriptions, details remain on 3853 items acquired illegally by the convict women. Over 400 different types of items were stolen, and a few were unusual. Someone stole a box of toys, another woman stole a feather bed; a kitchen range, empty bottles, even 'optician's bones' were nicked. No doubt victims—and presiding judges—were more disgruntled by the women who variously stole a gun, a pistol, grape(shot) and ammunition.

Figure 2.4 reveals the objects of criminal endeavours. It groups the 3800-odd items into six main categories plus one residual group, details of which may be found in Appendix 3. The story it tells is not what one might expect from a criminal class. Professional criminals living an uproarious life based entirely on the proceeds of their criminal activities would be expected to embezzle expensive, marketable items. Jewellery was both small (and therefore easily concealed), valuable, and pawnable. Prostitutes might have been in a better position than most to relieve a client of his watch (and clothes). Disposing of jewellery was, however, a risky business. Reading through sessions papers of the Central Criminal Court (Old Bailey), one becomes aware of the important role played by pawnbrokers in getting a defendant committed, as frequently pawnbrokers appeared to identify the accused as the individual who pawned the stolen property. The three silver balls of the pawnshop loomed ominously, offering a place of sale but threat of apprehension also. Rewards were high, even if there were dangers. And

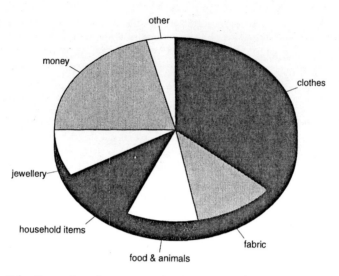

Figure 2.4   Categories of property stolen by women convicts.

yet, jewellery ranked sixth on the league table of favoured stolen objects. Some women stole watches, seven pinched rings, one thieved snuffboxes and another, trinkets. However, jewellery accounted for less than 8 per cent of stolen items. If Britain's criminal class earned its keep through trading in stolen jewels, either it was too proficient to get caught, or judges imposed punishments other than exile.

Eliminating dealings with a pawnbroker was a wise step. Many did this by stealing money. Money was the other obvious target for anyone seeking a criminal income from which to make their purchases, and it cut out the need for resale or pawning. Combined with notes, purses, basecoin, dollars, sterling, bad money and a cash book, money accounted for over one-fifth of stolen property and for around 12 per cent of thefts by women, ranking second on the league table. This proportion was very close to Gloucester criminals in the period 1815 to 1850 and Sussex offenders for 1805 to 1850, two rare groups of offenders so far analysed by historians.[50] But, as George Rudé noted when he made this study, money was an extremely ambiguous theft. Whether it represented 'acquisitive' or 'survival' crime is not easily assessed.[51] Such thefts may have funded illegal gambling or a generally illegal lifestyle, or they might have provided means of access to food, clothing or shelter as claimed by many in court.[52] Motives are not clear, and probably not uniform. It is worth remembering, however, that the theft of only five shillings—about one week's money wages for a housemaid—resulted in transportation, or just one shilling if it was a second offence.

What can be inferred from Figure 2.4 is that two-thirds of women were guilty of stealing goods at least as appropriate for immediate consumption as for resale. More typical than money, women snitched clothes. Clothing was particularly coveted. In 555 cases, convicts had stolen 'clothes'; when all other items of wearing apparel from frocks to socks are included, it transpires that 1394 items of clothing were purloined. Twenty per cent of transportees had earned their sentence for such thefts. Deirdre Beddoe in her study of Welsh convict women commented on the considerable irony that, journeying to the colony, 'the women were provided with more and better clothes than they had ever owned in their lives and many of them were being transported for stealing old garments of less value!'[53] Clothing thus accounted for 36 per cent of stolen property. Nearly half—some 47 per cent—of stolen goods were either clothes or fabric. Elizabeth had thieved silk, Hannah clothes, Caroline gowns. Another 10 per cent were household items such as blankets, cutlery, flat irons, pots and pans. Food and animals (who may have been stolen as food) contributed most of what remained, coming in at over 9 per cent. Again, these were the main objects of theft for other British criminals.[54] Rudé identified these very items as 'the typical means for survival for the labourer, craftsman, petty tradesman, or small consumer'.[55] Many of these goods might be traded in a second-hand market, or utilised directly.

What value might be allotted to such thefts? Old Bailey sessions papers recorded not only the items stolen, but their price also. Using a sample of this information, it is possible to gain some idea of the worth of convicts' criminal enterprise. Ann Andrews stole a watch worth 10s, and with it a passage on a transport ship.[56] Someone else went for quantity rather than pure quality: an ironmonger lost to his employee twenty-nine forks valued at £1, along with more than £2 worth of other goods (snuffers, canisters etc.). These earned James Bateman a year's confinement.[57] The second-hand pair of 'trowsers' and the frock stolen by Mary McCarthy were valued at 1s each.[58] A shift was worth 2s, as was a pillow; one blanket, 1s 6d; two sheets, 3s; one kettle, 1s; a shawl, 10s; and 30 yards of flannel, £1 14s.[59] If goods were stolen for resale rather than direct usage, these figures then need discounting. The three candlesticks purloined by James were worth 7s: the court heard that their resale value was only 3s. Eight silver spoons and two silver ladles worth a total of £4 had the potential to earn Anna Jardine a lesser 4s an ounce when melted down.[60] Maria Weston would have been lucky to receive a pawn value half the worth of her recently acquired candlesticks.[61] Maybe Maria and the others expected to gain more than they did, but if criminals were indulging regularly in theft and pawning, then surely they would soon have developed a feeling for the market and some ability to estimate worth. Pawn value appears rarely more than half the real value. If Ann

Andrews' 10s watch earned her 5s 3d, she could just afford to buy six standard loaves of bread. Mary McCarthy's venture into clothing was even less remunerative: her newly acquired purchasing power ran to one loaf, leaving her with the grand sum of three ha'pence (1¹/₂d). There was thus only limited money to be made this way, and it was insufficient to qualify as a primary income—at best, it was a supplement. Indeed, most of the thefts cited in the Old Bailey cases were committed by servants and other workers against their employers.[62]

It is possible that in bringing a charge the prosecutor might have underestimated the severity of the crime out of a humanitarian desire to see the offender punished but not executed. There was also a tendency for some juries and judges to exercise their discretionary powers in order to mitigate the severity of the legal system.[63] In one interesting trial a lodger, accused of pawning a sheet, was found not guilty on the grounds that the rental of 'furnished lodgings' entitled the rentee to the full use of the facilities and provisions.[64] More commonly, benevolence took the form of a 'partial verdict', that is, finding a criminal guilty of a lesser offence (with a lesser penalty) than the original indictment—'pious perjury'.[65] In practice this meant underestimating the value of the goods stolen, by as much as a half to two-thirds. No argument, then, should rely solely upon one potato having been stolen instead of two, or even two dozen.[66] Cited are single examples which suggest ball-park figures, but even assuming the worst of the data, if it is multiplied two or three times the ball-park itself does not really change.

Nor were the women stealing in the quantities that would surely have been needed to sustain a criminal lifestyle. Where this information can be assessed—for example, a distinction was made between stealing 'a shirt' or 'shirts'—it turns out that only 756 cases involved theft of more than one item. Often this involved stealing a couple of blankets or pigs, or, in ninety-one cases, goods were mixed: an umbrella and a book, bed and bedclothes, tea and sugar, boots and shoes, silk and butter, clothes and pistol, clothes and shoes, 'carpentering tools, butter, etc.', and the list goes on, objects of theft sometimes complementary, others not. The great majority of women, however, were charged with stealing a single item.

Even if a woman stole regularly, if these were the sort of items she thieved, it appears unlikely that she made an adequate income from it, or that her gains were of a wide enough variety to satisfy needs and wants directly and entirely. Alcohol is an interesting example of this. Crime was often thought to have been caused by the demon drink. Jelinger C. Symons wrote that 'perhaps of all the proximate causes of crime none is more fearfully powerful than that of drink'.[67] Sir W. Bovill reiterated these sentiments at the Denbighshire Assizes where he claimed that 'drunkenness, according to my experience, is at the root of nine-tenths of the crime committed in this Country'.[68] Given the image of nineteenth-century criminals, as habitual drunks as well as habitual criminals, it is something of a shock that only a paltry fourteen women were sent out for stealing alcohol.

By and large, the items stolen were petty, far from valuable, and were seemingly taken in small numbers—a blanket, a pair of gloves, a loaf of bread, a shirt. Betsey Brackingbury, transported in 1830 on the *Roslin Castle*, had stolen a prayer book. Of course, such items could have been sold to gain money to spend on what the ruling class considered to be frivolous luxuries—yet luxuries that they themselves were entitled to enjoy—such as gambling and alcohol and expensive dresses, which were not only detrimental to the obedience and regimentation of workers but a threat to social order as well.[69] But equally such items could have been stolen in order to alleviate suffering: such thefts might supplement income, or be useful in themselves, although they seem inadequate to sustain life for more than the briefest time. Ultimately, crime figures alone are inadequate to assess whether the motive was greed or need, acquisitiveness or survival. But perhaps such information is not all that relevant, unless the caretaker of that knowledge wants to make a case out for a professional criminal class, or to argue by inference that these criminals were good while those were bad. Convicts may have stolen for fun, greed, gluttony, on a whim, or through desperation. Whatever the case, it would seem unlikely that the theft of a loaf of bread or a single cloak represented a way of life commensurate with the expectations of a professional criminal element which believed it could gain more through crime than wage labour.

Convicts' victims, needs and opportunities

Nineteenth-century writings on the criminal or dangerous classes aimed at creating the image of an uncontrollable section of the people who posed a highly organised threat to the owners of property. This class who had chosen not to work but to live by crime was perceived as dedicated to the task of redistributing property away from the worthy to the unworthy. No person of property was safe from this danger and it was in this climate that Associations for the Prosecution of Felons, as well as local constabularies, proliferated.[70] But when the victims of the convicts become visible, it was not solely the stranger in the street who had fallen prey to these women.

Evidence suggests that when women murdered, they did not murder strangers but people whom they knew, lived and worked with, a tendency that persists today.[71] In his study of female criminals in the eighteenth century, John Beattie discerned the way in which violent crimes differed between women and men. Women committed these crimes not only less frequently but tended to commit them within the domestic sphere, against people known to them, and with a lesser use of violence.[72] Sometimes murder was a dramatic technique employed in terminating a problematic relationship. Was this the case for the two sisters Elizabeth and Constance (no surname supplied), aged nine and twelve years, two of the three females transported from the British colony of Mauritius for attempting to poison their master?[73] (These two girls would have been conspicuous in the colony, both because of their extreme youth among transportees and because of their colour: their eyes, hair and complexion were described simply as 'black', while their noses were 'broad' and 'pugged'.) Most violent crimes committed by convicts remain enigmatic, however, the indents revealing no insights. The crime of Mary Dennahy, for example, was listed simply as 'murder', and all we know about her is that she was an unmarried and childless 23-year-old Catholic, born and tried in Cork, short at 4 feet 10½ inches, with ruddy complexion, brown hair, hazel eyes and broad features, a country allworker and laundress with no history of offending.[74]

Yet sometimes this personal information hints at what happened. Ann Wilson and Catherine Harrington were the two women guilty of infanticide, and Rachael Atkinson, mentioned earlier, had attempted to murder her own child.[75] Ann was a nursemaid. She was twenty years old, Protestant, born in Cumberland and tried in neighbouring Westmoreland. Catherine was twice as old, a Catholic from County Cork where she worked as a dairymaid and maid of allwork. Standing in the dock in Kerry on 23 July 1835, this diminutive woman with dark brown hair and hazel eyes heard herself convicted of 'killing her child'. Both Ann and Catherine were sentenced to life transportation beyond the seas (although in New South Wales Ann received a pardon and Catherine a ticket-of-leave followed by a pardon). Nineteen-year-old Rachael was a country servant from Wigan in the North of England. She received the more lenient sentence of seven years' transportation. (Was this because she had botched the crime?) While the three had never met, coming as they did from various parts of two countries, they did have certain features in common. None of the three had any criminal record, all were otherwise childless, and all were unmarried domestic servants.

Being unmarried domestic servants had several implications. It meant the women were very vulnerable if they became pregnant. Single domestics were responsible for supporting themselves and were perhaps also contributing to their family's income.[76] Carrying an unsupported child was not only a social stigma but a threat to the whole family's living standards, for reasons both of lost earnings and of greater demands on household resources. Their work as domestics also meant the women were more vulnerable to becoming pregnant. This was an industry renowned for its high level of abuse. What was quaintly called 'seduction' was allegedly endemic in servant-employing households where sexual servicing and harassment were considered all part of the job.[77] Consensual sexual liaisons between household staff were also easier in this setting where young men and women lived in close proximity. Contraception was difficult and uncommon, and the other side of sexual liaisons, entered into willingly or otherwise, was unwanted and unsupported pregnancy. In nineteenth-century Britain, a single woman who found herself pregnant typically lost her job, living standard, status and any hope for a better future.[78] That so few convict women were guilty of these charges is perhaps what is surprising. Courts appear to have been disinclined to sentence women for infanticide, and certainly were averse to transporting them for it.[79] But was this vulnerability what motivated Ann, Catherine and Rachael to commit their offences? Certainly these do not appear profitable ventures. The indents are tantalising yet brutally concise.

Greater detail was listed in the indents in roughly one-tenth of offences, usually involving property. Locations were given in 260 cases. Shops, houses, an office, a window, a warehouse, an asylum, a hayloft, a lobby, a prison, a public house, a pawnbroker's, barracks and a garden all provided opportunities for attempts at anonymous crime. Dwellings and lodgings were popular, but more so were factories, targeted in half of incidents. Victims were listed in a further 340 indents. One-third of these cases described the victim simply as 'a person'. It is unclear whether the person was a stranger to the assailant or not. These incidents, like man robbery, sometimes indicated that prostitution was involved. Evidence in the Old Bailey sessions papers suggests that prostitutes 'took advantage' of their position to increase the value of their employment, or were accused of having done so, possibly by a dissatisfied client. Mary Revlet— later transported for a similar stealing offence—was accused of stealing money from a client availing himself of her prostitution services. Revlet argued that she 'had earned her £2 and would not give it up'. A witness in another case claimed that the offender 'deserved the money', and seemingly some judges agreed.[80] Many more crimes involved less transient encounters with individuals that the women knew personally. Husbands and relatives brought charges, but more common were masters, mistresses and other employers (57 per cent). Hannah Atkinson had robbed her mistress, and shipmate Susannah (alias Lavinia) Molton had robbed her master.[81] Some of these crimes were possibly committed by employees disgruntled at their working conditions who were attempting to 'get even'. What a worker saw as a perk of the job could, at the employer's discretion, be dealt with as a crime.[82] Other workers might have believed they had a justifiable right to supplement an income they perceived as simply too low, as in Mary Revlet's case. Or perhaps employers just made easy targets. Women might also have had scores to settle with relatives and employers. Intimacy was probably also a significant factor in the detection and prosecution of crime, with prosecution sometimes being made easier and sometimes being hindered by a personal knowledge of the offender.

Some of the convict women were obviously in employment at the time of committing their offence. From their employers the women had stolen, among other things, cloaks, shawls, gowns, handkerchiefs, coats, shirts, shoes, gloves, calico, cotton, linen, flannel, muslin, ribbons, sheets, blankets, quilts, tablecloths, pots and pans, plates, spoons, watches, money, meat, potatoes, bread, butter and cheese. They also purloined carpentry tools, a reaping hook, washing clothes, even washtubs. Indeed, crime often appeared to have been related to work even in cases where the victim was not specified. Needlewomen pilfered needles, thread and fabric. When dough was stolen, it was not startling to discover that the theft had been committed by a baker. Cooks sneaked food more frequently than most, but were less likely to steal clothes. Clothes were more the preserve of offenders like Caroline Humphries, housegirls, housemaids, laundrymaids, laundresses, needlewomen, dressmakers and children's maids—those women who made, cared for, washed, or worked with clothing. This is what May Davies, laundress and housemaid, had done to earn her passage on the *Princess Charlotte* in 1827, as had the Dublin needlewoman Mary Morris (alias Burke alias Morrison) transported six years later on the *Caroline* along with Margaret Shannahan.

Meanwhile, washerwomen filched the bedding and linen that they laundered: their rate of transportation for this offence was twice that of any other group. Theft of a tablecloth led the washerwoman Alice Dickson to New South Wales in 1834 on the *Andromeda*. On board ship with May Davies was Mary Condon. Mary was a 45-year-old Catholic, a mother and wife, who had practised both as a dairywoman and washerwoman before being sentenced for stealing sheets. As older women—many with children and often deserted or widowed—working for others but usually operating from within their own homes, washerwomen were unlikely to have been provided with necessary goods such as bedding by their employers other than for the purpose of laundering them. The poverty which drove so many women into this profession with its low entrance costs and wide demand was also likely to drive some women to steal, possibly pawn, or directly use the items temporarily in their possession. That food was also a high priority with these individuals would seem to confirm need as a typical motive.

Discrepancies in what was purloined by different groups of workers reflected that, to some extent, theft was determined by need coalescing with opportunity. Clothes were less prevalent than bedding among the goods stolen by washerwomen because these more delicate items were reserved for cleaning by the handiwork of women defined as 'laundresses' and 'laundrymaids', a distinction in nomenclature which reflected a specialisation in workplace, work and equipment. Cooks were prone to steal food more than most, but so too did general house servants. While cooks were in an obvious and direct relationship with food through their employment, the house servant, housemaid and other domestics would also have had some access to the kitchen. Dressmakers, too, were in want of food, but having no access through their trade they had to steal from a shop or barrow when the opportunity presented itself.

Convict women were casual offenders taking advantage of what chance openings they encountered, be they in their mistress's quarters, at home laundering sheets, in a dressmakers' workroom, on the street or in a shop. They stole irregularly, they failed to prig the items of greatest value, and they appear to have worked alone and not in gangs which might have maximised their efficiency. Even as thieves these women were not organised hardened professionals disinclined to any honest work. Professional and habitual criminals living entirely off illegal proceeds these were not. If these were the worst criminals Britain had to dispose of, then there was little to worry about other than rectifying some gross economic inequalities.

Sentencing

Transportation effectively banished convict women from their homes, their husbands, children, lovers, other family members and friends in England and Wales, Ireland and Scotland, for life. It was nearly impossible for a convict woman to return when her sentence had expired, as transport costs were prohibitive and women—unlike men—did not have the option of working their passage home as sailors. Nor did the authorities in Britain or New South Wales offer to repatriate the men and women whom they so willingly transported in the first place. Transportation was in this respect a very harsh sentence to impose on petty offenders. They were exiled for life irrespective of sentence length, but the original sentence did nonetheless matter. Colonial experiences were profoundly influenced by the duration of servitude. In practice, most women (four-fifths) received the minimum sentence of seven years. The rest got ten, fourteen or fifteen years, or life (see Figure 2.5). Life often represented a commuted death sentence as in the case of Sarah Oxley cited earlier.

The first point to note in sentencing was that courts treated various classes of crimes quite partially. Some crimes were immediately punished

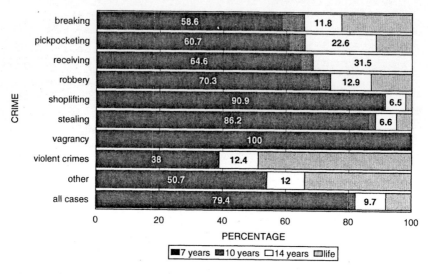

Figure 2.5   Crimes and duration of sentence of women convicts.

with transportation, while others were more leniently attended. One mistake that historians have made has been to employ criminal histories as a measure of 'criminality'. Repeat offenders were deemed hardened professionals, while first offenders were somehow less culpable. Looking separately at transportees who did repeatedly offend—that is, the 8 per cent with three or more convictions to their name including their transportable act—yields a criminal profile much like the first offenders who dominated, except that shoplifters offended more regularly than most. But prior convictions were in fact a poor measure of criminal status. They fail to identify members of a criminal class devoted to a life of crime, or the most aberrant offenders. Studying juvenile delinquency in early nineteenth-century England, Susan Magarey concluded that 'it is impossible to assume that one, two, or even ten previous convictions necessarily defined a hardened professional criminal, living by choice on the proceeds of theft'.[83] If deprivation was the dynamic behind criminal actions once, there is no reason to assume low wages or poverty were temporary. To have a previous conviction for stealing a loaf of bread before being transported for stealing butter does not make the woman socially aberrant, merely human with human needs but inadequate means. Conversely, not all first offenders can be assumed to be insignificant criminals. Indeed, to be transported for a first conviction might be evidence of a particularly brutal crime.

Court behaviour determined two elements in a convict's make-up: whether the offender had a criminal record (that is, whether or not she was transported for her first offence or given a second chance) and the duration of her colonial servitude. But what determined court behaviour? Was there a nexus between a crime's severity, the chance of being exiled for a first conviction, and sentence length? It will be remembered that Figure 2.3 illustrated prior conviction rates broken down by crime. Certainly there was a link between degrees of threat and punishment, although it is not an entirely clear one. Reoffending criminals tended to commit the same type of crime; it can be reasonably assumed that a second offender transported for picking pockets had been convicted of picking pockets before. On the whole, property crimes directly threatening no one were treated most leniently. Yet it was not vagrants and thieves who were most likely to have been let off transportation when previously dragged before the courts, but shoplifters. Earlier it was noted that 52 per cent of shoplifters had criminal histories when they appeared before the court that would finally transport them, 15 per cent of their number having been convicted on two or more occasions. Pickpockets and thieves came next, hovering around 40 per cent. Why shoplifters should be given a second chance more readily than thieves is difficult to guess. More worrying offences like breaking and robbery were permitted fewer opportunities for repeat performances, with only 31 and 32 per cent respectively possessing a criminal record, but strangely this put them on par with vagrancy, a crime involving no threat of force. Similarly, a past conviction rate of 25 per cent put violence on a level footing with receiving, another crime with no clear victim and threatening no one. In accordance with contemporary values, we might expect a severe crime involving threat of violence and intimidation to be punished promptly and austerely, but why were vagrants and receivers treated in the same harsh manner? Governing principles are difficult to ascertain, leaving the whole matter quite perplexing.

Was the correlation between severity of crime and punishment more clearly defined when imposing the sentence of transportation? Figure 2.5 compares the length of exile awarded to the different crimes. Less severe crimes—namely vagrancy, stealing and shoplifting—in the main were punished with the seven-year minimum. Conversely, overtly violent crimes were the most harshly dealt with. Crimes threatening personal safety were those most likely to be punished immediately and with a life sentence. Some 49 per cent of violent offenders received life sentences for this their first offence, although this still left 13 per cent with only mid-term sentences to serve and 38 per cent with the minimum seven years in exile. Beyond these offences the pattern becomes more muddled. Pickpockets were as likely as robbers to get life (12 and 13 per cent respectively), a sentence even more likely to be imposed on house-breakers (23 per cent). Breakers, pickpockets and receivers too also tended to fare worse than robbers, in that fewer gained the seven-year minimum (59, 61, 65 and 70 per cent respectively). While prior conviction rates and duration of exile did not clearly correlate, there is some logic evident: severe punishments were imposed on severe crimes, lighter sentences on less severe ones, but with grey areas in between. Receivers whose actions directly hurt no one were sentenced at the rate of violent offenders and for a length of time normally reserved for those engaged in threatening behaviour. Vagrants were promptly transported, but for the minimum period, perhaps reinforcing the idea that judges were bestowing a favour. But it should be borne in mind that while stealing was at the lower end of the punitive spectrum and a thief was transported for fewer years than were many pickpockets, this still meant many first offenders guilty of low-value thefts were being transported for seven, fourteen, fifteen years or even life when a few months' detention at home would have sufficed.

Irregularities in court practices were more pronounced when looked at case by case. Many rulings appear idiosyncratic, with judges exercising all the considerable discretion that had been built into the system over the centuries. Hannah Atkinson and Susannah Molton were mentioned earlier in the context of robbing their mistress and master respectively. Hannah received a life sentence, while Susannah's was for seven years. Neither had previous convictions. One obvious difference between them was age. Susannah was only fifteen, Hannah twenty-eight. There were other variations too. Hannah was married and travelled to Australia with one child. Born in Limerick, she had grown up a Catholic; eventually, she migrated to England, working in London either as a plain cook or as a housemaid in a hotel. She was illiterate. Susannah was single, childless, Protestant and, although young, she had already learned to read and write. She had not moved from London where she worked as a nurse-maid. Had any of these elements influenced the courts' decisions? Nineteen-year-old Rachael Atkinson received seven years' transportation for the attempted murder of her child, while the two Mauritian children Elizabeth and Constance got life for the attempted murder of their master. Such inconsistencies bespeak a certain capriciousness in sentencing.

Discrepancies in sentencing did not occur only among those transported. Even more glaring were those cases where similar offenders received wildly different punishments. Rudé noted marked disparities in sentencing. One 14-year-old boy found guilty of pickpocketing a handkerchief worth one shilling received a sentence of life transportation, while another 14-year-old lad guilty of stealing five pounds from his master was fined one shilling and discharged. The same judge presided in both cases.[84] Resonances ring out with the situation before 1706: it will be remembered that before everyone qualified for the benefit of clergy, two people guilty of the same type of crime might witness one of them walking free (though branded) while the other hung from the gallows. Discretion was once again being exercised in the nineteenth century, through the imposition of different sentences for very similar crimes. Indeed, reading the evidence of trial cases, it is difficult to discern what determined sentences.

Elizabeth Thomas had stolen from her master of four days, Charles Neville Smith, one spoon, one tablecloth and one shift, estimated at a combined value of ten shillings. This 30-year-old woman had seen better times, according to James Aldous, pawnbroker, and in spite of her history of pawning she was recommended to mercy by the jury and confined six months with three weeks in solitary.[85] On 22 December 1836 Ellen Coffee, a charwoman, had stolen from her employer a wide array of objects, here listed along with their value. One shawl (20s), one ring (20s), one shirt (3s), one spoon (3s), two sleeves (1s), one neckerchief (3d), one pillow-case (3d), carpet: one yard (8s), one wine glass (10d), one handkerchief (2d), two knives (1s), four forks (1s 6d), and three valances (3s).[86] Ellen was sentenced to three months confinement. Along with Elizabeth Scott (who was found to be innocent), Mary Ann Riley was accused of stealing shoes. Having entered the shop of Mr Charles Casey, a shoemaker in London, and after trying upon her feet a couple of pairs of shoes, Mary declared her business done, a fruitless search. The girls—for such they were—were questioned about a missing pair, knowledge of which they denied. Mary was searched bodily, and the said item located, held between her thighs. Confronted by Hannah Cunningham, the wife of a policeman, and interrogated 'How came you to do this?', the girl replied 'I do not know, I was in want of a pair of shoes, and had no money to buy them with'.[87] One month's confinement was generous. Eliza Blackwood—and forty-one other women—had not been so fortunate in their dealings with the law: for stealing shoes in the United Kingdom they were incarcerated in New South Wales. Essentially the same crime earned some women the sentence of transportation while others received verdicts such as 'Guilty—Recommended to mercy. Confined one month; one week in solitary'. These were not inconsiderable punishments, but they were by no means as extreme as transportation, the sentence awarded to so many other women guilty of no greater crimes and in many cases for crimes of considerably less value. How most sentences were arrived at remains an enigmatic calculation.

Puzzling out the story of founding White Australia requires us to understand more about the functioning of the legal systems of Great Britain and Ireland. We need to know why some women received verdicts of transportation and other women did not. There was enough leeway in the system to allow what appears to be a subterranean selection procedure operating at the point of sentencing which determined, in part, who was transported. In conjunction with the nature of the crime committed, other factors may have been influential. Did judges exercise discretion according to their hope that a particular offender might reform if given the chance in a new colony? Perhaps age, abilities, someone to testify of the accused's good character or the plea of distress influenced the verdict. Such decision-making had ramifications for the type of labour supplied to the Australian economies: were these the worst criminals with the poorest skills, or those women best equipped to take advantage of the move? And there was a second stage in selection: not everyone sentenced to transportation was in fact transported, about one-third being left behind.[88] Overt policies regarding sentences, health and age were clear: exile was ostensibly reserved for those awarded the severest punishments, women who were badly behaved while detained, along with others serving shorter sentences but whose health was strong and age was under forty-five years.[89] But were these the only determinants? Anne Summers has suggested that all women available for transporting were sent to satisfy the colonial demand for prostitutes, but the supporting evidence has not yet been collected and indeed there is some indication that the opposite was true.[90] For every one woman in gaol in England in 1841 there were 4.4 men, yet the ratio of women to men transported to New South Wales was 1 to 5.5.[91] Perhaps a gender-biased judiciary sentenced proportionally fewer women to transportation.[92] We simply do not know, yet it is imperative that we discover who out of that pool of potential transportees was actually sent to Australia, who was not, and why. Such questions regarding selection procedures will not be answered until further rigorous investigation is made of the British court records. Only then can hidden agendas in the colonisation of Australia be discerned.

On the issues of transported felons and crime, the findings are irresistible. Convict women were not habitual and organised criminals. Considerable doubt hangs over whether they were even regular offenders, let alone organised professionals sating all their wants through crime. They were not known recidivists, nor were most of them cruel and vicious criminals. One contemporary depiction, reproduced in Figure 2.6, suggests a much softer side to female prisoners. Very complex reasons govern why, and in what manner, crimes were committed. Some crimes were violent and disturbing. Some—like vagrancy—appear to us unjust. But the number of these cases is meagre. Overwhelmingly, convict women were first-time sneak thieves. Some women were driven by poverty. Others protested. Yet others found themselves in difficult positions foisted upon them by a sexual double standard which left them economically vulnerable. No

Figure 2.6 'The Daisy', frontispiece from F. W. Robinson, *Female life in prison by a prison matron* (London c. 1862, fourth edition), artist unknown. Note the 'General Rules for Female Prisoners' hanging dolefully on the wall.

doubt some were greedy. In most cases, we will never know what motivated their actions, although more can be discovered about the context and condition of their lives at the time of committing their offence by sifting through appeals for justice made by relatives requesting that sentences be overturned or mitigated. But the small-scale nature of their property crimes meant that convict women's stealing was quite inadequate to support a lifestyle based entirely on illegal proceeds. On the contrary, criminal earnings in most cases would have provided but a meagre supplement. These were casual criminals, many of whom committed their offences in familiar surrounds—at the shops, in lodgings, at work—and against familiar people. They stole from their masters and mistresses, other types of employers, and clients paying for laundry to be done or sexual services to be granted. Most appear to have acted alone. Little evidence suggests these women were organised molesters of anonymous wealthy victims in the crowd. For their sins, most women paid with seven years of their life spent in exile under the rule of colonial authorities in a country from which they were unlikely to return. That so few were murderous fiends or violent desperadoes does not gel with the image of convict women as utterly depraved criminals of 'the darkest complexion'.[93] Ill-fitting seems the nineteenth-century description of Britain's exiles as criminals from a dismal substratum, a hideous black band of society. Could it be, then, that a blacker truth about a criminal class operating in a particular area has been overlooked, in England perhaps, or maybe London?

CHAPTER THREE

Piso's Justice: Irish and English Offenders

A salutary tale is offered to us from Ancient Rome. Magistrate Piso believed a murder had been committed, and on circumstantial evidence he sentenced the perpetrator to death. But when the executioner was about to perform the deed, the alleged victim appeared, alive and well; in the changed circumstances the beheading was stopped and the three returned to Piso. But Piso was not happy. A capital sentence had been passed and it was to be fulfilled. One dead. The centurion had failed to carry out his duties as executioner, and for this he lost his life. Two dead. Finally, the chimerical victim forfeited his existence because he was deemed responsible for the deaths of two innocent men. Three dead. This has come to be known as Piso's justice: technically correct, but morally wrong. In *Les Misérables*, Victor Hugo's protagonist, Jean Valjean, reflected on the ethics of punishment in similar vein: while severe sentencing for small-time property crime might be required by law and was not, therefore, an injustice, it was an iniquity.

Something similar has operated in the minds of those commenting on Australia's convicts. Sentencing offenders to exile may have been just, but was it fair? Did convicts really deserve what appear to be such cruel sentences? Unlike the legal position, this moral dimension is never so easily settled. Perceptively, Bernard Smith recognised that 'the very word "convict" concealed moral issues to which, in one sense, there were no purely historical answers, but a great potential to divide and separate out historians along an ethico-political spectrum'.[1] Transportation was technically the correct sentence for convicts' crimes; yet by asking if it was morally right or wrong, historians effectively appointed themselves to the bench, but on what exactly were they adjudicating? No one was content to simply argue the pros and cons of transportation as a punishment without first tying it to the severity of the offence. Judgements regarding the morality of punitive measures then tended to become entwined with judgements on the crime and the morality of the offender. A simple equation operated. If convicts were immoral professional criminals, the sentence was morally justifiable; if they were victims of circumstances beyond their control, transportation was an iniquity.

It was a desire to exonerate convicts which led James Moore to declare of transportees that 'a very large proportion ... were neither hardened, nor vicious, nor even criminals'.[2] Technically convicts were lawbreakers, but Moore wished to deny this fact because he believed a moral injustice had occurred, that convicts were not such bad people, that the term 'criminal' had been invested with broader meanings embedding a set of derogatory values, and that redemption required innocence. This latter clause was wrong. Despite twentieth-century legal expectations that severe punishment is indicative of serious crime committed by morally reprehensible offenders, in the nineteenth century at least punishment, guilt and innocence had little to recommend them as predictors of personal morality. The very supposition that punishment, crime and personal immorality equated in any legal sense was wrong. Degrees of crime and punishment did not formally equate when transportation to New South Wales began and it is doubtful that they did so in practice even by 1840: death sentences were awarded for murder and petty theft alike before Peel's reforms. The harshest of sentences could be awarded irrespective of an individual's morality or, for much of the period, the nature of their crime. But the assumption that severity of punishment and seriousness of crime correlated was made and it had considerable influence, placing morality on the historical agenda and inviting the jury to reconsider.

Transportation seemed such harsh retribution to exact, and insinuated that those sent were so very degraded, that many historians felt the impulse to absolve. While convicts as a class were often dismissed as organised professional criminals, many transportees were exempted from castigation. If convicts were judged to be morally reprehensible, their punishment was not only legally but ethically justified and transportees fully deserved their sullied reputations. On the other hand, convicts who were the victims of difficult economic times or who were political protesters were more worthy, their sentences moral travesties.[3] Commentators exculpated these transgressors, believing their sentences were technically correct but morally wrong. Reprehensible and worthy categories overlapped with certain classes of offenders, specifically urban/rural and English/Irish criminals. Convicts from rural England, and convicts from Ireland like Margaret Shannahan, have not been tainted in quite the same way as Elizabeth Coltman's urban sisters. J. J. Tobias, crime historian, observed that 'contemporaries had no doubt that the criminal class was substantially a phenomenon of the large towns'.[4] In Britain this argument was put forward by men like Thomas Beggs, Patrick Colquhoun, Henry Fielding, Randle Jackson, Henry Mayhew, Jelinger C. Symons and Edward Gibbon Wakefield, to name but a few.[5] Modern historians agreed. The literature clearly establishes a dichotomy between urban 'guilt' and rural 'innocence': while the latter was perceived as the victim of poverty, the former was seen as the executor of crime.

Hence the ease with which Manning Clark refuted the earlier work of George Arnold Wood. Wood pronounced the convicts morally innocent village Hampdens. With the evidence that the majority were *not* rural born and bred, Clark, with equal nonchalance, condemned them as urban scum. He complained that Wood's argument 'stimulates two very misleading ideas in the mind: that convicts were mainly agricultural workers: that they were casual as distinct from professional criminals'.[6] Agricultural workers, it seems, tended to be casual criminals while their urban kin had a predisposition to professionalism. Clark delighted in pointing out that his figures 'show quite clearly that the majority of the convicts came from the towns, a fact', he claimed, 'which is blithely ignored by those historians who devote so much space to rural England, with special attention to the victims of enclosure, high prices, inadequate poor relief, and so little space to the towns'.[7] Were prices not high in urban centres? Was poor relief adequate there? And where were those workers dispossessed by Enclosure to be found if not in the towns? More recently, John Hirst pursued this theme:

> Fewer than half of the convicts sent to New South Wales came from the country. Nearly all of these were used to regular work and they were less likely to have been regularly involved in crime. Those sent from rural Ireland were often first offenders convicted on very minor or trumped up charges. A well-disposed country worker transported to Australia and assigned to a settler found it very easy to adapt to what was required of him ... Here was a proper servant who had a fit sense of the obligation not only to work but to serve and please his master; to do his duty. But most of the convicts had not been bred as proper servants. They came from the loose disorderly sort, chiefly from the towns; they were unused to regular hours, regular employment or hard manual labour; large numbers of them were professional thieves. The masters of New South Wales had to struggle hard to get these people to work at all ...[8]

Cemented was the identity of rural innocence and normality, juxtaposed with urban perversion. Another element in the equation is also evident here: the different treatment accorded the Irish.

The countryside generated casual crime, the cities professional criminals, or so it was thought. This identity had another reading in the division between the Irish and the English. It can be seen how these categories overlapped, given the predominantly pre-industrial and consequently rural basis of large sections of the Irish economy compared with the industrialising urban economy of much of Great Britain. Some observers and historians overstated this identity, creating all Irish offenders as rural and nearly all English criminals as urban. The corollary of this logic was a perception that the English were hardened malefactors while the Irish were victims of oppression and poverty. Furthermore, the equation was also taken to predict that the more urban a centre the more criminal its population, hence the description of London's convict women as being 'of the lowest and worst description, the very scum of the city and the country'.[9]

Critics last century dealt the Irish a lighter blow. Father William Ullathorne, writing in his *Catholic Mission* in 1837, expressed this theme. 'Many Irish Catholics, if I except those from the large cities, have been transported for the infringement of penal laws, for aggrarian [sic] offences, and minor delinquencies; whilst those from England are, with rare exceptions, punished for direct aggression on the property or the person'.[10] In 1887, the historian J. F. Hogan commented that 'these Celtic pioneers, it should be remembered, were transported in convict ships to Australia for alleged offences that were not crimes at all in the legitimate sense of the word, and nowadays are never regarded as such'.[11] Alexander Marjoribanks—a Scottish tourist to New South Wales—also communicated this more sympathetic perspective. He wrote, 'a man is banished from Scotland for a great crime, from England for a small one, and from Ireland, morally speaking, for no crime at all'.[12] This was unusually generous towards the English in terms of the current debate.

Twentieth-century historians conformed to this trend. Ireland's exiles were perceived less as immoral and more as the product of an oppressive social and economic regime. M. B. and C. B. Schedvin were explicit: 'The Irish are excluded from all that follows, for it is clear that the familial, religious and environmental background of the Irish convicts produced an identifiably different behavioural pattern'.[13] According to Patrick O'Farrell, 'it is true that all research suggests that ... generally, the Irish were a better type of convict ... their criminal impulses those of the destitute and desperate'.[14] Others agreed. A. G. L. Shaw calculated that 5000 Irish women and men were transported as either political or 'social' offenders, with most of the others guilty of only minor thefts. Interestingly, he concluded, 'save that they were more often driven to crime by desperate poverty, they were very like the English convicts' (quite a proviso!).[15] He also noted that those women forced into crime by the Famine 'were illiterate country-dwellers whose conduct in the colony was far better than that of the average convict'.[16] Francis J. Woodward blamed poverty and oppression 'for the lawlessness of a peasantry which in other respects was not criminal'.[17] Lloyd Robson, too, chimed in. 'The condition of the peasantry, then, was miserable in the extreme ... The offences of the Irish convicts reflect the state of the society from which they sprang' (apparently this was not so for the English and Scottish transportees).[18] Irish offenders were not habitual criminals from a professional criminal class. Discussing the early phase of transportation, T. J. Kiernan wrote, 'some 61 per cent of the total of the Irish convicts up to 1803 did not belong to the ordinary criminal class' and Clark, too, found that Irish convict ships 'contained a higher proportion of people not dependent on crime for a living than did similar ships from England and Scotland'.[19] John Williams discerned that 'more Irish male convicts conformed to the "Village Hampden" theory than did prisoners of other nationalities'.[20] On the women, Robson commented, 'that if there were any female village Hampdens, then they came not from England but from the Irish country-side'.[21] And while England's women, especially those from London, had a background of immorality and an 'apparent lack of any standards of decency or honesty', Portia Robinson found a sharp contrast in the Irish women, 'the only lifestyle familiar to them as wife and mother'.[22] The effect of this unequal treatment was to identify the dichotomy of good and bad with that of Irish and English.

While convicts *en masse* have been defamed as professional offenders, the Irish have been largely exempted. Throughout the literature Irish transportees have gained favourable positioning against the downgraded English. Interestingly, the Scots have been even more castigated, treated as the real dregs and described by Robson as 'the worst of a bad lot'.[23] There was thus a continuum created that ran from good to bad to very bad, as reflected in Marjoribanks' quotation. No Irish were sent to Van Diemen's Land while transportation to New South Wales was an option.[24] Consequently, the majority of convict women in New South Wales came from Ireland. Did this mean that the first colony inherited a better class of criminal? Was it true that the Irish were forced into crime through economic hardship while the English—and worse still, the Scots—chose crime as a preferable way of life, or because they knew nothing better?

Irish and English convicts

William Ullathorne had claimed that Irish transportees were minor and agrarian offenders, while the English were sentenced for direct aggression on property and the person. Was his assessment correct? Nearly 3000 women were tried in England, and over 3400 in Ireland, and we have information on offences for most of them. Their crimes are reported in Figure 3.1. Chapter Two observed that the one legal difference between the two countries was in their treatment of vagrants. It can be seen from Figure 3.1 that Irish alone were banished for vagrancy, because in England 'being without visible means of support' was a crime dealt with summarily and therefore not punishable by transportation.[25] The 5 per cent of Irish offenders who were vagrants perhaps best fitted Ullathorne's description of women transported for minor delinquencies. Over and above this, Irish and English offenders ranked crimes in roughly the same order. Direct aggression on property was what convict women from both countries did best. In both cases nearly four-fifths of women were guilty of stealing or robbery. Admittedly, the balance between these offences differed, although stealing predominated universally. Half of English women were guilty of stealing but even more Irish women—some two-thirds—had purloined their way to New South Wales. Conversely, proportionally more English women preferred to rob. At least superficially this appears to be true. The gap arises due to English women's propensity for 'person robbery' compared with the widespread Irish offence of 'stealing from the person', a gap that could be an artefact of the way crimes were labelled in the two countries. In any case, what do we infer from this gap: that Irish women were nicer, disapproving of the threat of force involved in robbery? The lower proportion of Irish robbers cannot easily be taken to indicate scruples because Irish women were twice as likely as the English to commit overtly violent crimes, yet caution should be exercised in interpreting such figures when so few women from either country had engaged in violent affrays. The numbers England failed to amass here and with vagrants were made up with pickpockets, receivers and to a lesser extent women guilty of breaking and entering and shoplifters, though once again the latter is compensated by the larger propor-

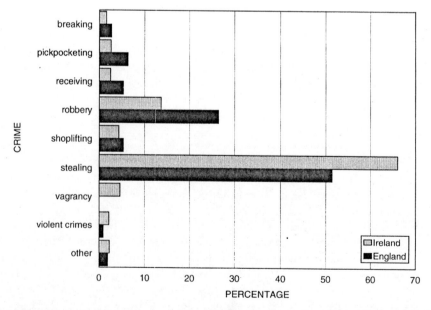

Figure 3.1 Female crime in Ireland and England.

tion of Irish women sentenced for 'stealing from a shop'. Some differences did exist between Irish and English offenders, but they were comparatively small and their meaning is inconclusive. Certainly, the Irish do not stand out as agrarian offenders and women guilty of crimes minor in comparison with their English sisters. Irish and English women held much in common and differed remarkably little, and in both cases two basic property crimes dominated.

Victims, and the objects of theft, did differ between English and Irish offenders. Factories were popular venues for crime in both countries, but far more of England's women were known to have exploited the homes and workplaces of their employers, masters and mistresses and their lodgings: together these comprised 52 per cent of known targets for English women, but in Ireland only 19 per cent. The Irish preferred houses, shops and less personal thefts, but also stole directly from 'the person' more so than did English women. Items thieved also varied. Both groups had a penchant for clothes and money, with the English tending a little more to cash and Irish women more prone to wearing apparel, as can be seen from Figure 3.2. Fabric, food and animals, as with clothes, were Irish predilections. The English favoured household items, jewellery and, to a lesser extent, money.

Such differences as did exist are easily explained, and were to be expected. In keeping with the argument made in Chapter Two, the nature of crime appears to have had much to do with circumstances and opportunities: maiming your master's cow or stealing their pig was easier for a

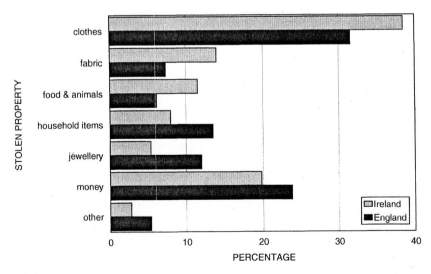

Figure 3.2 Property stolen by women convicts in Ireland and England.

country dairymaid than a housemaid in a town. Unlike the premeditated act of murder, or bank robbery, many thefts were opportunistic and items stolen reflected what goods were available. Avenues for crimes, and objects of theft, differed between England and Ireland. England had a more prominent urban sector and a larger and wealthier servant-employing middle class. English city streets provided pickpockets and thieves with richer pickings than could be found in most of Ireland, and predictably jewellery, other conspicuous items such as watches, and money led a more precarious existence in England. English convicts prigged these at twice the rate of Irish gals. Private homes and lodgings also promised profit. Given that English domestics were twice as likely as their Irish sisters to steal from their employers, it is not surprising to find they stole what was at hand: clothes, money, household items and jewellery. Theft in England was no doubt facilitated by the urban population's favoured access to pawnshops and second-hand markets. Only 1 per cent of Irish women were transported for pledging goods, while over 5 per cent of the English were. Not only jewellery, but clothes, fabric, cooking and household items, even bedding and linen could all be sold on if not used directly.[26]

Ireland was different. Proportionally it had a larger rural basis than did England. Consequently, Irish convicts stole animals at three times the British rate. Living in the countryside beyond the ready circulation of money, Ireland's country women were less likely to steal coins and cash. Black markets in all but clothes were less developed in Ireland and presumably the difficulties associated with processing stolen goods acted to limit crimes such as picking pockets, shoplifting and the like. When Irish women did steal, they fancied clothes. In some cases such theft bypassed the need for—and the dangers of—pawning, as clothes could themselves be worn or, less riskily, swapped for other ones, while those who wanted to translate clothes into cash could latch on to the illegal trade. Clothes may also have dominated because their victims possessed fewer movable items of value. Sentencing patterns and criminal propensities for Irish women who had migrated to work in England were closer to those of English than Irish transportees, stressing the primacy of environment in determining crime. Compared with women transported directly from Ireland, these Irish emigrants stole less from the unknown person on the street or in the crowd, but more from their masters, mistresses and lodging keepers. Clothes, fabric and animals were less regularly targeted. They chose instead cooking and household utensils, food, jewellery and money—objects consistent with urban living and domestic employment.

Returning to prior convictions as a yardstick for comparison, do they lend support to the notion of Irish criminal naivety? The Englishwoman

Elizabeth Coltman at thirty years of age had no previous conviction, while Margaret Shannahan from Cork, at the tender age of seventeen, was already on her second offence, this time robbery. But Elizabeth's shipmate Caroline Humphries, also seventeen, was thrice convicted. Were there any identifiable regional differences? Figure 3.3 indicates comparatively little disparity between English and Irish offenders: 67 per cent of English female convicts were first offenders, as were 63 per cent of the Irish. This would seem to indicate that the 'typical image of the English convict as an urban pickpocket, convicted many times before, does not apply in Ireland', nor, for that matter, in England.[27] James Moore had reached his generous conclusion quoted at the beginning of this chapter on the basis that neither English nor Irish offenders had significant criminal histories.[28] The reputation that Scottish convicts had of being particularly hardened offenders was predicated upon their tendency to have been previously convicted. Only 34 per cent were first offenders, meaning that twice the proportion of Scots possessed a criminal record compared with English and Irish convicts. This arose because the practice of the law was different in Scotland. Scottish authorities were hesitant to transport first offenders, but on principle exported women who transgressed a second time.[29] Euphemia Burnett (alias Buchanan) is one such example. She had managed to accumulate two previous convictions before being transported for life from Perthshire after stealing clothes.[30] Irish and English women sentenced in Scotland had similarly greater numbers of previous offences. Judicial sentencing patterns were also likely to have been responsible for the regional discrepancies in sentencing

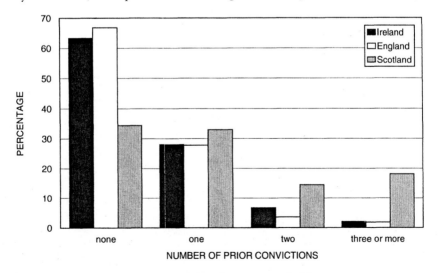

Figure 3.3 Women's prior convictions by country of trial.

obvious in Figure 3.4. Of those tried in Ireland, 93.5 per cent were sentenced for the minimum seven years, as were 73 per cent tried in Scotland and 63 per cent in England. Disparities in sentence length cannot be explained away in terms of one country or another sending its most aberrant and violent offenders. Quite simply, countries differed in their legal practice. For example, while 57 per cent of England's transported robbers received seven-year sentences, a staggering 97 per cent of Irish robbers were sentenced to that same statutory minimum. Irish judges were more lenient on this offence.

The criminal profiles of Irish and English women were dissimilar in small ways that were predictable, but what is startling is just how small these differences were, given that the English were meant to be professional and habitual criminals by choice, whereas the Irish were said to have been forced into casual crime by poverty. The overall ranking of crimes was the same: in both cases, stealing was overwhelmingly the main offence, followed a long way back by robbery. In both cases, clothes were the single most popular targets of wandering fingers, followed a long way back by money. What differences did exist were no greater than would be expected from women coming from varied economic backgrounds. And, using that traditional and dubious indicator of criminality—prior conviction rates— the women of England and Ireland differed little. What transpires is that the same factors that located the Irish in a poor socio-economic class had, ironically, also led to the placement of English convicts in a criminal class.

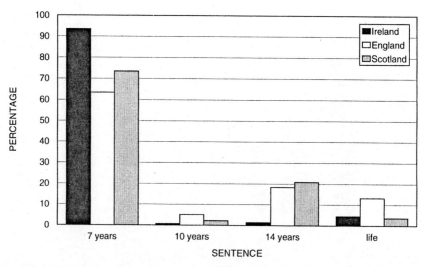

Figure 3.4 Women's sentences by country of trial.

Urban versus rural England

Irish and English convicts were not overtly different, but were England's criminal rejects themselves a homogeneous group? One theme in the literature stressed that the real difference lay between urban and rural offenders. Convict indents recorded whether a woman was born in a town or not, and from this we can judge who was urban-born and who rural. Convict women born in rural locations who were still living in the same spot when transported have been counted as country women, and conversely those born and living in towns have been classified town women. The question arises, was there an obvious difference between England's country and town convicts that was only explicable in terms of a casual/professional divide? The answer is no. This is not to say there were no differences—there were—but not the ones that might have been expected from assumptions regarding urban professionalism. Town and country criminal profiles can be seen in Figure 3.5. Urban dwellers were twice as likely to shoplift, marginally more likely to pick pockets, and more inclined to steal, while their country cousins had a penchant for man robbery, receiving and breaking. Offences present little evidence of a uniquely urban criminal sorority and, in spite of certain disparities,

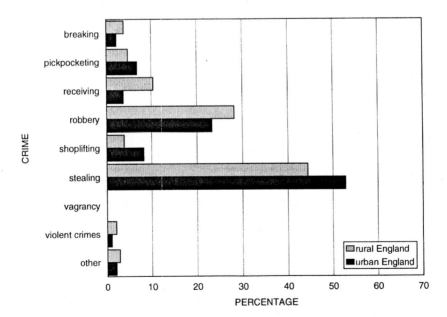

Figure 3.5 Female crime in village and town.

typically one offence shone out above all others: town or country, most
women engaged in theft. What did they pinch?

Immediately one is struck, not by the differences, but by the similarities
between urban and rural women. The comparison is represented graphically in Figure 3.6 Nearly identical proportions of town and country
women stole money, clothes, fabric, and homewares. Again thefts
seemed opportunistic. How need and opportunity coalesced did, however, vary between town and country in two important ways: in access to
animals and to jewellery. Country servants thieved animals far more than
any other group of women, only rivalled by country maids and dairywomen. Some 13 per cent of country women had stolen either animals or
food, compared with only 4 per cent of city women. The latter made up
their deficit by targeting jewellery: 14 per cent of their number thieved
jewels compared with only 5 per cent of rural convicts—a neat inversion
of the ratio for food and animals. Urban domestic servants in particular
filched jewellery, often the possessions of mistresses and masters,
reflecting two things: firstly, the predominance of indoor domestic service
in urban employment and hence opportunity (especially for servants
whose tasks brought them into their masters' and mistresses' private
quarters in cities where the demand for ostentatious display guaranteed a
supply of jewels); and secondly, the nature of the market. As with the
Irish, pawnshops were simply less accessible to rural women. Perhaps the
absence of this avenue of disposal accounts for rural women's receiving
activities. That rural workers poached or maliciously wounded sheep, that

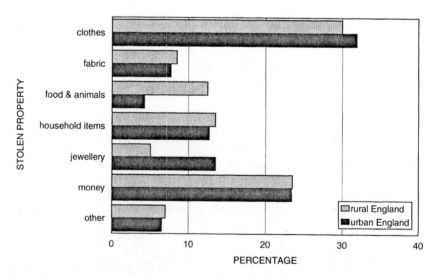

Figure 3.6   Property stolen by women convicts in village and town.

dairy women stole butter, that ladies' maids nicked rings and brooches, and so on, suggests the primacy of availability in determining the nature of the crime. Similarly, shoplifting was more an urban pursuit simply because there were more shops in towns and picking pockets was easier on busy streets. Clive Emsley attested to this opportunistic tendency in his study of crime in England finding 'the great majority of thieves—both urban and rural—acted not after detailed thought and planning, but because the occasion presented itself'.[31]

Yes, some differences existed between Clark's agricultural workers and town thieves, but no, their explanation does not require a fundamental divide between casual and professional offender, between crime driven by need and crime driven by greed. Indeed, townsfolk were *less* likely to possess a criminal history: 66 per cent had no previous conviction recorded against their name, compared with 58 per cent of country women, although in both cases the same proportion of women—two-thirds—was sentenced to the minimum seven years' transportation. Urban centres had bad reputations as homes of the inveterate classes because of perceptions that so much crime emanated from there. Crime may have been prevalent in urban areas—some three-quarters of England's convict women were sentenced in urban courts—because towns were unforgiving places. The urban situation intensified the experience of poverty: town workers were necessarily more alienated from the land than were their rural counterparts, and consequently were more reliant on the market for the satisfaction of their needs. Shortfalls of money denied urban workers access to the market, leaving them in want. But the countryside too was harsh. Revolutions in agriculture dispossessed farmers and created unemployment, while simultaneously the legal code redefined the nature of private property to include common lands and their assets, as noted in Chapter Two. Such redefinitions meant that hunting animals on once common grounds became poaching, taking firewood from once public forests became stealing, and walking on once common land became trespass. Widespread work practices such as gleaning fields after harvest for remnants of swede, turnips and other crops, or taking home fragments of unwanted coal, became criminal offences. Perks of the job were easily reclassified as crimes, a problem which any worker who fell out of favour with the boss quickly identified. But at least country folk had one choice denied city dwellers before turning to crime: they could migrate to towns in the hope of gaining fruitful paid employment (only in peak times such as harvest could town workers hope to pick up work in the countryside). Indeed, more than half the country lasses had migrated to urban centres before being transported. Upon arrival, they may have found work less forthcoming than anticipated. Away from their home parishes they would not have qualified for welfare support, and would have no families nearby to help them. What choices remained open to them then? Poverty? Prostitution? Crime?

Perceptions of high levels of professional urban criminality were based, at least in part, on prosecution rates. Crime may have been high in the towns, but it may also have been high in the countryside: levels of crime are always impossible to assess because not all crime is detected, nor is it always prosecuted. And yet, prosecution rates are taken to proxy crime rates. Such infected data mean that the comparison is not between regional patterns of crime but between regional prosecution rates. Higher levels of urban crime may have resulted from the very fact that most relevant courts were located in towns, or may have been artefacts arising from more effective detection methods and higher prosecution rates in cities. Prosecution and sentencing reflected more on local judicial behaviour than on the women. Rural communities found methods other than transportation for imposing discipline and punishment, and they apparently used these before seeking recourse to exile.[32] One outcome of this was the higher prior conviction rate among country women. It is therefore not possible for us to make quantitative judgements on comparative urban and rural crime rates. What is undeniable, however, is that no significant qualitative differences existed between country and town convicts that in any way implied the latter were professional and habitual ne'er-do-wells with the former holding a monopoly as the victims of inequality and economic change. Differences that existed were small and resulted from employment-related opportunities and varying methods of detection, prosecution and punishment between country and town.

There is no evidence to support Clark's harsh judgement. Many years after Clark, with many authors in between, Robert Hughes reiterated this logic, claiming that the 'popular', 'mythologised', 'stereotype' of convict identity which 'says that the convicts were innocent victims of unjust laws, torn from their families and flung into exile on the world's periphery for offenses that would hardly earn a fine today … insists that the human fodder of transportation sprang from the root of British decency, the yeoman in the rural village'.[33] Innocence, in fact, insists on no such thing. It is erroneous to identify urban living with an absence of need and it is wrong to equate the countryside, casual crime and innocence with poverty while conversely grouping towns, professional crime and guilt with laziness. Casual crime may be motivated by greed, just as professional pickpockets who worked in gangs may have chosen crime because no honest work was available. There is no justifiable reason to preclude poverty as the motivating factor in order to give preference to a specious argument that professional crime was urban and resulted from indolence and a disinclination to work. Further, this characterisation of rural decency juxtaposed with urban immorality misunderstands the nature of economic change with its dynamic interaction between country and town: so many women transported from the towns originated from those rural villages. Rather than dismissing convicts—urban or rural—as lazy, professional criminals it is more fruitful to enquire into what conditions either propelled them into crime or made crime an economic option.

London's ruffians: nineteenth-century perspectives

One avenue is left for those seeking a professional criminal class: the great metropolis, London. The equation of rural innocence and urban guilt predicted that the more urban a centre, the more criminal its population, with the outcome that the worst criminals were said to be those from London. The United Kingdom's largest city was taken by writers as the metonym for wealth, crime and—for other authors—poverty as well. Ostentatious wealth juxtaposed with declining working-class living standards created the appearance of wretchedness among many of London's inhabitants, providing to the 'morally weak' both motivation and opportunity for crime, or so it was claimed. London was seen as the very hub of vice and criminal culture, a mecca attracting criminals from all reaches of the world.

> Let it be remembered also, that this Metropolis is unquestionably not only the greatest Manufacturing and Commercial City in the world, but also the general receptacle for the idle and depraved of almost every country; particularly from every quarter of the Crown—Where the temptations and resources for criminal pleasures—Gambling, Fraud and Depredation, almost exceed imagination; since besides being the seat of Government it is the centre of *fashion, amusements, dissipation and folly*.[34]

This spectre of London as home for the inveterate criminal classes loomed large in the work of its author, Patrick Colquhoun, a man later described by the historian George Rudé as acceptable 'at best as a very prejudiced witness … who allowed his Gaelic imagination, or his middle-class prejudice, to run away with him'.[35] Colquhoun was one of the 'moral entrepreneurs' responsible for introducing the dramatic terminology and imagery of the criminal class onto the British scene.[36] Stipendiary magistrate and founder of the Thames Police Office at Wapping, Colquhoun was a vocal critic and wrote his *Treatise on the Police of the Metropolis* for a voracious audience: it was reissued five times within the first few years of its original publication.

Colquhoun's claim was that London in the 1790s supported a population, one-eighth of whose members 'regularly engaged in criminal pursuits'. This represented 115 000 people. Of these, half were prostitutes or 'lewd and immoral women'[37]. Devoid of its 'lurid trimmings', Colquhoun's work indicated a decline over time in violent crimes such as armed robberies, murder and hold-ups, but what it also indicated—and what it concentrated on—was the increasing number of 'economic' crimes, or crimes against property.[38] What such figures actually represented were not crime rates but prosecution rates and arguably it was the latter that was on the rise, but Colquhoun believed that crime itself was increasing at an alarming rate and attributed the cause to urbanisation and wealth, teamed with a general lower-class immorality.[39]

> The enlarged state of Society, the vast extent of moving property, and the unexampled wealth of the Metropolis, joined to the depraved habits and loose conduct of a great proportion of the lower classes of the people … will … reconcile the attentive mind to a belief of the actual existence of evils which could not otherwise have been credited … immorality, licentiousness and crimes are known to advance in proportion to the excessive accumulation of wealth.[40]

This was a theme frequently repeated by subsequent commentators. For example, in 1855 Lord Chief Justice Campbell stated that 'it will be a sad reflection to find that an increase in crime is a consequence of increased prosperity and that crime must follow in the train of affluence'.[41] Another theme readily adopted by later critics was the division Colquhoun made between casual and professional criminals, which had strong parallels with the division made between the casual or deserving and undeserving poor. It was at this point that economic categories effectively became imbued with moral meaning. Themes such as these were taken up with fervour throughout the first half of the nineteenth century, but it was a journalist from the middle of those momentous hundred years that so captured Australian historical thought, Henry Mayhew.[42]

In an advertisement in the front of *The Criminal Prisons of London and Scenes of Prison Life*, a study co-authored by Henry Mayhew and John Binny, Mayhew's earlier work on *London Labour and the London Poor* (to which Binny contributed) was praised for two significant achievements. Firstly, it had liberated the 'deserving poor'—that is, hard workers who were poorly paid, occasionally unemployed, and destitute —from the misnomer 'dangerous classes'. Secondly, the illustrative stories told by Mayhew in this work 'laid bare the really festering sores of London, and have shown which are in reality the dangerous classes, the idle, the profligate, and the criminal; those who prey upon the health and the property of others'.[43] In their joint book, Mayhew and Binny foreshadowed later arguments that punishment should fit the criminal and not the crime.[44] To illustrate, it was not what was stolen that mattered, but who did the stealing. British law, and the influential French philosopher Guerry, were rejected by Mayhew and Binny for placing too much emphasis on the object of the crime instead of the perpetrator. Mayhew and Binny recognised two classes of criminal: 'viz. (1) those who indulge in dishonest practices as a regular means of living; (2) those who are dishonest from some accidental cause'.[45] It is this grouping of criminals into professional and casual categories that has been so widely used in both the nineteenth and the twentieth centuries.

The second of the two groups were temporary criminals forced by circumstance to desperate action—'those who cannot work for their living, or rather, cannot live by their working'—and as such they posed little threat to society's values. Temporarily in need, and otherwise respectable, this class bore much in common with the 'casual poor'. By Mayhew and Binny's (enigmatic) calculation, at most these temporary criminals comprised $17\frac{1}{3}$ per cent of England's offenders between the years 1844 and 1853.[46] It was the first group, the professional criminal class—the other $82\frac{2}{3}$ per cent—who were constructed as evil, epitomising the opposite of hegemonic values. The 'predatory class are the non-working class', they wrote, whose disposition was 'to acquire property with a less degree of labour than ordinary industry'.[47] Like the 'undeserving poor' of the 1832 Poor Law, these were lazy people who *chose* not to work. It was this predatory class of criminal that proliferated in London. Mayhew and Binny thought ill of 'the criminality of the London people—whose pickpockets, it must be confessed, are among the most expert, and whose "dangerous classes" are certainly the most brutally ignorant in all Christendom'. London did not get a good write-up. It accounted for one-third of all criminals by their calculations, far in excess of its share of the population. An increasing tide of crime was washing upon the city, and in spite of a proliferation in various methods of social control such as religion, education and policing, Mayhew and Binny complained that crime was escalating, 'our felon population increases among us as fast as fungi in a rank and fetid atmosphere'.[48] Why was London such a sink of depravity?

The answer Mayhew and Binny presented is complex, and frequently contradictory. At length they detailed the various arguments put forward to explain crime in general, ranging from drunkenness and ignorance to wealth and poverty, vagrancy, lack of religious dedication, population density, 'unwholesome' urban dwellings, and finally to the fall of man and the inherent proneness to evil suffered by mere mortals. Then, through a cross-country analysis they displayed why all were unsatisfactory explanations: they were unable to discern any correlations between these factors and crime.[49] What, then, did they believe was the cause or causes of crime? Mayhew and Binny's conclusion: crime was due simply to that innate love of a life of ease, and aversion to hard work, which is common to all natures, and which, when accompanied with a lawlessness of disposition as well as a disregard for the rights of our fellow-creatures, and a want of self-dignity, can but end either in begging or stealing the earnings and possessions of others.[50]

For Mayhew and Binny, crime was the work of 'outcast parasitical tribes', 'mendicant races', 'a distinct body of people ... human parasites' who preferred to live by crime than by work. As with the rich and with workers, this class was a structural aspect of all societies, and this '*must ever be*'. It was a class to be feared, ridiculed and controlled, but it could not be eliminated, they asserted.[51] Yet while Mayhew and Binny saw love of idleness as propelling many into this criminal class, this assertion alone did not explain why London was unique, nor why patterns of crime changed over time. This prompts several questions: what did Mayhew and Binny believe caused this love of the easy life, why was it on the increase, and why in London? To answer these, Mayhew and Binny had to accept that crime was promoted by some of the factors that they had previously rejected—namely population density, changes in the provision of poor relief, and wealth—which they used in conjunction with genetic arguments to explain what they termed London's 'unique criminality'.

Themes of degeneracy, 'moral pestilence', the growth of criminal fungi and contamination were popular in the nineteenth century, and were much used by these two authors. As indicated, the language employed was vivid. Mayhew and Binny wrote of 'a criminal epidemic—a very plague, as it were, of profligacy—that diffuses itself among the people with as much fatality to society as even the putrid fever or black vomit'.[52] Contamination occurred through two mechanisms: through association and the spread of criminal values which were promoted by a large and close-living populace, and directly from parent to child—not solely through negative role modelling but genetically. The former is perhaps not *so* outlandish an argument. Indiscriminate mingling of professional criminals and others was considered educational in the worst sense. Prisons that had emerged by mid-century which made no attempt to separate hardened offenders from petty first-timers, or gaols that failed to segregate those awaiting trial from the guilty awaiting their removal to hulks, bridewells, houses of correction and prisons, were considered prime examples of learning centres in which the 'innocent' had their values corrupted. Resonances of this argument can be felt today in progressive thinking about the dangers of mixing juvenile offenders with more experienced and hardened criminals. Where nineteenth-century claims become more outlandish was in the type of 'bad behaviour' that commentators ascribed to this infectious criminal culture. Herded together in Cold Bath Fields Prison, 'smoking, gaming, singing and every species of brutalising conversation and demeanour tended to the unlimited advancement of crime and pollution'.[53] This value-laden theme was reiterated in New South Wales: as a result of public work teams, 'crowds of convict artisans were congregated in the towns, and countenanced each other in vice'[54]. Typical working-class culture was cast as a pollutant. Cities were prime sites for contamination, with more indiscriminate intermingling teamed with images of broken-down social control and loss of respectable values. Urbanisation with its density of population and lack of traditional forms of community control was believed to promote the spread of what was constructed as a kind of criminal disease.[55]

As well as being socially transmitted, this disease was also passed on from parents to child. It was a hereditary disease not dissimilar to other illnesses.

> Accordingly, ethnic crime and pauperism would appear, not only to be consistent with the ordinary laws of human life, but to be as natural as hereditary insanity, to which, indeed, it seems to bear a faint similitude; for, as in cases of mental disease, the faculty of attention is well known to be the first to exhibit symptoms of derangement, so the temperament of the habitual criminal is invariably marked by a comparative incapability of continuous application to any one subject or pursuit, whilst the same bodily restlessness as characterises the lunatic, is also the distinctive type of the vagrant.[56]

Mayhew and Binny claimed a genetic basis for the criminal class, meaning contamination commenced at conception. Employing a racist choice of metaphors, they claimed that as Jews begot Jews and Gipsies begot Gipsies (via the blood) 'then assuredly must there be a greater chance of habitual thieves and beggars begetting kindred natures to their own'. Graphic illustrations ensued when they wrote about the 'sanctuary men'—'a heterogeneous outcast tribe' of felons and debtors—who 'interbred with the lowest class of women, and so have served to render ... positive nests of vice, misery, and disease—hatching felons, lepers, and mendicants, like vipers in a muck-heap'. Almost with relief these authors wrote that 'it is no longer hard to tell how the predatory maggot got within the social nut, for here we detect the criminal ovum lying in the very blossom of the plant'.[57] Others agreed. Judge Alfred Stephen declared, 'crime *descends*, as surely as physical properties and individual temperament', and for Ernest W. Beckett this left New South Wales with 'a population in whose veins there is an hereditary taint of criminality'.[58] Parents passed on their criminality by example and breeding. In this manner the criminal class replicated itself, and multiplied.

Crime had increased over time, and in part Mayhew and Binny accepted that this arose from a decline in traditional forms of welfare, as outdoor relief was replaced by limited entry to strictly controlled workhouses. However, this was not because it increased the number of criminals belonging to the more respectable second class of temporary offenders driven into crime through low wages or inadequate demand for labour. Mayhew and Binny wrote, 'we proved, moreover, that crime is *not* referable to poverty'. Rather, diminishing welfare supports promoted the growth of professional criminals. How? Ending of the alms led the undeserving poor—'sturdy beggars' and 'valiant rogues' with their low moral fibre and unwillingness to work—to transfer their reliance on welfare to one on crime.[59] This highlights an equation evident in the literature: just as there were forced and elected criminals, there were deserving and undeserving poor; the poor and the criminal slipped easily between categories, as demonstrated by the vagrant. Terms used in describing the two groups were strikingly similar. It was the undeserving poor, those poor through their own choice, who were considered to have transferred their dependency onto crime, giving rise to a large profes-sional criminal element which thrived and multiplied in the nineteenth century. It found itself attracted to London because this large city offered remunerative pickings from affluent targets and anonymity to the 'predatory class'.[60]

Ultimately, the size and wealth—but not the poverty—of the city created London as particularly and increasingly criminal, in the view of Mayhew and Binny.[61] As the most urban centre, London was particularly prone to criminal contamination through overcrowding. In contradiction to claims made elsewhere that underplayed the role of opulence in generating crime, wealth was seen to attract those from outside who loved the easy life, those who loved to 'shake a free leg', and in particular those who could no longer rely on welfare for what were implied to be their ill-gotten gains.[62] These two authors were thus essentially, if unwittingly, in agreement with Colquhoun in blaming urbanisation, wealth and 'lower-class' failings for what was perceived as the unusually criminal nature of the metropolis with its ready money, movable property, entertainments and depredations. Poverty was not at issue; morality was. Repeatedly economic positions—be it unemployed, poor, destitute—were imbued with non-economic, moral values. Works by Colquhoun, Mayhew and Binny are selected illustrations from one side of an extensive and morally loaded nineteenth-century debate over the nature of crime and its practitioners. For us, their significance lies in the influence they exerted over Australian historians in the following century.

Twentieth-century perspectives

The tendency to confuse economic with moral categories continued in historical writings. Themes from the past century littered historical accounts. Australian historians found London's convicts emanated from an underworld of true professional criminals, the pickpockets and the less skilful 'common thieves ... ragged, squalid and unwashed'. 'The majority sprang "from the dregs of society", commonly trained from the cradle', and 'all in all they were a disreputable lot'.[63] Parents were blamed for the criminal propensities of their children.[64] Convict temperament was once more judged incapable of continuous application, demonstrating a preference for gambling and reliance on welfare or crime. These were wanderers and vagabonds, the nomadic tribes of urban Britain.[65]

Contemporaries had judged London's female offenders as 'scum', 'filthy in their persons, disgusting in their habits, obscene in their conversations'.[66] A disproportionately large number of convict women had indeed had their sentences passed at the Old Bailey. Isolating this group for study, Portia Robinson identified the class origins of London's convict women in the lower orders of society. Convict experience prior to their transportation was thus one of poverty, unemployment, starvation, filth, sickness, poor wages, the struggle to support dependants, and other forms of economic and social distress heightened by society's failure to provide sufficient welfare. Of London's criminals, 'all were familiar to a greater or lesser degree with the destitution London offered those without employment'. Those attracted to the capital in search of work suffered in particular because, outside their own parishes, they were not entitled to even meagre state welfare. Such factors motivated crime and the courts heard pleas of poverty and destitution: 'I was in dire need'; 'Distress drove me to it'. The vast majority of these women were guilty of property offences. Furthermore, Robinson demonstrated how the *colonial* behaviour of these women was not consistent with the vile image portrayed by authorities and other contemporaries, noting 'that, whatever may have been the reason, most of these London women merged into colonial society as the working and family women of Botany Bay'.[67]

However, according to Robinson, respectable commentators had been correct about the women's *British* reputation: undeniably these were 'criminals of the darkest complexion'.[68] It was only in colonial New South Wales that the women reformed. Having posed the question of whether these women really were the refuse of London, Robinson responded, 'from the individual histories of their offences, trials and convictions, there would seem little doubt': the answer was yes. Divisions between casual and professional criminals, deserving and undeserving poor, reasserted themselves. Convict reputations were tested by using information on crimes to infer whether offenders were casual and deserving poor or of the undeserving class. Casual poverty equated with respectable, while more regular poverty apparently indicated low character. Surprisingly the following conclusion was reached. 'Most could not be classified as the "casual poor". A more apt description was morally destitute, for they were women who, without scruple, could and did steal even from those who tried to help them'.[69] We cannot know what scruples the women did and did not possess, but with this assertion the women are robbed of their morality and their characters besmirched. Motivation and morality once more become the central issues, entwined in the consideration of whether convict women possessed good or bad characters.

Evidence for Robinson's conclusion included the 1814 case of a mother and her young daughter who were sentenced to death for coining and uttering. They pleaded 'distress caused me to infringe on the laws of my country'. Another case was Elizabeth Allen—Bett—who 'certainly did not fit any picture of the "casual poor" of London. Tried with two accomplices for highway robbery, she had "dragged him [the victim], while he was very drunk, out of a public house and robbed him".' Other women were guilty of stealing from fellow lodgers, and 'they stole almost as an occupation from their lodging-house keepers'. It was considered that 'one fact is indisputable: women who were transported for thefts from their benefactors could not, by any stretch of the imagination, be called "the deserving poor".[70]

Sceptically Robinson asked of the forgers, 'was it that same distress which had led to the mother's prior one-year term of imprisonment for the same offence? Or the daughter's one year in the House of Correction in 1810 at the age of nine, again for the same offence?'[71] The answer may well have been yes. Enforced poverty need not be short-term, and intermittent employment could see workers in and out of jobs and likewise in and out of crime, so there is no apparent reason to assume need was not the cause. Why did Bett *not* fit the picture of the casual poor? Because she employed force? Because she acted with others? Or was casual poverty meant to prevent its instruments from robbing imbibers? Even if this behaviour reflects badly on Bett's character, it tells us nothing about Bett's economic position. Similarly, thefts from lodgings and housemates do not imply the absence of poverty, of uninvited need, but they do indicate the role played by opportunity in committing offences. And one can dispute the meaning of robbing benefactors. Many of the benefactors listed were nothing more than employers, a group who inspired crime through low wages, poor conditions, grievances associated with the denial of perks, and even outright abuse. Agreed, robbing someone who displayed 'kindness and assistance' was not a particularly nice thing to do. Niceness should not be the issue. Irrespective of what judgement is made regarding the rights and wrongs of this behaviour, such 'ingratitude' does not reflect on the cause of crime or on the absence or presence of poverty.

So who were the casual poor? Patrick Colquhoun's classification is cited by Robinson. The casual poor were 'those virtuously brought up in the country ... unable to find employment ... left finally with nothing else to pawn ... [who] live in such miseries which often exceeds anything the human mind can conceive ... for they will not steal and are ashamed to beg'.[72] Robinson concluded that 'women fitting this description are not easy to find among those sentenced to transportation or death'. Nor should we expect to find those who 'will not steal' among a group of thieves. Members of the casual poor could be found by Robinson among the free passengers journeying to New South Wales. Specifically these included the wives of criminal men, although surprisingly few convict women were thought to be thus wedded. Many such wives petitioned the government seeking free passage to the colony, claiming distress arising from the loss of a husband to 'execution, imprisonment or transportation'. These were women who lived in 'inconceivable misery' but 'neither begged nor stole'.[73] How strange that convict men from the criminal class were married to such reputable women.

One particularly poignant example is given of a woman belonging to the 'casual poor' and it tells us much about the real meaning of the term. Her name was Elizabeth Surman.

> Women such as Elizabeth Surman could more aptly be called 'the casual poor'. Her body was found by an agent with those of two other women in an empty house in Stonecutter Street. She was the daughter of a respectable jeweller and only six years old when both her parents died. She then lived with a succession of friends and relatives, working as silk-winder or servant. She was discharged from her last employment (by a washerwomen with six children) because of her ill-health. Having no 'domicile rights', although her father had been a respected churchwarden, she ended up sleeping in the streets of London. She came to an empty house, starving, and lay down beside the corpses of two women who had died of starvation, not realising they were dead. She was found dead a few days later, literally starved to death. There were no avenues of poor relief or help open to her but she had neither begged, stolen nor prostituted herself. Death by starvation was the 'final solution' for those of the poor who would not beg or steal.[74]

The moral lesson is clear: if the poor fought back and displayed agency, if they tried to alleviate their own and their children's suffering through action, if they simply wanted more than they had, if they became embittered, twisted—perhaps violent—because of the harsh realities of poverty, then they were morally reprehensible individuals and they were damned, becoming 'criminals of the darkest complexion'. For the casual poor—preferably originating in the countryside—to remain morally pure it would seem that they needed literally to take what was dished up to them and lie down quietly and die. It seems ironic that if it came to light that Elizabeth Surman had stolen a bread roll, but not been prosecuted by a kindly baker or perhaps not even been caught, that seemingly her poverty would then cease to have been casual.

Convict women have been divided into two camps, the wholesome and the depraved, paralleling the divide between casual and undeserving which in turn reflected women who were either passive or aggressive. This is a preoccupation with character, but does character matter? Character is not independent of circumstances. Poverty and punishment can be deforming experiences, and violence, despair, confusion and breakdown can all be expected consequences. Unpleasant and even cruel offences were committed by women—such as stealing a child in order to gain its clothes, then leaving the child abandoned—and these illustrate the extremes to which individuals would go. But they do not illustrate motive. They do not prove poverty, but nor do they deny it. Causation and character have been muddled; women's behaviour is read backwards as a comment on their socio-economic position, with violent or unpalatable behaviour being read as a denial of poverty.

Economic concepts like poverty have been imbued with moral meanings. Poverty describes someone who from time to time slips below some imputed basic living standard or poverty line. Most of the 'lower classes'—a term that can be taken to mean the bulk of the working population—experienced poverty. Even for labour aristocrats, employment was rarely secure and even less likely to be full-time, and for the rest this uncertainty was magnified. Some were cushioned by high wages, others were not, but all were susceptible to dramatic fluctuations in purchasing power. How regularly a family or individual did fall into poverty may determine their classification as casual or not. Economic measures such as these have been transformed by the literature into measures of character, a subjective category at the best of times but particularly difficult to assess through impersonal market forces. Yet the term 'casual poor' came to symbolise one entire moral entity while those regularly in poverty became the undeserving, immoral poor who too easily turned to crime.

For Robinson, the London women were the quintessential criminal class, women of low moral character with few scruples. But her analysis left Robinson with one problem which she recognised: 'the difficulty is to explain why so few continued their "occupation" in New South Wales'.[75] This is indeed a problem. A starting point in its resolution is to ask, not what characters the women possessed, but whether an investigation of their criminal histories does indicate that London's convict women really were very different from the rest of England. Were these truly the essence of the criminal class?

London's convict women

London had been the last home of 1016 of the convict women who landed in New South Wales from 1826 onwards. Only one-seventh of all the female convicts, this was a hefty 35 per cent of those from England. Exactly what this magnitude indicates is difficult, if not impossible, to interpret. It might mean there was more crime in the capital than elsewhere, or it could reflect the growing efficiency of Peel's Bobbies, but perhaps more probably the explanation lies in prosecution and sentencing rates. Certainly there is evidence that women tried at the Old Bailey were far more likely to be transported than women whose cases were heard at other courts around the country.[76] But at least quantitatively there is something special about London. What remains to be done is to determine whether that something was a nefarious London criminal tendency. Was it true, as the surrounding literature suggests, that the women from that epitome of urbanisation were among the very worst criminals that Britain had to offer? Investigating London also presents the opportunity to test that other hypothesis, that England at least was populated by tribes of wandering felons.

Acting as a magnet, the capital supposedly attracted the criminal underworld from around the country and beyond. Colquhoun had complained bitterly that London was a receptacle for other countries' rejects as well as England's own. London's spellbinding powers derived from its ostentatious wealth and the promise of rich pickings, and was thus the very seat of temptation. It was also a city marked by seasons. Related to the weather, the rhythms of the calendar had their fashions. The fashionable 'London Season' of dances, nightclubbing, debuts, theatre, shopping, promenading, and other social functions was formed by the habits of the 'Quality'. The rich left London in droves in May and June to spend summer in the country. The Season began when they returned in October and November, when the hunting was over, Parliament met, and the Court returned from the summer palaces. From winter through spring and into early summer was the Season for the rich to be in town.

London's promise of movable property and anonymous crime was what identified the metropolis as mecca for those whom M. B. and C. B. Schedvin named 'the nomadic tribes of urban Britain', but the Season led to regular and predictable fluctuations in what was on offer. Along with the Quality, professional thieves were said to abandon London in summer when the city was out of fashion. Mayhew wrote of 'that multifarious tribe of "sturdy rogues", who ramble across the country during the summer, sleeping at the "casual wards" of the workhouses, and who return to London in the winter to avail themselves of the gratuitous lodgings and food attainable at the several metropolitan refuges' and to indulge in a little bit of illegal redistribution.[77] Similarly, the Schedvins argued that the criminal classes fled the cities in summer, choosing to take their criminal propensities to the countryside in search of racecourse meetings and fairs with opportunities for pilfering. They criticised the 'roving propensities and general restlessness of the London poor' and their 'consequent failure to inculcate the habit of industry and a sense of purpose', noting that 'aversion to continuity and steady work was prominent among boys and girls of this class and most professed to "like a roving life".'[78]

The case of London crystallises key elements of the criminal-class thesis. Crime belonged to a specific socio-economic grouping. Law-breakers were not workers who on occasion foundered, but were instead inadequate individuals with a repugnance to work who preferred roving and pilfering—a lifestyle choice. This thesis denies poverty as the cause of crime and conversely argues that crime was prosperity-based. For its validity, then, criminal activity must necessarily have been indexed to movable wealth, and this is what was argued for London. If the criminal-class thesis was accurate, if Colquhoun and company had been correct, then crime would flourish during the London Season, increasing with increased opportunity and subsequently declining. Is this what happened? Did crime escalate during the Season in that wicked metropolis?

London's Season has been taken here as running the six months from November to April, neatly dividing the year into two halves. Judging from those offenders whose crimes were bad enough to warrant deportation, what can be said of crime in the metropolis? Figure 3.7 displays seasonal conviction rates for Londoners, other town women and country women who ended up transported to New South Wales. The time elapsed between offending and conviction remained fairly standard over the course of the year: Quarter Sessions and Assize Courts capable of hearing such cases met regularly, so conviction rates approximated crime rates but with some constant time-lag built in. What is immediately apparent from this figure is that there was no criminal floodtide engulfing the city when opportunities for illegal endeavour were at their greatest. The split between when the Season was on and when it was off was very nearly fifty-fifty. The same was true for the rest of urban England. Elsewhere, however, the seasons did bring change. Country women (again meaning those born, bred and living in the country) were more likely to be sentenced in the winter-spring period: 61 per cent were sentenced then, compared with 39 per cent in summer and autumn.

Believing that crime arose from poverty rather than prosperity, it comes as no surprise to find that winter saw an increase in countryside sentencing rates. Notably, this was when employment was low but demands for food, shelter, clothes and heating were at their highest. Conversely, sentencing rates dropped at harvest and sowing times in summer and late autumn when women fared best. This was a pattern of 'summer work and winter gaol' that has been widely remarked upon.[79] Unlike workers directly engaged, or dependent upon those directly engaged, in agriculture, urban workers were better insulated from such seasonal shifts, although they were not entirely immune due to reliance upon rural factor inputs and local demand. London was best placed as the centre of commercial activities and trading links which continued independently of the weather. Additionally, counter-cyclical demand was afforded by the influx of the wealthy in winter and the run up to the London Season when manufacturers were anticipating demand, shops were stocking their shelves, and domestic servants were being recruited into the households of the visiting gentry and other fashionable folk. By comparison with the countryside, in towns work was a-plenty. The message of the data seems clear: when work was available, women worked, and when crime was the only alternative to poverty, some women stole. Consistent levels of urban un/employment maintained criminal activity at one basic level, while seasonal fluctuations induced cyclic trends in rural conviction rates.

Crime, measured by conviction rates for transportees in the metropolis, was not governed by seasonal swings as the Quality came and went,

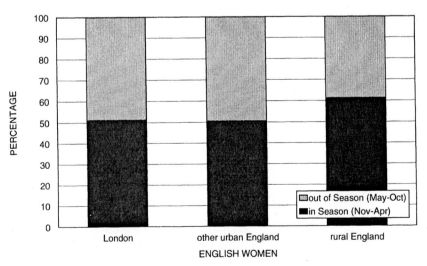

Figure 3.7 Female conviction rates and the London Season.

offering no support to contemporaries' and historians' claims about a wandering criminal fraternity. Fears of nomadic tribes, sturdy roving rogues and mendicant races arose from the migratory nature of London's populace and the perception that so many criminals were 'outsiders'. Certainly many London women were migrants. It was true that many of the women tried and transported from London had been born outside the metropolis; two-thirds in fact, and they came from a tremendous variety of places. Ninety-four different counties—and in some cases, different countries—had all lost women to London. Women came from all of England's counties, with the exception of Rutland, and from most of the Irish ones (excluding only Clare, Donegal, Down, Leitrim and Monaghan—some less accessible areas). Among other countries of origin were Holland, India, Jamaica, Gibraltar, Martinique, Madeira, Portugal, Prussia, Spain, France and even the United States. This was a truly cosmopolitan city. But while 69 per cent of London's convict women had been born elsewhere, London was not alone in attracting migrants. Some 57 per cent of convicts tried in Lancashire had immigrated there, and the national average beyond London with all its charms was in excess of 48 per cent. Such migration would be expected, not because the idle and depraved journeyed there *en masse* in search of enjoyable depredations, but because workers migrated in search of employment.

There is considerable evidence being unearthed by historians to suggest that the period of industrial revolution was one of considerable working-class mobility.[80] London in particular offered expanding employment opportunities in select trades such as dressmaking and needlework, plus charring and domestic service of all kinds.[81] It was thus not surprising that so many of the females convicted in London and other urban centres were migrants, nor that their geographical origins were so diverse. This was typical of migrants generally: migration was both rural to urban, and inter-urban, and while women came from most places within the British Isles, over two-fifths of the convict movers headed for the major urban industrial centres of Dublin, Manchester, Liverpool and, in particular, London. Conversely, labour demand also induced short-term migration in the opposite direction from town to country during summertime. Sowing late crops at the end of spring, but particularly harvesting in summer, were tasks dependent upon an influx of temporary workers from the towns.

Observers were correct in identifying the varied regional backgrounds of London's inhabitants and their migratory habits, although the imputed reason for this is contested. Next, we need to test whether assessments of crime were apt. London crime may not have demonstrated seasonal shifts, but were its criminals more aberrant than most? What sort of criminals did

London women make? One enduring stereotype was that of the pickpocket. The magazine *Punch* found mileage in this topic. *Punch* was introduced to the British public in July 1841. In its very first issue it portrayed the threat posed by young, nimble-fingered thieves to honest, upstanding citizens enjoying a day's outing, in a piece called 'The Gold Snuff-Box'. This was the story of a gentleman, one of many in a crowd at Buckingham Palace who had gone to see the Queen, who falls victim to a practised criminal mob who steal his one prized possession, his golden snuffbox.[82] It was clear where the readers' sympathies were intended to lie. Other literary mileage was gained from this topic and few are likely to forget the characters from Charles Dickens' *Oliver Twist*—the pickpocket John Dawkins who, along with Charley Bates, Tom Chitling, Betsy and Nancy, were the criminal apprentices of Fagin, 'a crafty old Jew, a receiver of stolen goods'[83]. Did London, with its easy pickings from among the conspicuously rich population of the city, possess a disproportionately large number of nimble-fingered pocket pickers? Not according to those it transported. Figure 3.8 compares crime in London with that in the rest of England. Surprisingly, picking pockets was no more common among London's convict women than those from elsewhere; indeed, it was marginally less, at 5 per cent compared with 7. Apparently this was a pursuit of declining value. Past its

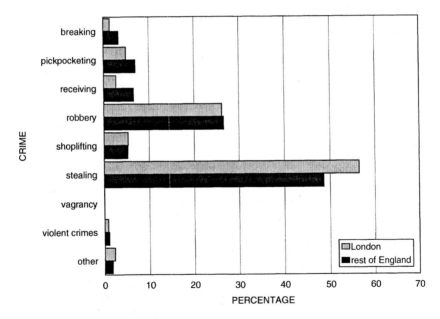

Figure 3.8 Female crime in London and England.

heyday in 1821, pickpocketing declined in the late 1820s and 1830s as fashions changed. Previously, watches were carried in 'fobs' that hung from the front waistline of breeches. These were replaced by less accessible lengthened waistcoats that provided pockets for storing such valuables. Only handkerchiefs were left in ready access, and consequently the value of pickings fell: a watch might be worth between £5 and £10; a handkerchief, between 2s and 5s 6d.[84]

Apart from dispelling the notion that picking pockets was a favoured convict pastime, Figure 3.8 paints the real picture of the crimes committed by London's convict women. Typical of every group investigated, be they Irish or English, country or town, two crimes predominated: stealing and robbery, always in that order. These two categories of crime were consistently a magnitude greater than any other class of offence. Shoplifting ranked third and picking pockets fourth, but between them these two offences accounted for little more than 10 per cent of the numbers involved while stealing and robbery combined to contribute some 83 per cent. These figures are nearly identical for criminal convictions in the metropolis more generally, including those punished less severely with short-term detention and the like.[85] Of every twenty women transported from the metropolis, twelve were sent for stealing, a further four for robbery, another one for shoplifting and one more for rifling pockets. The incidence of robbery was the same in the metropolis as elsewhere, but London's women were a little less likely than other English women to break and enter, or to receive stolen goods. The latter disinclination to engage in receiving presumably reflected that alternatives existed in the town where pawnshops were more readily found, as were those doing business on their premises: twice the proportion of Londoners were caught pledging stolen goods with pawnbrokers. London women compensated for the deficits they incurred in receiving, picking pockets and breaking by committing more theft.

Their thefts were also reasonably typical, as illustrated in Figure 3.9. Ever popular clothes topped the bill, with money, jewellery and household goods the other favoured objects. Londoners and other English women prigged clothes, fabric and other items at nearly identical rates, but differed elsewhere. London women stole considerably less money, food and animals than other English women (23 per cent compared with 34 per cent) but far more in the way of jewellery and homewares (32 per cent compared with 22 per cent). This related to the fact that when Londoners robbed and stole they did so, not from anonymous victims, but from masters, mistresses, other employers, and lodging keepers. Also, it would seem, they victimised clients. Watches in particular were thieved, and this was very much an urban crime stereotypically associated with prostitution, as indeed clothes often were. Such theft was sometimes seen

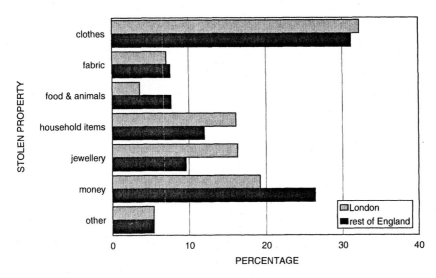

Figure 3.9 Property stolen by women convicts in London and England.

as recompense for services rendered and inadequately rewarded, as noted in Chapter Two.[86] Whatever the motive, many women did capitalise on the fact that purchasing and engaging in a sexual encounter made men vulnerable.

Sentenced, the women from London were treated harshly. Fewer than 60 per cent of other English transportees were first offenders, over 80 per cent of Londoners were. Those who had been previously convicted had, in general, received lengthier sentences than their counterparts throughout the country, having typically served nine months in detention compared with six months for women outside London. As noted, the Old Bailey judges seem to have been particularly prone to transporting women: while the Gloucestershire Assizes sentenced 5 per cent of female offenders to transportation, and the Quarter Sessions court 2 per cent, the Middlesex Assizes committed 23 per cent of women to this fate.[87] Perhaps judges and juries in the metropolis, conscious of the rhetoric that depicted London as a town besieged by crime, responded to the threat by emphasising the severity of the law in the hope of deterring would-be offenders.

London did not support a class who chose crime as a preferable way of life, offering good rewards to those with deft fingers who would do their best trade when wealthy individuals were in town, flaunting their watches and jewellery, carrying money and handkerchiefs, as they walked the London streets unguarded. Crime was a temporary solution, not an advantageous lifestyle, for most convict women; all year round London possessed wealth enough to rob and poverty enough to motivate, without relying on conjecture regarding a professional criminal class. Scouring the convict indents for evidence of repeated or organised criminal activity or serious crime has proved a fruitless quest. If the capital of the Empire was rent by a destructive, dangerous and acquisitive class, its criminal justice system was singularly unsuccessful in sifting it out. In point of truth, neither in Ireland, England nor even London did a criminal class exist.

Losing the criminal class

That a criminal class did not exist outside the nineteenth-century literary imagination and political debates where it had a heightened presence has been demonstrated by various recent British historical criminologists studying English offenders sentenced to punishments less severe than transportation. Some professionals operated, but they were few and did not constitute a *class*. To these historians, nineteenth-century crime was casual as distinct from professional, its cause poverty rather than greed. Conclusions were based on studies of court reports, offenders, the relationships between economic indicators and crime, and on the haphazard nature of offences.

Clive Emsley found for the first half of the nineteenth century that 'even in the cities organised crime, or crimes clearly committed by professionals, only ever constituted a fraction of the offences brought before the courts'.[88] Timothy Curtis and J. A. Sharpe reached similar conclusions on the basis of their research on Tudor and Stuart England.

> There have been claims for the existence of two different, though related, kinds of professional criminal organisation in early modern England: the itinerant vagabonds and the urban, especially London, gangs which survived on the profits of theft and prostitution ... Most of this evidence is part of a contemporary literary genre which can be shown evolving through its own dynamic ... Certainly wandering poor people existed, and committed crime: but in no serious sense did they threaten the fabric of society ... they [London court archives] reveal a world where the sneak-thief or small-time whore was more typical than the criminal entrepreneur.[89]

Having investigated crime in the three counties of Sussex, Gloucestershire and Middlesex for the period 1805–50, George Rudé posed the quintessential question, 'can one rightly speak of the existence of a "criminal class", or of "criminal classes"?' His answer: 'my conclusion must be that, even in London, for all its reputation as a centre of professional crime and "dangerous districts", the case for the existence of a definable 'criminal class' has not been made'. Hardened criminals existed, some were even organised, but their numbers were trivial.[90]

John Beattie argued for the female offenders of eighteenth-century Surrey and Sussex that property crimes were a function of want and necessity, and that 'the principal feature of crime against property was not its consistently high level, but its frequent and sizeable fluctuations. And this suggests that most theft was the work of people who chose to steal or not according to their circumstances and their ability to support themselves'.[91] Hence the violent swings in thefts by single women and widows—some of the most vulnerable members of the community— during periods of economic upheaval.[92] David Philips, in a comprehensive survey of nineteenth-century crime in the Black Country, found that criminals were offenders who normally worked, but who on occasion stole: crime was casual and haphazard, not the work of organised professionals.[93] Considering crime in its broader social context, David Jones found that 'theft and vice were calculated economic acts preferable to pauperism'.[94] Prices and employment fluctuated sharply in this period; numerous historians have detected direct correlations between price levels and crime, and the inverse relationship in which crime stood to employment and the trade cycle.[95] For Gatrell and Hadden, 'the conclusion is inescapable'. The higher number of summary property offences in the depressed years of the early nineteenth century 'has to be attributed to the fact that at such times quite ordinary people (the hypothetical "hitherto honest") were frequently obliged to steal in order to survive'.[96] In an author's note, B. J. Davey commented on crime in nineteenth-century Horncastle, England: 'Conditions in the 1840s were extremely harsh, and people were sometimes driven to occupations and actions out of a necessity which we find difficult to imagine. There are very few real villains in this book'.[97] The list goes on. The greatest concession made suggested that if there were any professional criminals operating they were too few to constitute a class, numbering at most only around 10 per cent, but even their existence was deemed uncertain.[98] If they did exist, these were the ones transported overseas. What the research undertaken here has shown is that even transported felons were simply small-time occasional crooks. Such findings mean that it is no longer tenable to simply accept the past description of Australia's convicts as professional and habitual criminals originating from a criminal class in Britain. There was no criminal class.

Conclusion

Rather than a marauding mass of Artful Dodgers seeking out easy targets in the crowd—as the criminal-class theory dictates—the female convicts appear as first-time offenders making criminal decisions based upon availability, need or even a sense of employment justice: seizing the perks of the job or compensating for low wages. Undeniably, some women were in employment at the time of committing their offence, and through crime, masters and mistresses were made victims. In a number of other cases, too, it is evident that criminal and victim were known to one another. Crimes were small-scale, violence was more readily eschewed than was work, the objects of thefts were petty and of limited resale value. Avarice may have been the motive, but the rewards appear low; the underlying purpose that might equally be inferred from these larcenies is that they offered some small supplement to income when unemployed, in periods of low pay, and during seasonal lulls. Many country workers settled into the familiar pattern of 'summer work, winter gaol'. This description fits the English as well as the Irish, women from both the country and the town, even from that supposed epitome of evil, London, but it is not the description one would expect of a group of women who chose to support themselves and their families through habitual crime. Perhaps the very fact they were apprehended indicates their lack of practice at criminal tasks. Further testimony that convicts were not in some way inherently criminal can be found in their post-conviction rates. In the colony, the convict women notably failed to amass considerable criminal records.[99] H. S. Payne found that one-third of women in Van Diemen's Land avoided any other sentences, forming 'a nucleus that was not normally criminal', and when crimes were committed they tended to be of the type that in England would have passed without comment: cheekiness to employers, swearing, drinking etc.—'bad behaviour' which in Australia was constructed as breach of law.[100]

The purpose of discerning whether convicts were professional crimi-nals or casual offenders as defined in the literature has not been to establish whether they were nice people or not. It is not even necessary to attribute their criminal actions to need rather than greed. The aim is to discover the inheritance convict workers brought with them to the task of building a new colony. Professional and habitual criminals, unskilled, refractory and unfamiliar with work, could be expected to contribute nothing to colonial development other than that which was beaten from them; no matter how harshly applied, neither the cat-o'-nine tails nor the treadmill could elicit skills where none existed, nor could reformation overcome an abject lack of training. If, on the other hand, convicts were workers not unlike others, with a range of skills and work experiences, who for whatever reason occasionally indulged in crime, then this would be a fine foundation for a new society. On the basis of the criminal statistics derived from the convict indents, it can be clearly stated that convict women were not habitual offenders from a professional criminal class. What we need to ask next is, before being transported, what sort of workers were these women?

Piso's spirit had reasserted itself. Whatever the morals of punishing offenders with exile, technically these women had broken their countries' legal codes and for this they were being expelled. Despite Moore's generous claim to the contrary, convicts *were* criminals and they had to pay for their sins. From the court where they heard the verdict proclaimed, Elizabeth Coltman and her like went back to their cells and waited, perhaps a few months, possibly several years. Once they were declared fit, and of an appropriate age, their transportation began. Collected from confinement, they were ushered to one of a small number of ports, eventually to embark upon a wooden vessel no larger than a Manly ferry today. Bobbing and tossing on the great ocean waves, it was expected to make its way to the other side of the world. Gathered on board, the women were allocated to messes for the duration of the voyage. Mixed together were different ages, varied religions, and women from all over Ireland, England, Scotland, Wales and elsewhere. How strange they must have seemed. Even people from a few counties distant appeared foreign, their accents nearly incomprehensible. For week upon week, month upon month, their only companions were each other and the crew, any of whom might prove to be friend or foe, or in the eyes of the dominant, disciple or rival. Together the women would share the space below deck, surfacing into fresh air at set intervals according to the regulations. Waiting at the dock they were ignorant of what to expect, on board and in Australia, their only information gleaned from a poster or two, a broadside, a popular song, and the odd well-read letter home. But they had to go. They had no choice. At the dockside they prepared to commence the long journey to New South Wales.

CHAPTER FOUR

Economic Accoutrements: The Skills of Convict Women

As Elizabeth Coltman boarded the *Competitor*, bound to dock at that distant Sydney quay, she had with her a meagre bag of clothing, a few material possessions, some cultural baggage and social capital (or more precisely, what many socially superior critics considered the lack of social capital, not approving of her working-class accent and less-refined comportment). But Elizabeth had another case, too, which we have heard less about. Written on its side, in a neat and even hand, were the words 'Economic Accoutrements'. Elizabeth was now a criminal, but she had also been a worker. The chances were, she would be again. While the contents of this interesting piece of economic luggage largely evaded careful examination, some observers did speculate on the quality of convict labour. Their musings were strikingly varied.

Transportation was a method of removing criminals from Britain and Ireland, but it was also a form of colonisation. Would Elizabeth and company, plus their male counterparts, make good colonial material or not? If the convict population comprised ordinary men and women possessed of ordinary skills, then it was a potentially useful labour source to be employed in the act of colonising a distant continent. But if, on the other hand, convicts were the work-shy untrained individuals of a criminal class, then their role in colonisation could be little other than detrimental, involving the expenditure of scarce and valuable resources in maintaining unproductive individuals whose only contribution would be to undermine progress through their continued criminal activity and vice. Any work would have to be beaten out of them. If this latter characterisation of the convicts had been true, then the dual functions of transportation as penal shovel and colonial pick would be fundamentally incompatible, suggesting poor planning and spelling doom for the colony.

And doom many expected. It was considered an unsound practice to construct a new society out of the rejects of an old one. At the beginning of the seventeenth century Francis Bacon warned against colonising America through transportation, protesting that it was 'a shameful and unblessed thing to take the scum of people and wicked condemned men, to be the people with whom you plant ... for they will ever live like rogues, and not fall to work, but be lazy, and do mischief, and spend victuals, and be quickly weary ...'.[1] In the nineteenth century Henry Mayhew and John Binny intoned that 'in our opinion, it is unworthy of a great and wise nation to make a moral dust-bin of its colonies ... by thrusting the refuse of its population from under its nose'.[2] Others referred to transportation as 'that great sewer which for so many years carried away the dregs of our population'.[3] To Arthur Griffiths, writing in 1884, transportation meant 'forming a new settlement thus from the dregs of society'.[4] This analysis was readily extended to 'pauper emigration'. *The Times* despaired: 'this is not the way in which a great and wealthy people, a mother of nations, ought to colonize'.[5]

Criminals were thought to be 'lazy' and 'quickly weary'. Earlier, the characteristics defining the criminal class were outlined: criminal professionalism and individual behavioural flaws of some considerable magnitude. It was said that criminals were both devoid of useful skills and unfamiliar with ordinary working life: its associated values, experiences of work and regimentation, stability and (supposed) respect for authority. Parents were often blamed for these shortcomings. Crime was hereditary, it was in the blood. When genes were not the problem, upbringing was. Criminals were not brought up in caring, loving families but by Fagins and drunken whores. This heritage was unstable, irreverent, immoral, drunken, work-shy and criminal. Even among commentators not wedded to the idea that criminals comprised a separate class, there was a widespread belief that crime was perpetrated by the morally aberrant members of the 'lowest orders' of society who cared little for work and too much for drink and debauchery.

Convict labour was certainly proclaimed recalcitrant by some contemporaries, notably employers.[6] Having spent a total of some two years in New South Wales after his time as surgeon-superintendent on board the *Recovery* in 1819, Peter Cunningham made the claim that it was 'a general maxim among English thieves to consider every thing in shape of work as a degradation' (unlike the more industrious Irish).[7] James Mudie, who wrote at length in his book *The Felonry of New South Wales* on the subject of convict depravity, noted that 'the convict labourers are most objectionable on the score of industry and morality', being 'in point either of industry or subordination, the very worst description of labourers and servants'.[8] The nineteenth-century historian and prison governor Arthur Griffiths, too, was a fervent believer in the poverty of convict work habits. In the colony, 'overseers were indispensable; for laziness is ingrained in the criminal class, and more than change of sky is needed to bring about any lasting change in character and habits'.[9] Further, 'the crowds of ex-criminals which might, by judicious treatment, have turned into virtuous bucolics, rapidly degenerated into a mass of drunken dissipated idlers'.[10] None of these men countenanced that the real source of tension was the more general phenomenon of worker resistance in the battle to extract labour from a coerced workforce.

Women convicts were considered even more reprobate than the men. Since 1810, when Governor Lachlan Macquarie claimed that 'female convicts are as great a drawback as the males are useful' (apparently with no sarcastic intent), this particular theme has demonstrated an insistent currency.[11] More so than male convicts, these women were a cargo both 'unnecessary and unprofitable'.[12] Frequent official complaints were made that these women were 'refractory and disobedient ... troublesome characters, who, to the disgrace of their sex, are far worse than the men, and are generally found at the bottom of every infamous transaction in this colony'.[13] James Mudie (author and employer) described the women thus to the Select Committee on Transportation: 'Of their character, I should say, in fact, that they are worse than the men in all descriptions of vice; you can have no conception of their depravity of character'.[14] Lieutenant-Colonel Henry Breton agreed: 'they are as bad as it is possible for human beings to be, the female convicts ... they gave more trouble than the whole of the 80 males belonging to the estates'.[15] Similarly, Bishop William Ullathorne pleaded, 'what shall I say of the female convict, acknowledged to be far worse and far more difficult of reformation than the man?'[16] Damnations were legion.

Convict women were 'dangerous and mischievous'.[17] Complaints centred on convict women's morality (frequently termed 'character'), rather than their employment performance. James Mudie informed the Select Committee that the female convicts in his service were 'savage'.[18] James Macarthur told the same body that his female domestic servants (drawn from the pool of convicts) were of a most dissolute character, necessitating constant recourse to the bench.[19] Mudie was interrogated by the Select Committee:

> 1508. Suppose a young female convict was to come out of fair character, or presumed to be of fair character?—I never knew an instance of any female convict coming out that I would consider a fair character.
> 1509. In point of chastity, I mean? There are several come out who have had good Education in England, and they have been applied for and they have been received into families as governesses, but always after they have been there a short time there was an intrigue with the son, if there was one, and they were always found to be bad subjects.[20]

Of course, such intrigue was the woman's fault. A couple of questions later, he was asked of the archetypal female convict, 'the impression in the colony is that she is bad?—Yes', Mudie replied. His evidence? They 'all smoke, drink and in fact, to speak in plain language, I consider them all prostitutes'.[21] In the colony female 'morality' was intimately tied up with perceptions about correct and proper female behaviour and work values, as it had been in Britain. Constantly the expectation was that, as criminals, these women were immoral, irreligious and poorly socialised.

Considered depraved whores and disobedient workers, female convicts were also expected to make very poor wives by some. Commissioner Bigge was concerned at the low official marriage rate, and commented specifically on the failure of free-born white men to marry convict women, partially resulting from 'the abandoned and dissolute habits of the female convicts, but chiefly to a sense of pride in the native born youths, approaching to contempt for the vices and depravity of the convicts even when manifested in the persons of their own parents'.[22] Convict men supposedly had similar scruples. Failed workers, failed wives, it comes as no surprise that convict women were expected to fail as mothers. Children of convict women were thought to 'imbibe vice with their mother's milk'.[23] Expounding on the evils of drink—considered the cause of much crime—George Laval Chesterton, Governor of the House of Correction at Cold Bath Fields and author of *Revelations of Prison Life*, wrote that 'in its vortex, every moral and social obligation alike becomes engulfed ... even of maternal ties ... It drowns all reflection, and plunges its willing votary into any excess of crime and dishonour for its own insatiate gratification'.[24] Governor King, too, expected disaster in the wake of these children's 'abandoned parents' profligate infamy'.[25]

Such beginnings did not bode well for the development of colonial New South Wales. Drawn from the criminal class, the building blocks of the new settlement in New South Wales were thought to be deficient: innately lawless, the convicts were judged to be 'for the most part idle, ignorant, and vicious ... England's social sewage'.[26] Colonial society was tainted: 'its prominent features were its drunkenness and its immorality'.[27] The Reverend Dr John Dunmore Lang was no more hopeful. 'The concentration of an emancipated convict population, as Governor Macquarie's experiment sufficiently proves, will infallibly be a concentration of vice and villainy, profligacy and misery, dissipation and ruin'.[28] Transportation thus meant pouring 'scum upon scum, dregs upon dregs ... building up with them a nation of crime'.[29] In short: at best convicts were not good workers, at worst they were not workers at all. In this guise they constituted a very poor labour supply. Convict labour was deemed deficient and inferior to that of free workers.

Paradox

The actual outcome of colonising New South Wales with forced convict labour was social and economic success. Growth was 'spectacular'.[30] As early as 1824, a visitor to New South Wales remarked, 'that colony is certainly the fruit of the convict's labour'.[31] The white economy grew at a rate that has never been surpassed. This was because growth occurred from a low base, because improved resources were being seized from the indigenous people, but also because valuable convict labour was being successfully exploited. From a very low economic base in 1820, the colony flourished. By mid-century 432 000 acres of land had been claimed for cultivation by the colonists; exports were worth £3.8 million and imports £4 million (a pattern of deficit in the balance of trade that continues today, somewhat problematically); 40 million pounds weight in wool were exported, providing England with over half its requirements; and the white population was in excess of 400 000 individuals, a significant proportion being the native-born offspring of convict mothers and fathers. Contrary to expectations, and despite financial, legal, social, religious and employment barriers plus the lure of cohabitation, many convict women did marry in the colony where there pertained a favourable 'marriage market' creating high official marriage rates measured by contemporary standards.[32] Currency lads and lasses, as the first generation of Australian-born whites were called, grew up strong and healthy, and found their pursuits best indulged legally rather than illegally. The growth of capital works, agriculture, the pastoral industry, small-scale domestic manufactures, the service sector, the population, families and the structure of society cannot be denied. Nor can it be explained away as the product of other labour: convicts and ex-convicts remained the single dominant element in the workforce in Australia until the late 1840s; they were on par with free migrants in 1850, and continued to be a significant element for decades to come.[33] Along with economic growth, a paradox emerged: dissipated convict idlers proved effective workers and citizens.

Not all contemporaries had regarded convicts and their labour with contempt. Many perceived Australia's convict fodder as useful workers skilled in a variety of occupations, individuals with a capacity to learn—and some a desire to do so—who provided a talented pool of labour available for exploitation in the service of colonial economic development.[34] Governor Macquarie criticised Bigge—the author of a rather damning report on the colony—for his having 'appeared to have come out with a strong and deep-rooted prejudice against all persons who had had the misfortune to come out as convicts, be their merits, talents and usefulness ever so conspicuous'.[35] Convict labour was acknowledged to be skilled, useful and needed in both public and private sectors.

Indeed, the very critics of convict labour cited have not always been consistent in their damnation of convict workers, or the system of transportation. Griffiths wrote that 'a plentiful supply of convict labour poured in at the cost of the Home Government is certain to be highly valuable',[36] and he highlighted the transformation of Sydney under Macquarie from 'a mere shanty town into a magnificent city'.[37] Cunningham, after complaining about the unwillingness of some convicts to work, continued that 'the great body, however, of the convicts turn out, as I have said, to be good servants, and you will exact as much labour from them in general as from free labourers in England'.[38] Governor King wrote to Lord Hobart about the women that 'the greater part are in general usefully employed in their domestic concerns', and Governor Hunter wrote to the Duke of Portland that 'if we establish their merits by the charming children with which they have fill'd the colony they will deserve our care'.[39] In a despatch sent to Governor Phillip from Grenville, he described the transportees upon the ship the *Lady Juliana*—much vilified by Lieutenant Ralph Clark—as 'unfortunate women' and requested of Phillip that 'you will cause them to be employed in such manner as may be most conducive to the advantage of the settlement'.[40] Lieutenant Clark himself took a young convict woman for his colonial wife, the mother of his child.[41] In government employ, the women made textiles, sewed the slop clothing that adorned convict bodies, crushed sea-shells for the mortar that held the hewn stone of colonial buildings together, cooked, cleaned and laundered. While convicts as a group were not 'very exemplary', King remarked that 'they certainly are not so generally depraved as may be imagined; nor have I any difficulty in saying that there are some very good characters among them'.[42]

In the conclusion to his book, Mudie eulogised at length about the overwhelming success of the colonial society and economy in attaining, in less than half a century, 'a state of things perfectly unexampled in the formation of an infant community ... with most of the distinguishing features hitherto belonging only to ancient and civilized states'.[43] The returns to capital were sensational.

So inordinately great, indeed, is the value of the productions of New South Wales, in comparison with the value or amount of the capital embarked in its formation, that the value of the productions of only two years is probably greater than the total amount of the capital as yet sunk in the formation of the colony'.[44]

Capital was not the source of wealth, labour was. Mudie continued: there was a 'striking peculiarity ... which certainly has had its share in causing so rapid a progression in wealth … The peculiarity referred to is the convict population …'.[45] What did the convicts have going for them?

> There is one circumstance regarding them which has been highly favourable to the interests of an infant colony; and that is, their being composed of almost every description of skilled labourers, and also of many men of very diversified knowledge and attainment, as well as of nearly every grade as to the rank in society which they had held in the mother country … There is no species, either of labour or of enterprise, which there are not to be found persons in the colony capable of undertaking.[46]

In addition to their skills, the convicts provided the *raison d'être* for the colony. Benefits accrued from the unprecedented financial input into public goods made by the British government in consequence of their penal policy of exiling miscreants.[47] Along with their gaolers, convicts 'formed a market for the productions of the industrious colonists'.[48] Mudie claimed that transportation had provided an 'instructive lesson' in imperialism; in how to create a wealthy colony that would earn money, furnish sound investments, provide a home for the excess population of the United Kingdom of Great Britain and Ireland, and be a market for British manufactures.[49] And 'all this accomplished in spite of the extreme moral depravity inherent in the constitution of the colonial society'.[50] But how could it have been *in spite* of its own labour force?

The penal shovel had not clashed with the colonial pick. On the contrary, the nature of this punitive settlement had been particularly conducive to growth and development, to the point where the expected outcome of pick and shovel meeting was reversed. Originally it had been thought that inept convicts would fail as workers; after a few decades of settlement, the fear was that life in the colony had become so prosperous that transportation was not a punishment to be dreaded but desired. An inherent contradiction developed as penal control came into conflict with economic prosperity.[51] Prison authorities reported that women awaiting transportation, held in Millbank Prison, were 'reconciled to the discipline [encountered there], however strict, by the knowledge that it would soon cease, and that it was only a necessary step towards all but absolute freedom in a colony'.[52] Lord Ellenborough, Chief Justice of the King's Bench and much in favour of capital punishment even for minor felonies such as picking pockets, considered exile to be 'a summer's excursion, in an easy migration, to a happier and better climate'.[53] Continuing the weather motif, Archbishop Richard Whately complained that transportation was effectively a free passage 'to a country whose climate is delightful'; and, in spite of his apparent sensitivity to the ferocity of life and work in the nineteenth century, Charles Dickens was distressed to find Australia viewed as a land of opportunity with a climate 'bright and hot', thus diluting the 'terrors' of transportation and reducing the potency of this form of punishment as a deterrent.[54] Satirically, the Reverend Sydney Smith wrote the following in *The Edinburgh Review*.

> Because you have committed this offence, the sentence of the Court is that you shall no longer be burdened with the support of your wife and family. You shall immediately be removed from a very bad climate and a country over-burdened with people to one of the finest regions of the earth, where the demand for human labour is every hour increasing, and where it is highly probable you may ultimately regain your character and improve your future. The Court have been induced to pass this sentence upon you in consequence of the many aggravating circumstances of your case, and they hope your fate will be a warning to others.[55]

Underpinning all these complaints and observations was the fact that development had turned Sydney into a flourishing town that now offered better economic opportunities than were available to many in England and particularly Ireland, where death by starvation was not uncommon.[56]

When transportation to New South Wales effectively ended in 1840 (later, in 1849, there was a brief but unsuccessful attempt to resurrect it) sections of the local employer population were despondent. They pleaded:

> In place, therefore, of the dribbling system of shipping small drafts at broken intervals, we say to England, Ship all your Crime and Poverty, which, whilst they reduce the remuneration of labour and lower the standard of comfort and subsistence at home, will produce a directly opposite effect if deported to a labour market where the demand may be described as unlimited ... Let our boundless labour fields be made available in the fullest extent for those millions of our starving and criminal brethren for whom England has hitherto provided no other place of refuge than—The Union or the New Bastille, the Spital or the Gaol.[57]

Employers welcomed British and Irish societies' 'dregs' with open arms. Convict labour was in demand. Convicts brought in associated capital investment, constructed capital works, enlarged the domestic market, and—of greatest significance—provided a supply of cheap, controlled and talented labour.

Historians and convict women

This paradox of degraded unskilled criminals producing rapid colonial development has gone unremarked. Historians have remained dubious about convict workers. On the basis of Henry Mayhew's evidence,

Manning Clark argued that 'mental imbecility and low cunning' were trademarks for convicts who were 'lazy in disposition and lacked energy both of body and mind'.[58] To an extent, there may have been an element of truth in Mayhew's observation of the low work effort of English workers. The lowest 3 per cent of the British workforce consumed inadequate nutrition to sustain any work, with the rest of the bottom 20 per cent possessing sufficient energy for only six hours' light work per day. Even the top half of the population were malnourished, stunted in growth, poor in health and went early to their graves.[59] Superior care and feeding in the colony should have improved worker productivity.[60] But for Clark and a number of other key historians, the problem was not physiological but psychological. Convicts suffered 'a deep-seated resistance to work' and 'they were ignorant to a degree which assumed comical proportions'.[61] Convicts were thought to suffer from an 'aversion to continuity and steady work', attributable 'in the main to the harshness of either parents or masters, and a consequent failure to inculcate the habits of industry and a sense of purpose'.[62] They had major attitudinal problems: 'these people knew what a good servant was but their whole lives turned on outraging that ideal'.[63]

Convicts were characterised as being devoid of any knowledge of working-class values and family relations. Their work histories—or more correctly, lack of them—and character values were not only inappropriate but antipathetic to the acquisition of skills. Character deficiencies both prevented criminal individuals from acquiring economically useful skills and prohibited them from willingly applying their labour. The prognosis made by many contemporaries and historians on the outcome of colonising New South Wales with criminal rejects had not been good. So how had colonial society made a silk purse from a sow's ear? No satisfactory attempt was even made to explain how poor economic material (convicts) was magically metamorphosised into economic miracle (colonial New South Wales). When, where, and (more importantly, perhaps) why did convicts who arrived unfamiliar with work learn to compensate for their lack of training? There was no one except other convicts to teach them. The silkiness of the purse required the sow's ear be re-evaluated.

Recognising this implicit contradiction, economic historians at the University of New South Wales employed quantitative and qualitative evidence to examine the convict economy. *Convict Workers* unravelled aspects of the workings of the convict system and reassessed convict origins, revealing the men to be appropriately skilled to meet colonial needs and demonstrating the vital roles these men played in the creation of the successful new society.[64] However, the jury remains out on convict women. The dominant theme in the literature remains one of deprivation. Convict women have been characterised as unskilled and illiterate non-workers, and in the sphere of unpaid labour as poor mothers. Labelled prostitutes, they were deemed members of the criminal class, the lowest order of society, who brought with them little in the way of work experience or traditional family values. In the colony, they were expected to fail as workers, wives and mothers. It was asserted that convict women did not contribute to economic success.

We hear that 'the women convicts sent out to the colony were often described as particularly poor types, and they rarely made any positive contribution to the public welfare or progress'.[65] In the years 1825 to 1831, 'many of those freshly landed were of such poor quality that settlers would not take them'.[66] Of Irish women transported to Tasmania, 'only a few had skills', with the rest limited by their 'religion, illiteracy and lack of skills'.[67] In Britain convicts had been 'despised, abandoned and worthless objects', 'women of no trade', 'members of the lowest order', who arrived 'as one class, the damned whores of the criminal haunts of Britain'.[68] This meant the women were 'illiterate and lacking in any skills' and 'did not, therefore, bring with them to New South Wales a familiarity with, or expectation of, those standards, values, customs, obligations and privileges which were an intrinsic part of the British hierarchical social system'.[69] In *Convict Workers* it has been claimed that the *lack* of convict women benefited economic growth, because 'women were imperfect substitutes for men'.[70]

Other nineteenth-century themes were resurrected. Lloyd Robson claimed that 'the male convict, desiring to marry, was more likely to marry a native-born girl, for he must have known that a convict woman was unlikely to make a satisfactory partner. Female convicts, especially those from London, were not the sort of women to attract men into marriage'.[71] Children who did not know their convict parents 'were better off than those who did, since most of the convict men were drunken and demoralized professional criminals, and most of the women equally drunken and demoralized prostitutes', according to Ken Macnab and Russel Ward.[72] Convict women's immorality was expected to corrupt their offspring, breeding immoral, unhealthy, shrivelled, stunted runts who would make the poorest of citizens. Partly this was due to the poverty of convicts' own upbringing. Inadequate parenting was blamed as a significant factor leading offenders into crime. This was observed by C. B. and M. B. Schedvin. 'Lack of self-confidence, negative self-image, weak super-ego resulting in poor control of impulses, and often delinquent behaviour round out the pattern resulting from parental neglect and emotional deprivation'.[73] Parents had failed 'to inculcate the habit of industry and a sense of purpose' in their offspring, characteristics necessary for participation in the legitimate workforce.[74] Worse than simply not inculcating the right work values, these neglectful parents promoted the opposite: 'the example of parents, siblings, peers and other associates was instrumental in representing the inducements of easy money, an idle and self-indulgent lifestyle, and the spice of defiance of law and society in such a way that the values of a criminal sub-culture were endowed with personal intimacy'.[75] As children, the convicts had not been raised in caring and loving families, but were brought up to crime by dissolute parents who demonstrated no loving, no caring, and whose treatment was harsh. Alternatively, they were orphans taken under the wing of Fagin-types who taught the skills of the pickpocket and organised gainful but illegal employment. Unaccustomed to family life, parental care, bonding and love, convict mothers would be neglectful, and they were accused of replicating in the colony that same criminal lifestyle and culture which spawned them. How could convicts' children do anything other than follow in their depraved parents' footsteps?

Recently a far more cheerful tale has started to emerge. Convict women at least did not establish a cold and barren criminal sub-culture, but one based on families, intimacy and warmth: they made good mothers, giving birth and successfully nurturing the first generations of native-born whites.[76] Welsh girls 'were well equipped to play a useful role in frontier life'.[77] Women 'with a skill or trade ... formed so high a proportion of women transported from England to Botany Bay'.[78] Transported women may have arrived as 'a uniform class of despised felons, tainted with all the vile and infamous connotations of that word "convict", but their responses to colonial opportunities and disadvantages were as stridently varied and determinative as were those of the women who came free and unconvicted'.[79] Something positive is now known of convict women's lives in the colonies—their reproductive roles, the relationships they formed and the ways in which they manoeuvred. And while some contemporaries denounced the women as worse workers than the men, being 'more disobedient and refractory', this was because more obedience was expected from women, especially as they laboured in close proximity to their employers and 'a surly servant was much harder to bear at the dinner table than in the field'.[80] No doubt a good proportion of women made poor mothers and indifferent workers, but the key finding was one of diversity: all convicts did not conform to the stereotype of degenerate professional criminals. However, those historians who did accept women's colonial achievements typically explained that better opportunities allowed convicts to reform: English women from the criminal class miraculously improved in colonial New South Wales, while the Irish, never so reprobate, benefited from improved life-chances.[81] It was not contemplated that what was wrong was the original characterisation of convict women as unskilled professional criminals.

Serious ramifications flow from whether we think of convict women as skilled or not, regarding their economic worth within the colony.

Economists and others have concluded that convict women (and women more generally) did not contribute greatly to colonial economic development. This was not because women were few in number. (As a labour supply, they could have been small but strategic.) The reason then? Convict women were unskilled, inculcated with the wrong values and were just plain useless, or 'the patriarchal society of emerging capitalism did not allow them [women] to work', or the women were skilled and potentially useful workers, perhaps appropriate to colonial needs, but the state failed to allocate women's labour efficiently.[82] Alternatively, economists and others have made a mistake.

For the moment, let us put aside that bigger question of whether convict women did or did not contribute significantly to economic development. (That must be the subject matter of a another book.) Let us ask instead, *could* they have done? The issue becomes one of unfit useless women, or potentially useful workers. This shifts the focus of debate from what happened to convict women once in Australia, to what had happened to them in terms of employment and skill acquisition back in England and Ireland. They were not part of a criminal class, but were convict women members of the lowest economic order of British society? Or did the majority arrive in New South Wales possessed of the necessary work skills and demographic characteristics that would allow them to participate in the colonial economy? Where can we turn for an answer? Elizabeth's box of Economic Accoutrements.

Elizabeth and her box: an inventory

Fortuitously—and interestingly—British administrators were also curious about Elizabeth's economic possessions. As noted in Chapter One, recording clerks spent some considerable energies in collecting information about the contents of the women's various boxes of social, cultural and economic luggage, with their findings stored for posterity in the convict indents. Of particular interest here is Elizabeth's box of economic tricks. What would we consider to be the women's economic assets? Age, mobility, health, literacy, numeracy, occupational training, and perhaps also experience of work and family life.

One most obvious economic asset was age. Transportees were chosen on the basis of the severity of their sentence, their health and their age. Selection was meant to be restricted to women under forty-five years, although this was treated as a guideline rather than a hard-and-fast rule.[83] Following in the footsteps of one of her two children, Catherine Finn was transported to New South Wales at the age of eighty for her first offence, passing 'bad money'. She was in the colony only six months before she

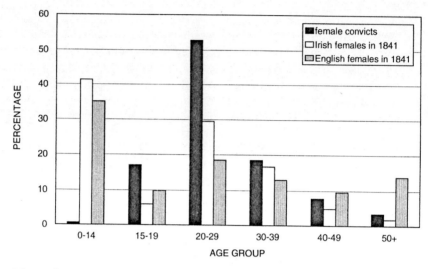

Figure 4.1   Age distributions of women convicts and Irish and English women.

died at the Female Factory at Parramatta in November 1826.[84] But Catherine was not typical. Indeed, she was the oldest woman sent out between 1826 and 1840. Convict women's age distribution is presented in Figure 4.1, alongside ages for non-criminal females in Ireland and England in 1841. What is striking about this graph is the dissimilarity between convicts and ordinary populations. Convicts were unique. Most convict women were aged between fifteen and thirty years. Certainly this had been the case for the women we met in Chapter One, Caroline Humphries, Harriet Wakefield, Margaret Shannahan (all seventeen), Rachel Bryant (twenty-three) and Elizabeth Coltman (thirty), although not for Hannah Buttledoor (thirty-six). In this age band between fifteen and thirty years were 70 per cent of female transportees, compared with 35 per cent of Ireland's non-criminal women and only 28 per cent of England's. Relatedly, among convicts there were fewer older women when compared with England, but even more noticeably, there was a nearly complete absence of children. Two-fifths of the Irish and over one-third of English females were pre-adolescent: this was the case for less than 1 per cent of convicts.

Was this outcome simply the result of the convicts being 'the sweep-ings of the gaols, hulks and prisons'? No, it was not, although the composition of prisoners was obviously influential. Figure 4.2 draws the comparison, with the choice of age groups determined by the statistics available for prisoners. There was no shortage of children in British gaols.[85] One in ten female prisoners in 1841 were aged sixteen years or less, compared with one in thirty-three convicts. Transported children

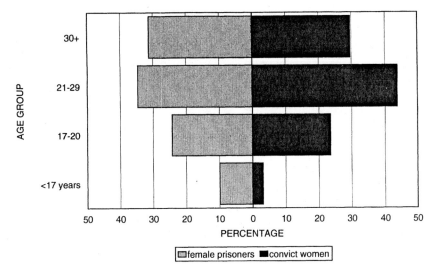

Figure 4.2 Age distributions of women convicts and female prisoners in British gaols.

were nearly all aged fifteen or sixteen, placing them on the borderline with those considered adult. Perhaps for altruistic reasons, authorities were hesitant to transport children, although before 1832 the Prison Discipline Society was in favour of sending juveniles.[86] Whatever the reason, selection on the basis of age was obviously practised even if not explicitly stated in the regulations. The relative shortfall caused by not exporting children was made up by transporting a higher proportion of women in their twenties. These decisions had economic implications.

Costly individuals with low or no productivity were missing from both ends of the age spectrum, and this skewed distribution was further accentuated by authorities who refused to allow convict mothers to bring their children with them, unless they were babes at the breast. This meant that convict women arrived in the colony with an age profile most conducive to economic growth. Currently, the Department of Immigration prefers immigrants between the ages of sixteen and thirty-five years. Today 47 per cent of immigrants fit this bill, compared with 82 per cent of female transportees landed between 1826 and 1840.[87] A comparable group of male and female free emigrants from the British Isles to the United States of America in 1831 also scored less well than convicts: 53 per cent were in the main productive age group between fifteen and thirty-nine years, as were 88 per cent of convict women.[88] Convicts were at their peak age for physical fitness, and young enough to adjust to a new environment, climate and social setting.

Adjusting to new environments was something many convict women were familiar with. Just as Rachel Bryant had moved from Taunton in Somerset, where she was born, to Bridgewater in Lancashire, so too had 3119 other convict women—46 per cent of their ranks—been tried in a county other than that of their birth. These women were movers. They were not wanderers and vagabonds, the nomadic tribes of urban Britain seeking out criminal mischief, but workers in search of employment. Workers often sold their labour in fairs, moving to wherever employment could be gained on the best terms they could negotiate. Anne Kussmaul's work on nineteenth-century labour markets revealed that the nature of hiring fairs for servant labour was 'designed to promote mobility over long distances' and Theresa McBride's research on one major form of women's employment led her to comment that 'the history of domestic service in the nineteenth century is the story of urban migration'.[89] At the same time that convicts were being shipped out to Australia, economic change was sweeping England and Ireland, and migration was a necessary feature of labour markets as workers shifted out of those sectors in decline and into areas of growing prosperity. Extensive movement covered both countries, particularly flowing from the countryside to urban centres.[90] Such internal migration appears to have been dominated by women, perhaps because they were the first displaced by economic reorganisation.[91] Two-fifths of convict migrants had flocked to just four towns out of all those in the United Kingdom: they had gone to Dublin, Manchester, Liverpool and—most of all—London. As will be seen in Chapters Five and Six, it was not the least skilled who migrated, pushed out by their own incompetence, but the most skilled and literate. Many convict women thus arrived in New South Wales already experienced at travel and the efforts required in re-establishing life in a new place.

Health was another of the three criteria employed in selecting who would be transported, and like age it had important implications for worker productivity. Various proxies can be used for health and living standards more generally. Height is one such indicator. How tall humans grow depends upon their genetic make-up and the amount of nutrition they consume, minus demands made on the body through work and fighting disease. Children denied sufficient food will not grow as tall as they otherwise would with higher calorific intake. Average height attained by a population of the same genetic background thus reveals something about the overall mix of work intensity, public health, the disease environment and nutrition. Economic historians have been keen to use this measure in comparing different groups and examining changes over time, and this would be a most useful indicator for convicts, but for one seemingly insurmountable hurdle.[92] While convict indents recorded women's heights in great detail—to the quarter-inch—there are no comparable measurements for other non-convict women in this period. Auxological research (as it is called) has relied upon recruitment data, and soldiers and sailors did not come in skirts. However, it will be seen in later chapters on Ireland and England that there are other ways of usefully employing this rare resource.

An alternative measure is mortality, with death a good proxy for ill-health. After disastrous experiences transporting convicts in the late eighteenth century, great care was taken with what appears a precious cargo.[93] Surgeon-superintendents responsible for the well-being of convicts accompanied every voyage from 1815, diet was considerately maintained with an eye on health, and arguably convict women received better treatment than their male counterparts and free immigrants.[94] Contractors shipping convicts were paid partly by results, and only healthy women were selected for transportation.[95] The outcome was positive. It can be seen from Figure 4.3 that 6876 women were sent to New South Wales between 1826 and 1840, and 6812 made it alive. Sixty-four deaths. A sad number, but a remarkably low one, with a mortality rate of less than 1 per cent.[96] Had these women stayed at home in Britain, a similar proportion could have been expected to die during the length of time a ship took to traverse half the globe.[97]

There were other deaths. Tragically, one female convict ship did not even make it out of the English Channel. On 31 August 1833 the *Amphitrite* went down in a savage and unexpected storm not a mile from French land, losing all 101 women convicts—unnecessarily, it would

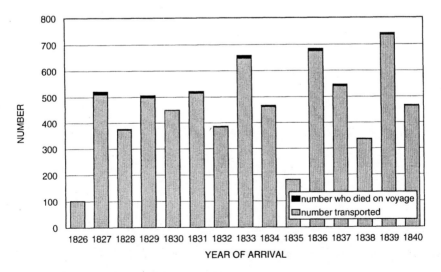

Figure 4.3 Female mortality on convict voyages.

seem from the report made to Parliament.[98] Gallant French sailors braved the waters, but all to no avail: their help was rejected. At one point the ship's surgeon ordered the longboat to be lowered that the convicts might yet effect an escape, but the unhelpful intervention of his wife, who would not tolerate the company of convicts, left the prisoners below deck, helpless. A return trip was too late. Crowds gathered on the beaches were subjected to a 'melancholy' scene, unaware passengers had been on board until the ship broke up and their drowned bodies washed ashore. Then in 1835 catastrophe similarly took the *Neva*. Having made the long journey from Cork across the world, it went down off King Island in the Bass Strait between what was then the southernmost part of New South Wales (now Victoria) and north-west Van Diemen's Land (Tasmania). One hundred and forty-five convict women died in that wreck; free women, children and crew also perished, leaving only six survivors.[99]

Including these shipwrecks, overall mortality crept up to 4.5 per cent. Even when incorporating deaths caused by misadventure, figures were surprisingly low for such a hazardous journey. Fatalities caused by shipwrecks, however, tell us nothing about the overall state of the women's health. Deaths through illness are more informative. At only sixty-four deaths, illness was not endemic. Nor was it evenly spread. Twenty-one of the fifty-one ships carrying women to New South Wales in this period suffered no deaths at all, while some convict vessels had disproportionately high death rates—*Fanny* had lost six women to cholera before setting sail from the Downs, losing a further two on the way. Such a concentration of mortality on selected voyages reflected the major causes of death: not chronic illness, but acute infections.[100] Diarrhoea was the cause of many deaths, with influenza, pneumonia, fever and scurvy also taking their toll on the women's health more generally.[101] In the absence of infectious illness, overall health standards were good by contemporary measures. Excluding disasters, the mortality rate on female convict ships at less than 1 per cent was much like that for free assisted immigrants arriving from England in 1838, with 40 out of 2416 adult women—1.7 per cent—lost at sea.[102] These rates were very low when considered against the backdrop of other coerced migrations. In the middle of the nineteenth century indentured Indians suffered an average mortality rate of 17 per cent.[103] Convict mortality contrasted markedly and favourably with crew and slaves on that other great intercontinental seaway, the slave route from Africa. Fatalities during England's Atlantic trade ranged between one death per fifty slaves to one death in every four, while mortality in the eighteenth-century French slave trade at times rose as high as 36 per cent.[104] By comparison, convict death rates were negligible. Such low death rates among convicts reflected care in selecting transportees from overcrowded and unsanitary detention centres and concern in their attendance, for example 'good and abundant' rations, making convict women comparatively healthy upon arrival.[105]

Literacy and numeracy are two other economic assets. Economists have identified the reading ability of a population to be a major determinant of economic growth: societies need to achieve a certain level of literacy before they are able to modernise. Clark had found illiteracy levels 'surprisingly low', and he was correct.[106] Australia was well served by its convict women, as can be seen from Figure 4.4. Upon arrival, 4322 women possessed the ability to read, 1489 of them additionally capable of writing. This left only about one-third who were functionally illiterate. Tutoring in reading and writing skills was provided while in transit to Australia, giving convicts the opportunity to improve or for the uneducated to learn, further investing in these potential workers. An experience of learning before embarkation no doubt assisted women to take best advantage of the opportunities with which they were presented, but Irish women began already disadvantaged. Some 64 per cent of all the women combined were able to read at least, but this figure masks significant differences between the Irish and the English: 80 per cent of women transported from England were literate compared with 48 per cent of Irish transportees. Elizabeth, Caroline, Hannah, Rachel and Harriet could all read, while Margaret from Ireland could not.

Convict women also appeared numerate. 'Age-heaping' is a technique for approximating numeracy. When the age distribution of a population is plotted (age on the horizontal axis, frequency on the vertical) it should

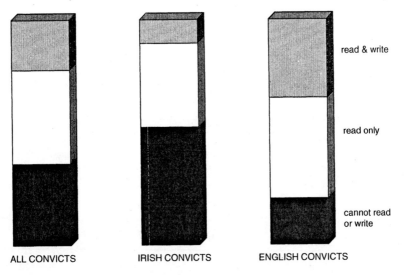

Figure 4.4 Literacy of Irish and English women convicts.

reveal a fairly smooth but decaying line. Instead, when semi-numerate populations are asked for their ages and this information is graphed, what appears are substantial perturbations at regular intervals: 'heaps' or 'clusters', to be found on rounded ages such as 20 years and 30 years rather than recording 19 or 21 years, and 29 or 31 years. This inexactitude is thought to reflect guessing. This is not to suggest that all women with rounded ages were innumerate, nor that failure to know one's age could only be the result of inadequate learning (many parents simply failed to impart this knowledge, often not knowing dates exactly themselves), but it does assume that a higher proportion of women with rounded ages were innumerate than those with non-rounded ages.[107] Convict women, on the whole, were precise. A truly random distribution would have 10 per cent of people sitting exactly on the decades; convict women had twice this number, 20 per cent giving rounded ages. There was comparatively little clustering around the half decade (25, 35 etc.). Four-fifths gave exact ages, and another 10 per cent could legitimately be expected to give rounded ages, suggesting that perhaps one-tenth of convict women were unsure of their year of birth. As with literacy, regional differences prevailed. Figure 4.5 illustrates the ages given by Irish and English convicts. About one-quarter of Irish women displayed heaping, a tendency nearly imperceptible among the English. Both literacy and numeracy are, however, more revealing when Irish and English convicts are separated and compared, not with each other, but with prevailing standards for Irish and English workers in the United Kingdom, the subject matter of the next two chapters. However, for a group of 'dissipated idlers', convict women were surprisingly literate and numerate, especially the English.

Such findings are significant for the criminal-class argument regarding the attainment of skills and convicts' ability to apply themselves. Convicts were not so idle and degenerate as to ignore their education. More than simply the ability to read and write, literacy suggests a higher level of worker productivity as it intimates exposure to the habits of industry—habits that the convicts supposedly failed to internalise.[108] While few convict women would have acquired their reading, writing and numeracy skills in a schoolroom, the act of learning in itself required discipline and taught obedience. That so many convicts displayed some degree of literacy and numeracy, and that more received and took advantage of training on their transport ships, suggests that the women brought with them to the colony a useful talent and appropriate attitudes.

Other talents were also packed among their economic possessions. Most women had experienced employment prior to their transportation. Information was missing for 109 convicts (including the 64 who had passed away), and 14 women were listed as 'unserviceable', 'unfit',

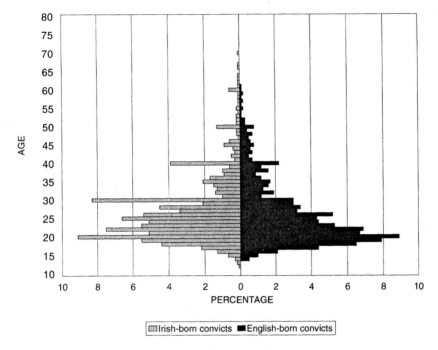

Figure 4.5 Female convict age distributions and clustering.

'incapable', 'crippled', 'asthmatic', 'sickly', 'feeble', 'infirm', 'deaf', 'rheumatic', 'lunatic', 'idiot' and 'silly'. Only 14 other women recorded 'no trade', although one woman filled in this column with the rather peculiar occupation of being the—presumably illegitimate—daughter of Lord Dundas. Of the 6738 women who listed one job, 2424 of them listed a second occupation, 326 listed a third and 24 even listed a fourth. Elizabeth Coltman was both a house servant and ribbon weaver, and her shipmate Rachel Bryant had worked as a silk weaver, needlewoman and allworker. In order to deal with all this data without losing any of it, all of these callings listed by each woman (jobs one, two, three and four) have been summated into one measure which I have called the 'stock of skills'. Elizabeth contributed two skills to this stock, Rachel three. Combined convict women brought to New South Wales a stock of some 9512 skills. Table 4.1 lists all these different callings in descending order, giving the raw frequency and the percentage contribution to the overall stock of skills. Much can be said of this material.

Elizabeth Coltman and her fellow deportees were very careful in specifying their job descriptions when asked by the recording clerk. One woman wanted it to be known that she was an allworker in a *lady's* house; another that she was a nurse in a hospital, as opposed to someone's home.

Weavers drew a distinction on the basis of their equipment, handloom or steam-driven. There were not just button makers but pearl button makers, not simply shoemakers and bootmakers, but shoe binders, shoe closers, boot closers, boot binders and boot corders—precise descriptions of tasks reflecting the extent of work-process fragmentation and the specialist skills acquired. Some fifteen different types of 'servant' were reported. There were general servants and general house servants, general country servants and general country house servants; indoors, outdoors, on farms, in houses—everywhere there were servants to be found, serving in different ways. Alongside them were housemaids, kitchenmaids, nursemaids, laundrymaids, dairymaids, and all manner of maids. This specificity is intriguing, and should not be overlooked. Some distinctions undoubtedly arose from idiosyncrasies among the recorders who compiled the convict indents, and also from regional differences in nomenclature, but these factors alone seem unlikely to account for all variations, particularly when some involved numerically large categories. Often distinctions reflected different employment demands: 'town allwork' would have involved different pursuits from 'country allwork'. The dividing line between 'laundress', 'laundrymaid' and 'washerwoman' was significant in terms of employment status, experience, age, ownership of the requisite tools, physical locality of employment, and whether a woman was single, married or widowed. Definitions are not always clear to us, yet this exactness in identifying their own particular responsibilities in the workplace suggests that the women themselves—and the recording authorities—were aware of specific employment responsibilities and skills associated with different jobs.

It is interesting that there was such depth to the occupations listed by female convicts. The manner in which women fell into these jobs is also noteworthy. Large numbers of women were concentrated in just a few of these pursuits. Although there are 160 jobs listed, about forty jobs accounted for the vast majority of women. Clearly convict women were concentrated in the service sector, in jobs that were extensions of women's domestic responsibilities such as cooking, cleaning, caring. But this does not demean the importance of these occupations nor the skills required to perform them. In the days before electrical household appliances (in the days before electricity!) domestic labours were extensive indeed. It took an army of workers to keep the big houses running. Service work was varied, detailed and in demand.

House servants and maids like Elizabeth Coltman and Margaret Shannahan abounded. Domestic service dominated both town and country employment. The listing of more than one trade or calling often reflected the complementary nature of domestic servants' multi-skilling. Such women tended to possess a range of domestic skills. Housemaids had worked as kitchenmaids, for example. But, as with Elizabeth, jobs

Table 4.1 Female convict occupations

Occupation (as on indents)[a]	Frequency of listing in the indents No.	Percentage of the stock of skills %
Housemaid	1 924	20.22
Allwork	1 720	18.08
Kitchenmaid	742	7.80
Nursemaid	659	6.93
Cook	591	6.21
Laundress	563	5.92
Dairymaid	509	5.35
Needlewoman	470	4.94
Country servant	379	3.98
Laundrymaid	262	2.75
Washerwoman	222	2.33
Child's maid	193	2.03
Country allwork	151	1.59
Dressmaker	122	1.28
Nurse	88	0.93
General house servant	67	0.70
Barmaid	66	0.69
Farm labourer	56	0.59
Housekeeper	37	0.39
Thorough servant	36	0.38
General servant	34	0.36
Inn-allwork	33	0.35
Servant	33	0.35
Farm servant	32	0.34
Ladies' maid	29	0.30
Milliner	21	0.22
Baker	19	0.20
Straw bonnet maker	19	0.20
Factory labourer	17	0.18
Silk weaver	16	0.17
Sempstress	15	0.16
Spinner	15	0.16
Boot binder	13	0.14
Bonnet maker	12	0.13
Brewer	12	0.13
Chambermaid	12	0.13
Confectioner	11	0.12
Inn-servant	10	0.11
Mantua maker	10	0.11
Shoe binder	10	0.11

Table 4.1 contd

Occupation (as on indents)[a]	Frequency of listing in the indents No.	Percentage of the stock of skills %
Stay maker	10	0.11
Silk winder	9	0.09
Straw plaiter	9	0.09
Governess	8	0.08
Cotton manufacturer	7	0.07
Boot closer	6	0.06
Cotton spinner	6	0.06
General indoor servant	6	0.06
Inn-house keeper	6	0.06
Lace maker	6	0.06
Tailoress	6	0.06
Town servant	6	0.06
Weaver	6	0.06
Button maker	5	0.05
Midwife	5	0.05
Plain work	5	0.05
Schoolmistress	5	0.05
Sews	5	0.05
Other[b]	166	1.75
Total stock of skills	9 512	100.00

Notes:

a   Includes apprentices where relevant (e.g. confectioner's apprentice, mantua maker's apprentice, under-waiter, under-housemaid).

b   The category 'Other' includes the following.

Four women listed under each of the following occupations: Charwoman, flax spinner, fruit dealer, hat trimmer, hawker, market woman, publican.

Three women listed under each of the following occupations: Basket maker, cheese maker, cotton winder, dealer, inn-kitchen maid, pastry cook, reaper, ribbon weaver, scullery maid, shoe closer, tambour worker, upholsterer.

Two women listed under each of the following occupations: Artificial flower maker, button maker, calico printer, chair carver, country house maid, country kitchen maid, embroiderer, farm servant indoors, general country servant, hotel cook, hotel chamber maid, inn-country allwork, inn-waiter, knitter, muslin sewer, pedlar, poultry dealer, shoe maker, tobacco maker, waiter.

One woman listed under each of the following occupations: Attendant in lunatic asylum, boot corder, boot maker, brace maker, bracelet maker, brush maker, calico hemper, catgut manufacturer, cloth cap maker, cotton weaver, comb stainer, country servant thorough, distiller, dyer, fancy trimmer, farm house girl, fishing net maker, fringe maker, furrier, general country house servant, gipsy, glass grinder, glass polisher, handloom weaver, hat binder, hat maker, hospital nurse, hotel house maid, house worker, huxter, in- and out-

were not always matched. A house servant who had practised as a ribbon weaver, or a reaper who also cooked, reflected the reality of nineteenth-century labour markets. Fluidity marked these places, as structural change within the economy necessitated retraining, and insecurity and season-ality of employment contracts required worker flexibility.

There is one other striking feature of Table 4.1: the extent of skilled and semi-skilled occupations among a group of women typified as the dregs of society. This result was arrived at by employing a widely used independent skill classification.[109] W. A. Armstrong employed census data, enumerators' books, and contemporary accounts in the painstaking task of defining the contours of the nineteenth-century English economy and stratifying occupations into five social-skill categories. How female convict skills were matched to these is given in Appendix 4. As can be seen from Figure 4.6, convict women fell into these groupings in the following way. Not surprisingly, none were 'professional' and only sixteen women were in the 'semi-professional' category, including six schoolmistresses (one from a village), four fruit dealers, four publicans and two poultry dealers. Nearly one-half—45 per cent—were 'skilled' and a further 31 per cent 'semi-skilled', with only 23 per cent classified as 'unskilled'. What did and did not count as 'skilled' work? All manner of trade was represented. Among convicts could be found midwives and dressmakers, housemaids, cooks including specialists in pastry, confec-tioners, cheese and butter makers. Other women had been employed as cotton manufacturers, winders, spinners and weavers, calico hempers and printers, fancy trimmers, catgut manufacturers, upholsterers, ostrich feather dressers, and also glass grinders and polishers, the makers of dresses, bonnets, mantuas, baskets, lint, tassels, artificial flowers, and much, much more. Relegated to 'semi-skilled' status were all those listed under the general rubric of 'servant', laundresses and washerwomen, distillers, dyers and fishing-net makers, to name a few. 'Unskilled' work-ers included factory labourers, huxters and hawkers, kitchenmaids and allworkers. As with literacy, again differences can be detected between the Irish and English, with the latter more highly trained as indicated in the figure.

Notes to Table 4.1 contd

door servant, indoor servant, inn-chamber maid, instrumental teacher, iron polisher, ladies' hairdresser, ladies' house allwork, ladies' nursery maid, linen draper, lint maker, nailer, ostrich feather dresser, pearl button maker, pin maker, picker, potter, pottery packer, public house servant, school house maid, shop man, stage dancer, steam weaver, stocking sitter, straw worker, tape weaver, tassel maker, tin hawker, tin ware manufacturer, town allwork, village schoolmistress, waiting maid, wool spinner.

Source: Convict indents

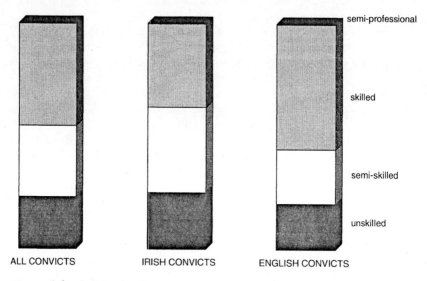

semi-professional

skilled

semi-skilled

unskilled

ALL CONVICTS   IRISH CONVICTS   ENGLISH CONVICTS

Figure 4.6   Skill levels of Irish and English women convicts.

Convict women thus appear to have largely been skilled and semi-skilled workers. Influencing this outcome was the reality that much domestic service—contrary to current expectations—did require extensive training and was in fact skilled work. Wage profiles confirm this. Comparatively unskilled workers commenced earning with relatively high wages which remained constant over their working lives, a quite dissimilar pattern to that for skilled workers; for the latter, starting wages were low (sometimes negative, as apprentices paid for the privilege of acquiring skills) but rose sharply, surpassing unskilled wages, as training increased labour productivity and returns to labour. (Investment in human capital—training—led to increased future returns—higher wages.) Wage profiles for domestic servants conform to this latter pattern.[110] Many domestic servants were skilled and semi-skilled workers.

Affirmation for this finding regarding the skill levels of convict women can be found by correlating skill with other information. Higher investment in education would be expected to yield improvements in other economic assets possessed by convicts, unless there was something wrong with the data or the skill classification.[111] Reassuringly, literacy and skill correlate. From Figure 4.7 it can be seen that skill and literacy levels improved together. *Il*-literacy rates are perhaps the most reliable indicators, given the primitive nature of measurement in the nineteenth century. Steadily illiteracy rates declined with evidence of greater investment in job training, making the more skilled workers also the more literate. While almost half the unskilled (47 per cent) were unable to read

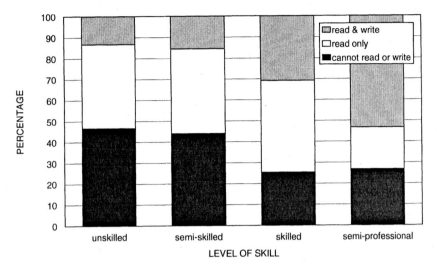

Figure 4.7 Female convict skill and literacy.

or write, only one-quarter of skilled workers remained ignorant of these accomplishments. Three-quarters of skilled workers able to read, a goodly number also capable of writing, was a remarkably high proportion for women growing up in Britain from the late eighteenth century and into the first quarter of the nineteenth century.

Additionally, we would expect skill to be a function of age, and indeed this was the case. As an individual matured, she experienced training; she became more highly skilled and, exposed to an ever-changing labour market, more widely equipped. The young Caroline was a housegirl, Harriet a needlewoman, Margaret a housemaid, while the slightly older Rachel had accomplishments as a needlewoman, silk weaver and all-worker, and Elizabeth as both a house servant and ribbon weaver. Skill tended to increase with age, as illustrated in Figure 4.8.[112] There was a rapid learning phase between childhood and the teenage years and through into the mid-twenties. The paths followed in Ireland and England then diverge, with England offering its women opportunities for higher levels of investment in education at older ages. For Irish women, stasis was reached at this point around the early twenties, even diminishing in later years, while in England women continued their training and retraining, not reaching anything like a plateau until into their thirties. It can also be seen from Figure 4.8 that overall levels of skill in England outstripped those in Ireland by some considerable degree, emphasising trends evident in measures of literacy and numeracy and reflecting the very different natures of the two economies. In both countries, although at different rates, women progressed from semi-skilled to skilled jobs, the

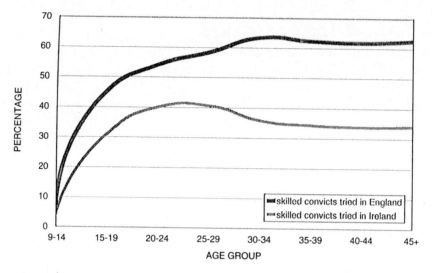

Figure 4.8   Skill acquisition of female convicts.

rewards of (sometimes informal) apprenticeships leading women into more highly prized occupations. Around twenty-seven years—the average age of convict women—probably represented the optimum balance between training and future practice: female convicts were old enough to have acquired skills, yet young enough to have a long working life in front of them.

Finally, there is one other dimension to female convict economic assets, associated with domestic labours, not normally paid and rarely considered: homemaking and motherhood. Prostitution and other forms of sexual encounters might also be added, especially since it has been argued that sexually gratifying male convicts and their gaolers, placating them and keeping them happy and heterosexual and working, was the main economic function of female convicts, even the reason that officials chose to transport women.[113] But in this we enter the realm of counter-factual history ('what would have happened if ...'), of unproved asser-tions, dubious interpretations of sexuality, difficult quantification, and the need to tease out an economic value from something—sex—that while sometimes in the marketplace was also often engaged in freely, willingly and to the satisfaction of both partners (one hopes). More clearly delineated was the colonial economy's need for labour, both in the short and long run. Be it coerced or free, immigration would be an important element in this, but eventually so too would natural increase. Children had to be born, and they needed to grow up strong, healthy, receptive to learning and keen to work. As we have already seen, convict women arrived in their peak productive and reproductive years. Some contemporaries and historians had, however, deemed convict women unfit both as wives and mothers. Unsubstantiated claims about the poverty of family formation incorrectly identified convict women's moral degeneracy and lack of familiarity with 'normal' family life as the cause. Convicts were said to have come from uncaring families—atomised collections of individuals rather than cohesive family units—or to be orphans brought up by crime bosses, a background leaving them incapable of forming satisfactory relationships.

Just how 'abnormal' their relationships had been prior to their departure seems open to dispute. When the women were transported to a destination 'beyond the seas', they left behind them mothers and fathers, brothers and sisters, husbands, lovers and children. That such family members existed and cared for their convicted relatives is evidenced by their activities in petitioning for clemency. Appeals lodged by relatives tell of offences committed in order to help a widowed mother or a starving sister.[114] Correspondence shuffled from southern to northern hemisphere and back repeatedly, again hinting at the strength of family ties.[115] These documented experiences would seem to mark many convicts as ordinary family women, thrown into hardship through sickness, loss of a breadwinner, dwindling employment, poor wages, or because there were too many mouths to feed. Convict women arrived in the colony familiar with family life, possibly even with a sense of domestic responsibility so active that it propelled them into crime. However, transportation did not discriminate between caring or brutal family relationships; it rent all asunder.

Figure 4.9 illustrates the women's conjugal status, and the proportion who already had children prior to their exile. It shows that 62 per cent were single women, another 14 per cent were widowed, and a quarter were married although effectively divorced by the distance. Deportation separated some 1598 women from their husbands, and broke who knows how many informal alliances. Perhaps some wives hoped that husbands might emigrate in pursuit, while a few others harboured the expectation of meeting partners or family who had themselves already been transported. Yet others would have been delighted to start afresh. Indeed, a previous marriage back in Britain did not deter some women from trying for a second go at wedded bliss in the colony, by sending themselves letters (or organising someone else to) via their old homes informing of the fictitious death of their dearly beloved spouse, thus making way for another.[116] Whatever the promise of greater opportunities, it is hard to believe that for most it was not also heart-wrenching to leave parents, siblings, friends, partners and children behind. Punishment's claws grasped at more than the offender alone. On departure, between them, convict women were forced to abandon most of their 4864 children.

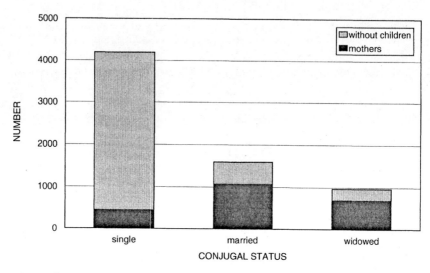

Figure 4.9   Female convict conjugal status and motherhood.

Widowed Hannah left behind two children. Who would care for them? Perhaps in other cases there was a husband around who was fit and willing, or relatives, or maybe an older child capable of keeping the family together. Some single mothers may have had boyfriends, but not all. Considerable literary use was made of the theme of the innocent servant girl propelled into crime through pregnancy and dismissal, after being 'led astray', 'seduced' or 'spoiled' by an evil man who then left her to bear the illegitimate offspring alone; this literary device was not without precedent in reality.[117] Whom would these single mothers have turned to? It is uncertain what informed the decision to prevent children from accompanying their convict parents. Perhaps this type of bereavement was part of the punishment of transportation. Or the decision may have been prompted by official concern for the children's safety during the voyage, a belief that hungry dependants were unsuited to colonial conditions, or simply cost. Whatever the motivation, the outcome was that through transportation many offspring were orphaned, left destitute and at the mercy of the state, while their mothers were left stripped of family responsibilities, no parents, no husbands, no children, just independent women easily allocated to employers, free to form the new social bonds that would shape colonial society, to make homes, engage in home production, and create families.

Convict women arrived in the colony capable of participating in the full range of human endeavour, be it as domestics, sex workers, wives, lovers or mothers. These women were young, healthy, single and—to use a term oft employed in colonial job advertisements—'unencumbered' by family responsibilities. Transportation offered to New South Wales a supply of independent female labourers who were surprisingly literate, numerate and trained, with all that suggested in terms of internalised work values and a sense of industry. Life in Britain and Ireland had also equipped many of these women with an experience of economic restructuring which required them to migrate, reskill and adapt. These women were multi-skilled workers, particularly domestic and farm servants supplemented with a smattering of artisans such as dressmakers and milliners. Of course, among convict women there would have been great diversity within the degree of proficiency attained by different individuals in their chosen employment, but this was typical of any group of workers. Information on wage rates, skill groupings, literacy levels, age patterns in training, and expected differences between England and Ireland all confirm the basic findings; combined, they indicate that convict women were not unskilled, as many first thought, but were instead skilled and semi-skilled workers. This is a most important finding for its implications regarding colonial economic development. However, skill and skill classifications remain difficult and contentious areas. Issue might be taken with Armstrong's schema. Some critics might believe too many occupations achieved high status. Others might note how few domestics appear in Armstrong's 'skilled' category. An allworker was deemed unskilled by Armstrong, yet an argument could be made that as the only domestic in a household, performing all jobs, she was more—not less—skilled than most. Whatever its faults, Armstrong's classification is most useful when applied as a common yardstick for comparing one group with another: if the scheme is flawed for one, it should be equally flawed for the other. The next task, then, is to compare convicts with Irish and English working women. Were convict women members of the lowest order of society or were they like their sisters left behind?

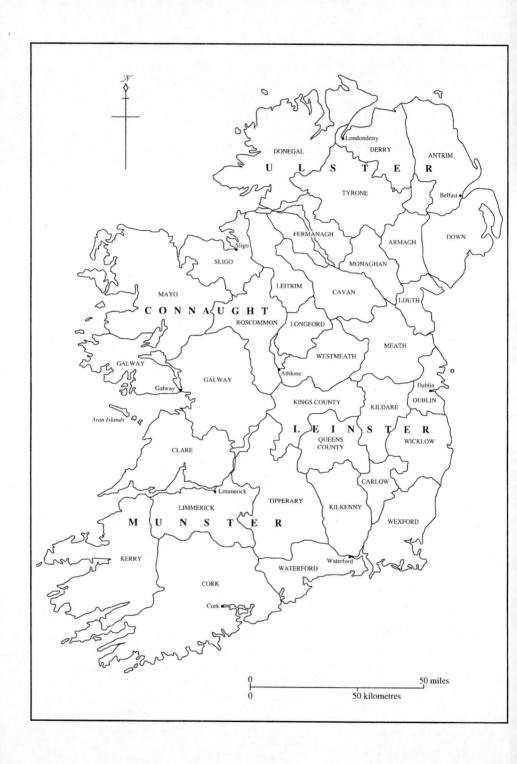

CHAPTER FIVE

Ireland's Distant Shores: Working Life in Ireland

Many courts tried and sentenced the women who were transported to New South Wales. Convicts came from every county in England, Ireland and Wales, from most of Scotland, from the Outer Hebrides and the Isle of Man.[1] In a small number of cases, the fingers of Britain's legal system stretched out across the oceans like tentacles, entangling others further afield in their grip. Jamaica, Dominica, Mauritius, Bermuda, Demerara, Essequebo and, with some irony, the Cape of Good Hope all had their emissaries present in the founding of white Australia. Yet very few convict women had such exotic beginnings. Convict origins can be seen in Figure 5.1. Overwhelmingly, just two countries dominated. Whether we measure by where a convict was born, or from where a transportee was sent, Ireland and England were responsible for propelling over 90 per cent of the women upon their forced Antipodean migration. Between them, these two nations provided the core of female labour supplied to the nascent colony. But they did not contribute evenly. Most convict women were Irish, disproportionately so. One-third of women in the British Isles had been born in Ireland, yet over half of female transportees to New South Wales were Irish.[2] Almost four thousand girls and women were shipped out directly from Ireland, or indirectly via England and Scotland. In respect to nationality, the colony's convict women bore an inverse relationship to the men. While 56 per cent of convict women had been born in the Emerald Isle, only 29 per cent of transported men shared these origins. The great bulk of convict men—some 63 per cent—were English; the comparable figure for women was only 34 per cent.[3] Irish women, then, were over-represented compared with their English sisters and their Irish brothers.

A policy of not transporting Irish prisoners to Van Diemen's Land before 1840 left New South Wales as the only alternative for these errant passengers, inflating the ratio of Irish to English offenders in the latter colony.[4] This explains why there were more Irish than English women, but not why there were so many more Irish women than Irish men. Irrespective of the cause, the upshot was that New South Wales acquired

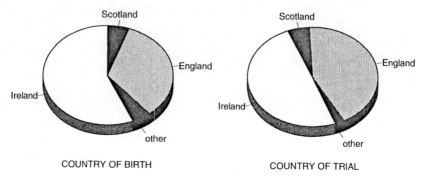

Figure 5.1   Regional origins of women convicts.

a strongly female Irish heritage. The impact of their countrymen on the colony has been considered.[5] Less is known about the impact of Irish women like Margaret Shannahan, the 17-year-old housemaid from King's County pictured when older in Figure 1.5. The extent to which these women arrived in the colony trained or not would have significant repercussions for economic development. What, then, were their skills? Already we know that Irish transportees differed from their English compatriots in a number of notable ways—they were less skilled, less literate, less numerate—but what we do not know is whether these errant Irish exiles were a cross-section of Irish working women.

Ireland

The Ireland that convict women left behind was a largely rural economy. Food production was wedded with domestic textile manufacture and was widespread throughout Ireland. Such domestic industries employed the labour of farming families, utilising their off-times, with intermediaries distributing raw or semi-processed materials to be cleaned, spun, and woven into cloth. Increasingly over the eighteenth century domestically produced cloths were substituted for imported ones, encouraged by government policies, and the industry supplied a variety of goods to be traded internationally. Financial institutions were supportive, and entre-preneurs came from England and Scotland to invest in linen, cotton, and shirt making, and also in shipbuilding and engineering firms, particularly in Ulster.[6] Ireland had not stood apart from the international economy, nor could it. The Napoleonic Wars stimulated the Irish economy. Farmers holding large, long, secure leases were responsive to market signals and had invested in the land through enclosure, weeding and improved

drainage. Crop yields were high, comparing favourably with British out-
puts, and wheat yields were increasing. This provided surplus for trade,
both domestically and for export. High prices for foodstuffs associated
with war demand had resulted in increases in output, farm employment,
and the number of farmers, simultaneously applying upward pressure on
rental costs.[7] Textiles were stimulated, with overseas demand for cotton
and a local market protected by their chief rival's involvement in war.

Economic disruption hit after 1815 when the French wars ended,
reversing the prevailing market facing Irish producers. It has been
remarked, 'it would have been better for the Irish farmer if Bonaparte had
never lived or never died': the problem was coping with dramatic
change.[8] Soon after hostilities ceased, there was an end to the high
demand and high prices Irish farmers had received from England.
Agricultural production suffered as demand, prices and profits fell. While
these declined, rents did not; they rose in real terms, a trend exacerbated
by population expansion.[9] Coinciding with this was greater market penetration by cheaper English manufactures. Exposure to English competition
increased from the 1820s, with pernicious consequences for one of
Ireland's most important industries, cotton. Still largely based on domestic
production, Irish industry did not possess equipment comparable with the
newer English machines. With lower factor productivity and increasing
rents, unable to compete with abundant, cheap, foreign supplies, Irish
industries collapsed. Paradoxically, while the Irish economy struggled to
come to grips with a new international environment, large sections arguably becoming poorer, a different diet bred healthier people.[10] Relying on
the nutritious potato, the population boomed and Irish women and men
grew taller. Convict women, mostly born between 1790 and 1820, gained
an average one-quarter inch over this period; town women gained even
more: half an inch. Irish girls' nutritional living standards were improving
in the early decades of the century, keeping pace with their brothers'.[11]

During the course of these women's lives, the Irish economy underwent profound economic transformation. The grey-haired Catherine Finn,
mentioned in Chapter Four, was the oldest woman sent out to New South
Wales. She had been born in 1746—one century before the Great
Famine—and witnessed much of this change at first hand. For Ireland's
convict women, theirs was a history characterised by very marked
regional variations. While the above story gives the broad brush strokes
of Irish economic history, no single description fits all of Ireland, because
Ireland was not a single, homogeneous economy. Different areas responded in different ways at different times to these often intrusive and
variable market forces. The ability to adapt resourcefully to shifts in
external market forces acted to delineate those regions of Ireland that
would survive well economically, and those that would suffer. Essentially,

this is the difference which arose between the north-east and elsewhere. Ireland can be roughly divided into three areas of basic tendency: the poverty-stricken rural west and south-west (Connaught and Munster), the fluctuating eastern economy (Leinster), and the more successful north-east (Ulster).

Exposure to external influences, and the ability to respond to them, varied widely by region. The western economies were vulnerable, marked by entrepreneurial failure and under-investment. Here, the penetration of market forces seems to have been of limited positive impact, becoming detrimental as the nineteenth century progressed. Landowners had been reticent to invest in agriculture because of their absenteeism, their insecure property rights, and agrarian violence. Failure to invest and to innovate led to a poverty of capital formation, and in turn to low levels of literacy, labour productivity, incomes and savings, and thence to endemic subsistence crises. That the greatest suffering during the 1845 Famine was experienced in the rural west and south-west, in the upland parts of Tipperary, speaks to the underlying weaknesses of these counties.[12]

Textile production was more positively affected by external influences, at least to begin with. Domestic textiles found ready markets. From the eighteenth century, in County Mayo on the far western side of Ireland, there developed a linen-yarn export industry targeting Ulster and England. Originating as a handicraft industry when landlords encouraged tenants to diversify their production (and thus to ensure the landlords' profits), this industry survived when others did not because of its external focus. War demand for expensive fabrics such as linen was limited to fulfilling displaced demand for cotton, leaving overall levels of consumption relatively immune to the shifts of 1815. However, the industry was not so safe from subsequent changes. Like cotton before it, the linen industry declined from the 1830s when it failed to match the mechanisation of linen-yarn production in Ulster, itself responding to English pressures.[13]

Beyond the west, in the east, the free play of market forces had encouraged growth. The English market acted as an engine for the commercialisation of agriculture on the border between Ulster and Leinster. Production for market was again encouraged by landlords, and there was a general demand for labour and other factors of production. After the 1820s, however, ecological limits were reached. Commercial agriculture remained but did not grow, pushing labourers out.[14] As workers lost their jobs, the effective local market shrank. At this time, domestic linen production declined, as it would in Mayo, unable to respond to and match the improved production techniques adopted elsewhere, or to compete with cheap English imports.[15]

The north-east was different again. While the rest of Ireland tended to de-industrialise, or remain essentially agrarian, significant parts of Ulster industrialised. Rather than attempting to compete with English suppliers through technological innovation in the cotton industry, investors capitalised on a comparative advantage that Ulster held in international trade. Cotton had a price advantage over other fabrics such as linen, but Ulster linen (still famed) had a quality advantage over other international producers. Unlike the production of cotton, with the more variable product associated with domestic manufacture, Ulster's pre-industrial linen trade had operated from the mid-eighteenth century under strict quality control that earned it an international reputation and market. Brown linens were exhibited and sold in public markets where quality was ensured by licensed sealmasters and a Linen Board. Bleachers could then buy materials appropriate to service overseas demand for high-quality products. Such was the reputation of these Ulster artisans that they even attracted bleaching business from overseas. Ulster linen thus possessed an established reputation for quality when investment decisions had to be made in the face of English competition. Capital was redeployed in mechanising the linen industry, which rapidly converted to power looms. By 1839, thirty-five powered linen mills were operating in the province, employing nearly 8000 workers, making substantial profits and creating a base from which the industry would continue to adopt new technology and prosper.[16]

Ulster, and a number of key ports in Antrim, Dublin, Cork and Limerick, emerged as prosperous economic centres. Why they succeeded while the economic fortunes of other provinces dwindled is not easily explained. Existing output structures, advantageous investment decisions, proximity to the English economy and easier access to imported sources of energy (Ireland suffered a scarcity of available power), along with direct cultural and economic links with England, may have helped the places that emerged successful. Simultaneously, English intrusion may have adversely affected other areas, with little positive influence to counterbalance the bad: English settlers and landowners whose major concerns lay not with Irish development; cultural and religious discrimination and conflict; unrestrained competition with English industrial production; exclusion from alternative markets; Union with Great Britain in 1801, and the progressive dismantling of protective policies thereafter.[17] Development in the first half of the nineteenth century was varied, localised, even dualistic: even though it is too simple to say that there were pockets of capitalist development in an otherwise pre-capitalist economy, the country was fragmented between areas that were industrialising, those that were de-industrialising, regions of growing commercial agriculture, and ones becoming increasingly reliant on subsistence farming and the potato.

In the future, it was these latter areas that would suffer most when widespread potato blight induced the Great Famine of 1845, laying Ireland waste for more than five years and leaving a barren landscape littered with the starving. A decade earlier, the hungry might have committed offences that would have had them journeying to New South Wales, as many who suffered localised famines in the 1820s and 1830s had done, but in 1840 that colony closed its ports to any more criminal exiles. Now, if lawbreakers were lucky, they might be rewarded with transportation to Van Diemen's Land. Hundreds and thousands of people sought refuge through paying their passage to America, Canada, Australia and elsewhere, and through assisted emigration schemes.[18] But not all could escape. One and a half million Irish women, men and children perished because the economy of Ireland could not feed them.[19]

Ireland's convict women

Brown hair, hazel eyes, ruddy, with skin pitted with pock marks, Bridget Kennedy looked typically Irish. Raised a Catholic in the Meath country-side, she remained in the rural sector employed as a housemaid, and also did some washing. Literacy was not her strong point, as she could neither read nor write. She had not married. At the age of twenty-four, Bridget was tried in nearby Wicklow for her second offence, stealing butter. Two years later she arrived in New South Wales aboard *Palambam*, with five years of her sentence left to run. Young, single, Catholic women who moved around the countryside, like Bridget, dominated Ireland's female cargo.

Uneven economic development meant that women from certain parts of Ireland were more likely than others to end up as convicts in New South Wales. While there was an inverse relationship between economic buoyancy and amounts of poverty and crime, low growth was not necessarily associated with high levels of transportation. Connaught's economy weakened over time. Increasing levels of unemployment, poverty and out-migration resulted, but with low levels of transportation. Disproportionately few women were transported directly from the poorer west, but why? Because the countryside provided those in need with alternatives to hardship, through a greater welfare net, local food production, and the possibility of migration. Further, when punishing women who did err, rural areas were less inclined to seek recourse to transportation, preferring other methods of community-based discipline and social control.

On the other hand, crime and punishment by transportation were more urban phenomena. Growing economies that could absorb workers were less likely to produce crime. Take Ulster, for example. Few women were transported from industrialising Ulster with its expanding employment opportunities (similarly, few women chose to emigrate from there). The rest of urban Ireland was not quite so buoyant. Poverty arose in the other towns where employment was insecure and limited, and welfare was stigmatised. Urban dwellers possessed fewer solutions to their misfortune than their country cousins, and perhaps this made them prone to commit crime. Additionally, anonymous urban centres lent themselves to more impersonal forms of punishment. Consequently, 80 per cent of Ireland's convict women were caught, tried and transported from urban centres, approaching half of them—some 1774 women—from Dublin, Cork and Limerick, and in England, from London, Liverpool and Manchester.

This is really quite fascinating. Four-fifths worked and committed offences in towns, yet most—the vast majority—of Irish women were born in the countryside. Two factors are indicated. Firstly, this bespeaks very high levels of migration within and beyond Ireland's borders. The Irish economy was characterised by migration, in particular seasonally based movement.[20] Between birth, and being tried and transported, we know that some 45 per cent of Irish convict women moved county at least once, one-third of migrants crossing the Irish Sea to Great Britain. Undetected by the indents, others migrated and returned home, and many more moved within county boundaries. Secondly, migration was largely from the country to urban centres. Women flocked to the bigger towns suggestive of opportunities, while few urban workers had the reverse expectation of finding work in the rural sector (except, perhaps, during harvest time). If migration and crime were alternatives to poverty, the former preferable to the latter (because migration did not entail the threat of deportation or hanging), then those suffering hardships in the countryside would seek recourse to migration before turning to crime. Such was the case for Bridget Gibbons and her daughter Mary Anne. Bridget, a widow, was a washerwoman, and Mary Anne was a nurse girl. They had migrated south-easterly from Mayo to Dublin where, on 12 May 1827, they were tried and sentenced to seven years' transportation for stealing money. Neither had previously offended.[21]

Some girls, like Mary Anne, migrated with families. Some women followed husbands. Compared with transportees who had not explored other counties, among convict women migrants there was a slightly higher proportion who were married, with children and a couple of years older than the rest. For most, the decision to migrate was influenced by local economic conditions and those pertaining elsewhere. Dislocation after 1815 encouraged migration. Areas in decline shed workers, who travelled to places like Paisley where the linen industry was expanding.[22] Pushed out of the poverty-stricken west, many women born in Connaught were tried in the more economically successful port areas, and also the more prosperous towns in England, Scotland and Wales. Most notably, Dublin acted as a magnet, pulling workers from a corridor stretching westward to County Mayo, and from adjacent and nearby counties, particularly Wicklow, Carlow, Kildare, Westmeath and Meath. Counties in the southern half of the country, and those in the north-east, with greater economic potential tended to lose fewer women to migration, while those in the west and middle lost most. Women from the port areas themselves—Belfast, Dublin, Cork, Limerick—were the least inclined of all to move. It would appear that while their geography facilitated overseas migration, comparative economic buoyancy in these entrepôts provided employment and opportunity, reducing the push-factors that acted upon natives of other counties. When these women did choose to roam, they did not move within Ireland to less economically advantageous areas, but went to places overseas with greater economic promise. Crossing the Irish sea, these women primarily went to Lancashire and London, a move which would seem consistent with a flight in search of employment in textile and domestic service industries.

Regional imbalance set the country awash with migrating individuals and families. Many Irish convicts had moved from poorer parts of Ireland to those of greater promise, leaving their homes—even their country— voluntarily, following husbands, parents, employment. However, their journey did not stop there, but in New South Wales. Migration was a perilous business. Women from the countryside took risks: they hoped for good jobs, better pay, greater prospects, but they left behind their social support systems, making them totally reliant for their survival upon gaining work. Yet employment was erratic, even in the more affluent sectors of the economy. Those perceived as 'foreigners' might have experienced inferior access to jobs, accommodation, character witnesses in court, etc. Welfare was at a premium for everyone in the crowded urban centres, but those recently arrived would be at a greater dis-advantage. Was transportation an act of kindness, as some have claimed?[23] To that, there can be no easy answer—it depends on the motives of many individuals, and on whether the colony was perceived to offer greater opportunities. What opportunities the colony did offer would be, at least in part, dependent upon the skills that Irish convict women could offer to it. What type of workers did these economies produce, and were the Irish exiles representative of the workers they left behind?

Irish working women and Irish convicts transported directly from Ireland possessed roughly similar levels of numeracy and literacy. Details are given in Figure 5.2. More than one-quarter of workers displayed age-heaping (28 per cent) compared with just less than one-quarter of Irish-born convicts (24 per cent), in both instances a significantly higher

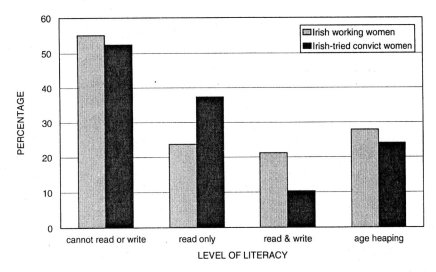

Figure 5.2   Literacy and numeracy among Irish women.

proportion than would be expected for a numerate population.[24] Literacy tells a similar tale. The 1841 Irish census recorded literacy in the same manner as the convict indents.[25] Over half of both groups were functionally illiterate, with convicts just edging in with a slightly better rate than workers (52 per cent compared with 55 per cent), although nearly twice as many workers (one-fifth) had mastered writing skills. On the score of literacy and numeracy, convicts and workers were much alike. However, there were significant differences between some groups of convicts.

Figure 5.3 presents literacy levels, distinguishing between Irish transportees born in the countryside and the town, and between those women who had migrated within or beyond Ireland and those who had stayed put, enabling something to be said about the quality of migrants. Convicts born in towns were markedly more literate than country girls (57 per cent compared with 46 per cent). Town work and life were more likely to require the ability to read than farm work was. Relatedly, many country women who had acquired those literacy skills headed for the towns where the rewards were greater. Women who migrated prior to their transportation had often experienced higher levels of training, being more literate than stayers (55 per cent and 45 per cent literate respectively). Both Bridget and Mary Anne Gibbons could read.

While the Irish census recorded literacy in great detail, it was less concerned with occupational details, tending to lump groups together, while convict occupational data were rich in nuances. This makes comparison difficult although not insurmountable. One comparison is between

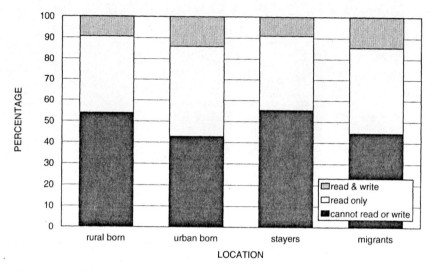

Figure 5.3   Literacy among Irish-born convict women.

skill levels. Classifying workers and convicts into Armstrong's social-skill schema permits the broad brushstrokes of the economy to be discerned.[26] Figure 5.4 indicates these results for workers and convicts. So few women were in professional and semi-professional occupations that these categories have been combined with 'skilled' workers in all subsequent analysis. Skill levels for Irish workers and convicts transported from Ireland were much alike, in that around one-quarter of both were unskilled by this measure. However, significantly more Irish-born convict women progressed from semi-skilled work to higher levels of skill attainment: 37 per cent of convicts compared with 22 per cent of workers. Problems with the census data preclude very strong statements, but it does appear that at the very least Irish convict women were no less skilled than their non-criminal counterparts. Once more, skill levels provide some evidence about the quality of migrants. Figure 5.5 presents details on different groups of Irish convict women. While differences were small they confirm the results on literacy. Movers were slightly more skilled than stayers, although figures in the next section are most revealing, when women who moved within Ireland are compared with those who ventured abroad. Resourceful women, it seems, migrated away from the countryside with its farm work to urban environments, and it is clear from the multiple trades listed in the indents that many women retrained, as one-time rural labourers shifted into domestic work. Rather than substandard workers pushed out by their failure, this suggests that it was women with marketable skills who travelled in search of better opportunities and greater returns on their investments.

semi-skilled

semi-skilled

unskilled

unskilled

skilled

skilled

IRISH WORKING WOMEN   IRISH-TRIED CONVICT WOMEN

Figure 5.4 Skill levels among Irish women.

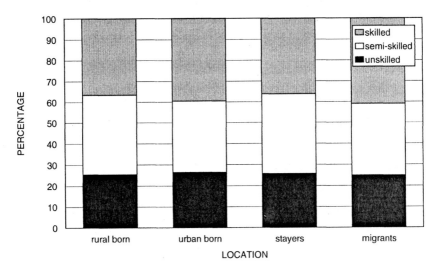

Figure 5.5 Skill levels among Irish-born convict women.

Improving their lot seems to have been a major consideration for migrants, facilitated by the ability to read the relevant literature and identify potential employment.

Divergence between worker and convict job training starts to appear clearly only when we look at the composition of their skills. Figure 5.6 represents five broad categories of employment based on the 1841 Irish census, and presents the data for adult Irish women and convicts transported from Ireland also aged fifteen years or over. Appendix 5 indicates exactly how convict occupations were classified into census groupings. Because the census lumped all domestic servants into one amorphous 'unclassified' category, and because difficulties arise in

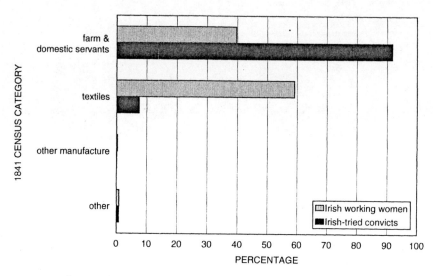

Figure 5.6   Female occupational structures in Ireland, convicts and workers 15 years and upwards.

determining whether convict 'allworkers' (as distinct from 'allworkers on farm') were domestics or farm servants, farm and domestic servants have been grouped together. Immediately it is apparent that there were significant differences between convicts and workers. Few Irish women were engaged in ministering to education, health, non-textile manufacture, charity, religion or justice; instead, they were concentrated in farm and domestic service and textile work. Convict women also congregated in the same two categories, but in markedly different ratio.

This disparity between the proportions of working women and convicts engaged as servants is striking. Two interrelated features stand out in this figure. Firstly, a disproportionate number of domestic and farm servants were transported. Of Irish convict women, 97 per cent had worked as domestics on farms or in homes, compared with 40 per cent of adult Irish women. Perhaps the extent of this over-representation is not so extreme as first appears. The fact that only 13 per cent of women were recorded in the census as 'ministering to food' (farm workers) in an economy with a large rural sector, in which three-quarters of Irish men were recorded as farm labourers ministering to food, hints at inaccuracies in the census. Considered appendages of the male kin they worked alongside, they may quite simply not have been counted.[27] Many farm women are missing, although not enough to make the imbalance disappear. Secondly and relatedly, this seeming over-representation of servants was at the cost of women engaged in textile production, specifically spinners. Spinners alone accounted for 45 per cent of Irish women enumerated in the census, some 485 089 of them. Sixteen convict women were spinners, less than half of 1 per cent. Textile production overall accounted for 59 per cent of Irish working women, and for 7 per cent of Irish convict women. Instead, housemaids, kitchenmaids, laundry workers and nursemaids proliferated among transportees. Whether working in the towns or in the countryside, convict women were labourers and servants, not textile workers. This did not mean that convicts were unskilled, although it did mean they possessed different skills from the majority of Irish women. Irish female convicts were not typical of Ireland's working women. Half of both convicts and workers were illiterate, one-quarter displayed age-heaping, and one-quarter of each were unskilled; but more convict women made it to loftier heights, possessed of different skills—trained not as textile manufacturers, but as farm and domestic servants.

From Ireland, to England, to New South Wales

Ireland's rapidly expanding population spilled into England, North America, even as far as Australia. Migration was a key feature of the Irish economy. North America was a popular destination for Irish migrants, but travelling such distances was costly; well-paying jobs were required in order to save the necessary fare to reach America. England, being closer, was more easily reached at cheaper cost. British counties were even feasible destinations for Irish seasonal workers. Nearly 200 000 Irish women were living in England, Scotland and Wales at the time of the 1841 British census.[28] Inevitably, some of these imported workers would commit offences. Some 535 Irish women made their way to the Antipodes via the legal systems of England and Scotland. Conversely, only 27 English gals were transported from Ireland.

But who was it that chose to emigrate? Were they the illiterate, innumerate, and unskilled; inept workers forced out by economic failure, a loss that Ireland could only celebrate? Or were they the cream of Irish workers; those people who could read about the promise of other places, more highly trained workers who travelled in search of greater pay and improved conditions, who sought to improve their lot in another land?[29]

Contemporary opinion was split. In marked contrast to the sympathetic view taken of Irish criminals discussed in Chapter Three, Irish workers abroad were heavily criticised. The Englishman Thomas Carlyle observed how 'crowds of miserable Irish darken all our towns'.[30] Ghettoised in England, Irish workers were slammed, their only strength—quite literally—their muscles. Scathingly, Friedrich Engels wrote, the dissolute, volatile, and drunken Irish are unfitted for tasks which demand either a regular apprenticeship or that degree of skill which can only be secured by a long period of unremitting application to one's job ... The Irishman, however, is just as capable as the Englishman of undertaking simple tasks involving brute strength rather than skill and precision'.[31]

Free immigrants to Australia were described as 'ignorant creatures', not only untaught but unteachable.[32] Irish emigration to North America has even been deemed an aid to Ireland by removing the 'less educated and less able'.[33] Yet the 'superior steadiness and docility' of Irish immigrants won them jobs over locals, a fact attested to by Mr Stuart, Factory Inspector for Scotland, who found 'preference being given to them as workers in the flax factories on account of their regular habits'.[34]

Irish emigrants may not have matched the skills of British workers— they did, after all, issue forth from very different economies—but that is hardly the relevant yardstick. More helpful is comparison with the Irish themselves, those who did emigrate with those who did not. Figures 5.7 and 5.8 compare Irish convict women who emigrated overseas prior to transportation, others who moved within Ireland and those who seemingly never left their homes. Both figures demonstrate that these emigrant workers were the pick of the crop, the most literate and by far the most highly skilled, women such as Catherine Grimes who was one of Elizabeth Coltman's shipmates on board the *Competitor* in 1828. Catherine was a chair carver and occasional washerwoman, who could both read and write. She had been born in Tralee, County Kerry, and thirty-five

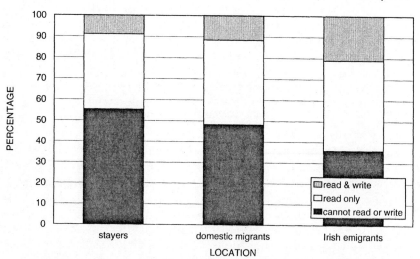

Figure 5.7   Literacy rates of Irish emigrant convict women.

years down the track, with one husband dead and buried, Catherine was in London being tried for stealing a bed. In Catherine we have one example of a tendency: Irish emigrants were more skilled and literate than the women they left behind. Stayers were less literate than domestic migrants (45 per cent as against 52 per cent), who were in turn less literate than those venturing further afield (64 per cent). The proportion of emigrant convicts who could both read and write was double that of women deported directly from Ireland. Similarly, fewer convict emigrants displayed age-heaping: 24 to 25 per cent of women tried in Ireland, both stayers and domestic migrants, gave rounded ages, compared with 19 per cent of Ireland's more adventurous types. Emigrants were also more numerate and less illiterate than non-convict Irish women. Little difference existed in skill levels between women who stayed where they were born and those who migrated within Ireland, but women who emigrated overseas had attained higher qualifications: nearly half (47 per cent) compared with about one-third. The Irish abroad thus displayed substantially greater occupational training, with many more in the most-skilled class. This suggests that chances for fulfilling apprenticeships improved upon migration, or that it was the most skilled workers who, having completed their training, then chose to move.

Compared with women transported directly from Ireland, Irish convict emigrants were on average marginally taller and about two years older; fewer were of the Catholic faith (77 per cent compared with 85 per cent) while more were Protestant (22 per cent as opposed to 15 per cent). Over one-half were married or widowed compared with one-third of stayers,

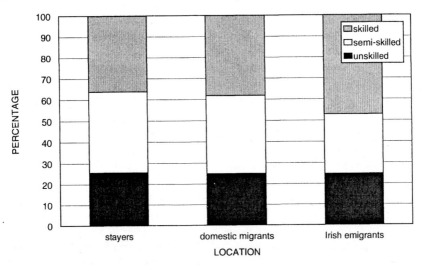

Figure 5.8   Skill levels of Irish emigrant convict women.

and following from this, more were mothers. Catherine Grimes, for example, was older, widowed but seemingly childless, and a Protestant. Catherine Barr, too, was typical. Born in the city of Waterford, she had been tried in Surrey for stealing a ham (she was a cook) and transported in 1839 on the *Planter*. Catherine Barr could read. She was thirty-six, a Protestant, married with three children. Perhaps these two Catherines had migrated with their husbands, or maybe they met their men after moving to England in search of work. Convict-emigrants had flocked to growing urban centres in England. They were well-enough informed by word-of-mouth or through literature to know when and where opportunities might be had. Nearly one-half of these adventurers ended up in London and its environs, and another quarter were to be found in Lancashire, places where they might work as domestics, or hope to find employment for their skills learned in small-scale farm-based cloth making.[35] Perhaps Protestants left because theirs was a minority religion, or because superior access to education bought them saleable skills that could earn more elsewhere. Their higher level of literacy reduced barriers to movement through facilitating knowledge of the new destination and its employment potentials.

Literate and skilled, migration represented a talented outflow of labour. Every county in Ireland contributed, some more than others: half came from Cork and Dublin, with lesser numbers from Limerick and Antrim. Derry, Galway, Kerry, Roscommon, Tipperary all offered up the human fruit of their land to Great Britain. Even before the famine, Ireland was experiencing a significant loss of talented workers that could only have hindered economic expansion. From the nineteenth century to the present, Irish officials have expressed concern at what is termed the 'brain drain': the loss to overseas destinations of the most highly trained and able workers, with obvious dire economic repercussions. In 1816 David Ricardo wrote, 'the young, the strong, the enterprising and industrious families leave us, whilst the old, the idle and the indolent portions stay with us'.[36] It was the loss of young, strong, enterprising and hard-working individuals which contributed to Irish economic backwardness. Cheap emigration allowed labour to seek out capital. Had this ex-rural workforce remained in Ireland, available for new exploits, capital may have been attracted to it.[37] This was a vicious circle: domestic economic failure 'pushed' migrants out while better opportunities elsewhere 'pulled' them away; the loss of skilled workers in turn inhibited productivity, investment, growth and development ... and the trap was set.

While Ireland would mourn this loss, such workers could assist the nations to which they migrated. Ireland provided New South Wales with the bulk of its female convict intake. In some respects, they were the pick of what Ireland had to offer. By Irish standards, these women were literate and numerate. They were in their prime productive and reproductive years, of healthy physical stock, trained as domestic servants and as farm workers, perhaps with some knowledge of local domestic textile production, but they were not factory workers. Resourcefully, many had reskilled as the economy underwent structural change, and nearly one-half had migrated within Ireland or beyond to neighbouring countries, looking to improve their lot. Adaptable to changed economic environments, familiar with migration, these young women were suited to the task that lay before them.

CHAPTER SIX

England's Castaways: Working Life in England

While nearly 3500 women were transported directly from Ireland, between 1826 and 1840 some 2946 women were banished to New South Wales from England, cast aside in the greatest economic upheaval the world had ever seen. Elizabeth Coltman and her fellow transportees came from a turbulent period in their country's history.[1] For many, these were exciting and creative times. Railways cut swathes through the English landscape, moving people and goods at undreamed-of speeds. The sweep of the countryside became less fragmented as land holdings were consolidated, and from small towns grew the great industrial cities of the north. Reorganisation of production trebled and quadrupled output, and the market was treated to new products and new ways of selling them. By 1851 nearly one million square feet of glass had been assembled over 14 acres of prime London real estate to create the Crystal Palace. Appearing to float in mid-air, Crystal Palace housed the Great Exhibition which celebrated Empire and ingenuity, presenting a veritable cornucopia of (mainly British) inventions in what has been described as 'the first outburst of the phantasmagoria of commodity culture'.[2] On the continent, Beethoven, Chopin, Mendelssohn and Wagner composed, while in England society was scrutinised by Jane Austen, Elizabeth Gaskell, the Brontë sisters, Charles Dickens and others. Partly, these examinations revealed that while change was exciting for some, it was bought at great cost to many.

Change dealt women a particularly hard blow. Women's status fell when England industrialised.[3] Revolutions in agriculture and industry transformed the socio-economic landscape, fundamentally altering the nature of work and the structure of the labour force. The basic unit of production in pre-industrial times was the family, normally comprising just two generations. Families worked together and earned a family wage. In agriculture and in mining this often involved many families coming together, whereas in domestic textile production—also known as the 'putting-out' industry—a single family unit operated. Here each member acted a part in a unified process, with specific tasks allocated according to age, sex and marital status. Children carded, women spun and men wove. This interdependent form of household production has been labelled 'gynocentric', meaning that 'the skills and work of women are indispensable to survival': each member of the family performed a vital role and each was dependent upon the others for the creation of the final product intended either for direct consumption or for market.[4]

Women were thus endowed with a certain degree of power within this structure because they were integral to the family's economic survival. This is not to suggest equality. A strong sexual division of labour operated. Within domestic industry and on family farms the male head of the family controlled the economic decision-making, acting as manager.[5] From God cast in the image of man, the King who always ruled in preference to a Queen, the lowest clergy always superior to the highest nun, to the lord who ruled the manor and the man who ruled his home, authority was masculine. Females had different, less powerful roles, but the extent of divisions and inequalities was subject to limitations.

Agricultural and industrial revolutions changed all this. Enclosure and consolidation of the lands, the decline of domestic textile production and the rise of factories led the unity and interdependence of family production to dwindle, and with them the barriers to intensive gender-based divisions disappeared. Production was no longer based on the family, but upon the individual wage worker, and the family wage designed to maintain the whole unit was replaced by the so-called independent wage.[6] The outcome was devastating. Two important shifts occurred. Firstly, production was cleaved off from reproduction, problematising childcare and creating a sphere of work that was unpaid. Secondly, forces were set in motion that led women to be excluded from certain areas of paid work, segmenting the labour market into male and female enclaves. The upshot of these two developments was that women in traditional areas of the economy suffered.

Women were responsible for the care of children, the sick, the aged, for the preparation of food and the maintenance of the home. This work was no longer carried out within the perimeters of family production. Nor was it rewarded with pay. Where the care of children entered the realm of the paid economy—wet nurses, nurserymaids, governesses, school-teachers—it was low-paying. Reproductive responsibilities conditioned the manner in which married women were able to participate in the paid economy. Demands on their time, availability in working hours, etc., were all factors that inhibited married women's bargaining power when it came to lobbying for work or better wages. It forced mothers to make employment decisions that enabled them to combine the tasks of child-care with that of earning money. Increasingly women became concentrated in those occupations that enabled them to mesh their employment with their domestic obligations, and to employ the skills they possessed or could extend. There was thus a marked sexual division of labour in the paid workforce. The occupations of married women were typically different from those of single women and of men (married or not) because their responsibilities differed: for example, married women and widows became laundresses and washerwomen or outworkers, professions that could be pursued at suitable times with children in attendance.[7]

But so too did the employment of single women differ from that of single men. In times of revolution, gender divisions achieve a greater degree of fluidity and are open to renegotiation, and women may have hoped for—and some would have achieved—more powerful economic positions. Most, however, did not. The nineteenth century witnessed an increasing feminisation of low-paying jobs and a diminishing range of employments open to women.[8] The paid-labour market became segmented into non-competing areas, with markedly different conditions for the labourers involved. Enclosure of the lands facilitated larger farming units and higher factor productivity. Agricultural output expanded. In the process, small-time landowners were dispossessed and a class of landless labourers created, freed for other employment. But the impact was gendered. In the space of fifty years, agriculture was transformed from a place where men and women worked alongside each other, to one characterised by a strident sexual division of labour.[9] By the end of the Napoleonic Wars in 1815, women were no longer employed equally with men. Born in 1788 and entering the workforce around the turn of the century, Susan Partridge would have observed the changing sex balance among her co-workers on the Gloucestershire farm where she laboured as a dairywoman, before being transported for receiving at the age of thirty-nine.[10] Widowed, with most of her seven children still dependent upon her, Susan would have felt acutely the grief caused as the already glaring gap between men's and women's earnings widened. Male wages increased but female wages fell.[11] Threatened by cheap female labour, men who wanted to keep their jobs and afford their families had little choice but to unite against the degradation of their wages, conditions and power. Rather than preventing cheap competition by pushing women's wages up (which may have brought other wages down), women were excluded from contending with men. High-paid crop-cutting jobs became the preserve of men, with women relegated to lower-paid crop-gathering ones. Technology was responsible, combined with male pressure to push women out.[12] Women like Susan were less successful at banding together to protect their interests. Demand for female labour diminished. As women's earning capacity fell, so the overall participation rates of women in agriculture declined as girls sought better employment elsewhere.

Craft production by skilled artisans was undergoing a similar process. Technology was changing the nature of work. At the heart of the industrial revolution lay the ability, and profit-imperative, to fragment the labour process. This meant dividing production into its constituent elements and placing these in the hands of specialist workers, some in factories and others at home. The skills required to manage the new equipment could be mastered more rapidly than a seven-year apprenticeship which taught each individual the entire production process from beginning to end. Workers still had to acquire skills, but not so many. No longer did employers have recourse only to a small pool of multi-skilled artisans, but to a much larger pool of workers who could be trained with greater speed. Reduced training requirements enlarged the available workforce and hence competition between labour suppliers. This was the case even when the new skills to be learned were extensive, as control over training now rested with employers and not masters of the trade.

Handicraft unions and craft guilds fought fragmentation, deskilling and loss of control by restricting entry to their professions, and they did so at the expense of women. The lower wage rates of women initially gave them a competitive edge in the labour market in areas where the sexual division of labour was ambivalent or undetermined. Male labour organised against female employment (though, again noticeably, not against the low wages of females), systematically excluding them from the formally apprenticed trades they had previously practised, from union membership and from union protection.[13] Women ceased working alongside men. For example, women were active throughout the eighteenth century in the apprenticed trade of hairdressing, but by 1800 they had lost out entirely to Frenchmen who came to dominate the London business.[14] Success came to those who could define the boundaries of their craft, and enforce a monopoly over skills by limiting entry. The strategic positioning which allowed some workers to carve out a niche for themselves while others floundered was based upon two factors: the nature of the product market (whether it was variable, demanding a flexible labour force with a wide skill base capable of adapting production to different demands, i.e. where technology was not a perfect substitute for labour); and the nature of skill acquisition (control over the labour supply, typically through formal apprenticeships and membership of trade bodies).[15] As history would have it, on both these counts women tended to miss out. Excluded from certain areas of apprenticed labour, women became concentrated in other, often less attractive, areas which were in long-term decline; or they suffered from an inability to resist cheaper production methods, or simply an incapacity to limit entry and to defend the prestige of the craft. Over the century, many of these feminised trades ceased to require apprenticeships as technology led to their restructuring; workers were not necessarily deskilled entirely, but guilds were weakened as barriers to entry were lowered and wages were depressed. Other women moved directly into unprotected branches developing outside guilds.[16]

The clothing and footwear industries afford key examples of these trends. Both sexes engaged in skilled work producing shoes, boots and other leather-goods, but by the nineteenth century women were rarely admitted to the trade societies. In the boot trade, for instance, most women were limited to closing and binding, trades practised by Ann Stewart, alias Curtis (shoe closer and binder), Ann Yellop (boot closer) and Mary Bates (boot binder) before their transportation.[17] (Mary Bates is one of the women followed through her colonial life in Babette Smith's book, *A Cargo of Women*.)[18] This was deemed 'light' work, which earned women considerably less than the men who were shoemakers and boot-makers. Women trained at these professions, such as Frances Nolan (shoemaker) and the multi-talented Elizabeth Wilkinson (boot and shoe maker and closer) were distinctly in a minority.[19] Any attempt to move into male preserves was strenuously and successfully resisted.[20]

In clothing and haberdashery, women continued to dominate in their traditional crafts of dressmaking, embroidery, tambouring, lace-making, pearl-stringing, millinery, the making of straw hats, bonnets, artificial flowers and many other refinements. Convict women had worked at all these pursuits and more: making braces, fringes, mantuas, as fancy trimmers, ostrich feather dressers, sempstresses, needlewomen, and many other trades. Dressmaking had been a popular choice for women like Mary Barrath of Manchester, transported on the *Sovereign* in 1829 for stealing clothes, and Eliza Grivell, guilty of the same offence and sent out in 1833 on the *Diana*. Elizabeth Watts from Middlesex, one of Elizabeth Coltman's compatriots on board the *Competitor* and sent to New South Wales for stealing a kettle, had opted for the more highly prized trade of millinery. Usually girls pursued their apprenticeships in the countryside, which was cheaper than the £30 to £50 premiums charged in London for an apprenticeship of two to five years, before moving to the city as 'improvers' for another nine months to two years at the cost of £10 to £15.[21] These women made ladies' dresses, bonnets and elegant gowns, and tailored for the emerging middle classes.

But dressmaking, needlework and the like were coming under attack from the 'dishonourable trades' serving the ready-made markets in the East and West Ends of London and in the city itself. This sector expanded rapidly in the hard years of the 1830s and 1840s on the strength of a dynamic cocktail: technological change, trained but cheap labour, and growing demand. Central to this development were innovations in the way work was subdivided. No longer did one artisan craft a single item, but a team comprised of members dedicated to different tasks produced a standardised garment in a fraction of the time. New equipment like sewing machines also increased output, and lowered costs: necessary skills required to operate technology would be taught on the job, with the supply of trained labour controlled by this new class of employer. Artisans beyond those catering to the elite could no longer command high wages. Abundant skilled and partially trained labour was easily found among the large group of distressed needlewomen resident in London, desperate for work and forced to vie against each other. In slop-work, factory workers competed with specialists, and outworkers competed with factory labourers, bringing down wages and conditions. Many women ended up sewing in poorly lit workshops for long and erratic hours, earning low wages or even paying employers for the privilege of learning their craft, while others laboured from home while they cared for small children. Girls as young as five would be enlisted to sew for their mothers. Fear that impoverished and unsupervised outworkers would be driven to pawn valuable items in their possession was the only force keeping finishing tasks like button-holing and topping in factories.[22] Cheap products found favour not only with middle-class consumers but with workers increasingly alienated from home production and dependent upon the market for satisfying their wants.[23] Apprenticed trades declined, and the new skills women learned would never be valued in the same way as had their traditional crafts. The same story was played out in industry after industry. Convict women were born and educated in a world when women served apprenticeships and learned trades, but it was a world of shrinking opportunities as gender divisions in artisan work intensified and the female crafts were increasingly undermined.

In addition to union constraints, technological change and growing competition, humanitarian legislation claimed that what was exploitative of women was not exploitative of men. This sabotaged women's partici-pation in wage-labour by reducing their ability (but not their need) to compete equally in the labour market, enforcing maximum hours but not minimum wages, and ideology explained why. Employment was con-sidered to lead women into moral and spiritual degradation.[24] Concepts of masculinity and femininity came into play when defining legislative controls, strengthening the limits that reproductive responsibilities already placed upon female labour-force participation. It was unrealistic to expect that working-class women could be excluded entirely from paid employ-ment. Many women actively chose to work for all the rewards it offered in terms of independence and camaraderie, in spite of conditions and pay. Others were propelled into work by economic necessity when husbands were sick, dead, absent, on inadequate incomes to support their family, or simply unwilling to do so. Single women worked to maintain self and family. Poverty was met, not by a friendly hand, but by a highly stigmatised and impoverished welfare system of workhouses, making even back-breaking laundry work preferable to tasting 'the crumb of charity or the loaf of lust', as one contemporary put it.[25] Others have estimated that conditions in gaol were more amenable than those in the workhouse.[26] For a variety of reasons, women workers would not be eliminated; they could, however, be ghettoised.

This tendency to sexual segregation in the workplace was exacerbated by the nature of girls' education. Parents distributing limited family resources were influenced by expected labour-market outcomes. Few jobs, dwindling pay, expectations regarding marriage and work, plus growing institutional barriers and hostile unions, all meant that anticipated returns on educating girls were less than for boys. Precious resources were allocated with a male bias. Boys were the more likely beneficiaries of investment in costly, formally acquired apprenticeships; girls gained an informal education. Nearly all girls in nineteenth-century Britain would have received an informal training in the home under the guidance of mothers, sisters, aunts etc. Women ended up concentrated in those jobs where the initial training was provided in their own homes, and further developed in the homes of their employers or in factories. This was knowledge gained 'sitting next to Nellie'. Consequently, much of women's work in the paid economy was similar to that of the domestic realm: caring, nurturing, food preparation, farm work, textile production and the provision of other services. Notably, this congregation of women in certain employment areas where required skills were abundant, or perhaps in over-supply, depressed wages.[27]

General laundry work, for example, commanded low pay. This was a form of employment with no official barriers to entry and minimal establishment costs; it was labour intensive and had flexible hours. As such it was favoured by many widows and married women who also used their children's and their husbands' labour (not always an easy task), often within the marital household. This was the case for Mary Condon, mentioned in Chapter Two. There was an abundant supply of laundresses (and laundry). It required more than hard physical labour alone. Washerwomen like Mary had to possess a good working knowledge of chemistry. In the absence of soap, these women needed to know, among many other things, the age at which urine developed its bleaching properties.[28] Laundresses and laundrymaids had to be adept with a needle. Knowledge was required of how different fabrics were to be treated, which garments needed unpicking and dismantling before laundering, which did not, and how they were to be reassembled. Beautiful dresses worn by aristocratic ladies were a nightmare to care for. A range of talents were employed in this demanding and repetitive pursuit, but the skills needed to wash and mend were, by and large, not attained through a formal apprenticeship. Those sections of the trade that were apprenticed were accorded a greater status and higher pay by contemporaries.[29] But for many laundry workers, skills were gained informally from other women who engaged in knowledge-sharing.

Women thus capitalised on the skills they attained at home, on the farm, and in domestic textile production. This equipped them for laundry work, garment making, textile manufacturing and the wide gamut of domestic service. As the rural sector shed labour, women moved to urban centres in search of these employments. Domestic service was a major employer of women, and one in which women outnumbered men.[30] This was work for single girls, with marriage a cause for dismissal.[31] Since the late eighteenth century domestic service had been growing, reaching its height at the peak of industrialisation.[32] Many employers kept but a single maidservant, the ubiquitous maid of all work—multi-skilling at its best.[33] One-third of servant-employing households employed no more than one girl, with a further 25 per cent employing only two.[34] Domestics were vital in some households, for example, those of shopkeepers or tradespeople, publicans, and craftspeople.[35] Even poor families would take on a girl to help with laundering and childcare.[36] For others, domestics were status symbols. As the century progressed and the middle class grew, individuals of these middle ranks sought to emulate their 'betters' and to display their new-found wealth. Possessing servants acted to define middle class status.[37] It was also an essential corollary to the rise of the dependent woman whose leisure was a sign of wealth and conspicuous consumption.[38] Such beliefs in the desirability of female idleness necessitated employment of women from other classes to perform domestic tasks. Demand was thus extensive.

Pushed out of agriculture, women who had trained in domestic service in the countryside migrated in search of employment. In 1851, two-thirds of domestic servants were the daughters of rural labourers.[39] Often work would be organised through family connections, with employers endowed with parental powers over these surrogate daughters, even the power to arrange marriages.[40] Entering into domestic service was very much like entering into another family: half member, half wage-earner.[41] In employment, behaviour would be carefully monitored. Both on the farm and in the home, domestic service perpetuated stringent controls over individual women and their morality, controls more readily escaped in the anonymity of the factory. Being monitored, however, did not guard their safety. One of many manuals was the 1840 London publication, *The Servant Girl in London, Showing the Dangers to which Young Country Girls are Exposed on their Arrival in Town, with Advice to Them, to their Parents, to their Masters, and to their Mistresses, respectfully dedicated to all Heads of Families & Benevolent Societies*. Girls were warned. 'Before placing you in a house where there are grown-up sons, your parents ought to make very strict inquiries. Such situations are always dangerous, and perhaps altogether improper for a girl just entering service'.[42] In service, domestics were targets of sexual harassment and abuse. Prostitution was even seen as part of the job description.[43] If rape, compliance, or illicit love led to pregnancy, the woman's choices were few: backyard abortion, infanticide, loss of employment and respectability, and then …?[44]

Importantly, for all its drawbacks, domestic service provided continuity and mobility between pre-industrial and industrial economies, playing a pivotal role in broadening women's horizons and expanding these beyond their immediate family.[45] Women were drawn into the urban economy, where occupational mobility was enhanced.[46] Many servants were hired on a yearly basis, enabling either side to terminate an unhappy working relationship, although workers only found this an option *if* alternative employment was forthcoming.[47] Domestic servitude, whilst hard work, did offer food and lodging, an independent wage (as opposed to a meagre supplement to a man's wage), some career path and a choice about remaining single rather than wed.[48] This was also an occupation which enabled women to employ skills they had commenced learning in their parents' homes.

Opportunities also arose in the newly mechanised textile industries: this was the other side of technological innovation. With industrialisation came a flood of new jobs, as handloom weavers, framework knitters, lace runners, in cotton manufacture and more. In manufacture, the sexual division of labour operative in the 1830s and 1840s reflected that of the domestic putting-out industry: because it was the traditional female tasks such as spinning which were first mechanised, women were the first pulled into the factory system.[49] The cotton industry provided tens of thousands of new jobs, representing massive employment opportunities for certain women, and at the start of the century over half of the workers in that field were female.[50] Factory work was the quintessential form of industrial employment, and that most readily associated with the gains of industrialisation. These workers have been described as feisty and rebellious, characteristics bred of their independent income and the bargaining power this granted them in their personal lives.[51] While factory work was was seen as liberating women, some critics feared it was at the expense of subjugating men.[52] Friedrich Engels shared in the misery of Jack, a worker from Lancashire, who bemoaned,

> there is work enough for women folks and childer hereabouts, but none for men; thou mayest sooner find a hundred pound on the road than work for men—but I should never have believed that either thou or anyone else would have seen me mending my wife's stockings, for it is bad work … it's a good bit

that she has been the man in the house and I the woman; it a bad work Joe ... [I] curse the damn factories, and the masters and the Government.[53]

To Engels, wage labour robbed men of their independence by making them dependent upon the bourgeoisie for work. Worse still, the bourgeoisie preferred to employ the cheap labour of women and children. This was the double heresy of drawing women out of their rightful sphere—the home—concomitantly leaving men there to rot. Factories, while bringing the clock and time-discipline, brought higher wages and greater personal freedoms than many women had known in rural production or in domestic service.

Yet not all was glowing in the textile sector. While factory work represented greater opportunities for women to work beyond the home, conditions were often poor. The story of dressmakers and needlewomen was played out again. Factories were cramped, inadequately lit and badly ventilated. Work was fragmented, sections feminised, and placed variously between factories and outworkers—'sweated' labour. The latter was an extremely exploitative practice. Outworkers operated from home, using their own capital, and were paid by the piece. These were married women who, like washerwomen and needlewomen, sought to blend family responsibilities with earning an income. Pay was low, seen as an adjunct to a more substantial male wage. Conditions for outworkers were not controlled, and the patterns of low pay readily adopted by employers ensured that the hours were long if something approaching a living was to be made. Additionally, the tens of thousands of jobs that mechanisation provided for some women had been bought at the cost of those women engaged in domestic textile manufacture, often located in areas other than those where the factories emerged. Ireland too, bore some of these costs. Impoverished domestic industries persisted but were unable to compete successfully with the cheaper factory product.[54] This was the demise of the putting-out industry. For those women who remained in the rural sector, life became increasingly hard.

Women were marginalised within agricultural work, excluded from apprenticed trades, disadvantaged in the labour market, and localised in a certain band of jobs. Urban centres offered the greatest hope, but there, too, demand for labour was erratic. When small-time traders, poor and even middle-class families suffered in times of economic downturn, their servants found themselves without a job and with little hope of finding one. The upshot of this growing economic vulnerability was that women's status fell, and it fell most where women's employment opportunities were in greatest decline. Women in the countryside, who once formed the backbone of agricultural and domestic production alongside their menfolk, had found their labour downgraded and cheapened.

Increasingly, wage workers were men. Yet the notion of the 'independent' wage worker did not fit reality. Replacing the family wage with an independent wage, while at the same time cutting women's earning powers, meant that family incomes fell. Households had to make savings somewhere. Discretionary income went on additional food, clothing and education, and cuts to these expenditures reduced living standards. Over time, education levels measured through literacy slipped and heights fell.

Girls were adversely affected more than boys. Men were the money-earners; if their share was reduced too much, their income-earning would be jeopardised. Girls and women, on the other hand, contributed less, were less vital—less than they had been, and less compared with brothers and husbands. In spite of easier access to higher-quality foodstuffs afforded by the countryside, it was rural England with its greater gender divisions and wage differentials where girls suffered most. Generation after generation, English children failed to match their parents' stature, falling around one-quarter of an inch during the convicts' lifetimes. But the gap was greatest between mothers and daughters in the countryside —nearly three-quarters of an inch marked their difference. Rural women ceased to grow as tall, had inferior access to education, and died earlier than their mothers' generation.[55] English country girls bore the brunt of industrialisation.

Rural Ireland—and much of Ireland was rural—told no such dismal tale. In good times and in tough, women's status *vis-à-vis* men was not equal but it held constant. Demand for female labour remained comparatively buoyant. Girls growing up in the late eighteenth and early nineteenth centuries shared in the country's economic fortune. Reliance on the nutritious potato meant Irish women's nutritional standards were improving in the early decades of the century and, significantly, keeping pace with those of men. So, while English heights were falling and those of women (particularly rural women) were falling fastest, Irish women were growing taller, gaining between one-quarter and one-half an inch. Irish women born in the late eighteenth century were shorter than England's country gals, a situation reversed by 1812. This supports the argument that family-based production systems, such as pertained in Ireland but were in decline in England, guaranteed girls and women a higher status and a more equitable distribution of family resources. The demise of family production in England meant that women no longer held that strategic power. Their claim on family resources weakened.

Outlined here are the maelstrom of forces acting to delineate the lives of workers. Born as far back as 1763, England's convict women experienced at first hand these drives working to create Great Britain as the most powerful industrial country in the nineteenth-century world. But with change, women's status declined. It fell as women were marginalised within the traditional sectors of the economy, and related to this, women's and girls' call on family resources dwindled. Quite simply, families had to spend their resources on those who could earn them back through paid work, and increasingly women could not. Country women neither grew so tall, nor lived as long, nor learnt as much as had their mothers and grandmothers. Pushed off the land and into unfamiliar urban settings, women found their labour put to work alongside other women, in the new factories and in providing the services required to make towns run: as domestics, laundresses, wives, mothers, and prostitutes. Many found jobs which afforded them independent wages and some authority, but this growth did not match the fall in agricultural jobs, apprenticed trades, and the domestic textile industry. Nor did it compensate those women who held on to their jobs, but not to their status and pay: the wage gap with men widened; women found themselves isolated in an ever decreasing number of agricultural tasks at the low-paid end of the market; and once highly-paid tradeswomen had their abilities downgraded, whilst others were excluded from learning trades entirely. Divisions occurred between family and work, girls and boys, women and men, the country-side and town. Australia's convict women were at the cutting edge of the greatest socio-economic change ever known.

England's convict women

Where did Elizabeth Coltman and her English compatriots fit in this picture? Some 2946 convict women had been tried in England, 43 per cent of the total transported to New South Wales between 1826 and 1840. It was these women, in particular the 608 born in the vicinity of the great metropolis and the equal number who migrated there, who had been tainted as 'scum'. Was Elizabeth one of the least capable of adjusting to the changes going on around her, or did she and her kin form part of the growing breed of female servants and factory workers in the new urban England?

Certainly, England's convict women were not stationary and unresponsive to the changes going on about them. Between birth and sentencing, over half the convict women had moved county on at least one occasion, and many others, undetected, migrated and then moved back home before offending. On board the *Competitor* with Elizabeth were some fifty-seven adventurers: Rachel Bryant, whose move from Taunton to Bridgewater was mentioned in Chapter Four, plus Esther Bowman, Augusta Downer, Abby Desmond, Lydia Hart, Gwenlliam Jones, Dinah Stanford, Sophia Sheppard and Sarah Racey, to name but a few. By comparison, only 17 per cent of English women enumerated in the census were not living in the county where they were born.[56] But this propensity to migrate has been cast in derogatory terms by some, as discussed in Chapter Three. For the criminal class was renowned for its wanderers, rovers, vagrants and tramps, the 'sturdy beggars' and 'valiant rogues' who 'delight in vagabondage'.[57] These 'English bedouins' were habitual mendicants and thieves 'who loved to "shake a free leg," as it is called by the fraternity, and who preferred cadging and pilfering to industry'.[58]

However, on closer examination, convict migrants did not display traits consistent with a criminal class of aberrant individuals unable or unwilling to learn, roving the countryside in search of criminal mischief. Rather than being the least equipped, these migrants were equal to and even more skilled and literate than those 'stayers' who did not move around the country, as demonstrated in Figure 6.1. Among movers, 16 per cent were illiterate while at the other extreme 41 per cent could both read and write, compared with stayers who were 18 per cent illiterate with 33 per cent learning to read and write. In terms of skill, 19 per cent of movers were unskilled, rising to 60 per cent skilled; for stayers, the figures were 21 per cent unskilled and 55 per cent skilled. These were only small differences, but at the very least they indicate that migrants and non-migrants possessed roughly similar levels of human capital, with migrants just edging in front.[59]

Just as Great Britain had attracted Ireland's most talented workers, towns exerted their magnetism on those who felt they could improve their lot by moving. Practitioners of the more prestigious and most skilled occupations were among the most mobile: three-quarters of house-keepers had migrated, keeping company with cooks, dressmakers and

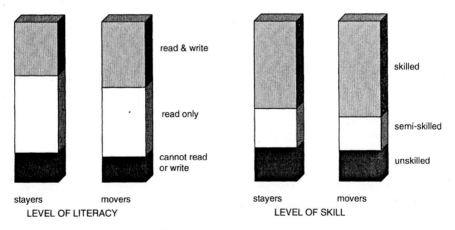

Figure 6.1   Literacy and skill among English-born convict women.

ladies' maids, and also dairywomen and farm labourers. Domestic and rural servants were particularly prone to migrate, in striking contrast with the comparatively stationary class of non-servants.[60] The history of migration amongst transported domestic servants matched that for the class of domestic servants in England as a whole: they moved around regularly, the majority of them having agricultural backgrounds at least until mid-century.[61] Three-fifths of convict women were rural workers who had migrated. This meant they brought with them experience of farms, small-scale domestic textile production, even mining. Farm workers shifted between agricultural work in different country areas, while those venturing to towns either retrained as indoor domestics or ended up as unskilled factory workers. Here are some examples. Accompanying Elizabeth Coltman were three dairymaids, each of whom had moved within England: Elizabeth Fisher left Somerset for Gloucester; Catherine Foster started life in Lincolnshire but was tried in Nottingham; while Maria Howells shifted from Hertfordshire to Hereford. The latter two also moved into domestic labour as allworkers. English factory labourers who were transported had nearly all started life in the country. Typically, convict women fled the countryside, seeking out urban centres like Liverpool, Manchester and, particularly, London in search of employment.

Geographic mobility was paralleled by mobility between employers.[62] Domestics and farm servants had few possessions to weigh them down, their skills were commonplace, and they were employed on individual contracts which terminated after a year or two, encouraging fresh starts. If they were unhappy with an employer or their workplace, if they wanted better pay or conditions, they could attempt to renegotiate their contract or travel instead to fairs where new contracts were to be had.[63] Of course, their bargaining power was also restrained by the very fact that their skills were so commonplace, meaning there was often stiff competition for jobs. Servants who stayed long-term with the one employer did so because the working and living conditions were good, or alternatives were absent.[64]

Conversely, those who moved on sought to improve their position. Migration allowed them to exploit the job market. A correspondent to the *London Chronicle* asserted that domestics saw a placement as an opportunity 'to make the most that they every way can for themselves'— an approach most consistent with the capitalist ethos that convicts were accused of failing to adopt.[65] The notion that English convicts suffered from a 'restlessness and unwillingness to accept the personal investment and self-discipline implied by continuity of work and purposeful action' is not sustainable, least of all for those who were 'restless'.[66] Instead, their mobility was evidence of contract employment, structural change in the economy, and a resourceful workforce aiming to maximise their worth.

But migration involved dangers. Leaving their home parish left them vulnerable, away from family and not qualifying for welfare supports. If work was not soon forthcoming, penury was.

Were England's convict women on the whole like the workers they left behind? Comparing levels of education is tricky. Ages were not carefully enumerated in the English census, excluding numeracy from our analysis. Unlike the Irish census, the English one did not record literacy either. The only measure available for working-class literacy is derived from signatures on marriage registers. People marrying were not a cross-section of the population, at least in terms of age, most being in their late twenties and thirties; by excluding earlier generations who may not have been exposed to the same levels of education, marriage registers may *over*-estimate literacy levels for the population as a whole. However, this age bias is ideal for comparing convicts with workers, as convicts were of a similar age. It also counterbalances another tendency. Using the ability to sign the marriage register as a measure *under*-estimates literacy in England by ignoring all those women who could read but had not learnt to write their name, but this is partly offset by the simplicity of the test, which deems literate women who could do no more than scrawl their name—a test of copying rather than writing or reading. Among English women who married, almost half (48 per cent) could sign their name on the marriage register.[67] What we know for English convict women is that 45 per cent could read and an additional 35 per cent could read and write. How the comparison is to be made is arguable. It has been noted that the proportion of the population signing the marriage register was greater than the proportion able to write, but probably less than the proportion able to read.[68] The proportion of married English women able to sign (around half) was greater than the 35 per cent of convicts able to write but less than the 80 per cent of convicts able to read, suggesting that in comparative terms convicts were at least as literate as—if not more literate than—workers.

Information on paupers and other criminals supports this claim. The government of England had seen fit to appoint a Select Committee whose purpose was to investigate the condition of education of the poorer classes in England and Wales.[69] Levels of literacy were assessed for adult paupers residing in Norfolk and Suffolk Unions and Incorporation (better known as workhouses) on 12 June 1837, distinguishing between the old and infirm, the temporarily disabled, and the able-bodied. Figure 6.2 presents the data for women paupers and convicts. Convicts consistently displayed greater literacy. Illiteracy levels among the poor ranged between 40 per cent for the able-bodied and temporarily disabled combined, and 64 per cent for the old and infirm. Both statistics compare unfavourably with transported women, only 20 per cent of whom could neither read nor write. Four times

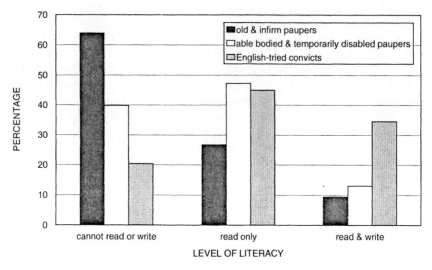

Figure 6.2   Literacy among English adult female paupers and convict women.

as many among the convicts could both read and write as among the old and infirm. Yet even when contrasted with the able-bodied or the temporarily disabled, still at least twice the proportion of convicts were able to read and write. Measuring literacy leads to the conclusion that convicts were not simply the poor transported.

How did convict literacy compare with criminals in Great Britain's gaols? Some contemporaries cited education as causing crime. Jelinger C. Symons expressed the fear that educating the poor meant 'giving mental power to moral evil', and Henry Mayhew cited an 'intelligent' policeman concerned that 'we are teaching our thieves to prig the articles marked at the highest figures'.[70] Criminal records collected information on literacy in the same way as the convict indents. Prisoners were not unlike paupers. In 1840, 44 per cent of women held in English gaols were functionally illiterate, being unable to either read or write. This was similar to able-bodied and temporarily disabled paupers, but was more than twice the proportion of uneducated transportees. If failing to sign the marriage register is treated as the inability to read or write in order to measure illiteracy, then workers, paupers, prisoners and transportees can all be compared. Figure 6.3 tells the story. England's working women and paupers were very much alike, with prison women marginally more literate. Gaol inmates, however, were not as literate as their criminal sisters exiled in New South Wales. Compared with prisoners, paupers and women more generally, convicts were among the more highly literate.

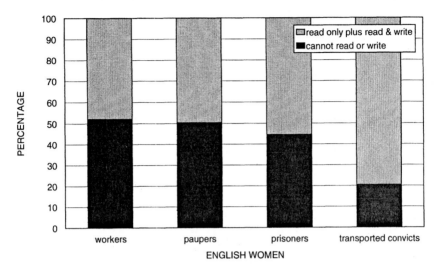

Figure 6.3 Female illiteracy in England: workers, paupers, prisoners and convicts.

Grouping workers and convicts into the same skill classification, and carefully matching convict descriptions to census occupations, are two ways in which we can assess how representative convicts were of the workforce in England. Convict indents demonstrated a clear focus on detail, as illustrated in Table 4.1. Between them, England's convict women brought a stock of some 4430 carefully itemised skills, facilitating comparison with census data. Early nineteenth-century census returns did not request the occupations of individuals, but by 1841 detailed, individual-specific descriptions were collected.[71] Yet, the 1841 census too had its problems. Virtually all men were enumerated on census night, 6 June 1841, yet only a fraction of England's women were counted.[72] Nearly three million women were bypassed. Sixty-eight per cent of women were recorded simply as the 'residue of the population' with a further 290 403 (7 per cent) classified as living by 'independent means', the details of which remained unspecified. Failure to count these women may have arisen when canvassing officers, or husbands answering questions, exercised discretion. Despite possessing a trade, a woman may have been unrecorded either because she was currently unoccupied at this profession, or because of assumptions regarding the role of wife and mother. She was expected to participate in the family enterprise: as helpmeet to her man, she may have been subsumed in his description. Seemingly, the decision not to record women's occupations was influenced by the nature of much female labour which, even when paid, was performed within

their own or someone's home. As Sally Alexander has noted, 'these traditional forms of women's work were quite compatible with the Victorian's
deification of the home, and so passed almost unnoticed'.[73] In quantitative
terms, this might have a quite literal meaning. It was not until Dr William
Farr revised the census programme for 1851 that the domestic roles of
women and children were elevated to the status of occupations. However, occupational information *was* recorded in the 1841 census for nearly
one-quarter of adult women (defined as twenty years of age or older),
and for 13 per cent of girls. The 1841 census thus has limitations, but
nonetheless offers the best possible source of occupational data for the
period when convict women were being transported. It affords us a
snapshot of the economy.

Skill levels for convicts and workers need to be compared. Unfortunately, another notable exception to the otherwise detailed recording of
occupational information in the 1841 English census occurred with
domestic servants. Unlike commerce, trade and manufacture, with
hundreds of occupations listed, the census class of domestic servants
comprised just three job titles: servant, domestic; groom and ostler;
keeper, game and gate. Women belonged exclusively to 'servant,
domestic'. Teasing out which English servants had how much training
was thus impossible, preventing a distinction being drawn between
skilled, semi-skilled and unskilled jobs. In the social-skill classification so
far employed, most domestic functions were deemed to be either skilled
or semi-skilled work. Collapsing these two categories into one, and
generously assuming no English domestic servants were unskilled, we
can make a comparison between convicts and workers, albeit one that
favours the latter. The results presented in Figure 6.4 are interesting.
Convicts and workers shared in overall levels of human capital. Applying
Armstrong's classification scheme to English women reveals that 77 per
cent of workers surveyed in 1841 were skilled or semi-skilled, compared
with 80 per cent of convicts. This high level of female skill also meant
that fewer convict women were unskilled than were convict men.[74] On
this basis, convict women appear as no way inferior to their working
sisters left behind, nor to the men transported with them.

The occupational profile of working women in England is given in
Figure 6.5. In this graph, English women aged twenty years and over are
classified into census categories. While there were ten census categories,
only four had real relevance to women (military, naval, etc. were empty
of women). It can be seen from Figure 6.5 that the great majority of
England's occupied women worked either as domestic servants, or were
engaged in commerce, trade or manufacture. The only other notable
employment for women was as labourers or agricultural workers. Men's
employment also tended to these same four categories but not to the

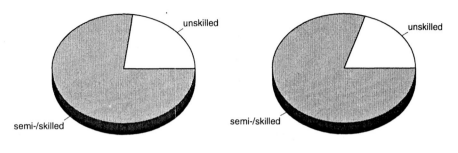

ENGLISH WORKING WOMEN   ENGLISH-TRIED CONVICT WOMEN

Figure 6.4   Skill levels among English women.

same degree, and within these overarching categories men worked at hundreds of different jobs while women were further concentrated into just a handful of areas. Within commerce, trade and manufacture, women were primarily employed as textile workers; as labourers, they did laundry work; in the countryside, they were farmers and agricultural labourers. Women's employment opportunities, outside domestic service, were considerably narrower than men's. Domestic service, however, was different. Although the census is silent on the matter, we know from other evidence that within domestic service women exercised more choice than men, and had scope to specialise in a wide range of tasks.[75] Domestic

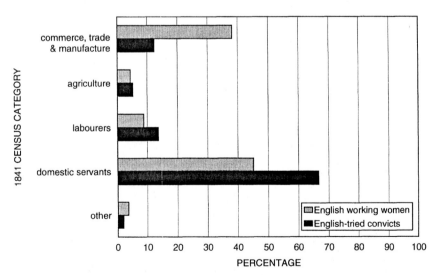

Figure 6.5   Female occupational structures in England, convicts and workers 20 years and upwards.

service also presented many women with their only opportunity to follow a career path, and perhaps this in part explains its popularity.[76]

Figure 6.5 also compares workers with convicts. Again, the four major employers dominated. Commerce, trade and manufacture, domestic service, agriculture and labouring work employed 97 per cent of working women, and 98 per cent of women convicts. Like their English sisters, transported women had found their employment prospects within three of these areas curtailed and limited to a smaller range of tasks than were available to their convicted brethren. Convict and working women were alike in terms of the scope of jobs they covered, but in other ways they were surprisingly dissimilar. Immediately it is apparent from Figure 6.5 that convicts were not like workers in respect of their distribution between the major census categories. Some 38 per cent of England's working women were engaged in commerce, trade and manufacture, a category accounting for less than one-third that proportion of convicts (12 per cent). Two-thirds of convicts in this category were employed in the apprenticed dressmaking, needleworking and millinery trades. What this meant was that among convict women there was a strange absence of textile workers, particularly cotton manufacturers, but also lace and silk manufacturers, seamstresses, and weavers. Only sixteen convict women described themselves as factory labourers or servants, in the main coming from Lancashire. Textile and other factory workers were missing among Australia's coerced immigrants. Conversely, more convicts belonged to the other three major categories. They were laundresses, laundrymaids and washerwomen, and a few more were agricultural workers, but most significantly of all, the vast majority of transported women were domestic servants. In England domestic service accounted for 45 per cent of workers—rising only to 51 per cent in the metropolis from where so many convicts came—but for 67 per cent of England's exiles.[77]

It is interesting to ponder what impact the numerical dominance of domestic servants had upon perceptions of convicts. Servanthood was often linked with prostitution. There was also a certain middle-class contempt for servants and the rest of the urban working classes, who were perceived as 'dirty, unhealthy and definitely dangerous'.[78] Employer dissatisfaction with servant performance was often expressed in terms of servant 'dishonesty, laziness, and sexual promiscuity'—just as it continued to be in colonial New South Wales.[79] Servants slipped easily between imputed classes, being at once urban, dangerous and sometimes criminal. Attitudes of this sort help explain the tainted nineteenth-century descriptions of Australia's convicts.

Why so many domestic servants yet so few textile workers? There are several possible reasons. Age is one. Domestic service was a job for young, single women, with many more girls than adult women engaged in this industry. According to the 1841 census, 60 per cent of females under the age of twenty worked as domestics, compared with 45 per cent of women aged twenty years and upwards. By their thirties, many women had married and left paid domestic labours for other pursuits; only between 9 and 18 per cent remained in service.[80] Skewed in favour of the young and single, transportation favoured the export of domestic servants. But discrepancies still existed even when compared with the relevant age cohort left behind: 78 per cent of convict girls but only 60 per cent of working girls were domestics; 67 per cent of convict adults but only 45 per cent of working women were employed as domestic servants. And in any case, factory textile work attracted over one-third of young working women and should have been similarly represented among convicts.

Another reason could have been the relative health of different sectors of the economy. The economically buoyant North—the heartland of industrialisation and textile production—propelled fewer women into the spiral of crime, detection, prosecution and transportation, leaving the northern counties under-represented among convict women, with the corollary that the south was over-represented. Perhaps, compared with southern domestic servants, northern factory workers were in less need, with less opportunity for crime, working in a less intimate environment than that required for detection. Maybe more domestics were transported because more domestics committed crime.

But this was not the case either. Domestic servants may have had greater recourse to the workhouse than some, but they were not more criminal than textile workers. In fact, the reverse was true. Figure 6.6 tells a revealing story. Census data were collected not only for the population at large, but also for workhouses, hospitals, lunatic asylums and, most importantly, gaols, allowing the occupations of prison inmates to be assessed. As a sizeable proportion of the gaol population (one-third) was defined as girls because they were aged twenty years or less, and with more than a quarter of England's convicts also in this category, girls have been included along with adult women in Figure 6.6. One-half of England's female workers practised domestic service of one sort or another. A similar proportion ended up in workhouses. In gaol, however, domestics were slightly under-represented. Had domestic servants been only as criminal as the rest of the population, their number in gaol should have been about 5 per cent greater. Certainly domestics were not *more* criminal than most. The same cannot be said of textile workers who were over-represented in gaols by some 5 per cent. Labourers—that is, laundresses, laundrymaids and washerwomen—were also over-represented in gaol, but even more so in workhouses, indicating the poverty of their trade.

Domestic servants did not display an unusual propensity for crime. What stands out in Figure 6.6 are not differences in the occupational profile of prisoners compared with workers: prisoners were much like

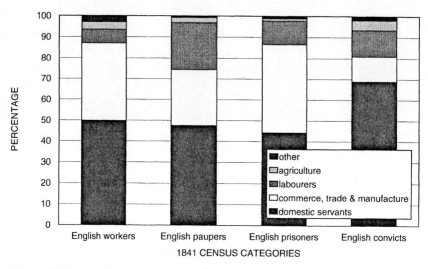

Figure 6.6   Female occupational spread of workers, paupers, prisoners and convicts.

workers. But what is clearly evident is the glaring disparity between the professions of women in gaol compared with those of convicts. Transported women did a poor job of representing gaol-birds. While 42 per cent of prisoners had engaged in commerce, trade or manufacture, the figure of 12 per cent for transported convicts is by comparison strikingly low. Textile and factory workers were over-represented in gaol, but under-represented among transportees. Compensating for this 30 per cent discrepancy were higher transportation rates for agricultural workers, labourers and most of all, domestics. Servants who broke the law were, it seems, more likely to be transported for their sins. Compared with the rest of the population, a domestic servant was in greater danger of ending up in hospital, in an asylum for lunatics, or in a workhouse than in prison, but even more likely than any of these options to end up in New South Wales. An element in the equation is missing. Not every prisoner under sentence of transportation was sent, but apart from age, health and the severity of crime, selection was ostensibly random. However, on the basis of census information, occupational training appears to have influenced the decision of who was transported. So an important question emerges: were domestic servants really being selected for Australia—in spite of their lesser criminality—and if so, why? This question will not be solved until selection procedures at the British end have been carefully disentangled.

There seems little evidence from the convict indents to support the claim by Mayhew, Binny and others that criminals were 'uncivilized professional thieves ... [who] look with scorn upon all who labour for their living as either mean or witless'.[81] Elizabeth Coltman and England's other female convicts were not overt political rebels seeking to undermine the system by rejecting paid employment and defiantly joining a subversive and alternative criminal class. Rather than being aberrant vagabonds, the restlessness that convict migrants were accused of indicated that they were part of a talented and mobile labour source in a dynamic period of English industrialisation. Many came from the countryside, and thus also brought with them knowledge of life on the land plus small-scale textile production. What does mark convicts out as unique, however, is the comparative absence of factory workers from the textile industry, and chronic over-representation of domestics. Convict women had worked as, among many pursuits, dressmakers, milliners, laundry workers, rural workers, nurses and—above all else—domestic servants of varying sorts. England's exiles, then, were young, single, domestic servants, with a few tradeswomen thrown in. They were skilled and literate, at least as talented as the women they left behind, and more so than female prisoners and paupers generally. But where would they fit in Australia's colonial economy?

AUSTRALIA.

GOVERNMENT EMIGRATION

TO

NEW SOUTH WALES.

Farmers, Mechanics, Agricultural and other Labourers and Small Working Capitalists,

MARRIED (with or without Children), NOT EXCEEDING 35 YEARS OF AGE; and

DOMESTIC SERVANTS,

NOT EXCEEDING 30 YEARS.

Are provided with Assisted Passages to

SYDNEY.

By the Agent-General for New South Wales.

Full Particulars and Forms of Application may be obtained from the Emigration Department, New South Wales Government Office, 5, Westminster Chambers, London, S.W.

Figure 7.1   Original poster, c. 1883. Document 93, AONSW.

CHAPTER SEVEN

Colonial Requirements: Coerced and Free Immigrants

Historians and economists seem to think that convict women contributed very little to colonial economic development.[1] Unsubstantiated claims that female transportees were unskilled are wrong. Convict women packed a range of occupational and literacy skills in the economic baggage they brought with them to Australia. They were much like the working women they left behind, but with two major exceptions: transportees were disproportionately young, and there was an inexplicably large number of domestic servants in their ranks at the cost of few factory workers. Otherwise, transported women shared with workers a common heritage and experience of life in two rapidly changing countries. So far we have established that the women had been instructed prior to their arrival, but not whether this training equipped them for participation in the colonial economy. Maybe women were irrelevant to the colonial economy, as some have argued. Perhaps the absence of textile workers, and excess of domestic and farm servants, meant that the colony suffered from a lack of appropriate skills, accounting for women's poor worth and the colony's failure to develop a manufacturing sector.[2] One way of answering the puzzle of whether convict skills matched colonial needs is to ask another question: when colonial authorities deliberately tried to attract workers into the colony through subsidised immigration, whom did they target? Whom did they receive? And how did convict women compare?

'A most valuable class'

At an official level, and also among private employers, there was a concerted effort to attract immigrants from the United Kingdom to the Australian colonies. Labour was in short supply, and immigrants equalled instant workers. Plenty of individuals wanted to emigrate from England and Ireland, but the problem was one of direction. Most preferred the

United States. For example, in 1831, 98 per cent of emigrants from the British Isles chose the United States and Canada as their destinations, while 2 per cent chose Australia and New Zealand.[3] An incentive scheme therefore had to be developed to attract immigrants to Australia, and in 1831 the Colonial Office made the first moves towards government-assisted emigration financed by the sale of colonial lands.[4] This would become an enduring policy. The poster in Figure 7.1 is an artefact from a late period, attesting to the continued importance of government-assisted schemes throughout white Australia's history. But not anyone would do. If public monies were to be spent, they were to be spent wisely, on the type of labour most needed. Authorities aimed at developing a policy through which 'a most valuable class of moral and industrious persons might be obtained'.[5] Once the right sort arrived, more would follow, or so the theory went.

Incentives envisaged were twofold. Financial support for the cost of passage was offered by the government either through a free passage which was to be reserved for 'the most eligible persons', or through a loan system whereby the cost of the fare would be provided upfront by the government and then repaid in the colony: repayment would be forfeited if colonial employment was not readily found. A second aspect of the plan was to assist immigrants in finding employment on their arrival in the colony.[6] Colonial employers also recruited overseas directly, through payment of a bounty and guaranteed work in New South Wales. In 1832 the first assisted scheme began with the arrival of eight single women and eight mechanics with their families on board the *Marianne* from England, and it accelerated thereafter. By 1838 the first immigration office had opened and the first agent for immigration was appointed. The plan worked. Although in 1839, 68 per cent of English emigrants still chose the United States, 27 per cent now opted for Australia.[7]

Although immigration was financed by the colonies, power over immigration decisions resided with the British government.[8] A committee on emigration from Great Britain to New South Wales was established in Britain under the chairmanship of Francis Forbes, with the intention of performing two major functions: 'The great objects to be obtained are care in the selection of emigrants, and economy in the application of public funds'.[9] The committee sought to gauge the demand for immigrants within the colony, in terms of number, gender and qualifications. Such matters, it was noted, depended upon colonial opinion. To form their views, they elicited information from 'some of the most experienced proprietors from each of the three principal sections of the colony'—men like the Honourable Alexander McLeay (Colonial Secretary), the Reverend J. D. Lang, John Blaxland and Thomas Potter Macqueen, to name but a few—gentlemen whose beliefs, it turned out, demonstrated 'a remarkable coincidence'. In practice, migration may have served multifarious purposes, impinging on the quality and appropriateness of the migrants actually received into the colony—Britain was accused of indiscriminately 'shovelling out paupers', a claim currently under attack—but immigration *policies* reflected who was in demand in the colonies.[10]

Policy aimed to minimise expense and maximise immigrants' utility: only the most suitable applicants would be financed to the extent of a subsidised voyage. What sort of people did they want? Among this 'most valuable class' was a strong contingent of women. Peter Cunningham, surgeon-superintendent, was greatly in favour of single female immigration, claiming that 'women are in fact one of the best and most patriotic consignments that could be sent out to our rising country'.[11] Between 1832 and 1836 the majority of colonial emigration funding was spent importing single women.[12] These years heralded the arrival of 2503 women, but only 475 men.[13] In 1837 the Emigration Committee found young single women to be 'desirable in the colony', placing them within the 'most eligible' category and recommending 'that young women between certain ages should be allowed a free passage'.[14] It was proposed that single women should comprise one-quarter of the projected inflow. This proportion was on a par with unmarried farm servants. Farm servants working in various capacities, from labourers clearing land to sheep-shearers and dairymaids, were essential to the productive enterprise and were deemed to be of considerable importance in the colony where, due to great demand but short supply, they commanded high wages. Upping their numbers would ease the shortage and bring down wages that many thought were too high.[15] Another quarter were to be married mechanics accompanied by their wives but without children. Married farm servants and married mechanics with their families made up the fourth quarter, although the number of children permitted was determined by the father's expected colonial wage rate: the higher the wage, the more children allowed, to a maximum of three.[16] Single women kept good company in the immigration stakes.

Single women were wanted in the colony, but in what capacity? Women were to be selected on the basis of two criteria: their morality and their employability. Unmarried women had to be of virtuous character.[17] They also had to be domestic and farm servants.

> Next in importance to character, it is essential to the success of the female emigrants that they should be useful. It has been observed, that of the young women who have hitherto arrived, many have been found so inexpert as servants as to give place to the convicts. To secure employment, therefore, it is necessary that such young women as are invited to come to the colony should be practised either as house-servants or in some of the more ordinary occupations of a farm. With such qualifications they will be able to command good places, and entirely supersede the employment of convict women in families.[18]

NOTICE

O. J. ~~~~~~~

TO

YOUNG WOMEN

DESIROUS OF BETTERING THEIR CONDITION BY AN

Emigration to New South Wales.

In New South Wales and Van Diemen's Land there are very few Women compared with the whole number of People, so that it is impossible to get Women enough as Female Servants or for other Female Employments. The consequence is, that desirable situations, with good wages, are easily obtained by Females in those Countries; but the Passage is so long that few can pay the expence of it without help. There is now, however, the following favourable opportunity of going to New South Wales.

The Committee has been formed in London for the purpose of facilitating Emigration, which intends to send out a Ship in the course of the Spring, expressly for the conveyance of Female Emigrants, under an experienced and respectable Man and his Wife, who have been engaged as Superintendents. The Parties who go in that Vessel must be *Unmarried Women or Widows;* must be *between the Ages of* 18 *and* 30; and must be of *good health and character.* They must also *be able to pay £6* towards the expense of their Passage. The remainder of the expense will be paid by the Society. Every arrangement will be made for the comfort of the Emigrants during the Voyage; and Medical Assistance provided: they also will be taken care of on their first landing in the Colonies; and they will find there, ready for them, a list of the different situations to be obtained, and of the wages offered, so that they may at once see the different opportunities of placing themselves. The Women sent out in this manner will not be bound to any person whatsoever, but will be, to all intents and purposes, Free Women.

Persons who on reading this Notice, may desire to emigrate in the manner pointed out, should apply by Letter to the " Emigration Committee, 18, Aldermanbury, London." If the Letter be sent by General Post, it should be sent under a cover addressed to " The Under Secretary of State, Colonial Department, London." It will be proper that the Application should be accompanied by recommendations from the Resident Minister of the Parish, and from any other respectable persons to whom the Applicant may be known; the same recommendations should state the fact that the Applicant will be able to pay £6. when she shall receive notice that it is time to embark.

All Applications made in the foregoing manner, will be answered; and it is requested that Parties will apply without delay, as the fine teak-built Ship " Bussorah Merchant," 530 tons burthen, now in the London Docks, is appointed to sail on the 13th April next expressly with Female Emigrants selected by the Committee.

Parties who may be desirous to obtain information by personal application in the City, may have further particulars from Mr. Thomas Hurt, 18, Aldermanbury, or from Mr. Hoskins, the Superintendant, 17, Warwick Square, Newgate Street; where arrangements are made for the temporary reception of Young Women who may not have other convenient places of residence in London.

(Signed) EDWARD FORSTER,
CHAIRMAN.

COMMITTEE ROOM,
18, Aldermanbury,

Figure 7.2 Broadsheet, 1833. Ref. D356/17: CY1118, f. 529, Mitchell.

This quotation is telling. Female immigrants were wanted as domestic workers, and they were to substitute for convict maids whose immorality made them undesirable in the homes of respectable citizens. It is also noted, at least for those arriving before 1837, that convict women were better workers and preferable to immigrants.

Advertising campaigns provide some interesting insights into the application of policy. Great energies were expended in trying to attract female immigrants. The Committee for Promoting the Emigration of Single Women (and widows) actively sought its clientele through posters. Figure 7.2 reproduces a tempting broadside from 1833 aimed at young, marriageable women, placed by Edward Forster, chairman of the committee. Good and plentiful employment, and care in placing migrants, were its key selling points.

In New South Wales and Van Diemen's Land there are very few Women compared with the whole number of People, so that it is impossible to get Women enough as Female Servants or for other Female Employments. The consequence is, that desirable situations, with good wages, are easily obtained by Females in those Countries.

Accommodation would be organised at both ends, in London and in Sydney, and on arrival they would be provided with a list of employment places with corresponding wages. Prospective emigrants had to be unmarried or widowed, aged between eighteen and thirty years, of good health and character, and capable of contributing £6 to the cost of passage.

Posters in Figure 7.3 (dated 1834) and Figure 7.4 (dated 1836) also targeted single or widowed women 'of Good Character', aged between fifteen and thirty years. English women were the audience for the first advertisement, and were offered a subsidised ticket costing 'FIVE POUNDS only', and even this would be waived under certain circumstances. New South Wales offered great promise, it declared. John Marshall, agent to the committee, was at pains to point out that the colony was a place 'where the number of Females compared with the entire Population is greatly deficient, and where consequently from the great demand for Servants, and other Female Employments, the Wages are comparatively high'. The second poster was aimed at Irish women. Beguilingly, the poster offered single Irish women 'A FREE PASSAGE' (in large bold letters) and the promise that 'all who may conduct themselves with discretion and industry, may calculate in time importantly to benefit their condition' from their Antipodean adventure. And there was more than this: accommodation with 'every essential comfort', immediate placement in employment with respectable families, good wages of the

Female Emigration
TO
AUSTRALIA.

COMMITTEE:

EDWARD FORSTER, Esq. *Chairman.*
SAMUEL HOARE, Esq.
JOHN TAYLOR. Esq.
THOMAS LEWIN, Esq.
S. H. STERRY. Esq.

CHARLES HOLTE BRACEBRIDGE. Esq.
JOHN S. REYNOLDS. Esq.
JOHN PIRIE. Esq.
CAPEL CURE, Esq.
WILLIAM CRAWFORD. Esq.

CHARLES LUSHINGTON, Esq.
JOHN ABEL SMITH, Esq. M.P.
GEORGE LONG, Esq.
COLONEL PHIPPS,
NADIR BAXTER. Esq.
CAPTAIN DANIEL PRING, R.N.

The Committee for promoting the Emigration
OF
Single Women

To AUSTRALIA, acting under the Sanction of His Majesty's Secretary of State for the Colonies, HEREBY GIVE NOTICE, That

THE SPLENDID TEAK-BUILT SHIP

"David Scott," of 773 Tons Register,

Carrying an experienced Surgeon, and a respectable Person and his Wife as Superintendents to secure the Comfort and Protection of the Emigrants during the Voyage, will sail from

GRAVESEND
On Thursday 10th of July next,

(Beyond which day she will on no account be detained) direct for

SYDNEY.

Single Women and Widows of good Character, from 15 to 30 Years of Age, desirous of bettering their Condition by Emigrating to that healthy and highly prosperous Colony, where the number of Females compared with the entire Population is greatly deficient, and where consequently from the great demand for Servants, and other Female Employments, the Wages are comparatively high, may obtain a Passage

On payment of FIVE POUNDS only.

Those who are unable to raise even that Sum here, may, when approved by the Committee, go *without any Money Payment whatever,* as their Notes of Hand will be taken, payable in the Colony within a reasonable time after their arrival, when they have acquired the means to do so: in both cases the Parties will have the advantage of the **Government Grant** in aid of their Passage.

The Females who proceed by this Conveyance will be taken care of on their first Landing at Sydney. They will find there a List of the various Situations to be obtained, and of the Wages offered, and will be perfectly free to make their own Election: they will not be bound to any person. or subjected to any restraint, but will be, to all intentsand purposes, perfectly free to act and decide for themselves.

Females in the Country who may desire to avail themselves of the important advantages thus offered them, should apply by Letter to "The Emigration Committee, London," under Cover addressed to "The UNDER SECRETARY OF STATE, COLONIAL DEPARTMENT, LONDON." It will be necessary that the Application be accompanied by a Certificate of Character from the Resident Minister of the Parish, or from some other respectable persons to whom the Applicant may be known; but the Certificate of the Resident Minister is in all cases most desirable. Such Female as may find it expedient may, when approved by the Committee as fit persons to go by this Conveyance, be boarded temporarily in London, prior to Embarkation, on Payment of 7s. per Week.

☞ All Applications made under cover in the foregoing manner, or personally, will receive early Answers, and all necessary Information, by applying to

JOHN MARSHALL, Agent to the Committee, 26, Birchin Lane, Cornhill, London.
EDWARD FORSTER, *Chairman.*

NOTE.—The Committee have the satisfaction to state that of 217 Females who went out by the "Bussorah Merchant," 180 obtained good Situations within three Days of their Landing, and the remainder were all well placed within a few Days, under the advice of a Ladies' Committee, formed in the Colony expressly to aid the Females on their arrival.

LONDON, 1st May, 1834.

By Authority:
PRINTED BY JOSEPH HARTNELL, FLEET STREET, FOR HIS MAJESTY'S STATIONERY OFFICE.

Figure 7.3 Original poster. 1834. Ref. D356/17: CY1118, f. 535, Mitchell.

Figure 7.4 Original poster. 1836. Ref. D356/17: CY1118, f. 534, Mitchell.

AUSTRALIA.

GOVERNMENT EMIGRATION

TO

NEW SOUTH WALES,

Farmers, Mechanics, Agricultural and other Labourers, Small Working Capitalists,

Female Domestic Servants, and other useful Classes,

Are provided by the AGENT-GENERAL FOR NEW SOUTH WALES, with Assisted Passages at Reduced Rates including Bedding and Mess Utensils, from **PLYMOUTH** to

SYDNEY,

AND THENCE BY RAIL OR STEAMER TO OTHER PARTS OF THE COLONY.

Married Couples not exceeding 40 years, £6 Each Couple. Single Men, £4. Single Women, £2. Children 3 and under 14 years, £1, under 3 years, Free.

An Experienced Surgeon accompanies each Ship: and the Single Women, for whom there exists a great demand in Colony, are placed under the care of a Matron during the Voyage.

Full Particulars and Forms of Application may be obtained from the EMIGRATION DEPARTMENT, NEW SOUTH GOVERNMENT OFFICE, 5. WESTMINSTER CHAMBERS, LONDON, S.W., or of the Local Agent

Figure 7.5 Original poster. c.1884. Document 102, AONSW.

women's own determination in '*this healthy and prosperous Colony*' (their emphasis), and the likelihood of marriage! A small detail affixed to the lower left corner provocatively asks, 'DO YOU WANT TO BE MARRIED?'

The penultimate paragraph in this 1836 poster is also interesting. Aimed at migrants more generally, it outlines appropriate skills that men should possess, with the similar promise 'that all such, *provided they are of industrious and steady character, are certain of immediate and constant employment*'. Good character mattered for men as well as women. In addition, the poster details the conditions of passage. For £10 a married couple could migrate; children under five years of age would be charged £3 each and those above that age a further £1 per year in addition, 'but Daughters above 12 years old, when accompanying their Parents, will be allowed a Free Passage' (as, indeed, were infants under one year of age). This latter age stipulation coincided with the age at which girls might be expected to commence their apprenticeships as servants.

Throughout this century and the next these themes continued: government posters declared that they wanted young single women, they wanted lots of them, and they wanted them as wives and workers.[19] Figure 7.5 is an Emigration Department poster from about 1884 which lists trades in demand. By itemising the cost of passage to be borne by each category of immigrant (and thus by implication the level of assistance provided by the government) this poster also gives an idea of the hierarchy operating among immigrants. A married couple, both under the age of forty years, could gain passage—inclusive of bedding and mess utensils—for £6. Single men would have to pay £4 each while, on the other hand, single women needed to pay just half of that, at £2. Only children between three and fourteen years of age gained a cheaper voyage. Why did single men have to pay more: were they more resource-expensive on the voyage than single women, married couples and children?

Single domestic servants were required in the colony to inhibit the increasingly high wages being paid to these types of workers, to boost living standards and to increase male labour productivity by releasing men from domestic chores.[20] In the Tasmanian House of Assembly, it was noted of the immigration of female domestic servants that 'there is perhaps nothing which more materially affects the comfort of families throughout the Colony'.[21] This demand for female labour was self-perpetuating: once married, these women themselves often sought domestic help. Female domestic workers were in demand, and the greater government subsidy of single women appears part of their deliberate policy to attract marriageable domestic servants. A similar advertisement was to be found on the back of a pamphlet issued gratis to intending emigrants by the agent-general for New South Wales in 1884:

while single men had to pay £4, and couples £6, 'Female Domestic Servants are much required in the Colony, and are taken on Payment of £2 each'.[22] The Emigration Department certainly did not want it to go unnoticed that female domestic servants were a group 'who may obtain high wages, and for whom there is a great demand in the Colony', and in the 1883 poster reproduced in Figure 7.1, the simple, bold description 'DOMESTIC SERVANTS' was not easily missed.

Good women

Immigration policies made it quite clear that young single women were desirable in more ways than one. Not only were these women required as domestic servants, but as wives and mothers—all jobs with considerable overlap. Women's domestic work, be it in the paid or unpaid sector, is one of the key areas that must be recognised if the story of economic development is to include women. Authorities in the nineteenth century seemed more aware of this than economists are today.

Migration posters referred to the great deficiency of single females in the colony, and to the favourable marriage market facing women there. This was intended to appeal to women, who were to be lured out with the enticement that 'a large proportion have married respectable settlers' (Figure 7.4). It was also a signpost to what colonial authorities wanted of women. In addition to their employability, single women were to be selected on the basis of their morality. They were required to be

> of virtuous character. This class of emigrants is by far the most important to the colony in a moral point of view. The great object of importing young women is not merely to supply the demand for servants; it is to restore the equilibrium of the sexes; to raise the value of female character; and to provide virtuous homes for the labouring classes of the community ... none but women of pure and unexceptionable character should be assisted in coming to the colony.[23]

'Good' women were valuable to the colony for their homemaking, and as God's police.[24]

The problem was a severe imbalance in the sex-ratio of the population, nowhere more noticeable than among convicts. Of the total 78 000 convicts landed in New South Wales between 1788 and 1840, about 12 000 were female.[25] Between 1826 and 1840, when 6812 women arrived in shackles—metaphorically if not literally—38 443 convict men descended on Sydney's shores.[26] This meant that women accounted for less than one-fifth of the convict inflow. In 1828 there were nearly ten convict men to every convict woman, and over three men for every woman in the population more generally.[27] The major impetus towards equality in the sex-ratio was the birth of the 'currency lads and lasses'—the native-born whites—who were, naturally enough, born in roughly equal numbers of girls and boys. Immigration could work either way, alleviating the problem, or exacerbating it.

Such discrepancies in the ratio between the sexes had numerous ramifications. Certainly the imbalance of the penal settlement and the ensuing search for 'partners'—long-term or short-term—had repercussions for Aboriginal women and their communities.[28] So, too, for white women. The dictum of supply and demand determining value conflicted with the old adage about safety in numbers, and must have influenced the status of women, but with what outcome is difficult to assess.[29] But authorities and social observers were more concerned with reproductive and moral problems that they believed were caused by this peculiar stratification. Imbalance between the sexes preoccupied policy-makers. Those responsible for the deliberate creation of the future population— the formulators of immigration policy—were particularly concerned with this state of affairs. The Emigration Committee, reporting in 1832, wished to stress that

> in appropriating the public funds to the promotion of emigration, your committee feel that they have a duty to perform towards the future as well as the present generation; and, impressed with a sense of the evil arising out of the existing disparity of the sexes, and admitted as that evil universally is, they cannot reconcile it with their duty to recommend to your Excellency and Council any measure which would tend directly to increase the evil, and to entail its consequences upon posterity. It is under this impression that they recommend the equal proportions of the sexes to be preserved in all importations made through the agency of Government ... The disproportion which at present exists between the sexes is nearly in the ratio of three males to one female. The effects of this unnatural state of things are powerfully felt at present; and unless an adequate remedy be applied, it may be impossible to calculate its consequences upon the future character and prosperity of the colony. It becomes, therefore, the duty of those in whose hands the destinies of this young country are placed to apply the remedy while it is yet within their power, but more especially to guard against an extension of the evil by every possible means.[30]

Evil arose from the lack of women which, they believed, led to excessive levels of prostitution and illegitimacy, and what was perceived as the threat of homosexuality.[31] Need to populate the colony was one problem, but making sure this occurred within marriage was another. The Molesworth Report was anxious about female convicts, that 'even if any of them were inclined to be well-conducted, the disproportion of the sexes in the penal colonies is so great, that they are exposed to irresistible temptations', of which prostitution was meant to be one.[32] Prostitution was not the only problem. Too few women meant men found other sexual partners, including each other.[33] In the course of his enquiries, Commissioner Bigge asked the Reverend William Cowper for his opinion regarding the impact of the shortage of women on the colony. Cowper responded 'that many evils arise from the great deficiency of their number … I think that from want of the happiness, or Domestic attach-ment, that arises from the marriage state, the convicts are induced to pursue various modes of dissipation, and leads to evil'.[34]

Moral and economic danger stemmed from inadequate numbers of female mates suitable for marriage. There were simply not enough women to go around, and those who were available were considered unsuitable. For the colony to thrive, some believed better women of higher morals were needed to fill colonial homes, and they were needed in significant quantity. Various plans were developed to increase the number of available women: through the importation of native women from nearby continents (as early as 1787 Governor Phillip was told to collect willing women from the Pacific Islands to marry soldiers resident in the settlement), to inter-racial marriages with Australia's indigenous women, through to requests to transport more women, and of course, via immigration schemes.[35] In practice, the latter two were the most successful strategies. Yet free immigrant women were not imported solely as marriage partners. Later, in Van Diemen's Land, even when women outnumbered men, female domestics were encouraged to immigrate, because as wives or workers these women materially improved living standards.[36] Single women, of good character, trained as domestics, and young enough to have a long future working and rearing children—these were the type of women the colony demanded.

Free immigrants and convict workers compared

Convict women were the dominant white female presence in the New South Wales colony well into the 1830s. It can be seen from Figure 7.6 (or more precisely in Table A1) that in the first three decades of settlement only 173 women arrived voluntarily, compared with the forced migration of some 4360 female transportees. During the 1820s convicted women maintained their prominence, arriving at ten times the rate of free immigrant women. Consequently, in 1830 women who were or had been convicts contributed over half the total female workforce, comprising 56 per cent, while their daughters accounted for nearly another fifth. It

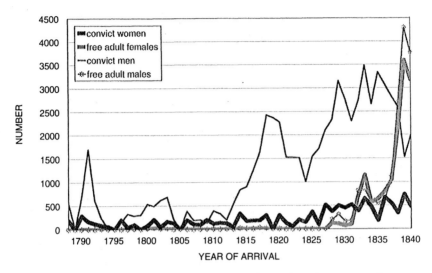

Figure 7.6 Free and forced immigration to New South Wales, 1788–1840.

was not until the later part of that decade that forcibly transported women would be surpassed by free immigrants as the single largest group of colonial women workers.[37]

The shift was finally brought about by the arrival of a substantial number of free women in the colony in the 1830s, particularly the late 1830s. This is when women like 18-year-old Mary MacCluskey, houseworker, and 20-year-old Catherine Fitzgerald, house servant, began to arrive, in their case on the *Red Rover*, landing on 10 August 1832.[38] During this decade women choosing to emigrate to this southern colony outnumbered female convicts sent as punishment. Figure 7.6 also reveals a unique phenomenon. What was so unusual for international migration in this period, and what foreshadowed the change that was to occur more widely in the last three decades of the nineteenth century, was that women arrived at a rate comparable with men, outstripping them in the early years of the 1830s.[39] This was not the case for all migrant groups. Some immigrants came to New South Wales paying their own fare, while others were encouraged to come through various incentive schemes. Among the *unassisted* travellers there were twice as many men as women between 1830 and 1850.[40] But with government-assisted passages between 1832 and 1836 women dominated, and it was only the shift away from individual and towards family migration that prevented this from continuing. In the immediate aftermath, near parity between the sexes was achieved. This inflow of women did not happen by accident. It was part of a deliberate policy aimed at attracting a large but select group of women competent at particular jobs.

But did they get the women they wanted? And how did convict women compare? Much work still needs to be done on this topic, but we do have some insights.[41] Age was a major determinant, along with occupational training and 'moral character', of who was assisted in migrating.[42] Various immigration regulations stipulated that immigrants be between the ages of eighteen and forty years, similar to today's requirements.[43] Sometimes the age band was even narrower. Edward Forster's notice in Figure 7.2 insisted that women 'must be *between the Ages of 18 and 30*' (his emphasis). Restrictive age limits continued throughout the century. The poster in Figure 7.1 declared that assisted passage would be offered to emigrants 'not exceeding 35 years of age', and in the case of domestic servants only to those 'not exceeding 30 years'. The aim was to ensure that most immigrants could be economically productive from the moment they disembarked. Australia would thus receive an active workforce without the costs of childbirth, rearing, education or, at the other end, care of the elderly with all the concomitant demands on services.

Some age data have been collected for immigrants, although they do not distinguish between women and men. Assisted immigrants were divided into those on government passage, and those termed bounty immigrants recruited by employers and their agents in the United Kingdom. The latter were expected to be the most suitable.[44] About one-half of bounty immigrants fell into this ideal age bracket of eighteen to forty years, as did one-third of government-assisted immigrants into New South Wales between 1837 and 1840.[45] Looking back on what had happened in the nineteenth century, the historian R. B. Madgwick found that 'on the whole … the age composition of the immigrants was fully as satisfactory as the colonists should have expected, and in this respect at least, the arrivals formed a desirable addition to the colonial population'.[46] If Madgwick thought the economy well-served by the age profile of the free immigrants, it was dealt an even better hand by the British judiciary. While between one-third and one-half of free immigrants were aged between eighteen and forty, so were 86 per cent of convict women.

Figure 7.7 compares the ages of immigrants with convicts. This figure shows that the age distribution of the immigrants was nowhere near as conducive to economic growth as was that of the transportees. The main difference lay in the higher number of dependants—children and young teenagers—among the immigrants: 40 per cent were under fourteen years of age, compared with only 0.2 per cent of female convicts. Many more convicts were aged between eighteen and thirty-five. With an average age of nearly twenty-seven years, convict women represented something close to the optimum balance between training and future practice, between investment in human capital and returns on that investment. These women were also in their prime reproductive years.

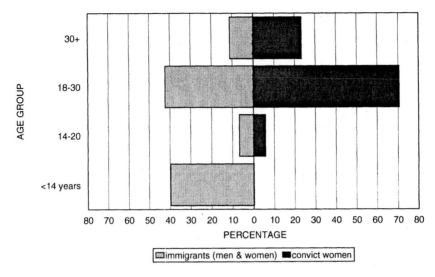

Figure 7.7 Age distributions of free and forced immigrants.

Marriageable women were assisted to Australia. Immigration policies targeted 'Single Women, for whom there exists a great demand in Colony'. The posters given in Figures 7.2 to 7.4, from the 1830s, were aimed exclusively at this group. As well as a rather harsh age-restriction, Edward Forster's immigrant women had to be '*Unmarried Women or Widows*' (again, his emphasis). Between 1831 and 1836 single women were brought out on their own, after that under the protection of their own or other families.[47] Young, single, adult women formed a high-priority group, according to immigration policies; and it was young, single, adult women who got transported, as was seen in Chapter Four. Convict women were effectively single, 76 per cent arriving unmarried or widowed. 'Single' may have included many women unsure of their status arising from *de facto* relationships, a common working-class practice—but along with the quarter who were officially married, they were all effectively divorced by the distance, forced to leave their spouses behind.[48] It was even suggested by Peter Cunningham that transportation should dissolve the legal ties of marriage, leaving the women free to remarry in the colony.[49] Additionally, few of the 2210 mothers transported were allowed to bring their offspring, leaving behind most of the 4864 children convict women were known to have borne, many destined to be orphans. Convict women thus arrived largely 'unencumbered' by maternal or marital responsibilities, if emotionally bereft at their situation.

How did immigrants rate in terms of literacy? Like transportees, some immigrants were required to state their level of education. Figure 7.8

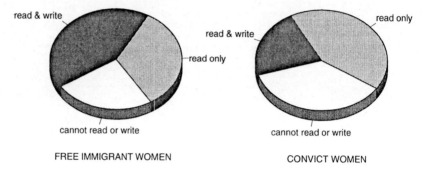

Figure 7.8   Literacy rates for free immigrant women and convict women.

presents figures on female literacy for a sample—combining single bounty immigrants in 1838, and single and married assisted immigrants in 1841—arriving in New South Wales.[50] Convict figures are also given. Overall, the colony received from its immigration an educated group of women, with three-quarters in some sense literate. Over time, these statistics improved further.[51] This fits well with the suggestion that it is usually the best-equipped who migrate, those able to read the literature in advance, make application, and adapt to new environments.

As a group, immigrant women were more literate than convict women. Breaking the group into its constituent elements—Ireland and England— is most revealing because, as we have seen in earlier chapters, Irish and English women were dissimilar in numerous ways. Among transportees, English women were more skilled and literate than Irish women: one-third of Irish were skilled, one-half of English. Reading was a skill mastered by less than half the Irish, but by four-fifths of English women. Irish women displayed age-heaping while the English did not. Fewer English women came from the countryside. It is therefore necessary to compare like with like, and Figure 7.9 does just this.

Immigrants and convicts from England were roughly similar. More immigrant women had mastered writing, but in both cases only one-fifth were illiterate. This compared favourably with English working women more generally, less than half of whom could sign their name when marrying, as will be remembered from Chapter Six. In stark contrast were the Irish. Women emigrating from Ireland had achieved a far higher level of literacy than had Irish convicts or Irish women in general. This was to be expected. Emigrants had to fill in forms, unlike their coerced counterparts. Indeed, these immigrant women bore more in common with those other Irish emigrants, the Irish convicts transported from England. Both were better educated than the women they left behind, leaving Ireland suffering a brain-drain.

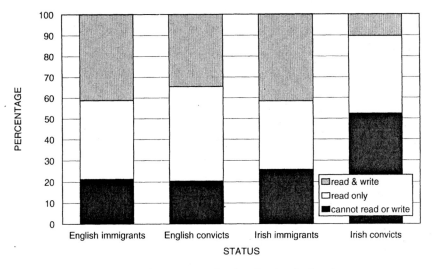

Figure 7.9 Literacy rates between England and Ireland's female immigrants and women convicts.

While a detailed study of immigrant skills awaits research, there does exist some readily available occupational information for single immigrant women who arrived in New South Wales in 1838 and 1839.[52] This comes from the 'Correspondence between the Secretary of State for the Colonies and the Governors of the Australian Colonies, respecting Emigration'. Included are both bounty immigrants and assisted immigrants who came on government-chartered vessels. Some problems exist with the job categories listed. The government's classification changed from ship to ship. Farm servants suddenly materialise when dairymaids and general servants cease to be recorded. While some 319 housemaids arrived on the bounty ships and on government vessels in 1838, none arrived on government vessels in 1839; however, house servants and housekeepers —previously non-existent categories—suddenly appeared. Profound shifts in the trades of immigrants in these adjacent years—indeed, in the same year—were unlikely, and it is far more probable that differences arose from irregularities in nomenclature. Additionally, it is unclear whether some convicts—general country servants, for example— belonged with other house and general servants or with farm servants. For these reasons, house, general and farm servants have been combined into one category, along with other related groups like cooks and nurse-maids. Sempstresses, needlewomen and dressmakers make up one other important category and laundresses another, leaving a small number of tradeswomen in one category, and midwives and schoolteachers in another along with dealers. Figure 7.10 employs this classification system, documenting the occupational profiles of these single female immigrants

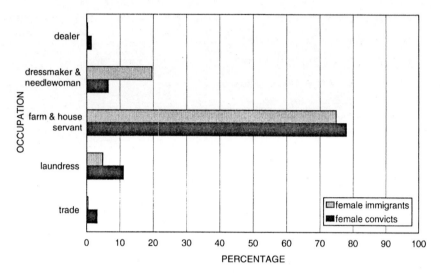

Figure 7.10   Occupational profiles of single immigrant women and convict women.

and listing female convict occupations alongside. Details of how convict trades were matched to those of immigrants can be found in Appendix 7.

The first striking feature of this figure to be noted is that immigration officials wanted domestic and farm servants, and this is who they got. More than seven out of every ten immigrant women were domestic and farm servants. There were cooks, nursemaids, housemaids and farm servants, to name but a few. Other trades also arrived in considerable numbers, most notably needlewomen, dressmakers and laundresses. In far smaller numbers were bonnet makers (four), straw hat makers (two), one milliner and one silk weaver, three midwives and three schoolmistresses. How did immigrant occupational backgrounds compare with those of convicts?

Overall, there are powerful similarities between the occupations of convict exiles and women voluntarily emigrating to New South Wales. Textile and other factory workers were noticeably missing in both cases, distinguishing free and convict migrants from Britain's working women. In their place were servants, in remarkably equal proportions. Domestics and farm servants combined accounted for 75 per cent of immigrants, corresponding closely with the figure for convict women at 78 per cent. Prying further into this exceptionally close match, some differences can be found. Seemingly fewer convicts were farm servants. This may be illusory. Difficulties in classifying rural jobs have already been mentioned. Additionally, in 1841 the New South Wales agent for immigration complained that casual urban labourers were calling themselves 'agricultural labourers' in order to gain the bounty, casting some doubt over the accuracy of immigrant claims to rural occupations and suggesting they overstated their familiarity with country work.[53] But it would not be altogether surprising if farm servants were somewhat less obvious among the convicts, given the latter's urban backgrounds. Equally expected were the higher number of convict cooks, laundresses, washerwomen and small-time trades associated with married women's work, trades understandably absent among single female immigrants. Less explicable is the relative deficiency among convicts of dressmakers and needlewomen. But while immigrant and convict skills were not identical, they did bear a striking resemblance to one another. The occupational categories that encompassed all immigrants were the same ones that accounted for nearly all convicts. Broadly speaking, officials received from immigrant women the types of skills and demographic profile they tried to attract. And, if they took the trouble to look, they would also have found the same set of skills and demographics among the convict women.

Convict women, like immigrant women, arrived in New South Wales with potentially useful skills. Advertisements for female workers such as those in Figure 7.11 appeared regularly in the *Sydney Gazette*. Taken collectively, these advertisements indicate the skills in short supply. By 1830, for women who could sew or do washing 'work was plentiful, as the demand for labour exceeded the supply', and employment was growing for housekeepers, nursemaids, kitchenmaids and cooks, laundry workers, other domestics and needlewomen.[54] In June 1833 the Committee of Emigrant Mechanics published an article in several newspapers which was described by William Macpherson (Clerk of the Councils) as 'a pretty correct list of the various descriptions of mechanics and labourers most required in the colony, and of their ordinary rates of wages'.[55] The list had been compiled after several meetings of the committee, and it was considered sufficiently accurate to reappear in the *Sydney Post-Office Directory* and in pamphlet form in London as an essay entitled 'Hints to emigrants' by the Reverend Henry Carmichael. His hints were well received: first published in 1834, this pamphlet subsequently ran into another two editions. The list informed cooks that in the colony they could expect four to six shillings a week plus rations, and that 'nearly every establishment employs them'. Dairywomen would receive between £10 and £12 per annum, their lodgings and rations; these women were 'in extensive demand'. This pay-rate put them on par with much demanded agricultural labourers, shepherds, sheep-shearers and ploughmen. In addition, farmers 'would be certain of employment, as would unmarried country girls, although not thorough servants, if active and willing to learn'. Single domestic servants might earn £8 to £15 in the year, and some employment in this field was even available to married women.[56]

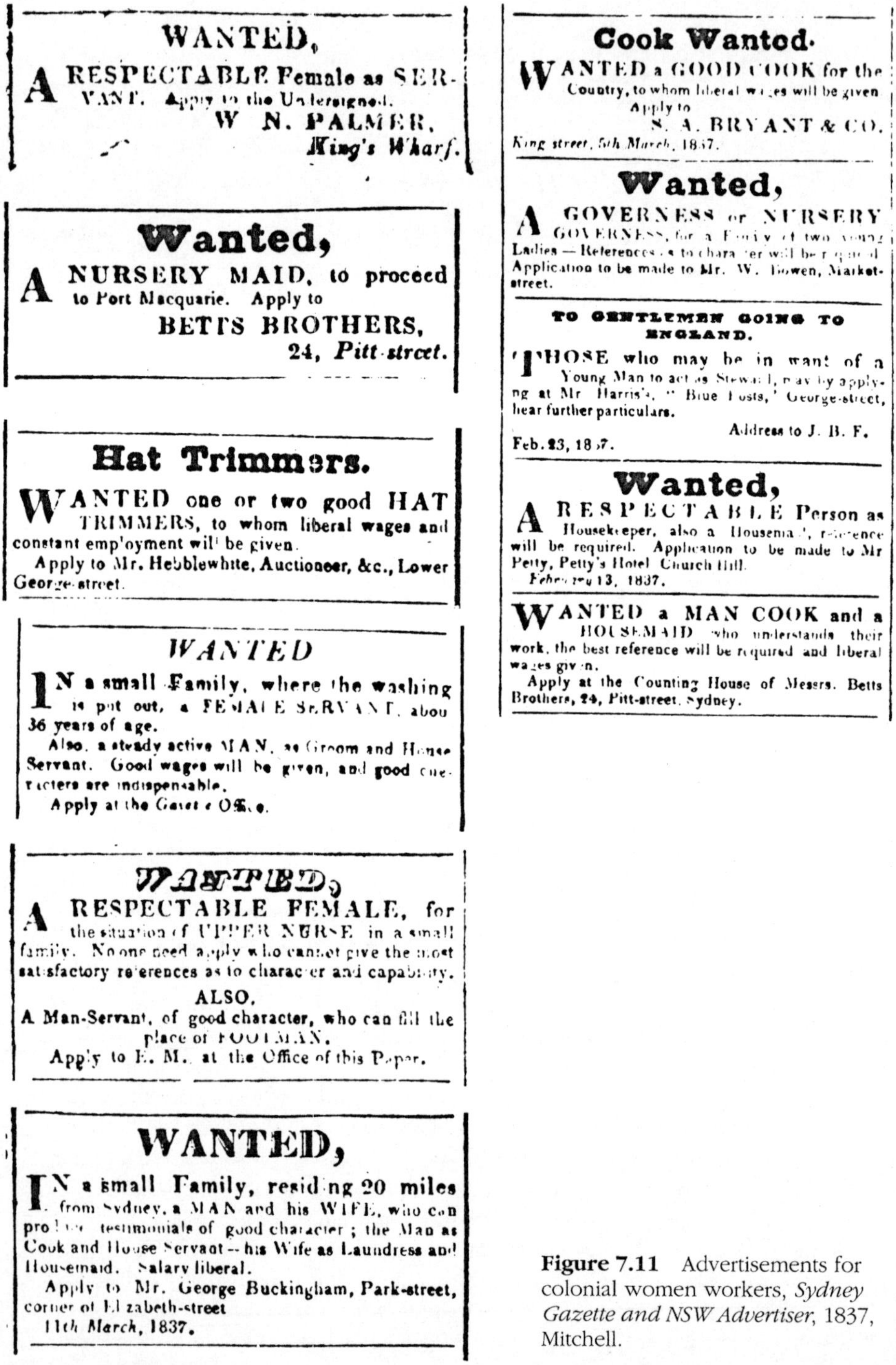

WANTED,

A RESPECTABLE Female as SER-VANT. Apply to the Undersigned.

W. N. PALMER,
King's Wharf.

Wanted,

A NURSERY MAID, to proceed to Port Macquarie. Apply to

BETTS BROTHERS,
24, Pitt-street.

Hat Trimmers.

WANTED one or two good HAT TRIMMERS, to whom liberal wages and constant employment will be given.

Apply to Mr. Hebblewhite, Auctioneer, &c., Lower George-street.

WANTED

IN a small Family, where the washing is put out, a FEMALE SERVANT, about 36 years of age.

Also, a steady active MAN, as Groom and House Servant. Good wages will be given, and good characters are indispensable.

Apply at the Gazette Office.

WANTED,

A RESPECTABLE FEMALE, for the situation of UPPER NURSE in a small family. No one need apply who cannot give the most satisfactory references as to character and capability.

ALSO,

A Man-Servant, of good character, who can fill the place of FOOTMAN.

Apply to E. M. at the Office of this Paper.

WANTED,

IN a small Family, residing 20 miles from Sydney, a MAN and his WIFE, who can produce testimonials of good character; the Man as Cook and House Servant—his Wife as Laundress and Housemaid. Salary liberal.

Apply to Mr. George Buckingham, Park-street, corner of Elizabeth-street

11th March, 1837.

Cook Wanted.

WANTED a GOOD COOK for the Country, to whom liberal wages will be given. Apply to

S. A. BRYANT & CO.
King street, 5th March, 1837.

Wanted,

A GOVERNESS or NURSERY GOVERNESS, for a Family of two young Ladies — References as to character will be required. Application to be made to Mr. W. Bowen, Market-street.

TO GENTLEMEN GOING TO ENGLAND.

THOSE who may be in want of a Young Man to act as Steward, may by applying at Mr Harris's, " Blue Posts,' George-street, hear further particulars.

Address to J. B. F.
Feb. 23, 1837.

Wanted,

A RESPECTABLE Person as Housekeeper, also a Housemaid, reference will be required. Application to be made to Mr Petty, Petty's Hotel Church Hill.

February 13, 1837.

WANTED a MAN COOK and a HOUSEMAID who understands their work, the best reference will be required and liberal wages given.

Apply at the Counting House of Messrs. Betts Brothers, 24, Pitt-street, Sydney.

Figure 7.11 Advertisements for colonial women workers, *Sydney Gazette and NSW Advertiser*, 1837, Mitchell.

Apart from thirty-six Irish 'thorough servants', convict women fitted the bill. Among the transportees there were cooks, dairywomen, farm servants and all sorts: the fifth most common occupation among them was cook; two categories further down the list was dairymaid; many others were country servants, that is, they were 'country girls' who (as noted above) 'would be certain of employment'. And overwhelmingly convict women were those much demanded domestic servants. In keeping with advertisements in the *Sydney Gazette*, there were 1934 housemaids and a further 37 housekeepers; 659 nursemaids and 193 children's maids; 747 kitchenmaids, and 596 cooks. Laundresses numbered 563, teamed with a further 262 laundrymaids and 222 washerwomen, plus an assortment of similar domestic employments and trade skills too. For example, there were 470 needlewomen, 122 dressmakers, 15 sempstresses and 5 women who sewed. The 'Return showing the average wages of mechanics and others, in the town of Sydney, for the six months ended 30th June 1836, and the number required in addition to those already employed', indicated that bakers received an average annual wage with board and lodging of £20, and another thirty-one were needed.[57] Dressmakers and milliners earned £10, board and lodgings, but there was only a shortfall of one in that field.[58] Straw bonnet makers—of whom there was employment for a further seven—received board, lodgings and £12 per annum.[59] Dyers were 'in great demand', as were

---

Government Notice.

COLONIAL SECRETARY'S OFFICE,
SYDNEY, MARCH 6, 1832.

NOTICE is hereby given, that Families who are in want of FEMALE SERVANTS may be supplied from the English Prisoners arrived in the Ship *Pyramus*, from London, provided they apply according to the established Form on or before Tuesday the 13th instant.

Printed Forms for the purpose may be obtained by applying at the Office of the Principal Superintendent of Convicts.

By Command of His Excellency the Governor,
ALEXANDER M'LEAY.

Figure 7.12 Convict women arrivals, *NSW Government Gazette*, 1, 7 March 1832, Mitchell.

Colonial Secretary's Office,
Sydney, 4th October, 1836.

FEMALE EMIGRANTS.

IT is intended that the Female Emigrants by the *Duchess of Northumberland,* shall be lodged in the premises provided for them in the rear of the Government House.   Persons desirous of engaging them are requested to make application to the Committee at Government House, on and after Friday next, at eleven o'clock ; such individuals as may not be known to the Committee producing testimonials of character.

The following Abstract of the Servants arrived, is published for general information.

Cooks	4
Country Servants . .	9
Dairymaids . . .	12
Dress-makers . . .	9
General Servants . .	15
Housekeepers . . .	2
Housemaids . . .	50
Kitchen Servants . .	16
Lady's Maids . . .	3
Laundresses . . .	12
Nursery Governesses . .	1
Nursemaids . . .	32
Staymaker . . .	1
Shopkeeper . . .	1
Waiting-maids . .	2

A few Gardeners and other useful men have also arrived, with their families.

By His Excellency's Command,
ALEXANDER M'LEAY.

Figure 7.13   Female immigrant arrivals, *NSW Government Gazette*, 242, 5 October 1836, Mitchell.

boot-closers; and there was employment to be had for a further sixty-four boot- and shoemakers and another thirty-three places for those specialising in shoes.[60] Upholsterers, weavers, woolspinners, stay-makers, hairdressers, hatters and confectioners were all employed in Sydney in 1836, and were all professions enjoying an excess of demand over supply. Convict women, like free immigrants, arrived already trained in the very skills being sought.

Distributing resources

Nor did the resemblance between free immigrant and convict women end when they disembarked. Perhaps conscious of the demand for these workers, authorities were quick to announce their availability for distribution. Figure 7.12 on the placement of female convicts bears much in common with Figure 7.13 on the distribution of female immigrants. Both announce the arrival of a ship, both emphasise the available female skills, both are dominated by servants, and both invite application from prospective employers. On the other hand, the assignment of convict women differed considerably from that of convict men. The latter was more laborious, and slow. An applicant for a male convict had to meet three criteria: firstly, to own a specific quantity of land; secondly, to be of good character and habits; and thirdly, to demonstrate adequate means of support for maintaining servants.[61] Less formal requirements operated in the case of females. Within certain limitations (request forms had to be submitted and specific procedures complied with), it was a case of help-yourself. With the arrival of every female convict ship—but not a male ship—the *Government Gazette* would publish the standard notice illustrated in Figure 7.12 in which only the details of the vessel changed. The words 'FEMALE SERVANTS' were always prominent in these advertisements.

Apart from choosing a convict at the dock, application could be made to the Female Factory at Parramatta, which housed unassigned convict women. The factory served a variety of functions, as a house of industry and place of secondary punishment, as a lying-in hospital, a marriage market and a labour bureau.[62] Eventually the Hyde Park Barracks would act a bit like the factory, holding and distributing immigrant women workers. Occupants of the factory were divided into three classes: women awaiting assignment belonged to the First Class; the Second Class comprised women returned from assignment as 'unsatisfactory, pregnant or both';[63] and to the Third Class belonged secondary offenders. Treatment, provisions and benefits were awarded depending on class, and an individual's ranking could alter according to how well, or how poorly, she behaved and worked. Class was also intended to influence assignment. The Committee of Management at Parramatta wished to take the

> opportunity of asserting their readiness, at all times, to assign any Female in the Factory, not under a Colonial sentence of imprisonment, to persons of good moral character; and if the supply of those Women, whose conduct offers a fair chance of their becoming useful servants, should at any time be unequal to the demand, the Committee would willingly assign those, of whose conduct it would, at the same time, be their duty to make an unfavourable report.[64]

Assigned convicts were provided with basic necessities from the government stores, providing a public subsidy to private employers. If an assigned convict servant became pregnant or refractory, she could be returned to the factory and exchanged for another one, very much as an item of faulty merchandise might be returned to the shop where purchased for replacement. Women remaining in detention made blankets and manufactured other forms of textiles, particularly the slop clothing worn by male convicts; they also washed, ironed and mended.[65] This was an institution where, according to Brian Fletcher, the 'emphasis was more on profit than welfare'; a harsh place (like its Van Diemen's Land equivalent) where infants died and women laboured in cramped and unpleasant surrounds, threatened with brutal punishments.[66] But the factory did not house a majority of convict women: typically, between two-thirds and four-fifths were in private service.[67] Most of the colony's women had been successfully assigned to private employment, with some considerable alacrity on behalf of both the state and employers.

Virtuous women

All their similarities—age, conjugal status, work experience, ease of access—left immigrant women with one advantage over convicts: their virtuous character. 'Good' women were needed to police the morals of the colony and to foster future generations that would populate and perpetuate the new white society and economy. For too long the convict women had lived with the converse of that stereotype—the damned whore image—to be considered for the role of God's police. Immigrant women were expected to be good, virtuous character being a prerequisite of passage. But free immigrants suffered the stigma of single women 'without male protectors'.[68] The same disparaging terms used to damn convict women were recycled. In particular, criticism was levelled at the immigrant women arriving under the bounty scheme between 1832 and 1836. Women on the *Red Rover* from Ireland in 1832 had been rapidly engaged as domestics and their morality lauded, but the *Princess Royal* which transported English paupers to Hobart Town brought immigrant women into disrepute with claims that it carried a licentious cargo 'far more depraved than the generality of convict women'.[69] The Reverend J. D. Lang reviled the female emigrants who arrived in Sydney in November 1834 on board the *David Scott*, the voyage advertised in the poster in Figure 7.3. He claimed that sixty of the women were prostitutes, forty unrivalled in the degree of their depravity by even the lewdest strumpet in England. In an interesting twist for the convict women, Lang wrote that

> we can recollect the time when, even in this convict colony, such a thing as 'street walking' was unheard of; but, thanks to Mr Marshall, we now vie with the vilest portions of the British metropolis itself in that evidence of advancing civilisation and refinement. No respectable female can now venture to cross any of the streets of Sydney in the evening for fear of being mistaken for one of Mr Marshall's proteges.

And this was the fault of the female immigrants![70] These bitter words come from a man who once described the convict women as profligate.[71] Emigrating Irish female orphans were vilified as 'refractory, insubordinate and extremely troublesome during the passage'.[72] Colonial employers also complained about the appropriateness and quality of incoming women workers. Too many were Irish, too few adequately trained in domestic service and sadly lacking in housekeeping skills, many were too young, and far too many were simply paupers 'brought up from their earliest years in habits inseparable from extreme indigence'.[73] Governor Bourke pursued a contrasting line, arguing that immigrant women were from too high a social class. In 1835 he complained that the women were 'upper female servants, too refined for hard work'.[74] Consistently there were complaints that there were inadequate numbers of (English Protestant) domestic servants.[75]

But colonial complaints should not be accepted without question. Perceptions of immigrant women seem far more negative than was justified. Quite simply, some employers demanded too much and were prepared to contribute too little.[76] Colonial officials viewed critical assessments of the women's work skills with great scepticism, noting 'we may be permitted to observe that the readiness with which the young women in question obtained situations and the wages paid them are scarcely reconcillable [*sic*] with the statement that they are "most unsuitable" to the wants of the colony'.[77] Nor was the rate of placement in employment slow. Positive testimony for the period up until 1838 came from Mr John Marshall, immigration agent responsible for the *David Scott*.

Appearing before the Select Committee on Transportation, he was asked: 'Have you any account of the condition of the emigrants on their arrival?' He answered,

> I believe that I may say that there is no instance where a woman, whose conduct after her arrival was what it should be, found the slightest difficulty in obtaining satisfactory employment ... either very happily circumstanced in service in the colony and, in very numerous instances, that they had married very satisfactorily.[78]

Noticeably, the supposedly bad experience of female immigrant arrivals did not ultimately prevent further attempts to lure out single women.[79] Subsequent policy abandoned attempts to attract lone single servants, opting instead to ensure the women's morality through promoting family migration which included unmarried daughters trained as domestics, and other single women under the protective authority of an adopted family. The outcome was that immigrant women arrived with heterogeneous class backgrounds. But if there was an inability to attract domestic servants, as some would-be employers complained, it was not for want of trying, as the posters have indicated.[80] Failure was not on the demand side. Faced with a supply-side shortage, the forced flow of convict women with appropriate training (many English Protestants), whose labour was readily directed, was all the more important.

Officials tried to attract free immigrants to New South Wales at a time when there was a shortage of convict labour in the colony, especially female labour. Convict women were at all times numerically subordinate to the male influx. The sex balance of immigrants was carefully managed, with women and men arriving in roughly equal proportions. This meant that, in the 1830s, while the vast majority of incoming males arrived in chains, the influx of women was dominated by free immigrants. Immigration promoters embarked on a deliberate and seemingly successful policy of attracting a group of single women much like convict women: young domestic and farm servants, with a smattering of other trades. The flow of female immigrants was intended to numerically supplement an existing supply of labour rather than to introduce hitherto missing skills. If the publicity from the immigration societies indicates the skills in demand in the colony—and this seems a fair assumption, given that demand was meant to be a function of informed colonial opinion—then both free immigrants and female convicts were desirable. Convict and immigrant women were appropriately trained, in an economically productive age group, and largely free from familial 'encumbrances'. On all counts save literacy, convict women scored highest. Pieces of a jigsaw puzzle are starting to fit together. Convict women were not evil malefactors, Britain's worst criminal rejects. Instead they were skilled and semi-skilled workers, as highly educated as the working women they left behind. And yet, they were strangely different from those Irish and English workers, not a representative cross-section. Most noticeably, the legal system failed to transport textile workers. Overwhelmingly, convict women had been trained in that variety of jobs that together comprised domestic service. Britain sent out convict maids. Fortuitously, maids were in demand.

CHAPTER EIGHT

Misconceptions

D isobedient, refractory, untalented, abandoned, vice-ridden creatures, a scourge upon the colony: these were typical representations of convict women (and free immigrant women also). Notwithstanding all their similarities to Irish and English working women, Elizabeth Coltman and company have been miscast as disreputable whores and misrepresented as members of a professional criminal class with a severe disinclination to work, unskilled in all but vice and unfit to contribute to colonial economic development. None of this was true. So why have convict women suffered such poor reputations? Because they have been gravely misunderstood. Convict women's invisibility in our economic history, and their shadowy presence more generally, has resulted from the undue influence exercised by a number of nineteenth-century observers on twentieth-century historical thought, commentators whose value judgements have been inadequately decoded and uncritically accepted. Gazing upon the nineteenth-century world, be it Britain or colonial New South Wales, through the eyes of contemporary social critics presents us with a view cluttered by their agendas, class biases, gendered expectations and experiences. Simply borrowing their vision leaves us accepting their set of values and beliefs. Notions of female depravity and criminal professionalism are the debilitating inheritance, excluding from consideration broader issues of economic assets and employability. But there are alternatives to uncritical acceptance. Sensitivity to their perspective and awareness of their amblyopia enable identification and discounting of subjective statements while retaining more reliable information. (It also gives us insight into the biases convict women had to contend with.) This helps us clarify the scene, peering over their shoulders to gain an independent position. The more shoulders the better. Had Elizabeth Coltman *et al.* left written records, they might have proved an interesting counterbalance to the assessments made of them by middle-class men, but if diaries and letters exist they have so far largely evaded capture.[1] Convict men also left few records. A broader range of opinion can nonetheless be canvassed and we can critique texts already employed.

Understanding why convict women have been so misconceived requires us to puzzle out what value judgements informed these nineteenth-century views and why themes of criminal degeneracy and immorality have so influenced historical thinking.

Colonial estimations

From the very commencement of transportation to New South Wales with the First Fleet that set sail in 1787, the female convicts received what is now widely recognised as a 'bad press'.[2] Why the women were so frowned upon is best answered by looking at the nature of the criticisms. Quotations litter this book, especially in Chapters Three and Four, but a few more examples will add immeasurably to the tenor of the appraisal. Arthur Bowes Smyth was the surgeon on board the First Fleet ship the *Lady Penrhyn*. He was distressed when, within one hour of a storm so ferocious as to have the female convicts on their knees praying for their survival, the women 'were uttering the most horrid Oaths & imprecations that cd. proceed out of the mouths of such abandon'd Prostitutes as they are!'[3] Lieutenant Ralph Clark, another First Fleet surgeon, complained that they were all 'damned whores' who 'the moment that they got below fel a fighting amongst one a nother and Capt. Meridith order the Sergt. not to part them but to let them fight it out.'[4] Clark's revulsion at the women's behaviour was shared by others, and in the nineteenth century this theme continued unabated. Governor Darling was in sympathy, believing transported women to be 'thoroughly abandoned' and of a 'depraved disposition' (although he at least accepted that not all were the same).[5] It will be remembered that Governor Macquarie thought the women a great drawback while Governor Hunter considered convict women to be the source of all evil, the disgrace of their sex.[6] To Thomas Potter MacQueen, a former member of the House of Commons and an Australian magistrate, these women were 'the most disgusting objects that ever disgraced the female form', while Bishop Ullathorne believed 'her general character is immodesty, drunkenness and the most horrible language'.[7] 'Loose, idle habits' marked the women's countenances, according to Alick Osborne, Royal Navy surgeon.[8]

The Select Committee appointed to enquire into transportation was treated to a barrage of abuse against these women articulated by a group of men who were often the employers of convict labour. Appearing before them on 21 April 1837, James Mudie informed the committee that these female miscreants were depraved and morally inferior even to convict men.[9] As an employer of convict women, Mudie could assure the committee, when still testifying on 5 May, that with the exception of only one woman, 'the others were bad beyond anything that you can fancy; some of them are exceedingly savage'.[10] The odd leading question did not go astray. When James Macarthur was asked, 'is it generally found that convict women who are assigned as domestic servants are of the most dissolute character?' his answer did not disappoint them. 'I believe so; ... there is no subject which occasions a greater amount of complaint to the different benches of magistrates than the conduct of the female convict servants. They are, generally speaking, such very bad characters, and so very troublesome'.[11] Lieutenant-Colonel Henry Breton was asked by the committee, 'were they dissolute?' 'Shockingly so; they are drunken, they are everything that is bad'.[12] On the basis of this mounting testimony, Sir William Molesworth, chair of the House of Commons Select Committee, was similarly unimpressed. In his report he denounced these women, declaring that 'at times they are excessively ferocious ... they are all of them, with scarcely an exception, drunken and abandoned prostitutes', words echoing with those given in evidence by Mudie.[13]

A great quantity of the evidence amassed incriminating convict women has been anecdotal, supplied by government officials and religious men attempting to impose authority on people little understood by them. Remarks were made by the women's gaolers, men of the cloth with strict moral codes, and by one other very significant group: employers. Class relations between employer and employee played their part in this discourse on convict women. Colonial New South Wales was an arena where employer and employee battled to establish work relations—a negotiation hardly unique to Australia. In the colony, however, the fight was weighted differently. Labour was scarce, and in demand. Catholic priest William Ullathorne commented in 1838 that

> since the year 1820, so great has been the increase of the number of emigrants and persons born in the colony, who hold property, and whose chief interest it is to have as many convict slaves as possible, because, from their sweat and sufferings the property of the free is enormously increased; that—although the number of criminal convictions is four times more in the year than it was thirty years since—yet the demand for the use of slave convicts in the colonies is now much greater than the three kingdoms, with all their crimes, can supply.[14]

Scarcity of labour was a bargaining point in free societies, but it held less sway in the colony where the state structure—and by extension the employer—had exceptional powers over convict workers. These powers included incarceration for the worker who had a quick tongue, a sharp wit, or a tendency to drink, who was rude, or who affronted a 'superior'. A Chief Justice of New South Wales made the following declaration.

In order to keep the convicts to their duty, they are subjected to a code of laws framed for such a purpose by the local legislature. These laws create a class of offences peculiar to the condition of the convicts—such as drunkenness, disobedience, neglect, absconding from service, abusive language, (to master or overseer) or other disorderly, (or dishonest) conduct—the breach of which is liable to be visited with summary, and in some cases, severe punishment.[15]

Sir George Arthur, Governor of Van Diemen's Land, told the 1837 Select Committee that

the convict is subject to the caprice of the family to which he is assigned, and subject to the most summary laws. He is liable to be sent to a chain gang, or to be scourged for idleness, for insolent words, for insolent looks, or for anything betraying the insurgent spirit.[16]

In spite of the male pronoun, criticisms of this 'giant lottery' were just as applicable to female convicts, although for them getting pregnant also needs to be added to the list of offending actions.

Lieutenant-Colonel Breton illustrated his claim that the women were 'everything that is bad' with the case of a woman who wanted rum for her labour, else she was back off to the Female Factory.[17] The factory may well have been perceived by some women as a place where refuge could be sought away from the dominant culture: a female enclave in a thoroughly male-dominated society. If women used this institution to escape from aggressive male employers, or men more generally, employers used the factory as a method of labour control. The majority of women in residence had not committed further crimes but had been returned for 'bad behaviour', such as drinking, swearing, or otherwise showing disrespect for their employers. Inside they could also be found guilty of disorderly, insolent or disobedient conduct, fighting and quarrelling, idleness and neglect of work, foul language— activities that would incur a loss of privileges. Working-class women found it remarkably easy to affront authority and, although they were not sent on chain gangs, in the factory they were subjected to often gruelling physical punishments, such as the treadmill, for what their employers considered insolence. These women were severely judged by harsh standards. In Britain these standards could not easily be enforced but in the colony they were institutionalised in law, a feature of settlement that did not escape the attention of Ullathorne, or the authorities.[18] S. Marsden, M. Anderson and S. Wright (the Female Factory's Committee of Management), in an article published in the *New South Wales Government Gazette* in May 1832, declared that they had observed, regretfully, how speedily a portion of the Female Convicts assigned from the ship, on their arrival from Europe, are returned to Government, and sent to the Factory at Parramatta ... in many cases, those persons have been returned for awkwardness or misbehaviour which, in free servants, would be noticed by a gentle reproof.[19]

To help remedy this 'injurious practice', the government instituted a penalty of forty shillings to be paid by employers who returned women after less than one month. Significantly, this sort of employer complaint was not restricted to convict maids. As we have seen in Chapter Seven, free female immigrants fell victim to their masters' acerbic tongues. One Irish servant, for example, was considered a very bad sort. She was brought before the magistrate because she insisted on wearing 'patent leather pumps' when working at the washtub![20] (I wonder if they were red.) Immigrant women were quickly labelled whores. This commonality of experience between immigrants and convicts highlights what the real issues were: not criminal professionalism, but class and gender. Women were damned for failing to work according to their masters' and mistresses' expectations.

Just as American plantation owners cannot be relied upon to give objective accounts of their slave workforce, neither can Australian employers be trusted to give accurate assessments of their convict workers. Thwarted expectations led to the condemnatory words of men who held power in the colony, and it is these that have repeatedly returned to haunt the convict women. No doubt, like their menfolk, many upper-class and middle-class women felt similar confusion and abhorrence when confronted by working women—perhaps their own domestic servants— whose behaviour did not conform to the strict code they themselves were meant to adhere to. By and large, however, it was not their offended thoughts that were left to litter the historical literature, but those of their husbands. But we need to ask if the men's expectations were reasonable before accepting their criticisms. Henry Breton's complaints were based on his personal knowledge as a member of the employing class, having 'seen a good deal of them in the employment of my own connexions, many in the same house'.[21] When James Macarthur, a large colonial landholder with a substantial convict labour force, described the female convicts as dissolute, it should be remembered that he was also describing women who worked for him as domestic servants: the women were 'such very bad characters' because they were 'so very troublesome' and because he, like other employers, was engaged in a traditional battle to extract labour which by his own account led him and his fellows regularly to the magistrates' bench.[22] Mudie was in the same boat, demonstrating distaste that his female workers chose to drink, smoke and act disobediently. This was the man, both a master and magistrate, who unremittingly lashed those who were not at work by sunrise, those who fell asleep on the job, and those who were disobedient and insolent by his measure. His brutality towards his convict workers, along with that of his son-in-law John Larnach, was so extreme that it inspired rebellion.[23] For the Irish—the majority of convict women— issues were further complicated by their language. Employer complaints that convict servants were obtuse and unresponsive to orders may have derived from simple misunderstandings as Gaelic speakers failed to grasp the meaning of commands. Employers were disgruntled at working-class morality, resistance and ineptitude, be it the workers' fault or not.

In the case of convict women, social dimensions of class, religion and ethnicity compacted with gender to exacerbate problems. Judged worse than the men, convict women were found guilty of unbecoming behaviour and in some respects this was their quintessential crime. Criticisms were that convict women were depraved, disgusting, ferocious, drunken, dissolute, loose, immodest, earning them disapprobation as abandoned prostitutes. Immoral, licentious, drunken and uncouth, they were more familiar with foul language than with decent womanly deportment. Dissatisfaction with the women was expressed in sexual terminology: they became whores, a metaphorical device distilling all the features that were the obverse of what became the Victorian feminine ideal. Disgracing their sex was a familiar reproach and one also levelled at other criminal women, as will be seen shortly. The cause of this name-calling was a clash of gendered cultural values which left a yawning chasm of misunderstandings between observer and observed, two very different groups. On the one hand were young and often Irish Catholic women (many Gaelic speakers) from the labouring classes who found themselves under coercive penal authority living in a society in which women were a scarce commodity, while on the other hand were English Protestant middle-class men who employed this forced labour, who (perhaps guilt-ridden) engaged in sexual liaisons with convicts, but who still judged convict women's morality and found it wanting.

Men such as those who did comment upon the women convicts would not, by and large, have been used to socialising with working-class women prior to their Australian experience. Many were more at ease in the company of elegant 'ladies', a term signifying not a biological entity but a moral being. These were upper-class and middle-class women of refined wit, 'good breeding', cultured accents, fine clothes, coiffured hair (or wigs), cared-for complexions, who spoke on appropriate subjects with only the correct amount of knowledge, and who, most importantly, shared the same set of values and cultural assumptions; for example, a belief that marriage was a necessary precursor to establishing a family, or that nice women averted their eyes when male strangers were present. There was, in short, a great difference in the cultural capital of convicts and their gaolers. As Marian Aveling has written, 'rather than their sexual morality it was the manners of the women—their demeanour, accent, language, and their deference, or lack thereof—which labelled them as good women or as whores in the eyes of the officers'.[24] Exposure to the female convicts—women of another class at a time when the gulf between the poor and the well-off was substantial and widening—would have been no less than a culture shock. Compounding this was a nearly insurmountable language barrier between English gentlefolk and Gaelic speakers. Some of these vocal males displayed every sign of suffering from a profound inability to come to terms with their situation, some of them repulsed by what they saw and yet simultaneously tempted.

An excellent example of the dilemma between desire and distaste is embodied in the well-cited Lieutenant Ralph Clark. Author of the infamous remark about damned whores, Clark held convict women in very low esteem. Surgeon on board the vessel *Friendship*, Clark joyously ditched the women in his care. 'About 1 oClock Sent the Women convicts away as order thank god that the[y] are all out of the Ship — I am very Glad of it for the[y] wair a great Trouble much more So than the [men]'.[25] He was delighted to exchange his cargo of women for one of sheep, believing of the latter 'we will find them much more agreeable shipmates than the women'.[26] Convict women were considered debased, the mirror-image of women like his beloved wife Betsey-Alicia, mother of his 'beautiful little engaging son', Ralph Clark junior. In his diary he eulogised at great length about Alicia's innocence, purity and goodness, and on Sundays he anointed her portrait with his lips 'a thousand times'. He found her virtues all the more creditable after his exposure to those transported women for whom he had such contempt and in whom he found positive attributes notably absent. Nonetheless, while stationed in the colony at Norfolk Island, Clark took a common-law wife, setting up home with 20-year-old Mary Branham, convict. The daughter born to this match was, curiously, christened Alicia. His fragmentary diary makes no mention of this his other family, nor his own back in Britain during this period. While apparently despising himself on occasions for his illicit involvement, he was neither so bound up by his scruples nor adequately repelled by the convict woman in question to alter his course of action. This internal conflict left Clark an unhappy man, and one whose bitter words hung in the air heavily and insistently, injuring the reputations of many.[27]

Gender differences also acted in other ways to create misunder-standings and misrepresentations. Arthur Bowes Smyth, mentioned earlier, was the surgeon on board another First Fleet vessel, *Lady Penrhyn*, and was thus responsible for the 109 women convicts that it carried. He described the women in particular, and the men incidentally, thus. After favourably outlining the food and medical provisions that had been made for the convicts, he stated:

> I wish I cd. with truth add that the behaviour of the Convicts merited such extream indulgence — but I believe I may venture to say there was never a more abandon'd set of wretches collected in one place at any period than are now to be met with in this Ship in particular & I am credibly informed the comparison holds wt. respect to all the Convicts in the fleet. The greater part of them are so totally abandoned & callous'd to all sense of shame & even of common decency that it frequently becomes indispensably necessary to inflict Corporal punishment upon them, and sorry I am to say that even this rigid mode of proceeding has not the desired Effect, since every day furnishes proofs of their being more harden'd in their Wickedness.[28]

To what proofs does Bowes Smyth refer? He continued:

> Nor can their matchless Hippocracy be equalled except by their base Ingratitude; many of them plundering the Sailors, (who have at every Port they arrived at spent almost the whole of the wages due to them in purchasing different Articles of wearing apparel & other things for their accommodation) of their necessary clothes & cutting them up for some purpose of their own—.[29]

'Some purpose', I wager, being rags to stem the flow of menstrual blood. It is somewhat surprising that a man like Bowes Smyth, with a considerable experience of midwifery, should have been so apparently unaware of the other aspects of the female reproductive system.[30] He considered provisions to be admirable, in spite of the absence of any rags or such like for menstruating women, and then criticised these women—seemingly out of ignorance—when they attempted to find their own solution to the shortage. For this they were abused as being ingrates beyond redemption. Bowes Smyth despaired, 'nor do I conceive it possible in their present situation to adopt any plan to induce them to behave like rational or even human Beings'.[31] On top of this, the women were badly regarded because of the language that they used: 'The Oaths & imprecations they daily make use of in their common conversation & little disputes with each other by far exceeds anything of the kind to be met wt. amongst the most profligate wretches in London'.[32] One wonders how much experience such a man would have had of London's profligates upon which to make his comparison. His assessment of colonial life was perhaps inevitable. 'The Anarchy & Confusion wh. prevails throughout the Camp, & the Audacity of the Convicts both Men & Women, is arrived to such a pitch as is not to be equalled, I believe, by any set of Villains in any other Spot upon the globe'.[33] A tradition of misunderstanding and misrepresenting women convicts thus began with the First Fleet, arising from cultural and gender differences.

Ultimately, the outcome of this cataclysmic contact between working-class women and middle- and upper-class men in colonial New South Wales was in the latter expressing their failure to grasp the cultural and economic differences which existed between them (and which were manifest in forms of worker resistance and even in clothes, complexion, etc.) in vitriolic attacks that then remained to be misinterpreted by historians. If the women had left written records, one wonders what portraits they might have painted of these nineteenth-century men! However, no person's comments should ever have been taken at face value and treated as evidence of life as it was. Comments such as those made by colonial employers, gaolers and clergy are evidence, but of something other than simply the objective world: class and gender biases and different cultural practices. The oft-quoted comment made by the colonist James Mudie is a very telling one. He dismissed the women as depraved whores, but not because they supported themselves by selling sex. Mudie chose his words carefully when he described the women convicts as 'the lowest possible ... they all smoke, drink and in fact, to speak in plain language, I consider them all prostitutes'.[34] Some of them had even attended the theatre! Convict women were damned because they did not behave like ladies nor sober workers and because they failed to adhere to Mudie's value system. They got drunk, they smoked, they gazed back, and they spoke in lewd ways their critics thought reserved for men. Or at least, some of them did. For this, they were all labelled whores.

Criminal classes and bad women

Significantly, descriptions of female convict depravity did not differ markedly from descriptions of other criminal women held in British gaols. Harlotry and criminality were closely entwined. Journalists Henry Mayhew and John Binny were 'rather inclined to connect female criminality with unchastity'.[35] Further,

> if it could be possible to obtain accurate returns as to the number of 'public women' throughout the country, it would be found that by far the greater proportion of the female offenders is derived from that class; and thus it would be proven, that among the chaste portion of the female sex crime is comparatively unknown.[36]

How they could reach their conclusion in the absence of such returns is a mystery, and flies in the face of the evidence they did possess. The matron from the female prison at Millbank made the following claim: 'The women are mostly in for common larcenies, and many of them have been servants; some have been gentlemen's servants, and a good number have been farm servants; but the fewest number are, strange to say, of the unfortunate class in the streets.' The warder concurred, 'Yes, not a great many of them come here'.[37] (Perhaps because it was better paid.) Apparently Mayhew and Binny found it inadequately strange to disconcert them. Consistent with convict rhetoric, being criminal put women's sexual behaviour and femininity on the line.

In 1866 an anonymous contributor (revealed from accounts payable to be Mrs M. E. Owen) felt it incumbent upon herself to notify the readership of the *Cornhill Magazine* of the following.[38]

> Criminal women, as a class, are found to be more uncivilised than the savage, more degraded than the slave, less true to all natural and womanly instincts than the untutored squaw of the North American Indian tribe ... From the mass of evil habits that these women have accumulated, it is not easy to select illustrations that shall convey a vivid impression to the reader's mind. As a class they are guilty of lying, theft, unchastity, drunkenness, slovenliness. To finish the picture, it may be added, they are ignorant, so obtuse, that instruction might as well be given in an unknown tongue, so little do they understand it. Lying may be said to be their native language.[39]

Prison reformer Joseph John Gurney, the man who so disparaged London's criminal women as filthy and disgusting 'scum', found the women incarcerated in Newgate Prison 'ignorant to the greatest degree, not only of religious truth, but of the most familiar duty and business of life'.[40]

Female criminals and female transportees shared other attributes: criminal women who sinned were more degenerate than criminal men. Major Arthur Griffiths, an Inspector of Prisons and one-time Deputy Governor of Millbank Prison, had this to say:

> It is a well-established fact in prison logistics that the women are far worse than the men. When given to misconduct they are far more persistent in their evil ways, more outrageously violent, less amenable to reason or reproof ... No doubt when a woman is really bad, when all the safeguards, natural and artificial, with which they have been protected are removed, further deterioration is sure to be rapid when it once begins.[41]

Mrs Owen continued:

> Again, it is notorious that a bad man—we mean one whose evil training has led him into crime—is not so vile as a bad woman. If we take a man and woman guilty of a similar offence in the eye of the law, we shall invariably find that there is more hope of influencing the former than the latter. Equally

criminal in one sense, in another sense there is a difference. The man's nature may be said to be hardened, the woman's destroyed. Women of this stamp are generally so bold and unblushing in crime, so indifferent to right and wrong, so lost to all sense of shame, so destitute of the instincts of womanhood, that they may be more justly compared to wild beasts than to women. To say the least, the honour of womanhood requires that a new appellation be invented for them.[42]

Like convicts, these women 'disgraced' their sex.

What bad behaviour did the criminal women of Britain indulge in to lead to this characterisation of utter abandonment? One example of their misconduct was to be found on entering Newgate Prison. 'On all sides the ear was assailed by awful imprecations, begging, swearing, singing, fighting, dancing, dressing up in men's clothes'.[43] Arthur Griffiths was horrified. Such behaviour was unfeminine, and there is the hint of Mrs Owen's wild beast metaphor when it came to begging. 'All visitors were clamorously attacked for alms, the wretched prisoners struggling wildly to get foremost and nearer the bars that parted them from the public, or stretching forth their wooden spoons, tied to the end of long staves, to collect the money. So great was the lawlessness …'.[44] The historian Peter Linebaugh noted the value-laden descriptions made by nineteenth-century men. James Guthrie, one-time Ordinary of Newgate, expounded upon 'the stupidity and hardness of these unthinking and miserable creatures'—the women and men in his cells—because they 'behaved very undecently, laughed and seemed to make a mock of everything that was serious and regular', by which he meant his sermons. One woman, Ann Mudd, 'used to sing obscene songs, and talked very indecently'. Another prisoner—a man—'was a very profane, unthinking hearer, for he could not abstain from laughing', and yet another individual was reproved for having 'a smiling countenance'.[45] American Quakers visiting Newgate Prison in 1813 were 'shocked and sickened … by the blaspheming, fighting, dram-drinking, half-naked women'.[46]

Similarly, when Mayhew enquired about the 'incorrigibles' brought down from Brixton, the warder from Millbank responded that these 'were the very worst women in existence. I don't fancy their equal could be found anywhere'.[47] Why this assessment? Because these women were guilty of singing, dancing, whistling and of using profane language—even in the punishment cells. The following interchange was recorded at length by Mayhew and Binny.

'That's one of the women under punishment who's singing now,' said the matron, and we stood still to listen. 'They generally sing. Oh! *that's* nothing—that's very quiet for them. Their language to the minister is sometimes so horrible, that I am obliged to run away with disgust.'

'Some that we've had,' went on the matron, 'have torn up their beds. They make songs themselves all about the officers of the prison. Oh! they'll have every one in the verses—the directors, the governor, and all of us.' She then repeated the following doggerel from one of the prison songs:—' "If you go to Millbank, and you want to see Miss Cosgrove, you must inquire at the round house;"—and they'll add something I can't tell you of.'

We went down stairs and listened to the woman in the dark cell, who was singing 'Buffalo Gals,' but we could not make out a word—we could only catch the tune ...

The matron now led us into a double cell, containing an iron bed and tressel. Here the windows were all broken, and many of the sashes shattered as well. This had been done by one of the women with a tin pot, we were informed.

'What is this, Miss Cosgrove?' asked the warder, pointing to a bundle of sticks like firewood in the corner.

'Oh, that's the remains of her table! And if we hadn't come in time, she would have broken up her bedstead as well, I dare say.' ...

'Some of our best-looking women are among the worst behaved of all the prisoners in the female ward,' says the matron.[48]

Other women had torn their own clothes, and yet others had the audacity to look a man—like Mayhew—full in the face, and in the schoolroom too. 'As we glanced along the three rows of white caps, there was not one abashed face or averted tearful eye to be seen, whilst many grinned impudently on meeting our gaze'.[49] Women were damned for not living up to expectations of polite and remorseful female behaviour, and the conclusion was reached about London's female prisoners that their 'most striking peculiarity ... is that of utter and imperturbable shamelessness'.[50]

Arthur Griffiths believed that criminal women could be made to behave in an even worse manner through poor conditions, concluding that such privations were wrong, that they could be righted, but that the depravity of the female prisoners could not be. They were essentially bad. Newgate, whence his earlier observation was drawn, was indeed 'a perfect sink of abomination'.[51] Three hundred women—tried, untried, felons and misdemeanants—plus their children were crammed altogether into 190 square yards of space, without beds, cooking on the floor where they slept, many half-naked or in rags.[52] Yes, the prison reformer Mrs Elizabeth Fry and her associates from the Society for the Reformation of Female Prisoners had the effect of improving these outward signs of depravity, having replaced

drunkenness, ferocity, and abandoned licentiousness by sober decency of demeanour; loud ribaldry and oaths by silence or edifying talk; squalor and semi-nudity by cleanliness and sufficiency in attire; to convert a den of wild beasts, where only filth, disgusting odours, and all abominations reigned, into a happy home of quiet and decorum'.[53]

But, he believed, Newgate was so awful that anything had to be an improvement, and such achievements were necessarily transitory. Women of the ladies' association were duped by the outward and 'most depraved and hypocritical' display of good behaviour put on by criminal women who momentarily hid their 'evil natures, which still rankled like hidden sores beneath'.[54]

How did he know this? Again the answer lay with the behaviour displayed whilst incarcerated. He described Mary McCarthy as 'a most artful, designing woman' because of her repeated attempts 'to destroy herself'.[55] Repeated attempts at suicide, self-mutilation and starvation, along with the use of 'dreadful' language, led Ann Williams' demeanour to be described as showing 'strongly of artifice' for which the doctor recommended punishment: a bread and water diet.[56]

For Griffiths, the most fascinating case—and the one that received his greatest attention at twenty pages, and his greatest damnation—was that of Julia St Clair Newman. Of all these 'very desperate characters' held in the confines of the penitentiaries, none were worse than Miss Newman, whose case, the reader is informed, can be taken 'as a type of the whole' (something of a contradiction).[57] In Millbank Prison, Julia Newman's history was one of repeated offences. Initially, these were her persistent attempts to gain writing materials with which to communicate with her mother (gaoled along with Julia but held separately) and to pass letters on via other prisoners. Throughout her offences Julia displayed a desire to free her mother, and to communicate with her. For these crimes she was persistently punished.

She continued in making 'clandestine writings' and invited disaster with 'a long and critical examination of the young Queen, who had just come to the throne'.[58] She further proved her immorality to the satisfaction of her gaolers through the destruction of property, by 'manifesting contempt of authority', through 'the frightful and horrible imprecations she uttered', and by singing, particularly little ditties about the infirmary warder Mrs King:

> What a pity hell's gates are not kept by dame King,
> So surly a cur would let nobody in.[59]

The primary reason the authorities were annoyed with Julia Newman changed over time, as her crime altered from one of letter-writing to 'trying it on' or 'doing the barmy'—feigning lunacy.[60] Evidence that she was pretending was weak. Attempted mutilation of herself (such as blackening her own eyes), violent tempers, refusal to eat, stating that she wished to be dead, attempting to hang herself on several occasions, and—most annoying to the authorities—indifference to punishment, all earned her repeated spells in the dark cell and in the straitjacket. Other mechanical devices aimed at restraining her were also tried; all fell victim to her amazing ability to dismantle and destroy. Various punishments were inflicted and none succeeded in bringing her to her senses or, more aptly, to the sensibilities of her gaolers. Mr Nihil, who was in charge of Millbank, had only one fear regarding this case, and that was that 'her own self-abandonment to violence may superinduce real madness, and then it will be said that our system at the Penitentiary had driven her out of her mind'.[61] Neither Nihil nor Griffiths wanted to countenance the possibility that it *was* the severity of the prison system that drove one woman to 'beat herself violently' and another to attempt 'to dash her brains out by striking her head violently against the wall'.[62] Rather, this conduct merely confirmed their belief that these women were the 'dregs of society', 'England's social sewage' and that Julia Newman was simply a 'violent and obstinate girl'.[63] It would be interesting to know if male prisoners were assessed as bad by these same criteria.

As with Australia's transportees, the reputation of criminal women in nineteenth-century Britain as depraved and disgusting was founded on behaviour such as singing, smiling, begging, dressing up in men's clothes, wanting to write to their mothers, or trying to kill themselves. More particularly, then, this reputation was founded on an interpretation of women's actions made by critics from a different class with no common experiential knowledge and perilously little understanding of their subjects' position. It is unlikely that the women themselves perceived singing or the desire to eat as fundamentally immoral. Different motives can be ascribed. Attempted suicide, for example, might be taken as evidence of emotional instability or extreme desolation at an intolerable situation, rather than as a method of irritating authorities. Self-mutilation is now known to be caused by such factors as distress: people, like other animals, turn upon themselves when caged and distraught.

It is interesting to note that a more lenient and sympathetic view of criminals prevailed among some of those individuals who had the greatest dealings with criminal women and who, as the following quotation will reveal, attested to their superior knowledge. A book was ghost-written by Frederick William Robinson for a long-time matron at the women's prison at Millbank. She was at pains to note that

> I am not alone in my conviction that these stories of erring and mistaken women—fallen sisters, but still sisters, whom we have no right to cast aside or shrink away from—do in many cases prove that there is no estate so low but

that the elements of the better nature are existent, and still struggling for the light.

Furthermore, she insisted,

> let me state that it is the humble officers of our female convict prisons that have the greatest—nay, the only—opportunity of estimating the true character of those whom they may have in charge ... The matrons are in constant communion with the prisoners; seeing them not for a few minutes each in a daily or weekly inspection, but passing their lives in their midst ... And of that better side to prison character which a matron has the greatest chance of observing, of that evidence of affection for some kind officer who has listened to some little story, in impulsive moments, about a mother, sister, brother, or child they loved once, the great report books utter not a word ... The report books bristle with statistics ... but of the life within the outward life that Blue Books speak of, and concerning which Parliament debates, there are no records kept.[64]

Indeed, if this matron had not recorded her thoughts on the matter, what total absence of evidence might cheat historians into erroneous beliefs? This matron did serve her duty to posterity, but even so, the historiography regarding female convict origins and characters rarely, if ever, uses testimony such as this.

Equally underplayed is that evidence compiled by socially superior women like the prison reformer Elizabeth Fry. Mrs Fry perceived criminal women as redeemable. Treated humanely, these 'poor women' would respond well and this was the great hope that transportation permitted. Under the auspices of Mrs Fry, women from the Society for the Reformation of Female Prisoners visited convict women on board their transport ships awaiting exile. Kind words fell on receptive ears, Mrs Fry assured the Select Committee on Secondary Punishments, and tales of 'the most dreadful iniquity, confusion, and frequently great distress' were replaced by ones of loyalty, love, and 'remarkable improvement'. Then was cited a litany of quotations from colonial sources providing testimony to the moral and behavioural improvement of women transported to Australia.[65] On the voyage, the women's deportment was 'exemplary', they 'evinced habits of industry' and were 'greatly improved'; in the colony, they 'turned out particularly well', with their labour in demand and many marrying.[66] Reformation was the informative philosophy. Presented with such evidence, the Select Committee were convinced, and in 1832 their report declared that it was the 'abandoned prostitute' and

> destitute female who, having neither friends nor home, has no alternative but a return to evil courses ... [and] should invariably be sent to New South Wales,

where, females being in great demand as servants by the settlers, the temptation to relapse into crime from the impossibility of obtaining employment, would be avoided, and the best chance of reformation afforded of which their situation is susceptible.[67]

Active engagement in prison life had bred empathetic views among some women from varied classes, and for their sympathies men like Griffiths considered them dupes.[68] That so little credence has subsequently been given to these female opinions suggests Griffiths was not alone in his thinking.

Criminal classes and antithetical values

Derogatory assessments of criminal women were part of a profoundly influential nineteenth-century discourse on the so-called criminal class, conceived as an organised group of professional prostitutes and outlaws choosing to live exclusively off immoral earnings. It is true that in nineteenth-century Britain there were criminals. Undoubtedly, too, in a setting of diminishing employment opportunities and increasing poverty there were many prostitutes supplying male demand for paid sex. There would also have been some professional lawbreakers who succeeded in making a living out of crime. But there was neither the number of criminals, the scale of crime, the imputed reasons and benefits encouraging an illegal lifestyle, nor the level of organisation necessary to constitute a criminal *class*. From the research undertaken here in *Convict Maids* and by British historians it appears that criminals did not form a unique group in these terms: they were largely workers who on occasion stole or robbed. Nor were systems of detection and prosecution adequately efficient to select such offenders even if they had existed. Yet such a class was created, at the level of myth. The criminal class was an ideological creation of some considerable force. A group of 'moral entrepreneurs' conjured up the threat posed by this imagined grouping of recidivists in their battles to increase police forces, modify systems of prosecution and punishment, change laws, alter welfare provisions, and in a host of other goals which if achieved would enhance the standing and political positions of their protagonists: Patrick Colquhoun, Edwin Chadwick, William Augustus Miles, Henry Mayhew, to name but a few.[69]

Part of the *raison d'être* of Mayhew's work on *London Labour and the London Poor*, for example, was to inform the reading population of working-class suffering and exploitation in England's great metropolis.[70] His work was also concerned with drawing a distinction: between the good and honest worker, and the shirker who deserved the contempt hitherto showered on the working class as a whole. Previously, the two categories had been conflated, and the former tainted by its association with the latter. When, in the 1750s, the author and magistrate Henry Fielding wrote of the ills besetting the London poor as 'the destruction of all morality, decency and modesty; the swearing, whoredom and drunkenness which is eternally carrying on in these houses ... and the excess of poverty and misery of most of the inhabitants', he was not referring to a small and isolated minority, but to the working classes more generally.[71] The term 'poor' had wide application. Definitions of class in this earlier period were marked by a considerable degree of fluidity, and 'poor', 'lower', 'working' seemed quite interchangeable prefixes. There was considerable justification for this identity of poverty with working-class experience (although not with the criticisms laid): the majority of workers were poor. In 1780 Arthur Young, farmer and traveller, claimed that eight million out of England's population of nine million were poor, and more recently R. B. Schwartz has suggested that some three-quarters of London's population in the early nineteenth century fell into that category.[72] However, during the century terminology underwent change, redefining 'poor' as a narrow band operating only at the margins.[73] Mayhew was part of this ongoing refinement of the definition of class.

Mayhew bought redemption from unjust criticism for the honest worker, in part, by accepting that criticism belonged elsewhere, in the province of a criminal class. Disapprobation had merely been indiscriminate and misdirected. On the one hand were the honest workers and 'deserving poor', and on the other a small and criminal element—some the 'undeserving poor'—comprised of indolent shirkers who preferred crime to work. Mary Carpenter, too, had created the 'dangerous classes' in contradistinction to the 'perishing classes': it was only the latter for whom assistance was both warranted and demanded by Christian duty.[74] If, as Stephen Garton suggests, 'under the Poor Law of the 17th century, criminality was a type of poverty', then under the dominant ideology of the nineteenth century, poverty was a type of crime.[75] Mayhew declared, 'I am anxious that the public should no longer confound the honest, independent working men with the vagrant beggars and pilferers of the country; and that they should see that the one class is as respectable and worthy, as the other is degraded and vicious'.[76] Cleaving off one group from the other was a necessary step in implementing more standardised mechanisms of welfare if they were to be popularly introduced and financed, in terms acceptable to landowners (taxpayers) and dominant work values. By constructing crime as the preserve of the criminal class, the working classes could be freed from stigma.

While Mayhew was critical of inadequate working conditions and rewards, his rhetoric helped to create the criminal—like the 'undeserving' poor—as 'other', obscuring the connection between inadequate wages, intermittent employment, poverty and crime. Charles Darwin unwittingly summed up the threat such knowledge would have posed, commenting that, 'if the misery of our poor be caused not by the laws of nature, but by our institutions, great is our sin', for institutions are made by humans and can therefore be remade.[77] Denying the link between work and poverty that suggested a structural flaw in the mode of production helped undermine criticism and resistance. How much safer and politically expedient for those in power (employers and the like) if people believed that the poor were poor because they chose to be, rather than because their wages were insufficient to live on or their employment intermittent and seasonal. How much less threatening if criminals committed offences because they were the scum of the earth, rather than because they needed food, because they resented and rebelled against their loss of customary rights on common lands, or because unofficial employment perks could be re-termed illegal acts at the whim of an employer. It was almost a policy of divide and conquer.

Reversing that same coin, the creation of a class of others who need not be defended furnished the possibility of others who might be actively despised. As with social welfare, crime and criminality provided an arena which allowed for the clear articulation of hegemonic values. Importantly, as noted by Clive Emsley, 'crime is not, and never was, confined to one social class, yet middle-class offenders were not included among the criminal class'.[78] Rhetoric was about workers, not criminals. Designed in the minds of these moral entrepreneurs, the criminal class embodied all that was unacceptable in the industrial working classes. Industrialisation, urbanisation, modernisation brought massive changes in what was required of workers. A tricky transformation was under way, guiding individuals away from pre-industrial rural lifestyles. Previously, work, leisure and family life melded, all governed by the daily passage of the sun and overarched by seasonal events, and welfare was a right; now, a new system of industrial labour employed individuals according to fluctuating demands determined they knew not where, for regimented hours on unfamiliar machines, sometimes paid by the piece but nearly always required to live in urban centres and to satisfy their wants via the marketplace, with entitlements to welfare limited to those indisputably unable to work. Monumental transitions such as these brought conflict and tested employers' abilities to overcome entrenched social practices.[79] It was within this context that there emerged imperatives to label old practices as dysfunctional and wrong, while sanctioning and celebrating the new. Juxtaposed to the good worker was an evil criminal class created in contradistinction to capitalist production, its social organisation and values; this class epitomised all that was antipathetical to the emerging industrial society of urban England. Mayhew and others made it clear: the criminal class, and all it was designed to stand for, was to be feared and hated by rich and poor alike.

Appropriating the words of Lieutenant-Colonel Breton, criminals embodied everything that was bad. Consider the stereotype of the criminal class. The 1839 Royal Commission on the Constabulary found the suggestion that crime was linked with unemployment and poverty 'disproved at every step'; it commented disparagingly that criminals rejected legitimate work, preferring to succumb to 'the temptations of the profit of a career of depredation'.[80] Writing in the nineteenth century when a wave of crime was feared to be engulfing the country (particularly the metropolis), Mary Carpenter drew attention to the 'dangerous classes ... notoriously living by plunder,- who unblushingly acknowledge that they can gain more for the support of themselves and their parents by stealing than by working'.[81] As with most classes, gender acted to stratify the criminal class, and women belonged there not for their illegal activities, but for their sexual impropriety. As early as the seventeenth century, Thomas Dekker denounced criminals because 'the Devil is their tutor, Hell their school, thieves' roguery and whoredom the arts they study'.[82]

Throughout an extensive literature, the criminal class was created as the antithesis of an equally stylised and honourable working class; the imputed dominant values of one were anathema to the other. Use of the term 'class' was pivotal. Class denotes a relationship to the means of production, and the ideologically-created and gender-stratified criminal class bore a unique relationship to those means; it was placed outside the accepted class structure, its members neither capitalists nor workers (not even intermittent ones) but professional criminals. Distinct from the other classes of society, this criminal element was entirely parasitical. It threatened. Illegal acts were nearly the exclusive preserve of organised professional criminals, dedicated to offending; they were motivated by greed, the desire for an easy life, and their own failure to adopt appropriate values of hard work, dedication, abstemiousness and sobriety. Criminals were guilty of rebellion, unwillingness to work and disrespect for authority. The mythical members of this criminal substratum were unfamiliar with morality, villains who even rejected the King's English and who denied and threatened the integrity of private property.[83] Brought up badly by parents who failed to teach appropriate values, in turn they made poor parents themselves.

Which persons found certain characteristics to be desirable or not remained implicit in this discourse, although naturally it was the author of any given piece. Invariably, these values promoted industrial work practices and a system based on private property, and consistency was maintained when it came to the gender order. A new order was struggling to emerge, in which women and femininity were being reconstructed as entities belonging to a realm outside wage labour. The emerging 'feminine ideal' was defined in strict middle-class and patriarchal terms, involving a prescription for the good woman of not only sexual and moral purity but also female supplication, subordination and economic dependence to be maintained within the limited confines of the domestic realm. Idle, modest, monogamous marriage partners who might ensure genetic lines for the transmission of private property were the objects of praise.[84] While such values might be essentially middle class—working-class women would always participate in paid labour of some sort—they were nonetheless culturally active, pervading the literature. Importantly—and in contrast with convict men—in the antithetical light cast by the criminal-class theorem, convict women would not be damned for failing to work but precisely for doing so, particularly at the point where their labours entered the paid sector as prostitutes. Prostitutes were caught between this public morality and public demand in a period when the classic double standard was held vehemently. Through the dominant ideology the prostitute was constructed as aberrant, as an immoral entity rather than as an economic agent. Whoredom became the symbol representing the opposite of the feminine ideal. Once it has been realised that the language used to define the female convicts and other aberrant women—argot such as 'damned whores', 'abandoned women', 'prostitutes'—was not necessarily a description of a woman who sold sex, but was in fact an expression of morality and power, then that language can be deconstructed and reread to reveal the morality and power structure which produced it. A whore was a woman who had violated the moral code of the observer. The condemnation of convict women as immoral whores fed into a wider narrative in which women who 'erred' were described in similar terms intended to have negative connotations. If the essence of femininity was the 'angel at the hearth', the residue of rejected elements was poured into the 'damned whore'.

A domestic servant was particularly prone to be stigmatised as licentious, both because her employment was often predicated upon her remaining unwed and thus limiting her to informal relationships, and because she was an easy target for the sexual advances and sexual attacks of men in her master's family or employ. These men, having seduced or raped her, then proceeded to condemn her as a whore for not adhering to middle-class and implicitly correct cultural practice which dictated that women did not have sex outside formal marriage.[85] A related example is the class conflict which arose over the status of informal weddings, a battle being fought bureaucratically with legislation attempting to compel workers into legally recognised unions.[86] Church marriages were at this time simply irrelevant to many people, and many from the working classes married informally by exchanging vows in front of family and peers. Consequently, when viewed by members of another social group who valued church marriages and certification more highly, working-class coupling appeared as informal and immoral. Social superiors considered such women no better than prostitutes, whereas with the sanctity of formal marriage their morality would have been secured. It was this logic which had informed Samuel Marsden's infamous calculation regarding concubines, a fact recognised by Michael Sturma and Portia Robinson, as noted in the Introduction.

In Britain, other working women also found censure expressed in terms of immorality. Even when criticism was completely unrelated to matters sexual, when it was the actual work performance or even work-place that was being scrutinised, the language used was that of sexual impropriety. Disapproval was easy to earn within the ascendant feminine ideal of Victorian England which was so proscriptive of women's behaviour. Any woman who stepped outside the domestic realm left a certain security behind: on one side of the threshold stood the good woman, on its other the bad. A new obsession was with unrelated women and men working alongside each other. The outcome of hetero-sexual employment was thought necessarily to lead to immorality, 'no other result could accrue'.[87] Mining provides one example. So intense was the obsession with working girls' morality that tales of gross exploitation of women workers down coal mines led Subcommissioner Symons, enquiring into the state of this industry, not to draw parallels with slavery or some other such harsh labour system, but to liken the pits to a brothel. In so doing, given negative attitudes held about prostitutes, he effectively shifted the burden of guilt from the perpetrator to the victim (a technique known to psychologists as projection). The women were deemed a disgrace. Immorality perceived to arise from women doing paid work, either in the proximity of men or in competition with them, was thus expressed in terms intended to denote sexual depravity and fuelled the dual moves to exclude women from the paid workforce and to concentrate them in selected all-female tasks.

Nor is it accidental that 'inappropriate' female employment should have been intertwined not only with immorality and loss of femininity, but with criminality also. In the nineteenth century Samuel Redgrave linked criminality to aspects of female employment. Redgrave was the Criminal Registrar in the Home Office, responsible for preparing the annual official 'Returns of Criminal Offenders'. He wrote, 'the greatest proportion of female commitments has taken place in those counties where females are employed in the rudest and most unfeminine labours'.[88] In 1849 another social critic expressed this complementary view and causal explanation. Jelinger C. Symons wrote in his treatise entitled *Tactics for the Times*, as regards the condition and treatment of the dangerous classes that

> so true is it that the extremes of vice as well as virtue co-exist in the female character ... Of the criminal classes in England there can be little doubt that the criminal mind is quite as strong in women as in men. The lesser number of female offences arises, it is to be feared, chiefly from their lesser power rather than their better disposition. This view derives confirmation from the fact, that wherever women are much employed in masculine pursuits which tend to increase their power and opportunities of committing offences, the proportion of female to male offenders increases.[89]

As we have already noted, Mayhew and Binny did not concur but believed criminality to be caused by unchastity 'rather than "rude" employment among women'.[90] Unchastity, and hence criminality by this equation, was a feature others associated with the less-rude feminine labours of domestic service. Immorality, criminality, and paid female employment made an unholy tripartite alliance.

Women who were labelled as whores had, in their own way, offended by stepping outside the sphere defined for them by the dominant ideology: a woman stigmatised as 'abandoned' might be a wife in all but the legal sense of the word, a worker in a mixed-sex environment, a woman living beyond the direct control of a male guardian, even a sex worker. What they all had in common was disapproval conferred upon them because they had violated some moral code. Most certainly, a woman who had threatened the sanctity of private property through thieving would fall into this category. Even if convict women in the colony forsook drink, gambling and the theatre—the charges levelled by Mudie—and became diligent workers, they were still tarred with the same brush. In breaking the legal code they had offended morally and were at once beyond redemption, all of them, with scarcely an exception, being considered abandoned prostitutes. As Portia Robinson noted, the very fact 'that they *were* criminal women meant, to contemporaries, that they were also degraded, vicious, depraved and dissolute whores'.[91] Views such as these were not held by all members of society, but certainly by many critics who found the female convicts an exciting subject for comment.

The practice was to transport women and men who had violated the sanctity of private property, but it was more than this. As indicated by the quotation from the Reverend Sydney Smith at the beginning of this book, transportation was created as an education, to teach the arts of self-discipline, control and gender relations. Similarly, in the following century Douglas Hay identified the criminal law as an ideological system which 'contributed to the maintenance of order and deference'.[92] This educational feature was no less true of criminal mythology. The theory crystallised in the term 'criminal class' represented emergent values as appropriate, and thus functioned to promote them. Intended to be despised as the enemy of property owners and workers alike, the symbolic criminal was dysfunctional in terms of a wide set of values which varied only slightly between authors. Rhetoric punished offenders who failed to internalise the necessary values of a capitalist-patriarchal society, while their parents were blamed for inadequately inculcating these canons. Distaste for women's paid labour meant that a criminal class representing all that was bad chastised women, not for failing to work, but for engaging in the market, depicting them as low types, with the lowest possible being prostitutes. The construction of the criminal class at the level of ideas was thus an important ideological tool: more than simply controlling the poor, it aided in limiting opposition and in imposing new, regimented work values, new attitudes to property, and new social limitations on a working-class population which maintained pre-industrial attitudes to marriage and family formation, moral economies, women's work and more leisurely and less fragmented work processes.[93]

Significantly, popular culture did not always ascribe to the criminal-class theory. Often it chose to romanticise and glorify criminals in widely circulated and devoured broadsides, ballads, newspapers, pamphlets and picaresque novels. In broadsides such as 'The London Convict Maid', reproduced in Figure 1.1, the criminal was also a victim of injustice—a worker led astray, rather than a professional criminal indulging their favoured pursuit. Many critics were horrified by these popular forms, and the novels in particular were decried as 'socially dangerous'.[94] Yet not all popular culture escaped class stereotyping. Footpads and robbers remained unpleasant shadowy figures emanating from the lower classes, while the highwayman possessed genteel origins and appropriate manners. Working alone, Dick Turpin and other highway robbers were perceived 'to be brave men defying the world of structured authority, escaping from the hum drum', surrounded by 'the aura of gentility and politeness … refusing to point their pistol at ladies, witty repartee'.[95] Often—but not always—the literature ended on a moralistic note of criminal repentance. This was indeed the function of the *Newgate Calendars* and other publications that recorded the remorseful last dying speeches of capital offenders before they 'danced' or were 'turned off'— popular terms for death by hanging. These stories were circulated at the event and read rapaciously. Broadsides etc. were not pure expressions of working-class resistance, yet they had not been totally subverted by other interests. They serve to illustrate the ongoing conflict between different value systems that occurs in all societies at all times, but particularly at those junctions when the beneficiaries of a new mode of production are asserting beliefs that differ from those of the old mode. Such adversaries were engaged in numerous fields of battle: antagonists fought to influence the ideological creation of the criminal, as well as the definition of crime itself.

Undue influence

Not all contemporaries judged lawbreakers in the same way. Some nineteenth-century commentators portrayed criminals and convicts, not as professional parasites, but as individuals forced into crime through poverty. In 1787 a pamphlet declared that 'the very best education will scarcely keep a man honest and virtuous whose family is perishing for want of necessaries', and in 1827 the Earl of Malmesbury attributed the increase in poaching to 'the present distressed condition of the humbler classes of society. The people were too apt, from want of lawful employment to encounter the dangers of poaching'.[96] Sir George Arthur, Governor of Van Diemen's Land for twelve years and a witness before the 1837 Select Committee on Transportation, explained that 'I think that many of those who have been sent out have been driven to commit the offence for which they have been sent out through want'.[97] Even Mayhew and Binny acknowledged that some small number of workers on low pay, or who were out of employment, were faced with few alternatives other than to steal in order to survive.[98] Views such as these, however, held little sway by the middle of the twentieth century, by which time they were unceremoniously dismissed in favour of something spicier.

Historians have been unduly influenced by nineteenth-century opinions on the so-called criminal class, seeming unaware of the complexity and interplay of forces generating these texts. Manning Clark, Lloyd Robson, A. G. L. Shaw did not return to the idea of a criminal class because their studies of the convict indents led them inexorably to no other conclusion, but on the basis of qualitative evidence amassed in selective contemporary works. Henry Mayhew was particularly notable. While Mayhew was not alone in influencing historians, he laid foundations which made twentieth-century readers receptive to other similar views, supporting the evidence of earlier writers such as Patrick Colquhoun and Peter Cunningham.[99] His words resonated with the widely read fictional works of Charles Dickens, convincing some that '*Oliver Twist* is only partly a work of fiction'.[100]

Historical opinion shifted in the 1950s away from viewing convicts sympathetically to labelling them as professional members of a criminal class, a shift which coincided with the reissuing of works by Mayhew. Rescued from oblivion, Mayhew's writings appeared as a hitherto neglected source: rich in detail, it possessed a wealth of information regarding life, labour and crime in London. Upon republication they were immediately influential. Mayhew was rediscovered with a vengeance. His presence is to be found in the early articles by Clark, in the books written by Robson and Shaw, and in later articles such as that by M. B. and C. B. Schedvin in which some 45 out of 106 footnotes were made directly to Mayhew, with more notes citing related works.[101] It was indeed appropriate that good use should have been made of this valuable source material. With it, however, this source brought its own value judgements and political agenda. Heavy reliance upon Mayhew's evidence, teamed with the sometimes less than critical adoption of the views expressed, meant that biases implicit in Mayhew's standpoint, the paradoxes and contradictions, translated into the modern studies and permeated the historiography. Fear of the criminal class was resurrected. It is not accidental that Mayhew was notable only for his complete absence in the 1922 seminal article written by George Arnold Wood, which established the earlier orthodoxy portraying convicts as village Hampdens 'more sinned against than sinning'.[102] Nor can a Mayhewian presence be detected in the sympathetic work by Payne, contemporaneous with Clark *et al.* but generally unrecognised.[103]

Powerful imagery, evocative language and vivid formulations by nineteenth-century writers captivated the minds of a number of historians. Support for this contention can be found in the ready way in which their prose mimics earlier writings. Burglary, robbery, poaching, coining, working illicit stills, housebreaking, pickpocketing, etc. were for the habitual criminal 'regular crafts, requiring almost the same apprenticeships as any other mode of life': these were the words of Mayhew and his associate, John Binny.[104] In the twentieth century Manning Clark echoed this theme with these words: 'crime is an occupation just as plumbing, carpentering, etc., are occupations for other members of the working classes'.[105] A. G. L. Shaw wrote that the majority of convicts were not casual offenders but 'professional and habitual criminals'.[106] Approvingly, Mayhew and Binny quoted the finding of the 1839 *Report of the Constabulary Commissioners*, that crime proceeded 'from a disposition to acquire property with a less degree of labour than ordinary industry'.[107] Clark thought the transportees to be 'men [sic] with a deep-seated resistance to work'.[108] The former two observed, 'it is well known that such persons [as criminals] are distinguished by a comparative incapability of protracted attention ... and an indomitable repugnance to regular labour'.[109] To Clark, the convicts were 'characterised by mental imbecility and low cunning. Many of them were lazy in disposition and lacked energy both of body and mind', while Keith Hancock deemed convicts a 'lump, which was wretched and listless and forlorn'.[110] Mayhew and Binny continued: 'Hence the predatory class are the non-working class—that is to say, those who love to "shake a free leg", and lead a roving life, as they term it, rather than settle down to any continuous employment'.[111] To Shaw, convicts became 'wanderers' and 'vagabonds' roving the countryside committing crimes, rather than paid workers contributing to the good of the economy.[112] Lloyd Robson wrote of travelling 'mobs' of criminals.[113]

Mayhew and Binny's leverage continued throughout the 1970s, this time supported by the weight of empirical evidence furnished by Clark and Robson. In the nineteenth century,

> habitual criminals ... are those persons who feel labour to be more irksome than others, owing to their being not only less capable of continued application to one subject or object, but more fond of immediate pleasure, and, consequently, less willing to devote themselves to those pursuits which yield only prospective ones.

Such types possessed 'an inordinate love of amusement'.[114] A century later, in psycho-sociological terms, Schedvin and Schedvin observed the convicts' traits of 'restlessness and unwillingness to accept the personal investment and self-discipline implied by continuity of work and purposeful action', noting their 'reliance on chance and addiction to gambling on the one hand and a tendency to rely on externally-provided support on the other'.[115] Mayhew and Binny calculated that $82^2/_3$ per cent of criminals were 'uncivilised professional thieves ... who look with scorn upon all who labour for their living as either mean or witless'.[116] Six score years later John Hirst, pursuing this theme, wrote of 'the true underworld of professional pickpockets, thieves and prostitutes. These people knew what a good servant was but their whole lives turned on outraging that ideal—only the suckers worked and touched their caps to the masters, the flash man tricked and robbed them'.[117] The chasm between the working and supposed criminal classes was as great in the late twentieth century as many had believed it to be in the nineteenth.

Reliance on such nineteenth-century accounts proved particularly detrimental to women, who were judged harshly by Mayhew and his fellow observers. The criminal class was bad, but it was believed that within their midst lay a core of even greater depravity: the female criminals. Women qualified for membership of the criminal class, not so much as thieves and robbers, but as whores. Vituperative terms such as 'prostitutes', 'abandoned women', 'notorious strumpets' and 'damned whores' littered nineteenth-century accounts of convict women. Too easily this nineteenth-century terminology was taken out of context and misunderstood: these labels described what was deemed unfeminine behaviour (such as smoking, drinking and swearing) but historians gave it literal meaning, as noted in the Introduction. Time and again convict women were classified as prostitutes, not on the basis of objective criteria which measured how many women engaged in sex work, but on subjective statements and interpretations of their behaviour for which they were then castigated.

Once more convict women were criticised for what observers considered bad behaviour. Suspending his otherwise quantitative approach, Robson found that the convict women's urban backgrounds, criminal records, stolen goods and press accounts 'all drive the researcher to the conclusion that, for whatever reasons, most of Australia's prospective mothers for the foundation years were no better than they should have been'.[118] His evidence? One-third of the women surveyed were from London, Lancashire and Dublin, and somewhere between 41 and 60 per cent had previously offended—not particularly culpable features. What, then, of these prior convictions? Did their character, frequency, type of goods stolen, and circumstances truly compel Robson to his unpalatable conclusion? Here the proof becomes anecdotal, and subjective.

> The previous offences were not all petty—to take some examples: four months for clothes, six days for a shawl and eight days for being disorderly; 60 days three times for theft, three times for quarrelling; 60 days for a gown, 60 days twice for bottles, nine months for a muslin gown; 60 days for being drunk, 20 or 30 times for drunkenness. Previous offences were usually the theft of clothes and of such objects as mirrors [a hint of vanity, perhaps?], as well as for vagrancy, 'leaving her place', and especially for being 'disorderly' or involved in 'rows'.[119]

Without claiming the above behaviour as particularly 'lady-like' (was this their real sin?) these examples are hardly the work of aberrant and irredeemable rogues. Leaving a workplace, rowing, even being drunk, are not inherently evil doings. The evidence is open to alternative interpretation, and it should be noted that such material is not marshalled and dealt with in the same quantified manner as the other major issues in his study. In Robson's account, Mayhew's voice is again being heard, with tales of boys and girls 'all huddled promiscuously together', breeding an atmosphere, so Mayhew and Robson believed, in which prostitution was the inevitable next step.[120] This was the real reason the women were considered to be of 'generally bad character', presenting an unattractive picture.[121] Mayhew enters the stage on the third page of Robson's book, and never leaves.

Recently, historians have brought a critical eye to bear on the problem of who created the historical record, who was its subject, and how differences between the two groups—observer and observed—influenced the product.

Nineteenth-century commentators were part of the socio-political scene which produced transportation, and as such they had not only insights into the problems of the time, but the biases of the time as well. Consequently, the wealth of information generated by nineteenth-century criminologists, social commentators, commission witnesses and government institutions does not provide a definitive account of convict origins. But this recognition came too late for the convict origins debate which stagnated for much of the 1960s, 1970s and 1980s. Mid-twentieth-century historians of convict origins concluded that Australia's convict women presented what they considered to be a rather revolting picture. Constantly, the women were described as prostitutes. This characterisation arose, not on the basis of objective evidence, but from the colourful but amblyopic accounts made by contemporaries, all of which can be found repeatedly cited in the literature on female convict character (notably singular) while competing views were unceremoniously dismissed, or more typically, ignored altogether. Calumnious contemporary remarks were taken at face-value. Even the definition of prostitution was assumed unquestioningly. Failure to perceive the none-too-subtle nuances of terms like 'whore' and 'prostitute' led to them being taken as literal descriptions rather than as terms of abuse.[122] Had historians of convict origins taken the trouble to look at the use of pejoratives such as 'damned whore' and 'abandoned woman' in early nineteenth-century Britain, then they would have found that different meanings prevailed then compared to now.

Concentrating on those nineteenth-century discourses in which prostitution was a recurrent and negative theme (and not those numerous alternative voices that can be heard echoing from the same distant past), it is evident that the charge of prostitution was made for a variety of reasons. The term did, naturally, denote women who sold sex, although this fact was never left lying in a moral vacuum: prostitution was evidence of wrongdoing. But the charge was far from limited to that observation. Many women were labelled whores, not because they were such in any literal sense, but because the term had been appropriated as a reproach to be levelled at women who erred in any one of a variety of ways. Certainly the emerging feminine ideal of submissive, passive woman located at the hearth was outraged by single women working for money outside the home, which many female convicts had done. Even more, these women also affronted the integrity of private property, through exercising agency, through theft, stealing, picking pockets, and—worse— man robbery. Consequently, female convicts have been labelled 'abandoned', 'whores', and these terms have been misinterpreted. It is not altogether surprising that women who threatened the sanctity of private property, as well as the developing values about femininity, should have had such a perverted logic used against them in the nineteenth century.

However, it is disappointing that these opprobrious contentions continued comparatively unabated, unquestioned and misunderstood into the twentieth century.

The worth of convict women

In Aphra Behn's play *The Rover*, written in 1678, the courtesan Angelica asks the following.

> Who made the laws by which you judge me? Men!
> Men who would rove and ramble, but require
> That women must be nice.[123]

Convict women had not been 'nice'—by definition they had broken at least one law—and the criticisms they incurred were loud and clamorous. Myopic contemporary accounts misled undiscerning historians into constantly mistaking economic categories of poverty, prostitution and other forms of female labour for moral issues, and dismissing convict women as whores as if this alone defined their entirety and signalled their worthlessness. Such misconceptions about convict women bore great costs. Convict women never emerged in the literature as potential workers: instead, they were bad mothers, undesirable marriage partners, and whores. Precluded from analysis were questions of the work histories these women brought with them; what training they possessed; whether they could read, write, count; how they might have contributed to the colonial economy; what their roles were as domestic labourers, traders, mothers and as sex workers in the male-dominated colony. In particular, there has been great resistance to the notion that convict women were skilled and semi-skilled workers. Blinkered vision led historians to underrate the worth of convict women. Three key points need to be made. One, the extent of apprenticed skills brought by the convict women has not been adequately recognised. Two, equating 'skill' with formally apprenticed trades alone ignores recent arguments about the historical specificity of the term, a factor which has militated against women who in particular acquired their skills informally. Finally and relatedly, adherence to notions of the market economy has led to the undervaluing of women's work performed in the unpaid or non-market sector. Combined, these three factors have led historians to underplay the significance of convict women in the development of Australia's colonial economy.

Commonly, men who served apprenticeships have been considered highly skilled. The works of Sally Alexander, K. D. M. Snell and Eve Hostettler permit a listing of apprenticed trades to be drawn up for the early to mid-nineteenth century.[124] The listing is incomplete, and therefore gives a lower-bound estimate. Matching convict trades to the list reveals that some 30 per cent of skills brought to Australia by convict women had been acquired through formal apprenticeships. These included such professions as millinery, dressmaking, straw bonnet making, embroidery, tambour working, lace-making, needlework and some areas of laundry work, to name but a few.[125] So, even by a very traditional measure (apprenticed trades), a significant number of convict women appear skilled, yet historians have largely failed to recognise and value these economic assets. That in the twentieth century the value of past female labour has been so readily doubted has something to do with the declining status of women in industrial societies. Sceptical historians might best be seen as victims of the ideology of skill. Historically contingent, the parameters of skill were certainly in flux in the eighteenth and nineteenth centuries, as noted in Chapter 6. This was a crucial period in the transformation of the gender order and of production processes which saw women marginalised within agriculture, excluded from the prestigious trade areas that once they had traditionally occupied, until finally localised in feminised occupations unable to carve out a labour-market niche. Unfamiliar with women as skilled artisans, historians writing in the twentieth century might not have expected to find apprenticed craft workers among women convicts or indeed among British working women.[126]

A second and most important point to be made relates to the validity of the equation of formal apprenticeships with skill. Historians might unintentionally have bought the argument that only formally apprenticed work was skilled. It is an equation that can only exist in an ahistorical context which ignores the processes which define skill.[127] A corollary of the argument that skill was a category constructed according to political and economic power, rather than some objective and absolute proficiency, is that not all work involving 'expertness, practised ability, facility in an action ... dexterity, tact'—the dictionary definition and actual meaning of the term—was awarded the accolade 'skill'. This label has come to be associated with those areas of employment where the supply of labour could be limited, specifically through control of the training process, and did not necessarily correlate with high levels of expertise. But this is where women have come a cropper, so to speak: in the *informal* nature of much of their training—gained 'sitting next to Nellie'—and in the widespread availability of their skills. Early nineteenth-century British families continued, as they had in pre-industrial times, to be a seat of production for both use and exchange. More than this, they were major training grounds. Girls were more likely than boys to receive their share of household resources in the form of cheaper informal training. This was because parents distributed limited family resources on the basis of gendered expectations about declining labour-market opportunities that were exacerbated by the emergence of institutional barriers to female choice (restraints on hours, conditions, etc.). Such informal investment in human resources has been under-counted—indeed, ignored—because it took place outside the market sector. It also meant that these types of labour were supplied in quantity. Extensive supply made workers easy to replace, depressing wages and status, but not the talents required to exercise the trade. To be analogous for a moment: literacy is a vital tool in employment and in living generally; it involves training and a great deal of practice; it could rightly be termed a 'skill' and tends to be considered such when few individuals possess the ability. When it becomes widespread, its usage increases, but its status as a 'skill' diminishes.

Specifically, both these factors (informal training and extensive supply) have meant that women's work such as domestic service has been under-valued. Despite all the features that convicts held in common with English and Irish working women, commentators have been blind to convict women as workers. Time and again they have tended to regard convicted women as aberrant in the sphere of work as well as crime, as was seen in Chapter Four, derogatorily describing them as belonging to 'the vague, general category "domestic servant"'.[128] Nursegirls, kitchenmaids and allworkers were considered 'unskilled'. Informally trained in 'women's work', convict women failed to fit the description of a skilled worker. Yet the work of the kitchenhand was in no way vague. It was not general. It was located in a particular physical place, it involved specific tasks, and it acted as an informal apprenticeship for the profession of cook. If historians think lowly of cooks, nineteenth-century employers—even with their class and gender biases—were aware of the value of a good, proficiently cooked meal which arrived on the table intact and on time. Armstrong's social-skill classification used earlier revealed a remarkably high level of skill among convict women, and this classification was based in part on nineteenth-century evaluations. The status of domestic servants was not formally downgraded until the *Classification of Occupations, 1950*, when they were relegated from Class III (skilled occupations) to Class IV (intermediate skills).[129] Throughout the nineteenth century the traditional work of women continued to hold—although increasingly shakily—a status unrecognised by the late twentieth century.[130]

Convict women have suffered because their formally attained skills have not been duly recognised, nor have the informal skills that they put to work in the paid economy. A third problem arises when trying to estimate the economic worth of women, convict or otherwise. Much valuable women's work occurred outside the paid economy in the unpaid household (or non-market) sector. We need to consider the non-market sector, not only as the provider of informal training but as a site of work and consumption. In a market economy, work that is not paid is not formally valued. (As with trees and fresh air, people are more conscious of its absence than its presence.) Sleight of hand in accounting procedures excluded reproduction, unpaid housework and production for family consumption from estimates of output and wealth and from the approbatory category 'productive employment'. This was not always the case, as the battle to control the Australian census reveals, but the household sector was ultimately defeated and today we continue to live with that heritage.[131] Women found themselves on the periphery of legitimate economic enterprise, with the value of their work downgraded. This invisibility has not been readily questioned.[132] Instead, historians and economists continue to write about the significance to economic growth of roads, but not of children, nor the clothes that workers wore, nor the food that they ate. While the birth of a lamb is counted in the measurement of national wealth, the birth of a human infant is not, nor is all the unpaid labour invested in nurturing the child to productive adulthood recognised. That certain historians have concluded that the female convicts were unskilled and, if anything, a drain on the colony is a position derived from an uncritical understanding not only of the nature and worth of women's paid work, but of the unpaid work of women also.

Discussing the roles of women in economic development, R. B. Madgwick wrote that there 'are definite reasons why women cannot produce as much as men, and an excess of females in the population will normally lead to a smaller production per head of the population'. He believed that 'granted a population of working age, it is economically more desirable to have a slight excess of males over females than an excess of females'.[133] Stephen Nicholas and Peter Shergold argued in *Convict Workers* that colonial economic development benefited from the 'exceptional workforce' that transportation provided, in which not only the young and the elderly (commonly considered to have low-productivity rates and to be resource-expensive) were under-represented, but women also.[134] They claimed that 'women were imperfect substitutes for men' in terms of strength, and that infrastructural development, such as road building, would have been hindered had the sex-ratio been less skewed or in their terms, less favourable. They recognised that women manufactured substitutes for imports, worked as domestic servants, and—apart from childbearing—there was little reason why female participation rates should have been lower than men's, but they were. Nicholas and Shergold asserted that 'because their labour was undervalued, women convicts were also underemployed'. Put simply, 'the patriarchal society of emerging capitalism did not allow them [women] to work'.[135] The evidence supporting or refuting this has yet to be collected.

Hazarding a guess—prompted by the growing body of work by numerous historians—I think it unlikely that all or most convict women sat around twiddling their thumbs all day.[136] How did those big and little colonial houses operate without domestic servants? Women might not have built these houses, but they were often instrumental in running these establishments.[137] Meals were cooked, kitchens scrubbed and children minded. Someone was out there milking cows, nurturing chickens, turning raw materials into edible foodstuffs, making clothes, trying to make loose dirt into floors. Struggling at the frontier, these were mistresses of ingenuity, making do with what could be obtained, creating pots, pans, cupboards, the lot, from whatever came to hand. Did convict men work alone at these tasks? Certainly it was not they who risked their lives in childbirth. Colonial women did work, but their work has not always been valued or recognised. Michael Roe's assertion that the female convicts 'rarely made any positive contribution to the public welfare or progress' was made at the same time as acknowledging that these women spun wool, flax and hemp, that a few succeeded in trade, and that the majority were domestic servants who 'very often' ended up as their employer's mistress or wife, and went on to bear and nurture children.[138] This latter aspect of women's lives has been greatly undervalued. When Madgwick wrote of there being 'definite reasons' why women were 'less productive', he was alluding to women's reproductive responsibilities (and to their social responsibilities also, in guarding against the threat of 'social and moral evils') which he termed 'non-economic' considerations. And Nicholas and Shergold might have considered that men were imperfect substitutes for women in that very vital role of reproducing the labour force: perfectly imperfect, in fact. All this unpaid work failed to be counted, but would life and the economy have been the same without it? Despite efforts by historians like Beverley Kingston, Portia Robinson, Katrina Alford and others, there is still the tendency among economists to divide in two these interrelated processes of production and reproduction and to see them and their practitioners as distinct, one important, the other not. Yet it was production *and* reproduction which governed lives, and ultimately it was the success of these combined strategies that would determine Australia's economic fortune.

Misconceived as whores, convict women have suffered badly from this stigma. Apart from its inaccuracy, such moral judgements have meant that prostitution was not considered work, and nor have those labelled prostitutes been conceived as working in any other capacity. Kay Daniels observed, 'the woman who works as a prostitute is given no identity apart from this role and no location beyond the territory of her workplace. Deprived of any other life she appears, in this literature, as less than human, the archetypal "bad woman" or as a sexual "deviant".'[139] Judith Allen and Hilary Golder argued that prostitution (wifery, motherhood) was work, but of a nature so intimate that it involved the sale of something more than labour-power alone, making untenable the claim that in a patriarchal system female work and male work were essentially the same. Many found this realisation so unpalatable that they readily perpetuated a mythical separation of work and sex that was too readily accepted by some mid-century historians.[140] But this *was* a myth, too often denied by the lives of working women in nineteenth-century Britain familiar with sexual harassment, abuse and other less coercive sexual encounters. For convict women, the outcome of such misconceptions has been debilitating. Daniels' observation was correct. Convict women's identities as workers, mothers, homemakers, partners, entrepreneurs, citizens and colonists have all been obfuscated and are only now being slowly excavated from the ruinous legacy of the convict origins debate. Elizabeth Coltman, Caroline Humphries, Hannah Buttledoor and all the other women transported so far across the seas would be most displeased at being so ignored in the past. With their compatriots they slapped thighs, sang rowdy songs, and generally did their best to gain attention, but we have tended to shut our eyes and our ears to their protestations and demands in a manner that few of their contemporaries could. Exiled from Britain, they resent this second exile from white history (even from its nasty bits). And yet they are not the only ones to have suffered. Australia's economic history has been robbed of a vital dimension, leaving a tale only half told.

CHAPTER NINE

Britain's Loss, Australia's Gain?
Concluding Remarks

Colonial authorities attempting to exert control and employers battling to extract labour were annoyed by convict women. It was the behaviour of these transported female felons which so shocked and disappointed their detractors. Convict women were denigrated because they made refractory servants who enjoyed drinking and partying, uttered oaths and imprecations, tore sailors' clothes into rags, acted licentiously, and because they tempted yet simultaneously repelled the men who had charge of them as criminals, workers or parishioners. Gender, class values and relations, ethnicity, religion, language, even sexual attraction all contributed to a damaging cocktail of misunderstanding and contempt. In the colony, forced and free immigrant women alike were disparaged in terms expressed in sexual phraseology, such as damned whore and abandoned woman. Prostitution became the metaphorical device, not solely identifying women who sold sex, but used to castigate any woman who broke the rules of civilised womanhood, be it through crime, work or personal morality. Femininity proscribed female activity. Dangerously this teamed with the highly influential criminal-class theorem propounded by contemporary journalists and politicians with their own barrows to push as they formed public opinion, policy and institutions. George Rudé noted that crime in nineteenth-century London did not fit the lurid image conjured up in theatrical style by Charles Dickens, Patrick Colquhoun or Henry Mayhew, and that their scripts were 'formed by too narrow a focus on records in which crime was made to respond to the needs of the drama'.[1] The characterisation of their female roles was particularly poor, though predictable: they fell back on stereotypical cardboard depictions; their female *dramatis personae* were unchaste, unwomanly whores. The criminal class was complete: it exactly mirrored the values desirable in 'good' men and women, as defined by selected but vocal interests. The outcome was that lawbreakers like Elizabeth Coltman transported to New South Wales were depicted as professional and habitual criminals and prostitutes, as individuals making an unfettered decision to maximise utility: actively choosing a life of crime because it was more profitable

232

than a life of wage labour. Through bad parenting and poor upbringing, certain individuals, family groupings and even social strata were incapable of conventional work and family life, concepts with which they were thought totally unfamiliar.

Vivid rhetoric from Britain and colonial Australia captured the imaginations of a number of key historians. Earlier writers like George Arnold Wood seemed unaffected by past utterances and wrote sympathetic accounts of convict origins, while those who engaged with those earlier political writings—such as Manning Clark, A. G. L. Shaw, Lloyd Robson—reshaped Australia's first white settlers into Britain's professional criminal class. Relying on accounts made by individuals with vested interests and imperfect understanding of class and gender differences, ignoring other evaluations when these were found to diverge, and failing to rigorously define terms and mine more objective information, they erected a myth about who the convict women were and what skills and graces they failed to possess. On frighteningly subjective evidence, too many historians demonstrated an overwhelming desire to judge these convicts as good or bad, leading to a profound misconception of who the convict women were. These findings underscored much subsequent historiography, arguably distorting it. In standard accounts of colonial economic development, convict women failed to appear as potential workers, were rejected as suitable marriage partners, and made drunken and demoralised mothers. This was so debilitating an inheritance that subsequent claims that transported women came from skilled and semi-skilled professions were met flatly with disbelief. Convict women were elided in Australia's economic history, undermined in three ways: their apprenticed skills went unrecognised, their informal education was denied, their unpaid labours were ignored. But, increasingly, the negative conception of convict origins came into conflict with other research.

As work focusing on colonial experiences progressed, different and more dynamic conclusions were reached about the roles played by convicts in colonial society. Convict women made good mothers and were—if Irish—poor criminals forced into illicit acts by deprivation: in New South Wales they made homes, gave birth and successfully nurtured the next generations of white Australians; as whores and wives they helped control their coerced male brethren and bring social stability; as agents protecting their own interests they manipulated the male-dominated marriage market, the courts, the Female Factory and any institution they encountered; when given the chance, they achieved in business. A creative tension emerged in the literature. How had all these achievements been possible if colonial fodder was poor, tainted, derived from the criminal class? Typically composed of individuals who had never experienced any of the more traditionally expected values of family life such as loving and caring, how then had convicts become fit parents? When, where, and (more importantly, perhaps) why did English women who arrived unfamiliar with work and industrious habits learn to compensate for their lack of training?[2] Colonial society was not so different from other, free societies of the nineteenth century according to John Hirst, and Michael Roe before him. The emerging theme was one of normality. A 'normal' colonial existence approximating established societies was surely more likely to have evolved from an average working population than from a criminal underclass of rogues. Portia Robinson's earlier work identified convicts as ordinary working-class women, experienced in ordinary family and working life, who were 'the victims of British social conditions'; this is far more consistent with her analysis of the emergence of convict women as successful parents and economic agents in the colonial economy than with her later depiction of English convict women as emanating from the lowest classes of British society and thus being unfamiliar with ordinary work and family life.[3] Tensions thus developed between a colonial success story juxtaposed with the extremely dubious criminal-class origins of its workforce, demanding those origins be reappraised.

Perceptively, in *The World Moves Slowly*, published in 1977, Beverley Kingston made the following observation regarding convicts.

> Perhaps the question which asks what kind of people they really were under the label of bad or vicious, and which increasingly is becoming more satisfying to answer by sophisticated re-examination of the convict records and court reports, will set us all free of that old set of value judgements out of which there seemed nothing more to say.[4]

In conjunction with a wealth of other historical endeavours, *Convict Maids* has demonstrated the inadequacy of the criminal-class hypothesis and 'that old set of value judgements' which hindered historical thinking. In reality, convict women were not overt political rebels seeking to undermine the system by rejecting paid employment and defiantly joining a subversive and alternative criminal class. These women forcibly exiled from their homes were not known recidivists and hardened violent criminals, but mainly casual first offenders indulging in small-scale property crime that often victimised those around them, their employers, landlords, shopkeepers, clients. Their criminal labours were unorganised and undifferentiated: whether they were from Ireland, England, countryside or town, even from the great metropolis of London reputed to be crime's mecca, convict women were essentially sneak-thieves and robbers. What varied most were the opportunities that their environments presented them with. Rather than being aberrant vagabonds seeking criminal mischief and a quick quid, the restlessness of which convict migrants were accused seems consistent with membership of a talented and mobile labour source in a dynamic period of English industrialisation and Irish internationalisation.

Convict women brought with them a range of valuable economic assets. Selected to be young and healthy, cared for on the voyage and exposed to further education, the workers that New South Wales received were at the height of their powers. Aged mainly in their late twenties and early thirties, these young women were at the peak of their productive and reproductive years. They were old enough to have acquired skills, and young enough to look forward to a long future employing them. And they had acquired skills. By the standards of the time they were literate, numerate, trained and practised at work. Mainly, convict women had been domestic servants, covering the full gamut of that catch-all label. Overwhelmingly this category dominated, mixed with a smattering of other trade skills. New South Wales received convict maids. Mostly the women were single, with transportation proving something like divorce for the rest. Many brought with them an experienced eye and hand as mothers, making convict women well suited to perform one role typical of women throughout the world, to have babies and to rear them. These girls and women arrived in the colony already familiar with life and work as members of the labouring classes of England and Ireland.

They left behind them countries undergoing profound economic restructuring as industrialisation reshaped both Ireland and England. Agricultural and industrial revolutions in England transformed the economic landscapes, demanding that workers respond or perish. Production processes were reorganised and sometimes mechanised; the family production unit was replaced by the individual wage worker, simultaneously problematising childcare; labour markets became contested terrain; living standards fell; and in particular women suffered as their work became increasingly feminised, limited in scope, and badly paid. Increases in industrial employment were inadequate to soak up labour displaced from the declining domestic sector. Vulnerable since the end of the Napoleonic Wars, Ireland was sensitive to these developments. As English output grew, it changed the game in international competition; it displaced domestic production in countries like Ireland, which could not match the low prices of industrial manufacturing based on low wages and highly specialised work processes, occurring in such close proximity to its own shores. Nor did Ireland have the political strength to exclude imports after Union with Great Britain in 1801. While a niche could be found by the Ulster linen trade which buoyed that region, and some parts of the country responded dynamically to external stimuli, many other areas sank. Resourceful individuals from both Ireland and England, attempting to negotiate these monumental and rapid developments, responded by retraining and relocating. Turbulence thus bred multi-skilling and migration, and also uncertainty, poverty, crime and convicts.

Australia's criminal refugees brought with them a diverse set of experiences, emanating from all over Ireland and England. Many were country girls whose experience of agriculture and the putting-out industry had encouraged them to retrain and go searching for better opportunities elsewhere. For many, domestic service was the answer. Widespread demand made their work transportable and enabled them to capitalise on training already received at home and on the farm. English women were more skilled, literate and numerate than their Irish sisters, but this reflected the economies whence they came. Comparing Irish convicts with Irish workers, and doing the same for the English, revealed an interesting story. Irish convicts were much like their non-criminal counterparts, with the notable difference that those who had moved within Ireland—and especially those emigrating to England—were more highly trained, confirming arguments that Ireland suffered a brain drain. Similarly, English convicts were at least as talented as the women they left behind, judging by skill and literacy, and more so than female prisoners and paupers generally, suggesting that convict women were not simply the sweepings of the gaols. Related to this, convicts differed from gaol inmates in another highly significant aspect: occupational training.

While transported women bore much in common with other workers, and certainly differed insufficiently to suggest they belonged to a non-working criminal class, a significant difference did nonetheless exist between working women, prisoners and Britain's coerced emigrants. Disproportionate numbers of domestic servants were transported, both from Ireland and England. Over-representation was bought at the cost of textile manufacturers who, but for a handful of transportees, were totally absent. True, domestic service was a job for young single women, and young single women dominated the convict flow, but this alone cannot account for the magnitude of the discrepancy. Comparing census data with occupational information in the indents, and controlling for age, diminishes the gap but does not destroy it. And in any case, textile work was also typically associated with young women. Domestics had an unusually high propensity to be transported. Nor was this imbalance explicable in terms of domestics' greater criminality. On the contrary: textile workers dominated the prisons, with servants surprisingly under-represented. What was happening? Domestic servants were less likely to offend, but more likely to end up transported to Australia. Either convict women systematically lied on all four occasions on which occupational data was collected from them, or a selection procedure was occurring at some point in the lengthy chain between offending, being detected, caught, charged, prosecuted, found guilty, sentenced and picked out of the gaol before finally being deported. Tantalisingly, this whole selection process remains a mystery.

Coerced criminal migration delivered to the colony of New South Wales trained, healthy, convict maids of productive age, but were their work skills of the type required in the colony? Seemingly, the answer was yes. One way of establishing this was to analyse who was targeted through assisted immigration. Limited funds were being spent in order to stock the colony with those individuals deemed 'most desirable'. From the first assisted venture and throughout the nineteenth century, this target group comprised single women under the age of thirty-five years, trained as domestic servants of a variety of sorts. Investigating a small group of these immigrants revealed that immigrant and convict women were remarkably alike. Within the colony, they were also distributed in surprisingly similar fashion. Judging from colonial policies regarding the construction of the female labour force through immigration, convict women arrived appropriately trained to fulfil colonial requirements. Transported women had come from skilled and semi-skilled professions, had undergone apprenticeships, been trained informally in their own and their employers' homes, arrived equipped with experience of ordinary working and family life, and were of an age where they could benefit from enhanced opportunities, while their colonial employers, the economy and society generally could benefit from them. Britain's loss of convict maids may well have been Australia's gain.

Future directions

Frequently depicted as immoral and dissolute harlots, the female convicts were said to have contributed nothing to the colony other than vice. Earlier it was noted that the bulk of the literature on colonial economic development denied convict women any productive role, with a repetitive theme of the fewer women, the better. Several possibilities were presented as to why convict women had not participated in invasion and colonial expansion: because they were (1) unskilled and useless, (2) skilled but inappropriate to colonial needs, or (3) a worthy resource misspent by a wasteful state. A fourth option was that women *had* contributed to economic growth and development, but in ways not recognised and valued.

On the basis of an investigation of the convict indents, the first point was demonstrably incorrect. Convict women arrived bearing economic luggage well packed with a range of employment skills, many with the ability to communicate with the written word, and numerate. Was it perhaps that the women were ill suited to colonial requirements? Immigration policy casts considerable doubt over the verisimilitude of this second option, though there is scope for greater exploration of this point. Desperately the colony craved women with domestic skills (preferably from ordinary rather than grand households) also experienced at small-scale production. Their presence raised living standards, freed men from domestic duties, and made middle-class life more recognisably British. This supply of convict maids was supplemented with a smaller quantity of artisans, who found their labours in demand in just about the same ratio in which they arrived. But it has been argued by K. M. Dallas that colonial economic development suffered from the nature of the female convict labour flow: it delivered *too few* convict women. Dallas believed that in general women played an instrumental role in colonisation. Approvingly he quoted Beard's *Rise of American Civilization*: 'Absolutely imperative to the successful development of European civilization in America was the participation of women in every sphere of life and labour … Even the women of landed families were not idly rich.' In Australia, 'the low proportion of women was a great restriction on development'.[5] Particularly, the colony was starved by the lack of female textile workers necessary for the growth of an indigenous manufacturing industry. In their absence no such growth occurred, with fleeces left to rot.[6] This failure to add value to raw materials remains a problem to this day. If Dallas is correct, the problem female transportation imposed on the colony was not that convict women's stock of skills were inappropriate, but that the women were numerically deficient and their skills were inadequate in scope.

Convict women had arrived from Great Britain and Ireland bearing economic luggage loaded down with substantial skills, social baggage well-packed with experiences of ordinary working life, and a conducive age distribution which should have served colonial development singularly well. These exiles were accused of 'not in general being transported until there is no longer any hope of their reformation at home';[7] in reality, they were not in general transported until they had attained the optimum age at which skills had been learned, productive life lay ahead, and family formation might peak. Convicts bore more human capital assets in common with free immigrant women who elected to live in New South Wales than with the women who remained in British gaols. They landed employable as domestic workers, tradeswomen, prostitutes, wives, lovers and mothers. These women were certainly capable of contributing a good deal more than vice to the development of white Australia. But the problem remains of whether this potential was fulfilled—the third possible explanation for their perceived inactivity. Were convict women a resource squandered by a careless state?

Comparatively little is understood of how the state allocated these potentially valuable assets. Evidence collected on the colonial lives of transportees indicates that women did work in the colony, but the period covered is restricted and we do not know if *best* use was made of them. Research suggests the state dealt carefully in distributing convict men, maximising their worth by allocating them to jobs for which they were already trained, or ones where their past experience gave them an advantage in adapting to new tasks.[8]

Were authorities equally assiduous in their treatment of convict women? Preliminary studies suggest they were.[9] The 1828 muster was a colonial census and as such recorded occupations. Many women were listed ambiguously as 'wives', but sometimes the information was more revealing, permitting cross-referencing with the indents. Here are some examples. Back home, Ellen Nichols was a house servant, the same job she practised in the colony in the employ of one E. Bunker. Hannah Pritchard, twenty-eight, had been born in Bengal before migrating to Manchester, where she worked as a washerwoman; in New South Wales she was a laundress working for A. M. Baxter. Susan Barnett had been, and remained, a house servant. So too had Sarah Ludlow, Elizabeth Nichols, and Elizabeth McKey. Mary Hague, stealer of shoes, had been a country servant back in the Midlands and was designated a 'servant' in the muster. Ann Silk had been an allworker in Warwickshire, and in the colony was a servant. At home, Elizabeth Brooks had been a house servant and a nursemaid; in the colony, she practised the latter (and rarer) trade. Other women, such as Sarah Williams, had married and probably put their skills to good effect labouring alongside their husbands. Allocated to jobs consistent with those held in Great Britain and Ireland, many women appear to have continued in their assigned jobs once freed and unconstrained by the convict labour market, indicating that the state had made a good decision. For example, Jane Dundas was assigned as a housemaid and chose to remain in service with the same family after her period of servitude ended, and in time was duly promoted to housekeeper.[10]

Option four is looking most likely: convict women found a blind-spot in historians' and economists' field of vision. It seems likely that these exiles *did* contribute to colonial development, but in ways not always recorded or recognised. Certainly many of the currency lads and lasses were the fruit of convict loins. Who bore the children? Who suckled them and coddled them? Who worked the big and little houses? Who made the meals? Who worked the nurseries? Who spun the fibres? Who made the clothes? Who laundered them? Who battled at the frontier? Certainly convict men were there, but they were not always alone, their company not always white, nor always male. More needs to be known of these colonial pursuits which have been hidden from history. Convict women have been given short shrift. Their apprenticed skills have been ignored, their informal education down-graded, and their roles as wives and mothers producing in the household sector and striving alongside their husbands left an enigmatic mystery. Convict and ex-convict women accounted for 58 per cent of the female labour force in the colony in 1825, and for 43 per cent ten years later; in 1840, when their numbers became static with the cessation of transportation to New South Wales, they still numbered 30 per cent.[11] Numeric dominance subsided only as convict women gave birth to daughters, and free women voluntarily immigrated into the colony. More than free immigrants, convict labour could be directed by the state to work in the service of the colony. Given the importance of Australia's convict heritage, if we are to gender colonial economic development we must understand the roles played by convict women. The last two decades of research has begun to rectify the imbalance, with work by historians like Katrina Alford, Susan Thomas, Babette Smith, Portia Robinson, Monica Perrott, Annette Salt, Hilary Weatherburn, Marian Quartly (once Aveling), Marilyn Lake, Lyndall Ryan, Beverley Kingston and many others placing women on the agenda. But in spite of all this interesting work, many questions remain unanswered. I think we know remarkably little about convict women as workers in Australia; I think economists are unsure of how to evaluate the roles of women in the household sector (as domestic workers, wives, mothers); and I believe we are similarly uninformed about how gender influenced labour relations and other broader social relations.

Now we know what skills and talents convict women did bring with them, a number of issues arise. Census employment data suggests that convict women were not a cross-section of women held in British gaols: was some selection process occurring on the basis of job skills, and if so, at what point, under whose orders, and with what intent? Was deliberate care being taken in managing the flow of convict labour to Australia? Convict women, I have argued, did arrive in New South Wales with skills, attitudes and demographic characteristics much like those of other British and Irish working women, but even more favourable to economic development (in their most productive years, literate, etc.). Convict women were economically well equipped, and *could* have played a pivotal role. The challenge now is to examine the actual roles women played in promoting the colonial economy. We need to penetrate the issue of the nature of labour demand and the impact of labour supply on the economy, of how free and coerced flows compared, of how efficiently this labour was allocated, and whether these issues differed between colonies and over time. It would be interesting to compare the roles played by Australia's women with women in other lands of recent invasion, such as Canada, the United States, and Australia's close neighbour, New Zealand. And before we even begin to probe how women contributed to development, we need to broaden our definition of economy to include both the market *and* non-market sectors. How important was reproduction of the labour force? What were marriage rates like, and what did marriage involve apart from the obvious—labouring on the farm and in other family enterprises? If women were imported as prostitutes, as some historians have suggested, did this have an economic value? All this will require painstaking work on the colonial economy, and imagination and innovation in attempting to quantify the economic worth of assets and services which currently evade accounting sheets.

Next to nothing has been said in this book comparing the treatment of women with that of men, but most realities are gendered and this is a topic now waiting to be tackled. To what extent did being female alter the experiences of being a convict? And to what extent did being a convict alter the experiences of being female? Female convicts faced an added dimension in unfree labour relations, that of sex-work and sexual harassment. Were they more open to abuse than male convicts? And did this differ much from the experience of free English and Irish workers? Domestic workers in Britain all too often were expected to sexually service the men of the household: prostitution was part of the job. If convict women in Australia found themselves in a similar position, was this because they were women or because they were convicts? At least in theory, English and Irish workers could change employers. Or did being your employer's mistress make for better employment conditions? Were convict women forced into prostitution by the 'imperial whoremaster', adding another dimension to punishment not experienced by their male counterparts? Mothers and fathers, on the other hand, had something in common not shared by other transportees: they were forcibly parted from their children, who were left behind in England and Ireland, often abandoned and alone: how did this bereavement affect colonial life? Small in number, did convict women form an outcast group who suffered in a male-dominated society, or as a scarce resource did they wield more power in their personal relationships? Were female convicts more likely than men to negotiate the marriage they wanted? Perhaps convict women had greater control over their colonial lives than did men. Just how much autonomy did convict and ex-convict women exercise over reproduction, sexuality, work? All are topics worthy of further investigation. All this work must be done if women—convict and otherwise—are to be accurately located in Australia's economic history.

Arrival

One hundred and nineteen days after the *Competitor* left London, Elizabeth and her cohorts sailed into Sydney Harbour. It was Friday, 10 October 1828.

Commander Steward had safely negotiated the journey and Thomas Hunter, surgeon-superintendent on board, had not lost a single woman to illness or misadventure. Their cargo arrived intact. Mercury, patron of thieves, was also god of commerce; his miscreants had proved a profitable trade for the shippers and accountants like John Clark, who arranged their passage to Australia. In the colony these lawbreakers would become the very basis of commerce, providing a key element in the supply of labour. The forced migration of criminal women provided the colony with a rare asset. These were women who had demonstrated their ability to learn and their enthusiasm to adapt to new situations, and the very fact that they committed crime indicates they were resourceful if not honest. Some convicts may have been motivated to illegal acts by avarice, some by revenge, a small number may even have been forced by elders running rackets, but it seems likely that convicts were often workers deported because they occasionally sought refuge from the vagaries of unemployment and underemployment in crime. Irrespective of motive, nearly all appear to have been workers; as such, they brought with them to the colony a useful range of skills available for colonising a newly invaded land. They arrived familiar with obligations, work relations, social order and hierarchy, and also the need to adapt to changed economic conditions. Some were prostitutes, others were not, but that was part of working life. Overwhelmingly they were convict maids. Young, healthy women, effectively without families but with a range of employment experiences, literate, numerate, and many already familiar with migration and adjustment were an advantage to any new colony. This was good material suited to the task of building a new society and economy. Convict maids were well equipped to be homemakers, for themselves and their families or as somebody else's employees, and to labour at a variety of tasks.

On arrival, what now awaited these female exiles? They would not be freed upon disembarking; their punishment was only just beginning. Would the government house them, clothe them, feed them while they idly waited for their servitude to pass, or would work be found for them? Would Elizabeth Coltman, Caroline Humphries, Hannah Buttledoor and all the others become cooks, kitchenhands, housemaids, laundresses, dressmakers and children's maids, working in jobs they already understood which might only need adapting to local conditions, or would they be required to retrain yet again as they had done in the changing economic climate back home? Elizabeth was promptly assigned to Elizabeth Raine, although in what capacity the indents remain mute. Some might stay in the Female Factory, or at least be regular visitors there. Perhaps they would quickly wed or find partners, and give their labours freely. Margaret Shannahan, pictured in Figure 1.5, had been a housemaid in Ireland and in the colony was assigned as a domestic servant before bearing a daughter in 1837. Three years later she married the child's father, William Greenwood, an 'esteemed' and 'greatly respected' citizen of Araluen district in New South Wales.[12] Together they successfully reared eight children to adulthood, but lost one other as an infant. On what terms would such partnerships be made, and how much control did Elizabeth and her kin exercise over issues of sexuality, conception, childrearing and other employment? Did free immigrant women like 20-year-old house servant Catherine Fitzgerald or 18-year-old house worker Mary MacCluskey, travelling out on the *Red Rover* in 1832, have more or fewer choices than convict women, both at work and in bed? What happened to all of them as they grew older? After a seemingly fruitful life progressing from assigned servant to wife and mother, Margaret Greenwood's life fell apart upon the death of her husband in a cart accident on his way home from work. Margaret relapsed into crime, becoming a derelict, finally perishing under a tram on Elizabeth Street, Sydney, the efforts of passers-by ultimately failing to halt her repeated wanderings onto the busy road. Was hers a typical story? And how did these women act when they found themselves at the interface between an invading force displacing the legitimate inhabitants of the nation? So many questions beg answers. This story has already been played out, but seats in the audience have been hard to come by, particularly ones with unobstructed vision. If we try, just a little harder, we might yet snatch a view.

Appendices

1. CONVICT VESSELS

The following is a list of all vessels arriving in New South Wales carrying female convicts from 1826 until the end of transportation to that colony, and is in chronological order by year of arrival. Every woman embarked upon these ships and brigs as a convicted felon has been surveyed to create the database upon which this book is based. All information—the spelling of the vessel's name, the date of arrival, the number of female convicts that embarked and the place from where they sailed—is recorded here as it appears on the indents themselves. Convict indents exist in a variety of forms: in the original handwritten manuscripts and in the printed and bound versions that were produced from 1831 onwards, both held at the State Archives Office of New South Wales. The State Archives have made reproductions of these both on microfilm and, more recently, on microfiche that are now readily available through many libraries and genealogical societies. *Convict indents of transported prisoners* 4/4003–4019, and *convict indents of transported Irish prisoners* 4/7076–7078, State Archives Office of New South Wales, also reproduced as *Convict indents 1788–1842*, F614–744, Genealogical research kit stage 1, State Archive Office of New South Wales.

Female convict ships arriving in New South Wales, 1826–1842

Vessel[a]	Arrived	Sailed from	Embarked
Lady Rowena	17.5.1826	Ireland	101
Grenada 4	26.1.1827	England	88
Brothers	4.2.1827	Ireland	161
Prince Charlotte	6.8.1827	England	90
Governor Ready	1.9.1827	England[b]	1
Harvey	5.9.1827	England[b]	1
Harmony	27.9.1827	England	80
Louisa	3.12.1827	England	90
Elizabeth 4	12.1.1828	Ireland	194
Eliza	14.5.1828	England[b]	1

Female convict ships *contd*

Vessel[a]	Arrived	Sailed from	Embarked
Competitor 2	10.10.1828	England	99
City of Edinburgh	12.11.1828	Ireland	80
Edward	26.4.1829	Ireland	178
Princess Royal 2	12.5.1829	England	100
Sovereign	3.8.1829	England	119
Lucy Davidson	29.11.1829	England	101
Asia 7	13.1.1830	Ireland	201
Roslin Castle 2	29.6.1830	England	128
Forth 2	12.10.1830	Ireland	120
Kains	11.3.1831	England	120
Celia	11.3.1831	Mauritius	1
Earl of Liverpool	5.4.1831	England	89
Palambam	31.7.1831	Ireland	117
Hooghley 3	27.9.1831	Ireland	187
Strathfieldsay	19.12.1831	England[b]	1
Pyramus	4.3.1832	England	149
Burrell 2	20.5.1832	England	101
Southworth 2	14.6.1832	Ireland	134
Fanny	2.2.1833	England	106
Surry 6	9.3.1833	Ireland	142
Diana	25.5.1833	England	101
Caroline	6.8.1833	Ireland	120
Buffalo	5.10.1833	England	179
Dart	31.12.1833	Mauritius	1
Numa	13.6.1834	London	140
Dart 2	9.7.1834	Mauritius	2
Andromeda 3	22.9.1834	Ireland	176
George Hibbert	1.12.1834	England	144
Siren	27.2.1835	England[b]	1
Spence	20.6.1835	England[b]	1
Mary 5	7.9.1835	England	179
Henry Wellesley	7.2.1836	England	118
Roslin Castle 4	25.2.1836	Ireland	165
Thomas Harrison	9.6.1836	Ireland	112
Elizabeth 5	12.10.1836	England	161
Pyramus 2	14.12.1836	Ireland	120
Sarah and Elizabeth	3.4.1837	England	98
Margaret	30.5.1837	Ireland	153
Henry Wellesley 2	22.12.1837	England	140
Sir Charles Forbes	25.12.1837	Ireland	150

Female convict ships *contd*

Vessel[a]	Arrived	Sailed from	Embarked
Diamond	28.3.1838	Ireland	162
John Renwick	31.8.1838	England	173
Margaret 2	5.1.1839	Ireland	169
Planter 2	13.3.1839	England	171
Whitby	23.6.1839	Ireland	133
Mary Anne 5	10.11.1839	England	143
Minerva 6	26.12.1839	Ireland	119
Kate	26.12.1839	Adelaide, SA	1
Surry 9	14.7.1840	England	213
Isabella	24.7.1840	Ireland	119
Margaret 3	17.8.1840	Ireland	131
Emma	18.1.1842	Adelaide, SA	1
		Total embarked	6 876

a   The number following the name of a ship denotes a ship that made multiple voyages, and identifies the particular journey in question.
b   via Hobart Town.
Source: Convict indents; also see the *Guide to the State Archives of New South Wales: Information Leaflet No. 12.*

2. CRIME CLASSIFICATION

Since crime was the *raison d'être* behind the convict indents, it is not surprising that some considerable detail was recorded. After 1826, information was collected rigorously and has left for the historian a wealth of material with only fragmentary losses—a mere 3.6 per cent of cases suffer from missing values, and this is largely the result of deterioration in the records themselves rather than any deficiency in the collection of the information. Recorded were each convict's crime, objects of theft, sentence, previous criminal record, and sometimes the victim. Between them, the female convicts sent out to New South Wales had committed hundreds of different crimes, ranging from concealing stolen clothes to stealing fruit, pewter pots, cabbages, and many other items.

To make analysis possible, crimes have then been grouped into nine categories compiled, as closely as possible, according to nineteenth-century attitudes towards crime, many not all that different from today's. For example, a distinction is made within property crimes between offences that threatened violence (robbery), those that brought the victim and the assailant into direct contact (picking pockets), those that invaded private property and thus potentially involved contact (breaking, shoplifting), and those offences where the victim was absent (stealing, receiving). The categorisation was made as follows.

Breaking: breaking into premises, burglary, enter and steal, housebreaking.
Picking pockets.
Receiving: buying stolen goods, receiving.

Robbery: accessory to highway robbery, bleach-green robbery, highway robbery, house robbery, man robbery, man robbery and stealing money, person robbery, robbery and breach of trust, robbery and burglary, robbery, street robbery.

Shoplifting.

Stealing: concealing clothes, defrauding, embezzlement, false pretences, larceny, obtaining goods, pawning, pledging, possession, privately stealing, stealing and shoplifting, stealing, stealing and larceny, stealing and receiving, stolen goods.

Vagrancy.

Violent crimes: accessory to rape, administering poison, aggravated assault, assault and vagrancy, assault, assault with intent to kill, attempted murder, attempted poisoning, concealing murder, conspiring to murder, drowning, infanticide, maiming, malicious assault, manslaughter, murder, robbery and manslaughter, robbery and attempted murder, robbery with assault, robbery and accessory to rape, robbery with assault and stealing, robbery and murder, stabbing, suspicion of murder, violent assault.

Other: arson, bad notes, bed ticking, bigamy, breach of trust, brothel keeping, coining, conspiracy, cutting and maiming animals, feloniously killing animals, felony, firearms, forgery, fraud, house burning, incendiarism, incest, offering her child for sale to a surgeon, passing bad notes, perjury, procuring an abortion, rioting, sacrilege, selling her child, stealing and stripping children, stripping children, uttering base coin.

3. STOLEN GOODS CLASSIFICATION

Details on the goods stolen by convict women have been classified into eight groups. The following lists detail the way in which items were grouped. A solidus followed by an *s*, '/s', indicates that a multiple of the same item was stolen. For example, 'hat/s' includes Catherine Burke who was guilty of 'stg hats' plus someone else content with purloining one 'hat'. Ambiguously recorded items that tell us nothing about what was stolen have been excluded from the calculations and tables. These items were: a bundle, forged item/s, good/s, miscellaneous good/s, other article/s, and a parcel.

Clothes: apparel, bombazine, bonnet/s, boots, brogues, cap/s, cape/s, child's dress, cloak/s, clothes, coat/s, dress, frock/s, garment, gloves, gown/s, handkerchief/s, hat/s, jacket, lace veil, lace cap/s, mantle, military clothes, parasol, pelerine, pelisse/s, petticoat, reticule, scarve/s, shawl/s, shift/s, shirt/s, shoes, silk handkerchief/s, silk ˙cloak, silk gown, socks, stays, stockings, trousers, waistcoat, washing clothes, wearing apparel.

Fabric: calico, canvas, cashmere, cloth, corduroy, cotton, fabric, flannel, flax, gingham, gown piece/s, lace, leather, linen, muslin, piece of cloth, piece of woollen cloth, plaids, ribbon/s, satin, silk, stuff/s, a piece of stuff, thread, ticking, toil net, tuscan plait, velvet, wool, worsted, yarn.

Food and animals: apple, bacon, bread, bullock/s, butter, cabbage, calf, cattle, cheese, chook, coffee, cow/s, dough, duck/s, fish, flour, fowl/s, fruit, goose/geese, groceries, ham, heifer/s, honey, horse, lamb, loaf, meat, merino, milk, mutton, oatmeal, oats, pig/s, potato/es, poultry, sheep, spirit/s, suet, sugar, tea, tobacco, turkey/s, turnip/s, vinegar, wheat, wine, yam.

Household items: apron/s, bag/s, bain, basket, bed/s, bedclothes, blanket/s, bolster, bottle/s, bowl, box of toys, box, broad cloth, bucket, candle/s, candlestick/s, carpet, casement cloth, chair cover/s, chair/s, china, clock/s, comb/s, copper kettle, copper boiler, counterpane, cup and saucer/s, curtain/s, cushion, cutlery, decanter/s, dish/es, empty bottles, feather bed, fender, fire grate/s, flat iron, frieze, furniture, glass/es, glassware, grate/s, grid iron, hair comb, hairbrush, house utensil/s, iron pot, kettle/s, kitchen range, knife/s, looking glass, mug, napkin, needle/s, oil cloth, pan/s, paper, pencil, penknife/s, perfumery, pewter pot/s, pillow, plate/s, pot/s, quilt/s, rag, rug, sheet/s, silver spoon/s, silver knife, silver plate, snuffer/s, soap, spoon/s, sugar tongs, table linen, table, tea pot, tea caddy, tea tray, towel/s, tumbler/s, tureen, umbrella/s, washtub/s, writing desk.

Jewellery: bead/s, brooch, chain/s, diamond ring, earrings, eye glass, gold watch, gold ring/s, jewellery, necklace, ring/s, silver snuff box, snuff box/es, spectacles, timepiece, trinket, watch/es.

Money: £50 sterling, bad note/s, bad money, bank note/s, base coin, bill/s, cash book, cheque, dollar/s, money, note/s, note for £60, promissory note/s, purse, ticket, till.

Other: 4 lb weights, a cart, a keg, ammunition, ballad, book/s, brass rod, brass, brass collar, bridlebit, cage, carpentry tool/s, compass, copper, feather/s, file/s, grape, gun, hammer/s, hardware, hay, horse collar, horse cloth, iron, key, lead, machinery, mahogany, nail/s, optician's bones, pewter, pistol, prayer book, print/s, reaping hook, rope/s, sack, saddlery, seal/s, sextant, silver, spade, stone, tool/s, trunk/s, tub/s, turf, violin, wood.

4. SOCIAL-SKILL CLASSIFICATION

The following schema details the way in which convict occupational categories were ranked using Armstrong's social-skill classification. This classification—based in part on the enumerator's books for York in 1841 and 1851—did not include all the occupations listed by the convicts. Consequently, I have made decisions about the location of these occupations in accordance with the system adopted by Armstrong, and influenced by the Nicholas–Shergold adaptations listed in Table A18 of *Convict Workers* (Melbourne 1988). This system has been maintained without adjustments for masculine biases. I have also kept the nomenclature with which I am not totally in agreement, notably the term 'unskilled' which I doubt can justifiably be applied to many jobs. Apprentices, of whom there were very few, have been classified in the level of the occupations they were striving to attain.

Class 1: professional occupations: No female convict (and very few male convicts) belonged to this class—a comment on the class nature of crime and punishment.

Class 2: intermediate occupations: Fruit dealer, poultry dealer, publican, school mistress, village schoolmistress.

Class 3: skilled occupations: Artificial flower maker, attendant at a lunatic asylum, baker, basket maker, bonnet maker, boot binder, boot closer, boot corder, bootmaker, bracelet maker, brace maker, brush maker, butter maker, button maker, catgut manufacturer, calico hemper, calico printer, chair carver, cheese maker, cloth cap maker, comb stainer, confectioner, cook, cook—hotel, cotton manufacturer, cotton spinner, cotton weaver, cotton winder, dealer, dressmaker, embroiderer, fancy trimmer, flax spinner, fringe maker, furrier, glass grinder, glass polisher, handloom weaver, hat binder, hat maker, hat trimmer, hospital nurse, house keeper, housemaid, housemaid—country, housemaid—hotel, housemaid—inn, housemaid—school, instrument maker, instrument teacher, iron polisher, knitter, lace maker, ladies' hairdresser, linen draper, lint maker, mantua maker, market woman, midwife, milliner, muslin sewer, nailer, needlewoman, nurse, ostrich feather dresser, pastry-cook, pearl button maker, pin maker, potter, ribbon weaver, sewer, shoe binder, shoe closer, shoemaker, shop man, silk weaver, silk winder, spinner, stay maker, steam weaver, stocking sitter, straw bonnet maker, straw plaiter, straw worker, tailor, tambour worker, tape weaver, tassel maker, tin hawker, tinware manufacturer, tobacco maker, upholsterer, waiter, waiter—inn, waiting maid, weaver, wool spinner.

Class 4: semi-skilled occupations: Barmaid, brewer, charwoman, child's maid, chambermaid, chambermaid—hotel, chambermaid—inn, country servant, dairymaid, dairywoman, distiller, dyer, farm house girl, farm labourer, farm servant, farm servant indoors, fishing-net maker, general country house servant, general country servant, general house servant, general indoor servant, general servant, governess, in- and out-door servant, indoor servant, ladies' maid, ladies' nursery maid, laundress, laundrymaid, nursemaid, picker, reaper, scullerymaid, sempstress, servant, servant—inn, stage dancer, thorough country servant, thorough servant, town servant, washerwoman.

Class 5: unskilled occupations: Allwork, allwork—country, allwork—country inn, allwork—inn, allwork—ladies' house, allwork—town, factory labourer, factory servant, gipsy, hawker, huxter, kitchenmaid, kitchenmaid—country, kitchenmaid—inn, pedlar, plain worker, pottery packer, house worker.

5. IRISH CENSUS CLASSIFICATION

The following organises census categories into six groups, and provides a detailed listing of how convict occupations were matched to these groups.

Farm and domestic servants (ministering to food plus unclassified): allwork, baker, barmaid, butter maker, cheese maker, child's maid, confectioner, cook, country servant thorough, country housemaid, country allwork, country servant, dairymaid, dealer, farm servant, farm servant indoors, farm labourer, fruit dealer, general house servant, general indoor servant, general country servant, general servant, housemaid, housekeeper, huxter, kitchenmaid, ladies' maid, laundress, laundrymaid, market woman, nursemaid, pastry-cook, pedlar, plain work, poultry dealer, reaper, servant, thorough servant, waiter, waiting maid, washerwoman.

Textiles (ministering to clothing): bonnet maker, boot binder, boot closer, brace maker, calico hemper, calico printer, comb stainer, cotton manufacturer, dressmaker, dyer, factory labourer, flax spinner, fringe maker, hat maker, hat trimmer, knitter, lace maker, mantua maker, milliner, needlewoman, ribbon weaver, sempstress, sews, shoe binder, shoemaker, silk winder, spinner, stay maker, straw bonnet maker, straw plaiter, straw worker.

Other manufacturing (ministering to lodging, furniture, machinery etc.): basket maker, fishing-net maker, tinware manufacturer, upholsterer.

Other (ministering to health, education, religion, charity, justice): governess, midwife, nurse, schoolmistress.

6. ENGLISH CENSUS CLASSIFICATION

The following organises census categories into six groups, and provides a detailed listing of how convict occupations were matched to these groups.

Commerce, trade and manufacture: baker, basket maker, bonnet maker, boot binder, boot closer, boot corder, bootmaker, brewer, button maker, pearl button maker, butter maker, brush maker, brace maker, cloth cap maker, catgut manufacturer, chair carver, cheese maker, cotton manufacturer, cotton spinner, cotton weaver, cotton winder, dealer, distiller, dressmaker, dyer, embroiderer, factory labourer, artificial flower maker, fancy trimmer, ostrich feather dresser, fishing-net maker, flax spinner, fringe maker, fruit dealer, furrier, glass grinder, glass polisher, ladies' hairdresser, hat binder, hat maker, hat trimmer, hawker, huxter, pedlar, iron polisher, bracelet maker, knitter, lace maker, linen draper, lint maker, market woman, mantua maker, milliner, nailer, needlewoman, pin maker, potter, pottery packer, calico printer, publican, ribbon weaver, sempstress, sews, shoe binder, shoe closer, shoemaker, shop man, silk weaver, silk winder, spinner, stay maker, straw bonnet maker, straw plaiter, straw worker, tassel-maker, tailoress, tambour worker, tape weaver, instrumental teacher, tin hawker, tinware manufacturer, tobacco maker, handloom weaver, steam weaver, weaver, wool spinner.

Agriculture: dairy maid, farm labourer, picker, reaper.

Labourers: charwoman, laundress, laundrymaid, nurse, nurse in hospital, washerwoman.

Domestic servants: allwork, allwork in a country inn, allwork in an inn, allwork in a ladies' house, country allwork, town allwork, chambermaid, chambermaid in a hotel, chambermaid in an inn, child's maid, cook, cook in a hotel, country housemaid, housemaid, housemaid in a hotel, housemaid in an inn, housemaid in a school, housekeeper, house worker, country kitchenmaid, kitchenmaid, kitchenmaid in an inn, ladies' maid, farmhouse girl, farm servant, country servant, general country servant, general country house servant, general house servant, general indoor servant, general servant, in and outdoor servant, indoor farm servant, indoor servant, nursemaid, ladies' nursery maid, pastry-cook, public house servant, servant, servant in an inn, thorough country servant, thorough servant, town servant, scullerymaid, waiting maid.

Other (professional persons, other educated persons following miscellaneous pursuits, persons engaged in the government civil service, unclassified):

attendant at a lunatic asylum, barmaid, confectioner, gipsy, governess, midwife, plain work, schoolmistress, stage dancer, stocking sitter, upholsterer, village schoolmistress, waiter, waiter in an inn.

7. FREE IMMIGRANT CLASSIFICATION

Convict occupations were matched to the list of immigrant occupations recorded from free single migrant women who arrived in New South Wales in 1838 and 1839. Minor distinctions made in the indents have been subsumed within the generic category in the following classification for simplicity, for example, country kitchenmaids and hotel kitchenmaids are all under 'kitchenmaid'.

Dealers and others: attendant at a lunatic asylum, barmaids, charwomen, dealers, factory labourers, fruit dealers, gipsy, hawkers, huxters, instrument teachers, ladies' hairdressers, market women, midwives, pedlars, plain workers, pottery packers, poultry dealers, publicans, schoolmistresses, shop men, stage dancers, tin hawkers.

Dressmakers and needlewomen: dressmakers, embroiderers, muslin sewers, needlewomen, sempstresses, sewers, tailors.

House and farm servants: all types of allworkers, chambermaids, child's maids, cooks, dairymaids, farm labourers, farm servants, governesses, house workers, housekeepers, housemaids, kitchenmaids, ladies' maids, nursemaids, nurses, pickers, reapers, scullerymaids, servants, waiters, waiting maids.

Laundresses: laundrymaids, laundresses, washerwomen.

Trades: artificial flower makers, bakers, basket makers, bonnet makers, boot makers, boot binders, boot closers, boot corders, brace makers, bracelet makers, brewers, brush makers, butter makers, button makers, calico hempers, calico printers, catgut manufacturers, chair carvers, cheese makers, cloth cap makers, comb stainers, confectioners, cotton spinners, cotton winders, cotton weavers, cotton manufacturers, distillers, dyers, fancy trimmers, fishing-net makers, flax spinners, fringe makers, furriers, glass polishers, glass grinders, handloom weavers, hat binders, hat makers, hat trimmers, iron polishers, knitters, lace makers, linen drapers, lint makers, mantua makers, milliners, nailers, ostrich feather dressers, pearl button makers, pin makers, potters, ribbon weavers, shoe binders, shoe closers, shoemakers, silk winders, silk weavers, spinners, stay makers, steam weavers, stocking sitters, straw workers, straw plaiters, tambour workers, tape weavers, tassel makers, tinware manufacturers, tobacco makers, upholsterers, weavers, wool spinners.

8. STATISTICAL APPENDIX

Convict Maids has been a quantitative study based upon data collected for the 6876 convict women landed in Sydney in the years 1826 to 1840. This information came from the *Convict indents of transported prisoners* 4/4003–4019, and *Convict indents of transported Irish prisoners* 4/7076–7078, also reproduced as *Convict indents 1788–1842,* F614–744, Genealogical research kit stage 1, AONSW. This appendix gives summaries of the statistical information upon which the figures contained in the text are based. I have attempted to group them into six logical categories.

Three points should be noted. Firstly, raw figures do not always add up to 6876 women because information was missing on select variables in certain cases. 'Valid cases' refers to the number of women for whom information was available. Secondly, throughout these tables a distinction is drawn between 'convicts', meaning those offenders transported to New South Wales, and 'criminals' and 'prisoners' meaning offenders incarcerated in the UK. Thirdly, calculations have been made only to one decimal point. Due to rounding errors, columns do not always add up to exactly 100 per cent. However, I have followed the custom of rounding totals to 100 per cent.

General
A1   Free and forced immigration into New South Wales 1788–1840   253
A2   Convicts' regional origins   255
A3   Mortality on convict voyages   255
A4   Convict conjugal status and motherhood   255

Age
A5   Age distributions of convicts and Irish and English working women   256
A6   Age distributions of convicts and prisoners   256
A7   Irish and English convict age distributions and clustering   257
A8   Age distributions of forced and free immigrants   259

Crime
A9   Offences for which convict women were transported   260
A10 Property stolen by convicts   261
A11 Prior convictions of convicts   262
A12 Crime and prior-conviction rates of convicts   263
A13 Duration of transportation sentence   264
A14 Sentencing of convicts by crime   265
A15 Conviction rates during the London Season (winter–spring)   265

Literacy
A16 Literacy rates for convicts and free immigrants   265
A17 Literacy rates for convicts, working women and free immigrants from England and Ireland   266
A18 Literacy among Irish-born convict women: birthplace and migratory status   267
A19 Literacy among English women: convict stayers and movers plus adult paupers and prisoners   268

Occupation
A20 Occupational structures in Ireland: workers and convicts 15 years and upwards   269
A21 Occupational structures in England: workers and convicts 20 years and upwards   269
A22 Occupational spread of workers, paupers, prisoners and convicts (all ages), Great Britain   270

A23 Occupational profiles of single immigrants and convicts   270

Skills
A24 Skill classification for convicts by country of trial plus Irish workers 271
A25 Convict skill and literacy   271
A26 Convict skill acquisition   271
A27 Skill levels among Irish-born convict women: birthplace and
      migratory status   272
A28 Literacy and skill among English-born convict stayers and movers   273

Table A1   Free and forced immigration into New South Wales, 1788–1840

Year of arrival	Convict women	Free adult females	Convict men	Free adult males
1788 188	– 548	–		
1789	–	–	–	–
1790	288	6	692	–
1791	169	6	1 696	–
1792	121	–	610	–
1793	87	2	233	7
1794	60	2	23	2
1795	–	–	1	–
1796	200	–	152	–
1797	43	–	324	–
1798	94	–	287	–
1799	–	–	305	5
1800	76	12	533	10
1801	207	32	493	26
1802	51	15	618	15
1803	162	10	680	10
1804	130	13	202	11
1805	–	1	–	3
1806	193	3	382	2
1807	110	–	193	–
1808	97	–	197	1
1809	200	–	134	–
1810	121	1	389	8
1811	138	–	333	1
1812	125	–	199	6
1813	54	–	537	–
1814	332	20	839	20
1815	171	3	902	10

Table A1 contd

Year of arrival	Convict women	Free adult females	Convict men	Free adult males
1816	182	16	1 242	11
1817	188	12	1 642	34
1818	292	5	2 425	19
1819	–	4	2 371	11
1820	296	10	2 278	10
1821	130	–	1 528	–
1822	62	–	1 524	–
1823	199	–	1 515	–
1824	147	–	1 006	–
1825	366	–	1 544	–
1826	101	–	1 699	–
1827	511	–	2 103	–
1828	374	122	2 327	200
1829	498	113	3 151	306
1830	449	70	2 767	166
1831	515	98	2 295	185
1832	384	706	2 720	819
1833	649	1 146	3 479	838
1834	462	569	2 658	571
1835	181	644	3 333	551
1836	676	807	3 084	624
1837	541	1 040	2 815	1 125
1838	335	2 111	2 595	2 692
1839	736	3 593	1 529	4 288
1840	464	3 160	1 991	3 760
Total	12 155	14 352	67 123	16 347

Sources: 1788–1800, Shaw, *Convicts and the colonies*, pp. 363–4; 1801–25, Bateson, *The convict ships*, pp. 381–91; 1826–40 *Convict indents*. Immigrant data from Butlin, Ginswick and Statham, 'Colonial statistics before 1850', pp. 10–11, 14–15.

Table A2   Convicts' regional origins

| | Born | | Tried | |
Country	No.	%	No.	%
England	2 326	33.8	2 946	42.8
Ireland	3 868	56.3	3 407	49.5
Scotland	351	5.1	361	5.3
Wales	101	1.5	57	0.8
Outside the United Kingdom	98	1.4	20	0.3
Unknown	132	1.9	85	1.2
Totals	6 876	100	6 876	100

Source: Convict indents.

Table A3   Mortality on convict voyages

Year of arrival	Number transported	Died on voyage No.	%
1826	101	–	–
1827	511	10	2.0
1828	374	2	0.5
1829	498	8	1.6
1830	449	–	–
1831	515	6	1.2
1832	384	2	0.5
1833	649	10	1.5
1834	462	4	0.9
1835	181	–	–
1836	676	8	1.2
1837	541	5	0.9
1838	335	2	0.6
1839	736	5	0.7
1840	464	2	0.4
Total	6 876	64	0.9

Source: Convict indents.

Table A4   Convict conjugal status and motherhood

Conjugal status	No.	%	No. with children	% with children
Single	4 194	62.0	440	10.5
Married	1 598	23.6	1 071	67.0
Widowed	970	14.3	697	71.9
Valid cases	6 762	100	2 208	average 32.7

Source: Convict indents.

Table A5   Age distribution of convicts and Irish and English working women

Age group	Female convicts No.	%	Irish females in 1841 %	English females in 1841 %
0–14	42	0.6	41.3	35.1
15–19	1 151	17.0	5.9	9.9
20–24	2 168	32.1	14.7	18.5
25–29	1 396	20.7	14.8	
30–34	803	11.9	10.9	13.0
35–39	443	6.6	5.8	
40–44	356	5.3	3.4	9.6
45–49	172	2.5	1.4	
50+	227	3.4	1.8	13.9
Valid cases	6 758	100	100	100

Source: Convict indents; 'Report of the commissioners … census of Ireland 1841',
pp. 488–9; 'GB census 1841', p. 20.

Table A6   Age distribution of convicts and prisoners

Age group	Convict women 1826–40 %	Female prisoners in England, 1841 %
<17	3.1	9.9
17–20	23.5	24.3
21–29	43.8	34.6
30+	29.6	31.2
Totals	100	100

Sources: Convict indents; Gatrell and Hadden, 'Criminal statistics', p. 384.

Table A7 Irish and English convict age distributions and clustering

Age	Irish-born convicts No.	%	English-born convicts No.	%
10	1	–	–	–
11	1	–	–	–
12	3	0.1	1	–
13	6	0.2	1	–
14	13	0.3	11	0.5
15	28	0.7	23	1.0
16	49	1.3	48	2.1
17	85	2.2	103	4.4
18	170	4.4	151	6.5
19	213	5.5	183	7.9
20	350	9.1	207	8.9
21	196	5.1	156	6.7
22	288	7.5	161	6.9
23	212	5.5	122	5.3
24	197	5.1	103	4.4
25	256	6.6	100	4.3
26	208	5.4	121	5.2
27	130	3.4	74	3.2
28	174	4.5	80	3.4
29	80	2.1	69	3.0
30	319	8.3	70	3.0
31	37	1.0	28	1.2
32	55	1.4	43	1.9
33	50	1.3	31	1.3
34	58	1.5	38	1.6
35	82	2.1	40	1.7
36	66	1.7	28	1.2
37	33	0.9	20	0.9
38	39	1.0	37	1.6
39	25	0.6	27	1.2
40	149	3.9	50	2.2
41	12	0.3	17	0.7
42	21	0.5	12	0.5
43	12	0.3	16	0.7
44	17	0.4	14	0.6
45	34	0.9	19	0.8
46	25	0.6	15	0.6
47	5	0.1	11	0.5
48	8	0.2	17	0.7
49	6	0.2	10	0.4
50	52	1.3	18	0.8

Table A7 contd

Age	Irish-born convicts		English-born convicts	
---	No.	%	No.	%
51	6	0.2	8	0.3
52	6	0.2	6	0.3
53	6	0.2	3	0.1
54	4	0.1	2	0.1
55	9	0.2	5	0.2
56	3	0.1	2	0.1
57	5	0.1	5	0.2
58	3	0.1	3	0.1
59	2	0.1	4	0.2
60	25	0.6	3	0.1
61	3	0.1	2	0.1
62	3	0.1	–	–
63	2	0.1	1	–
64	2	0.1	–	–
65	1	–	–	–
66	2	0.1	1	–
67	2	0.1	–	–
68	1	–	–	–
69	1	–	–	–
70	4	0.1	–	–
71	–	–	–	–
72	1	–	–	–
73	–	–	–	–
74	–	–	–	–
75	–	–	–	–
76	1	–	–	–
77	–	–	–	–
78	1	–	–	–
79	–	–	–	–
80	1	–	–	–
Valid cases	3 859	100	2 320	100

Source: Convict indents.

Table A8   Age distribution of forced and free immigrants

Age group	Female convicts		Male and female immigrants	
	No.	%	No.	%
Less than 14	16	0.2	39 456	39.7
14–17	395	5.8	6 706	6.8
18–30	4 764	70.5	42 139	42.4
Above 30	1 583	23.4	10 991	11.1
Totals	6 758	100	99 292	100

Sources: Convict indents; Shultz, 'Immigration into Eastern Australia', p. 275.

Table A9 Offences for which convict women were transported

Crimes	All convicts		Irish convicts		English convicts		Rural English (never moved)		Urban English (never moved)		London convicts		Non-London English	
	No.	%	No.	%	No.	%	No.	%	No.	%	No.	%	No.	%
Breaking	169	2.5	55	1.6	76	2.7	17	3.8	18	2.2	14	1.4	62	3.3
Pickpocketing	271	4.1	86	2.6	179	6.3	21	4.7	57	6.8	49	4.9	130	7.0
Receiving	258	3.9	85	2.5	150	5.3	46	10.4	31	3.7	27	2.7	123	6.6
Robbery	1 300	19.6	459	13.7	755	26.4	125	28.2	194	23.3	262	26.2	493	26.6
Shoplifting	309	4.7	145	4.3	150	5.3	17	3.8	68	8.2	53	5.3	97	5.2
Stealing	3 909	58.9	2 204	66.0	1 467	51.4	197	44.4	440	52.8	565	56.5	902	48.6
Vagrancy	154	2.3	154	4.6	–	–	–	–	–	–	–	–	–	–
Violent crimes	121	1.8	74	2.2	26	0.9	9	2.0	8	1.0	8	0.8	18	1.0
Other	150	2.3	78	2.3	53	1.9	12	2.7	17	2.0	22	2.2	31	1.7
Valid cases	6 641	100	3 340	100	2 856	100	444	100	833	100	1 000	100	1 856	100

Source: Convict indents.

Table A10 Property stolen by convicts

Stolen property	All convicts		Irish convicts		English convicts		Rural English (never moved)		Urban English (never moved)		London convicts		Other English convicts	
	No.	%	No.	%	No.	%	No.	%	No.	%	No.	%	No.	%
Clothes	1 394	36.3	861	38.5	435	31.6	60	30.0	128	31.9	160	32.3	275	31.2
Fabric	423	11.0	313	14.0	102	7.4	17	8.5	31	7.7	35	7.1	67	7.6
Food and animals	360	9.3	258	11.5	86	6.2	25	12.5	17	4.2	18	3.6	68	7.7
Household items	394	10.2	179	8.0	186	13.5	27	13.5	51	12.7	80	16.1	106	12.0
Jewellery	317	8.2	122	5.4	166	12.0	10	5.0	54	13.5	81	16.3	85	9.6
Money	821	21.3	444	19.8	328	23.8	47	23.5	94	23.4	95	19.2	233	26.4
Other	144	3.7	62	2.8	75	5.4	14	7.0	26	6.5	27	5.4	48	5.4
Total of stolen goods	3 843	100	2 239	100	1 378	100	200	100	401	100	496	100	882	100

Source: Convict indents.

Table A11 Prior convictions of convicts

Number of prior convictions	All convicts		Irish convicts		English convicts		Rural English (never moved)		Urban English (never moved)		London convicts		Other English convicts	
	No.	%	No.	%	No.	%	No.	%	No.	%	No.	%	No.	%
None	4 288	65.3	2 135	63.3	1 955	66.8	263	57.5	555	65.6	823	81.4	1 132	59.1
One	1 896	28.1	945	28.0	814	27.8	154	33.7	238	28.1	176	17.4	638	33.3
Two	386	5.7	226	6.7	105	3.6	27	5.9	34	4.0	9	0.9	96	5.0
Three	105	1.6	50	1.5	19	0.6	4	0.9	7	0.8	3	0.3	16	0.8
Four	19	0.3	8	0.2	3	0.1	–	–	2	0.2	–	–	3	0.2
Five	11	0.2	1	–	3	0.1	1	0.2	2	0.2	–	–	3	0.2
Repeatedly	48	0.7	8	0.2	26	0.9	8	1.8	8	0.9	–	–	26	1.4
Valid cases	6 753	100	3 373	100	2 925	100	457	100	846	100	1 011	100	1 914	100

Source: Convict indents.

Table A12 Crime and prior conviction rates of convicts

Crimes	None No.	None %	One No.	One %	Two or more No.	Two or more %
Breaking	114	67.5	33	19.5	22	13.0
Pickpocketing	160	59.0	87	32.1	24	8.9
Receiving	191	74.6	53	20.7	12	4.7
Robbery	900	69.4	298	23.0	99	7.6
Shoplifting	147	47.7	116	37.7	45	14.6
Stealing	2 372	61.0	1 191	30.6	327	8.4
Vagrancy	102	67.1	39	25.7	11	7.2
Violent crimes	89	75.4	20	16.9	9	7.6
Other	108	72.5	27	18.1	14	9.4
Valid cases	4 183	63.3	1 864	28.2	563	8.5

Source: Convict indents.

Table A13 Duration of transportation sentence

Sentence	All convicts		Irish convicts		English convicts		Rural English (never moved)		Urban English (never moved)		London convicts		Other English convicts	
	No.	%	No.	%	No.	%	No.	%	No.	%	No.	%	No.	%
Four years	1	–	–	–	1	–	–	–	1	0.1	–	–	1	0.1
Five years	1	–	–	–	–	–	–	–	–	–	–	–	–	–
Seven years	5 366	78.9	3 178	93.5	1 867	63.4	297	65.1	579	68.2	654	64.4	1 213	62.9
Ten years	180	2.6	23	0.7	148	5.0	26	5.7	45	5.3	49	4.8	99	5.1
Fourteen years	637	9.4	34	1.0	506	17.2	67	14.7	129	15.2	160	15.7	346	17.9
Fifteen years	46	0.7	13	0.4	32	1.1	5	1.1	7	0.8	12	1.2	20	1.0
Life	572	8.4	151	4.4	390	13.2	61	13.4	88	10.4	141	13.9	249	12.9
Valid cases	6 803	100	3 399	100	2 944	100	456	100	849	100	1 016	100	1 928	100

Source: Convict indents.

Table A14 Sentencing of convicts by crime

| | Duration of sentence in years | | | | | | | |
| | 7 | | 10 | | 14–15 | | Life | |
Crimes	*No.*	*%*	*No.*	*%*	*No.*	*%*	*No.*	*%*
Breaking	99	58.6	12	7.1	20	11.8	38	22.5
Pickpocketing	164	60.7	14	5.2	61	22.6	31	11.5
Receiving	166	64.6	10	3.9	81	31.5	–	–
Robbery	913	70.3	49	3.8	168	12.9	168	12.9
Shoplifting	281	90.9	2	0.6	20	6.5	6	1.9
Stealing	3 368	86.3	84	2.2	257	6.6	194	5.0
Vagrancy	154	100.0	–	–	–	–	–	–
Violent crimes	46	38.0	1	0.8	15	12.4	59	48.8
Other	76	50.7	5	3.3	18	12.0	51	34.0
Valid cases	5 267	79.4	177	2.7	640	9.7	547	8.2

Source: Convict indents.

Table A15 Conviction rates during the London Season (winter–spring)

| | London | | Rest of urban England | | Rural England | |
Season	*No.*	*%*	*No.*	*%*	*No.*	*%*
In Season (November–April)	519	51.1	274	50.5	273	61.2
Out of Season (May–October)	497	48.9	269	49.5	173	38.8
Valid cases	1 016	100	543	100	446	100

Source: Convict indents.

Table A16 Literacy rates for convicts and free immigrants

| | Convict women | | Free immigrant women | |
Level of literacy	*No.*	*%*	*No.*	*%*
Cannot read or write	2 443	36.1	95	24.7
Read only	2 833	41.9	128	33.2
Read and write	1 489	22.0	162	42.1
Valid cases	6 765	100	385	100

Sources: Convict indents; calculated for samples of single female bounty immigrants into New South Wales in 1838 and for single and married female assisted immigrants into New South Wales in 1841, from Penglase, 'Enquiry into literacy', pp. 45–9.

Table A17 Literacy rates of convicts, working women and free immigrants from England and Ireland

| | From England | | | | | | From Ireland | | | | | |
| | Convicts* | | Working women | | Immigrants | | Convicts* | | Working women | | Immigrants | |
Level of literacy	No.	%	No.	%	No.	%	No.	%	No.	%	No.	%
Cannot read or write	597	20.4	52		17	21.3	1 773	52.4	1 394 273	55.1	77	25.7
Read only	1 318	45.0	48		30	37.5	1 261	37.3	598 527	23.7	98	32.7
Read and write	1 011	34.6			33	41.3	348	10.3	536 860	21.2	125	41.7
Valid cases	2 926	100	100		80	100	3 382	100	2 529 660	100	300	100

*Convicts transported from that country.

Sources: Calculated for samples of single female bounty immigrants into New South Wales in 1838 and for single and married female assisted immigrants into New South Wales in 1841, from Penglase, 'Enquiry into literacy', pp. 45–9; *Convict indents.*

Table A18 Literacy among Irish-born convict women: birthplace and migratory status

| | Rural born | | Urban born | | Stayers | | Migrants | | | |
| | | | | | | | Domestic | | Emigrants | |
Level of literacy	No.	%	No.	%	No.	%	No.	%	No.	%
Cannot read or write	1 618	53.9	137	42.8	1 171	55.4	584	48.3	192	35.9
Read only	1 101	36.7	138	43.1	754	35.7	485	40.1	230	43.0
Read and write	284	9.5	45	14.1	188	8.9	141	11.7	113	21.1
Totals	3 003	100	320	100	2 113	100	1 210	100	535	100

Source: Convict indents.

Table A19 Literacy among English women: convict stayers and movers plus adult paupers and prisoners

Level of literacy	Convict stayers		Convict movers		Adult paupers 1837				Female prisoners 1840
					Old and infirm		Able-bodied and temporarily disabled		
	No.	%	No.	%	No.	%	No.	%	%
Cannot read or write	239	18.3	157	15.7	232	63.9	187	39.8	44.5
Read	631	48.4	436	43.5	97	26.7	222	47.2	53.3
Read and write	434	33.3	410	40.9	34	9.4	61	13.0	1.9
Valid cases	1 304	100	1 003	100	363	100	470	100	100

Sources: Convict indents; 'SC on education', p. 42; Gatrell and Hadden, 'Criminal statistics', p. 380. For criminals, only percentages were given, and the category recorded here as 'read' also includes those who could only read and write imperfectly.

Table A20 Occupational structures in Ireland: workers and convicts 15 years and upwards

1841 Irish census category	Irish working women No.	%	Convicts transported from Ireland* No.	%
Farm and domestic servants	427 875	39.7	4 065	91.7
Textiles	636 909	59.1	330	7.4
Other manufacture	3 488	0.3	4	0.1
Other	9 542	0.9	36	0.8
Total occupied	1 077 814	100	4 435	100

*Figures based on convicts' stock of skills.
Source: 'Report of the commissioners . . . census of Ireland 1841', p. 440; *Convict indents.*

Table A21 Occupational structures in England: workers and convicts 20 years and upwards

1841 British census category	English working women No.	%	Convicts transported from England* No.	%
Commerce, trade and manufacture	379 458	38.2	450	12.4
Agriculture	43 354	4.4	190	5.2
Labourers	86 652	8.8	498	13.7
Domestic servants	447 896	45.1	2 418	66.7
Others	35 421	3.6	68	1.9
Total occupied	992 781	100	3 624	100

*Figures based on convicts' stock of skills.
Sources: 'GB census 1841. Occupational abstract', pp. 31–44; *Convict indents.*

Table A22   Occupational spread of workers, paupers, prisoners and convicts (all ages), Great Britain

1841 British census category	English workers No.	%	English workhouses No.	%	Gaols in Great Britain No.	%	English-tried convicts* No.	%
Commerce, trade and manufacture	533 400	37.2	2 936	26.9	717	42.4	539	12.2
Agriculture	51 938	3.6	270	2.5	19	1.1	211	4.8
Labourers	93 233	6.5	2 439	22.4	191	11.3	547	12.4
Domestic servants	712 790	49.8	5 180	47.5	747	44.1	3 029	68.8
Others	40 822	2.9	76	0.7	19	1.1	79	1.8
Total occupied	1 432 183	100	10 901	100	1 693	100	4 405	100

*Figures based on convicts' stock of skills.
Sources: 'GB census 1841. Occupational abstract', pp. 31–44, 62–70; *Convict indents.*

Table A23   Occupational profiles of single immigrants and convicts

Occupation	Single female immigrants,[a] 1838 and 1839 No.	%	Female convicts,[b] 1826–1840 No.	%
Dealers and others	6	0.3	135	1.4
Dressmakers and needlewomen	439	19.6	622	6.5
House and farm servants	1 681	74.9	7 407	77.9
Laundresses	111	4.9	1 047	11.0
Trades	8	0.4	301	3.2
Total occupied	2 245	100	9 512	100

a   Those travelling in bounty and government-chartered vessels.
b   Figures based on convicts' stock of skills.
Sources: 'Report from the agent-general for emigration', pp. 25, 27, 33, 35; *Convict indents.*

Table A24 Skill classification for convicts by country of trial plus Irish workers

Level of skill	All convict women No.	%	Tried in England No.	%	Tried in Ireland No.	%	Irish working women %
Unskilled	1 555	23.1	592	20.3	844	25.1	25.5
Semi-skilled	2 106	31.3	700	23.9	1 264	37.6	52.7
Skilled	3 062	45.4	1 622	55.5	1 245	37.1	21.8
Middling	15	0.2	9	0.3	5	0.1	
Valid cases	6 738	100	2 923	100	3 358	100	100

Sources: Convict indents; figures for Irish working women taken from Nicholas and Shergold, 'Convicts as workers', p. 73.

Table A25 Convict skill and literacy

Level of literacy	Unskilled No.	%	Semi-skilled No.	%	Skilled No.	%	Middling No.	%
Cannot read or write	725	46.6	924	44.0	774	25.3	4	26.7
Read	623	40.1	854	40.6	1 341	43.8	3	20.0
Read and write	207	13.3	324	15.4	944	30.9	8	53.3
Valid cases	1 555	100	2 102	100	3 059	100	15	100

Source: Convict indents.

Table A26 Convict skill acquisition

Age group	Tried in Ireland Total No.	Skilled workers No.	%	Tried in England Total No.	Skilled workers No.	%
9–14	23	1	4.3	13	1	7.7
15–19	488	152	31.1	570	259	45.4
20–24	1 108	444	40.1	921	499	54.2
25–29	744	302	40.6	568	332	58.5
30–34	441	158	35.8	306	194	63.4
35–39	186	64	34.4	212	132	62.3
40–44	183	62	33.9	144	89	61.8
45+	176	60	34.1	184	115	62.5
Valid cases	3 349	1 243	37.1	2 918	1 621	55.6

Source: Convict indents.

Table A27 Skill levels among Irish-born convict women: birthplace and migratory status

| Level of skill | Rural born | | Urban born | | Stayers | | Migrants | | | |
| | | | | | | | Domestic | | Emigrants | |
	No.	%	No.	%	No.	%	No.	%	No.	%
Unskilled	754	25.3	83	26.3	538	25.6	229	24.9	132	24.7
Semi-skilled	1 137	38.1	108	34.2	802	38.2	443	36.9	150	28.1
Skilled	1 092	36.6	125	39.6	758	36.1	459	38.2	252	47.2
Total occupied	2 983	100	316	100	2 098	100	1 201	100	534	100

Source: Convict indents.

Table A28 Literacy and skill among English-born convict stayers and movers

	Stayers		Movers	
Level of skill	*No.*	*%*	*No.*	*%*
Unskilled	273	21.0	193	19.2
Semi-skilled	319	24.5	211	21.0
Skilled	708	54.5	602	59.8
Valid cases	1 300	100	1 006	100

Source: Convict indents.

Notes

ABBREVIATIONS

AONSW   Archives Office of New South Wales
HRA   *Historical Records of Australia*
IUP   Irish University Press Reprint Series
Mitchell   Mitchell Library, State Library of New South Wales
MLNLA   Manuscript Library, National Library of Australia
PP   *British Parliamentary Papers*

INTRODUCTION

1. For some examples, see B. Attwood, *The making of the Aborigines* (Sydney 1989); N. G. Butlin, *Economics and the dreamtime: A hypothetical history* (Cambridge 1993); J. Huggins, 'Experiences of a Queensland Aboriginal domestic servant: Agnes Williams talks to Jackie Huggins', *Labour History* 61 (1991); A. McGrath, *Born in the cattle* (Sydney 1987); H. Reynolds, *The other side of the frontier* (Ringwood 1982); H. Reynolds, *Frontier* (Sydney 1987); H. Reynolds, *With the white people* (Ringwood, 1990); H. Reynolds, *Law of the land* (Ringwood 1992); L. Ryan, *The Aboriginal Tasmanians* (Brisbane 1989).
2. S. Nicholas (ed.), *Convict workers: Reinterpreting Australia's past* (Melbourne 1988).
3. Pioneering work was done in this area by Beverley Kingston in *My wife, my daughter and poor Mary Ann: Women and work in Australia* (Melbourne 1975). For recent work on this topic, see K. Reiger, *The disenchantment of the home* (Melbourne 1986); G. Snooks, *Portrait of the family within the total economy: A study in longrun dynamics, Australia 1788–1990* (Cambridge 1994). For a critique of this latter publication see K. Alford, book review, *Labour History* 67 (1994).
4. For a review of this literature see S.Garton, 'The convict origins debate: Historians and the problem of the "criminal class"', *Australian New Zealand Journal of Criminology* 24 (1991); most recently B. Dyster, 'Convicts', *Labour History* 67 (1994).
5. These figures are for the whole of Australia and include all forms of penal experiments. L. L. Robson, *The convict settlers of Australia: An enquiry into the origin and character of the convicts transported to New South Wales and Van Diemen's Land, 1787–1852* (Melbourne 1965), p. 4.

6. His paper on this topic was seminal: G. A. Wood, 'Convicts', *Royal Australian Historical Society Journal and Proceedings* 8 (1922). For a biography of Wood, see R. M. Crawford, *'A bit of a rebel'. The life and work of George Arnold Wood* (Sydney 1975).

7. J. L. Hammond and B. Hammond, *The town labourer, 1760–1832: The new civilization*, second impression (London 1917); J. L. Hammond and B. Hammond, *The village labourer, 1760–1832: A study in the government of England before the Reform Bill*, new edition (London 1913); S. Webb and B. Webb, *The history of trade unionism*, new edition (London 1911).

8. Wood, 'Convicts', pp. 181–2.

9. Wood, 'Convicts', p. 181.

10. Wood, 'Convicts', p. 196.

11. Wood, 'Convicts', pp. 180–1.

12. Wood, 'Convicts', p. 189.

13. C. M. H. Clark, 'The origins of the convicts transported to Eastern Australia, 1787-1852', *Historical Studies: Australia and New Zealand* 7 (1956); H. S. Payne, 'A statistical study of female convicts in Tasmania, 1843–53', *Tasmanian Historical Research Association Papers and Proceedings* 9 (1961); L. L. Robson, 'The origin of the women convicts sent to Australia, 1787–1852', *Historical Studies, Australia and New Zealand* 11 (1963); Robson, *Convict settlers*; A. G. L. Shaw, *Convicts and the colonies: A study of penal transportation from Great Britain and Ireland to Australia and other parts of the British Empire* (Melbourne 1981).

14. R. Hughes, *The fatal shore: A history of the transportation of convicts to Australia, 1787-1868* (London 1987).

15. Shaw, *Convicts and the colonies*, p.165.

16. Robson, *Convict settlers*, pp. 157–8.

17. Clark, 'Origins', p. 327; Clark quoted in F. B. Smith, 'The fatal subject', *Scripsi* 4 (1987), pp. 60–1.

18. Clark, 'Origins', p. 134.

19. Clark, 'Origins', p. 134.

20. Wood, 'Convicts', p. 194.

21. Robson, 'Origin of women convicts', p. 53.

22. Shaw, *Convicts and the colonies*, p. 164.

23. Robson, 'Origin of women convicts', p. 47.

24. Robson, 'Origin of women convicts', p. 46.

25. Robson, 'Origin of women convicts', p. 53.

26. P. Robinson, 'The first forty years', in J. Mackinolty and H. Radi (eds), *In pursuit of justice: Australian women and the law, 1788-1979* (Sydney 1979), p. 5.

27. See P. Tardiff, *Notorious strumpets and dangerous girls: Convict women in Van Diemen's Land, 1803–1829* (North Ryde 1990).

28. K. Macnab and R. Ward, 'The nature and nurture of the first generation of native-born Australians', *Historical Studies: Australia and New Zealand* 10 (1962), p. 290.

29. At least among the Irish female convicts according to P. O'Farrell, *The Irish in Australia* (Sydney 1987), p. 24.

30. J. McQuilton, 'Women convicts', in J. C. R. Camm and J. McQuilton (eds), *Australians: A historical atlas* (Canberra 1988), p. 205.

31. M. B. Schedvin and C. B. Schedvin, 'The nomadic tribes of urban Britain: A prelude to Botany Bay', *Historical Studies: Australia and New Zealand* 18 (1978), p. 254; J. B. Hirst, *Convict society and its enemies: A history of early New South Wales* (Sydney 1983), p. 33; Hughes, *Fatal shore*, pp. 158–63.

32. C. M. H. Clark, *A history of Australia* (Melbourne 1962); M. Dixson, *The real Matilda: Woman and identity in Australia, 1788 to the present* (Victoria 1976); H. McQueen, *A new Britannia: An argument concerning the social origins of Australian radicalism and nationalism* (Victoria 1980).

33. Hirst, *Convict society*; F. D. Lewis, 'The cost of convict transportation from Britain to Australia, 1796–1810', *Economic History Review* 41 (1988); Macnab and Ward, Nature and nurture'; P. Robinson, *The hatch and brood of time: A study of the first generation of native-born white Australians, 1788–1828*, volume 1 (Oxford 1985).

34. For some examples, see T. A. Coghlan, *Labour and industry in Australia: From the first settlement in 1788 to the establishment of the commonwealth in 1901*, volume 1, first published 1918 (Melbourne 1969); B. Fitzpatrick, *British imperialism and Australia, 1788–1833* (London 1939); R. M. Hartwell, *The economic development of Van Diemen's Land, 1820–1850* (Melbourne 1954); E. Shann, *An economic history of Australia*, first published 1930 (Cambridge 1948). For a recent appraisal of this problem, and an attempted resolution, see S. Nicholas and D. Oxley, 'Convict economies', in R. Jackson (ed.), *The Cambridge economic history of Australia*, volume 1 (forthcoming).

35. Both of these books were reissued in 1994. Dixson, *The real Matilda*; Summers, *Damned whores and God's police* (Victoria 1976).

36. Summers, *Damned whores*, pp. 270–3.

37. M. Sturma, 'Eye of the beholder: The stereotype of women convicts, 1788–1852', *Labour History* 34 (1978).

38. Sturma, 'Eye of the beholder', p. 4.

39. Robinson, 'First forty years', p. 9; Robinson, *Hatch and brood*, p. 75.

40. D. Beddoe, *Welsh convict women: A study of women transported from Wales to Australia, 1787–1852* (Wales 1979), p. 37.

41. H. S. Payne, Deirdre Beddoe and John Williams all hazarded guesses about the numbers involved, but like Wood, they reached somewhat different conclusions from Robson. Beddoe, *Welsh convict women*, p. 37; Payne, 'Statistical study', p. 58; J. Williams, 'Irish female convicts and Tasmania', *Labour History* 44 (1983), p. 5. Williams' subsequent work has been published posthumously; J. Williams, *Ordered to the Island: Irish convicts and Van Diemen's Land* (Sydney 1994).

42. For example, see K. Daniels (ed.), *So much hard work: Women and prostitution in Australian history* (Sydney 1984).

43. Beddoe, *Welsh convict women*, p. 38.

44. Defoe, quoted in A. W. Baker, *Death is a good solution: The convict experience in early Australia* (St Lucia 1984), p. 8.

45. H. Mayhew and J. Binny, *The criminal prisons of London and scenes of prison life* (London 1862), p. 454.

46. Mayhew devoted considerable attention to prostitutes. See H. Mayhew, *London labour and the London poor: A cyclopaedia of the condition and earnings of those that will work, those that cannot work, and those that will not work, comprising prostitutes, thieves, swindlers, beggars*, volume 4 (London 1862). Also see F. B. Smith, 'Mayhew's convict', *Victorian Studies* 22 (1979); E. P. Thompson and E. Yeo (eds), *The unknown Mayhew: Selections from the 'Morning Chronicle', 1849–50* (London 1973).

47. J. W. Scott and L. A. Tilly, 'Women's work and the family in nineteenth-century Europe', *Comparative Studies in Society and History* 17 (1975), p. 58.

48. Mayhew, *London labour*, p. 216.

49. Robinson, *Hatch and brood*, p. 73.

50. Robinson, 'First forty years'.

51. Beddoe, *Welsh convict women*.

52. Williams, 'Female convicts'.

53. Macnab and Ward, 'Nature and nurture', p. 289.

54. Robinson, *Hatch and brood*.

55. M. Perrott, *A tolerable good success: Economic opportunities for women in New South Wales, 1788–1830* (Sydney 1983).

56. A. Salt, *These outcast women: The Parramatta female factory 1821–1848* (Sydney 1984); H. Weatherburn, 'The female factory', in Mackinolty and Radi (eds), *In pursuit of justice*. Similar work has been done for the factory in Van Diemen's Land; see K. Daniels, 'Prostitution in Tasmania during the transition from penal settlement to "civilized" society', in Daniels (ed.), *So much hard work*; T. Rayner, *Historical survey of the female factory historic site, Cascades* (Tasmania 1981).

57. K. Alford, *Production or reproduction? An economic history of women in Australia, 1788–1850* (Oxford 1984).

58. For some examples see K. Alford, 'Convict and immigrant women before 1851', in J. Jupp (ed.), *The Australian people* (Sydney 1988); A. Atkinson, 'Four patterns of convict protest', *Labour History* 37 (1979); A. Atkinson, *Camden: Farm and village life in early New South Wales* (Oxford 1988); M. Aveling, 'She only married to be free: Or, Cleopatra vindicated', *Push from the Bush* 2 (1978); M. Aveling, 'Gender in early New South Wales', *Push from the Bush* 24 (1987); M. Aveling, 'Bending the bars: Convict women and the state', in K. Saunders and R. Evans (eds), *Gender relations in Australia: Domination and negotiation* (Sydney 1992); M. J. Belcher, 'The child in New South Wales society: 1820–1837' (unpublished PhD thesis, University of New England, 1982); P. J. Byrne, 'Women and the criminal law: Sydney 1810–1821', *Push from the Bush* 21 (1985); P. J. Byrne, *Criminal law and colonial subject: New South Wales, 1810–1830* (Melbourne 1993); K. Daniels and M. Murnane (eds), *Uphill all the way: A documentary history of women in Australia* (St Lucia 1980); M. Sullivan, 'Ann McNally: Convict servant', in M. Lake and F. Kelly (eds), *Double time: Women in Victoria—150 years* (Melbourne 1985).

59. M. Sturma, *Vice in a vicious society: Crime and convicts in mid-nineteenth century New South Wales* (St Lucia 1983).

60. M. Roe, 'Colonial society in embryo', *Historical Studies: Australia and New Zealand* 7 (1956); Hirst, *Convict society.*

61. M. Lake, 'Convict women as objects of male vision: An historiographical review', *Bulletin of the Centre for Tasmanian Historical Studies* 2 (1988). Also see D. Kent and N. Townsend, 'Deborah Oxley's "female convicts": An accurate view of working-class women?', *Labour History* 65 (1993); D. Oxley, 'Exercising agency', *Labour History* 65 (1993).

62. P. Robinson, *The women of Botany Bay: A reinterpretation of the role of women in the origins of Australian society* (Macquarie 1988).

63. B. Smith, *A cargo of women: Susannah Watson and the convicts of the 'Princess Royal'* (Sydney 1988).

64. L. Ryan, 'The governed: Convict women in Tasmania, 1803–1853', *Bulletin of the Centre for Tasmanian Historical Studies* 3 (1990–91).

65. An unresolved tension identified years ago by Beverley Kingston: *The world moves slowly* (Cornell 1977), p. 7.

66. Robinson, *Women of Botany Bay*, p. 6.

67. Robinson, *Women of Botany Bay*, pp. 4–8, 235–6.

68. Robinson, *Women of Botany Bay*, p. 236.

69. Robinson, *Women of Botany Bay*, p. 5.

70. Robinson, *Women of Botany Bay*, pp. 34–6.

71. Robinson, 'First forty years', p. 10; Robinson, *Hatch and brood*, p. 10; Robinson, *Women of Botany Bay*, pp. 13–14.

72. Robinson, *Women of Botany Bay*, pp. 3, 236.

73. Robinson, *Women of Botany Bay*, p. 3.

74. Robinson, *Women of Botany Bay*, p. 38.

75. Robinson, *Women of Botany Bay*, p. 235.

76. In addition to those studies already mentioned, see A. Needham, *The women transported on the 1790 'Neptune'* (Sydney 1988), and M. Tipping, *Convicts unbound: The story of the 'Calcutta' convicts and their settlement in Australia* (Victoria 1988).

77. Nicholas (ed.), *Convict workers.*

78. S. Nicholas and P. Shergold, 'Unshackling the past', in Nicholas (ed.), *Convict workers*, pp. 7–11.

1   ELIZABETH

1. L. L. Robson, *The convict settlers of Australia: An enquiry into the origin and character of the convicts transported to New South Wales and Van Diemen's Land, 1787–1852* (Melbourne 1965), p.173. For a discussion of how the convict records were generated, see Robson's appendix 3, and P. R. Eldershaw, *Guide to the public records of Tasmania. Section three: Convict department record group* (Hobart 1965).

2. 5 George IV, cap. 84, quoted in Robson, *Convict settlers*, p. 174.

3. The Corporation of London Records Office holds these transportation accounts submitted by John Clark from 13 July 1829 to the end of 1840. It is unclear whether Clark was the man responsible in the years 1824 to 1828. *Transportation accounts*, Australian joint copying project, Reel FM4/2283.

4. 'Report from the select committee on transportation together with minutes of evidence, appendix and index', *Parliamentary Papers* (hereafter *PP*) 1837 (518) XIX, pp. 281–2 (Irish University Press reprint series (hereafter IUP) *Crime and Punishment—Transportation* 2).

5. 'SC on transportation', p. 282.

6. *Convict indents of transported prisoners* 4/4003–4019, and *convict indents of transported Irish prisoners* 4/7076–7078, also reproduced as *Convict indents 1788–1842*, F614–744, Genealogical research kit stage 1, both at the State Archives Office of New South Wales.

7. P. Cunningham (ed.), D. S. Macmillan, *Two years in New South Wales: Comprising sketches of the actual state of society in that colony; of its peculiar advantages to emigrants; of its topography, natural history, &c. &c.*, (1827; reproduction Sydney 1966), pp. 301–2.

8. Robson, *Convict settlers*, pp. 181–2; John Hirst's address quoted in K. Bishop and I. Gray, 'HTAA National Conference—Hobart 1989', *The History Teacher* 27 (1989), p. 10.

9. B. Dyster, 'Employment and assignment', in S. Nicholas (ed.), *Convict workers: Reinterpreting Australia's past* (Melbourne 1988), p. 148.

10. J. T. Bigge, quoted in Robson, *Convict settlers*, p. 173.

11. This is noted in Robson, *Convict settlers*, p. 174.

12. J. Williams, 'Irish female convicts and Tasmania', *Labour History* 44 (1983), p. 2.

13. 'SC on transportation', p. 282.

14. D. Meredith, 'Full circle? Contemporary views on transportation', in Nicholas (ed.), *Convict workers*, p. 15.

15. Age-heaping is discussed in Chapter Four.

16. W. B. Stephens, *Education, literacy and society, 1830-70: The geography of diversity in provincial England* (Manchester 1987), p. 29.

17. S. Nicholas, 'Understanding Convict Workers', *Australian Economic History Review* 31 (1991), pp. 103–4.

18. S. Nicholas and P. Shergold, 'Convicts as workers', in Nicholas (ed.), *Convict workers*, pp. 62–84.

19. For comparison, see the criminal registers of the Home Office or the Old Bailey records. Both are available at the Mitchell Library, Sydney: for example, *Criminal registers*, Australian Joint Copying Project, HO26, 27; *Central criminal court (Old Bailey) sessions papers*, 1835/36–1836/37 FM4/5851 Reel No. 41; 1836/37–1837/38 FM4/5852 Reel No. 42. For some examples of historical works, see V. Bailey (ed.), *Policing and punishment in nineteenth-century Britain* (London 1981); J. M. Beattie, 'The criminality of women in eighteenth-century England', *Journal of Social History* 8 (1975); J. S. Cockburn (ed.), *Crime and the courts in Surrey 1550–1800* (London 1977); D. Hay, P. Linebaugh and E. P. Thompson, *Albion's fatal tree: Crime and society in eighteenth-century England* (London 1975), pp. 255–308; D. Philips, *Crime and authority in Victorian England: The Black Country, 1835-1860* (London 1977); G. Rudé, *Criminal and victim: Crime and society in early nineteenth-century England* (Oxford 1985).

20. Thanks to Peter Roberts, one of Margaret's descendants, for drawing this invaluable historical record to my attention.

21. D. Oxley, 'History and mythology: Researching female convicts', *Locality* 3 (1989).

22. D. Beddoe, *Welsh convict women: A study of women transported from Wales to Australia, 1787–1852* (Wales 1979); Williams, 'Irish female convicts'.

23. P. Robinson, *The women of Botany Bay: A reinterpretation of the role of women in the origins of Australian society* (Macquarie 1988).

24. A. Needham, *The women transported on the 1790 'Neptune'* (Sydney 1988); M. Tipping, *Convicts unbound: The story of the 'Calcutta' convicts and their settlement in Australia* (Victoria 1988).

25. B. Smith, *A cargo of women: Susannah Watson and the convicts of the 'Princess Royal'* (Sydney 1988).

26. J. J. Bachofen, quoted in E. Gould-Davis, *The first sex* (London 1973), p. 33.

2   MERCURY'S CHARGES

1. There is a lengthy debate over the motives behind colonising Australia, divided between those who view transportation as simply a dumping measure, and those who believe strategic naval and/or trade reasons drove the move. Conveniently, many of the salient articles have been gathered together in G. Martin (ed.), *The founding of Australia* (Hale and Iremonger 1978). For recent contributions, see A. Frost, *Convicts and empire: A naval question, 1776–1811* (Oxford 1980), and M. Gillen, 'The Botany Bay decision, 1786— convicts, not empire', *English Historical Review* 97 (1982).

2. A useful discussion of the context and nature of change from 1780 to 1850 can be found in D. Philips, 'Crime, law and punishment in the industrial revolution', in P. O'Brien and R. Quinault (eds), *The industrial revolution and British society* (Cambridge 1993).

3. For a short and very useful discussion of the differences between felonies and misdemeanours, and also indictable and summary offences, see D. Philips, *Crime and authority in Victorian England: The Black Country, 1835–1860* (London 1977), pp. 298–300.

4. J. M. Beattie, *Crime and the courts in England, 1660–1800* (Princeton 1986), pp. 141–6. Also see J. M. Beattie, 'Crime and the courts in Surrey, 1736–1753', in J. S. Cockburn (ed.), *Crime in England, 1550–1800* (London 1977).

5. Beattie, *Crime and the courts*, pp. 440–9.

6. Beattie, *Crime and the courts*, p. 142.

7. Beattie, *Crime and the courts*, p. 491.

8. Beattie 'Crime and the courts', p. 158.

9. Beattie, *Crime and the courts*, pp. 142, 490–1.

10. Beattie, *Crime and the courts*, p. 143.

11. Beattie, *Crime and the courts*, p. 146.

12. Beattie, *Crime and the courts*, pp. 144–6; J. M. Beattie, 'The criminality of women in eighteenth-century England', *Journal of Social History* 8 (1975), p. 88; D. Hay, P. Linebaugh and E. P. Thompson, *Albion's fatal tree: Crime and society in eighteenth-century England* (London 1975); D. Jones, *Crime, protest, community and police in nineteenth-century Britain* (London 1982), pp. 11–14; A. J. Peacock, 'Village radicalism in East Anglia, 1800–50', in J. P. D. Dunbabin (ed.), *Rural discontent in nineteenth-century Britain* (New

York 1974); E. P. Thompson, *Whigs and hunters: The origins of the Black Act* (London 1975).

13. Quoted in G. A. Wood, 'Convicts', *Royal Australian Historical Society Journal and Proceedings* 8 (1922), p. 193.

14. Beattie, 'Crime and the courts', p. 157.

15. Beattie, *Crime and the courts*, pp. 142–3.

16. Beattie, *Crime and the courts*, p. 88.

17. W. Oldham, *Britain's convicts to the colonies* (Sydney 1990). Also see Beattie, *Crime and the courts*, pp. 470–83.

18. *Act for punishment of rogues, vagabonds and sturdy beggars*, 39 Elizabeth, c. 4 (1597). *Act for the further preventing of robbery, burglary, and other felonies, and for the more effectual transportation of felons, etc.*, 4 George. 1, c. 11 (1717). Also see L. Radzinowicz and R. Hood, *A history of English criminal law and its administration from 1750*, volume 5, chapter 14.

19. See C. Sweeney, *Transported: In place of death. Convicts in Australia* (Melbourne 1981).

20. Beattie, *Crime and the courts*, pp. 506–13.

21. Beattie, *Crime and the courts*, pp. 182, 287; A. R. Ekirch, *Bound for America: The transportation of British convicts to the colonies, 1718–1775* (Oxford 1987), pp. 29–30; Philips, *Crime and authority*, p. 299.

22. Beattie, *Crime and the courts*, p. 89.

23. *An Act to authorise, for a limited time, the punishment by hard labour of offenders who, for certain crimes, are or shall become liable to be transported to any of His Majesty's colonies and plantations*, 16 George. 3, c. 43 (1776). Also see Ekirch, *Bound for America*, p. 1. Subsequent Acts relating to transportation were: *An Act to explain and amend the laws relating to transportation, imprisonment, and other punishment, of certain offenders*, 19 George. 3, c. 74 (1779); *An Act for the effectual transportation of felons and other offenders, etc.*, 24 George. 3, session 2, c. 56 (1784); *An Act for the transportation of offenders from Great Britain*, 5 George. 4, c. 84 (1824).

24. G. Rudé, *Criminal and victim: Crime and society in early nineteenth-century England* (Oxford 1985), p. 108. Also see V. A. C. Gatrell and T. B. Hadden, 'Criminal statistics and their interpretation', in E. A. Wrigley (ed.), *Nineteenth-century society: Essays in the use of quantitative methods for the study of social data* (Cambridge 1972), p. 352.

25. V. Bailey, 'Introduction', in V. Bailey (ed.), *Policing and punishment in nineteenth-century Britain* (London 1981), p. 16.

26. V. Bailey, 'Introduction', pp. 11–12; V. Bailey, 'The Metropolitan police, the Home Office and the threat of outcast London', in Bailey (ed.), *Policing and punishment*; A. Shubert, 'Private initiative in law enforcement: Associations for the Prosecution of Felons, 1744–1856', in Bailey (ed.) *Policing and punishment*; R. Swift, 'Urban policing in early Victorian England, 1835–86: A reappraisal', *History* 73 (1988); J. J. Tobias, *Crime and police in England, 1700–1900* (Dublin 1979).

27. C. Emsley, *Crime and society in England, 1750–1900* (London 1987), pp. 145–6; Rudé, *Criminal and victim*, pp. 89–90.

28. Gatrell and Hadden, 'Criminal statistics', p. 352.
29. Rudé, *Criminal and victim*, pp. 109–10.
30. Rudé, *Criminal and victim*, p. 112.
31. Cesare Lombroso, quoted in D. Beddoe, *Welsh convict women: A study of women transported from Wales to Australia, 1787–1852* (Wales 1979), p. 33. Themes of genetic criminality will be touched on in Chapter Three, while the association of female criminality with lack of femininity will be pursued in Chapter Eight.
32. H. Mayhew and J. Binny, *The criminal prisons of London and scenes of prison life* (London 1862), p. 87.
33. Quoted in A. W. Baker, *Death is a good solution: The convict experience in early Australia* (St Lucia 1984), p. 31.
34. Mayhew and Binny, *Criminal prisons*, pp. 84–9, 356–8; Mary Carpenter, *Reformatory schools for the children of the perishing and dangerous classes and for juvenile offenders*, quoted in Beddoe, *Welsh convict women*, p. 75.
35. Anonymous nineteenth-century commentator, quoted in Gatrell and Hadden, 'Criminal statistics', p. 381. For more on the defining characteristics of the criminal class, see D.Oxley, 'Female convicts', in S. Nicholas (ed.), *Convict workers: reinterpreting Australia's past* (Melbourne 1988) and D. Oxley, 'Women transported: gendered images and realities', *Australian New Zealand Journal of Criminology* 24.2 (July 1991).
36. Mayhew and Binny, *Criminal prisons*, p. 396.
37. C. M. H. Clark, 'The origins of the convicts transported to Eastern Australia, 1787–1852', *Historical Studies: Australia and New Zealand* 7 (1956), p. 314; M. B. Schedvin and C. B. Schedvin, 'The nomadic tribes of urban Britain: A prelude to Botany Bay', *Historical Studies: Australia and New Zealand* 18 (1978), pp. 263–4.
38. Beddoe, *Welsh convict women*, p. 40; L. L. Robson, *The convict settlers of Australia: An enquiry into the origin and character of the convicts transported to New South Wales and Van Diemen's Land, 1787–1852* (Melbourne 1965), p. 9; J. Williams, 'Irish female convicts and Tasmania', *Labour History* 44 (1983), p. 7.
39. For descriptions of the meanings of various crimes see Beattie, *Crime and the courts*. Interestingly, while robbery was classified as violent crime, the indents drew a distinction between robbery, and robbery committed with assaults of one sort or another
40. Rachael Atkinson, *Henry Wellesley* 1837. Throughout this book, convicts who have not been thoroughly identified within the text will be listed along with their transport ship and its year of arrival in Sydney. All information comes from the *Convict indents of transported prisoners* 4/4003–4019, and *convict indents of transported Irish prisoners* 4/7076–7078, State Archives Office of New South Wales, as discussed in Chapter One.
41. Beattie, *Crime and the courts*, p. 191.
42. Beattie, *Crime and the courts*, p. 143.
43. Beattie, *Crime and the courts*, p. 423.
44. M. A. Crowther, *The workhouse system, 1834–1929: The history of an English social institution* (London 1981), p. 249.

45. Crowther, *The workhouse system*, p. 251.
46. Quoted in Williams, 'Irish female convicts', pp. 9–10.
47. Quoted in Williams, 'Irish female convicts', p. 8.
48. See the case of Henry McCave and Julia Smith, found in possession of two penny-piece counterfeiting moulds; *Old Bailey Sessions Papers* (8 January 1840) case no. 453.
49. R. Richardson, *Death, dissection, and the destitute* (London 1987).
50. Rudé, *Criminal and victim*, p. 18.
51. Rudé, *Criminal and victim*, p. 79.
52. For examples, see cases quoted in: Beddoe, *Welsh convict women*, p. 79; P. Robinson, *The women of Botany Bay: A reinterpretation of the role of women in the origins of Australian society* (Macquarie 1988), p. 54; Rudé, *Criminal and victim*, p. 81.
53. Beddoe, *Welsh convict women*, p. 109.
54. Rudé, *Criminal and victim*, p. 18.
55. Rudé, *Criminal and victim*, p. 79.
56. *Old Bailey Sessions Papers* (2 January 1837) case no. 326.
57. *Old Bailey Sessions Papers* (4 January 1837) case no. 349.
58. *Old Bailey Sessions Papers* (4 January 1837) case no. 376.
59. *Old Bailey Sessions Papers* (4 January 1837) case no. 357; (6 January 1840) case no. 405; (8 January 1840) case no. 458; (8 January 1840) case no. 455.
60. *Old Bailey Sessions Papers* (4 January 1837) case no. 354.
61. *Old Bailey Sessions Papers* (4 January 1837) case no. 362.
62. There are always exceptions that test the rule. Ann Cronin was one such unusual case. After five days in employment, Ann succeeded in making off with £80 worth of her new mistress' household goods before being found out! *Old Bailey Sessions Papers* (6 January 1840) case no. 437.
63. Beattie, *Crime and the courts*, pp. 424–30; Rudé, *Criminal and victim*, pp. 104–9.
64. Rudé, *Criminal and victim*, p. 109.
65. Blackstone quoted in M. Tipping, *Convicts unbound: The story of the 'Calcutta' convicts and their settlement in Australia* (Victoria 1988), p. 12.
66. Rudé, *Criminal and victim*, p. 109.
67. J. C. Symons quoted in Beddoe, *Welsh convict women*, p. 73.
68. Beddoe, *Welsh convict women*, p. 72.
69. N. McKendrick, 'Home demand and economic growth: A new view of the role of women and children in the industrial revolution', in N. McKendrick (ed.), *Historical perspectives: Studies in English thought and society in honour of J. H. Plumb* (London 1974), pp. 167, 195–208.
70. Shubert, 'Private initiative in law enforcement'; Swift, 'Urban policing'.
71. J. Howard, 'Why are there not more women law-breakers?', *The Australian*, 5 June 1985, p. 23.
72. Beattie, 'Criminality of women', p. 84–9.
73. Elizabeth and Constance, the brig *Dart* 1834. Thanks to Ian Duffield for supplying the information on their victim.
74. Mary Dennahy transported for life, *Andromeda* 1834.

75. Ann Wilson, *Planter* 1839; Catherine Harrington, *Thomas Harrison* 1836; and Rachael Atkinson, *Henry Wellesley* 1837.
76. J. W. Scott and L. A. Tilly, 'Women's work and the family in nineteenth-century Europe', *Comparative Studies in Society and History* 17 (1975), pp. 50–4.
77. T. McBride, *The domestic revolution: The modernisation of household service in England and France, 1820–1920* (London 1976), p. 22.
78. See U. R. Q. Henriques, 'Bastardy and the New Poor Law', *Past and Present* 37 (1967), pp. 103–29.
79. Beattie, 'Criminality of women', p. 84.
80. Rudé, *Criminal and victim*, pp. 56–7.
81. Hannah Atkinson and Susannah Molton, *Numa* 1834.
82. Emsley, *Crime and society*, chapter 5.
83. S. Magarey, 'The invention of juvenile delinquency in early nineteenth-century England', *Labour History* 34 (1978), p. 24.
84. Rudé, *Criminal and victim*, pp. 102–7.
85. *Old Bailey Sessions Papers* (4 January 1837) case no. 357.
86. *Old Bailey Sessions Papers* (5 January 1837) case no. 441.
87. *Old Bailey Sessions Papers* (4 January 1837) case no. 365.
88. A. G. L. Shaw, *Convicts and the colonies: A study of penal transportation from Great Britain and Ireland to Australia and other parts of the British Empire* (Melbourne 1981), p. 150.
89. D. Meredith, 'Full circle? Contemporary views on transportation', in Nicholas (ed.), *Convict workers*, p. 14.
90. A. Summers, *Damned whores and God's police: The colonization of women in Australia* (Melbourne 1976), p. 268.
91. 'Great Britain census 1841. Part I England and Wales, occupational abstract', *PP*, 1844 (587) XXVII, p. 67 (IUP *Population* 5); Robson, *Convict settlers*, p. 4.
92. Rudé, *Criminal and victim*, p. 62.
93. Robinson, *Women of Botany Bay*, pp. 13, 36.

3.   PISO'S JUSTICE

1. B. Smith, 'The fatal subject', *Scripsi* 4 (1987), p. 59.
2. J. F. H. Moore, *The convicts of Van Diemen's Land, 1840–1853* (Hobart 1976), p. 94.
3. G. Rudé, *Protest and punishment: The story of the social and political protesters transported to Australia, 1788–1868* (Melbourne 1978). Also see K. Amos, *The Fenians in Australia, 1865–1880* (Sydney 1988).
4. Tobias, quoted in Moore, *Convicts of Van Diemen's Land*, p. 2.
5. For a discussion, see L. Radzinowicz and R. Hood, *A history of English criminal law and its administration from 1750: The emergence of penal policy*, volume 5 (London 1986), pp. 73–107.
6. C. M. H. Clark, 'The origins of the convicts transported to Eastern Australia, 1787–1852', *Historical Studies: Australia and New Zealand* 7 (1956), p. 121.
7. Clark, 'Origins', p. 130.

8. J. B. Hirst, *Convict society and its enemies: A history of early New South Wales* (Sydney 1983), pp. 32–3.

9. J. J. Gurney, quoted in R. P. Dobash, R. E. Dobash and S. Gutteridge, *The imprisonment of women* (Oxford 1986), p. 43.

10. Ullathorne quoted in J. Waldersee, *Catholic society in New South Wales, 1788–1860* (Sydney 1974), p. 43.

11. Hogan, quoted in Waldersee, *Catholic society*, p. 44.

12. Marjoribanks, quoted in L. L. Robson, *The convict settlers of Australia: An enquiry into the origin and character of the convicts transported to New South Wales and Van Diemen's Land, 1787–1852* (Melbourne 1965), p. 10.

13. M. B. Schedvin and C. B. Schedvin, 'The nomadic tribes of urban Britain: A prelude to Botany Bay', *Historical Studies: Australia and New Zealand* 18 (1978), p. 258.

14. P. O'Farrell, *The Irish in Australia* (Sydney 1987), p. 24.

15. A. G. L. Shaw, *Convicts and the colonies: A study of penal transportation from Great Britain and Ireland to Australia and other parts of the British Empire* (Melbourne 1981), p. 183.

16. Shaw, *Convicts and the colonies*, p. 183.

17. Woodward, quoted in H. S. Payne, 'A statistical study of female convicts in Tasmania, 1843–53', *Tasmanian Historical Research Association Papers and Proceedings* 9 (1961), p. 58.

18. Robson, *Convict settlers*, p. 28.

19. Kiernan, quoted in Waldersee, *Catholic society*, p. 44. Also see W. K. Hancock, *Australia* (Melbourne 1966), pp. 24–5; Clark, quoted in A. W. Baker, *Death is a good solution: The convict experience in early Australia* (St Lucia 1984), p. 53.

20. Williams, quoted in Baker, *Death is a good solution*, p. 53.

21. L. L. Robson, 'The origin of the women convicts sent to Australia, 1787–1852', *Historical Studies: Australia and New Zealand* 11 (1963), p. 53.

22. P. Robinson, *The women of Botany Bay: A reinterpretation of the role of women in the origins of Australian society* (Macquarie 1988), p. 100.

23. Robson, 'Origin of women convicts', p. 46.

24. Robson, *Convict settlers*, p. 89.

25. A. R. Ekirch, *Bound for America: The transportation of British convicts to the colonies, 1718–1775* (Oxford 1987), p. 31; D. Philips, *Crime and authority in Victorian England: The Black Country, 1835–1860* (London 1977), p. 298.

26. B. Fine and E. Leopold, 'Consumerism and the industrial revolution', *Social History* 15 (1990).

27. J. Williams, 'Irish female convicts and Tasmania', *Labour History* 44 (1983), p. 7.

28. Moore, *Convicts of Van Diemen's Land*, p. 94.

29. Robson, 'Origins of women convicts', p. 46.

30. Euphemia Burnett, *Princess Charlotte* 1827.

31. C. Emsley, *Crime and society in England, 1750–1900* (London 1987), p. 44.

32. J. M. Beattie, 'The criminality of women in eighteenth-century England', *Journal of Social History* 8 (1975), pp. 107–16.

33. R. Hughes, *The fatal shore: A history of the transportation of convicts to Australia, 1787–1868* (London 1987), pp. 158–9.

34. P. Colquhoun, *A treatise on the police of the Metropolis: Containing a detail of the various crimes and misdemeanours by which public and private property and security are, at present, injured and endangered: and suggesting remedies for their prevention* (London 1805), preface.
35. G. Rudé, *Criminal and victim: Crime and society in early nineteenth-century England* (Oxford 1985), p. 123.
36. David Philips has done interesting work on the moral entrepreneurs. D. Philips, 'Moral entrepreneurs and the construction of a "criminal class" in England, c.1800-1840', paper presented to the Australian Historical Association Conference (Sydney University 1988).
37. Colquhoun, *Treatise on the police*, pp. vii–xi, 5, 230.
38. Rudé, *Criminal and victim*, p. 123.
39. For some explanations of the pitfalls of interpreting criminal figures, see D. Philips, 'Crime, law and punishment in the Industrial Revolution', in P. O'Brien and R. Quinault (eds), *The industrial revolution and British society* (Cambridge 1993), p. 159, and M. Sturma, *Vice in a vicious society: Crime and convicts in mid-nineteenth century New South Wales* (St Lucia 1983), chapter 4.
40. Colquhoun, *Treatise on the police*, preface.
41. Campbell, quoted in D. Jones, *Crime, protest, community and police in nineteenth-century Britain* (London 1982), p. 4.
42. Evidence from the various authors is collated in J. J. Tobias, *Crime and industrial society in the nineteenth century* (London 1967). Tobias is, however, mustering this evidence to demonstrate that a criminal class did in fact exist.
43. Advert at the commencement of H. Mayhew and J. Binny, *The criminal prisons of London and scenes of prison life* (London 1862).
44. Mayhew and Binny, *Criminal prisons*, pp. 87–9; Cesare Lombroso discussed in S. J. Gould, *The mismeasure of man* (New York 1981), pp. 140–3.
45. Mayhew and Binny, *Criminal prisons*, p. 87.
46. Mayhew and Binny, *Criminal prisons*, pp. 89, 395–6.
47. Constabulary Commissioners, quoted in Mayhew and Binny, *Criminal prisons*, p. 84.
48. Mayhew and Binny, *Criminal prisons*, pp. 28, 95, 96.
49. Mayhew and Binny, *Criminal prisons*, pp. 383, 381–3.
50. Mayhew and Binny, *Criminal prisons*, pp. 385–6.
51. Mayhew and Binny, *Criminal prisons*, pp. 87–90, 357, 383.
52. Mayhew and Binny, *Criminal prisons*, pp. 358, 90.
53. Mayhew and Binny, *Criminal prisons*, pp. 285–6.
54. A. Griffiths, *Memorials of Millbank and chapters in prison history* (London 1884), p. 262.
55. Mayhew and Binny, *Criminal prisons*, p. 379.
56. Mayhew and Binny, *Criminal prisons*, p. 357.
57. Mayhew and Binny, *Criminal prisons*, pp. 357, 356, 381.
58. Quoted in Sturma, *Vice in a vicious society*, pp. 2, 6.
59. Mayhew and Binny, *Criminal prisons*, pp. 88, 357–62.
60. Mayhew and Binny, *Criminal prisons*, p. 84.
61. Mayhew and Binny, *Criminal prisons*, p. 28.

62. Mayhew and Binny, *Criminal prisons*, pp. 87, 382.
63. Shaw, *Convict and the colonies*, p. 165.
64. Robson, *Convict settlers*, p. 150.
65. Schedvin and Schedvin, 'Nomadic tribes'; Shaw, *Convicts and the colonies*, p. 160.
66. J. J. Gurney, quoted in Dobash *et al.*, *Imprisonment of women*, p. 43.
67. Robinson, *Women of Botany Bay*, pp. 37, 40–1, 67, 51–5, 36, 63.
68. Robinson, *Women of Botany Bay*, p. 63.
69. Robinson, *Women of Botany Bay*, p. 78.
70. Robinson, *Women of Botany Bay*, pp. 56, 74, 58.
71. Robinson, *Women of Botany Bay*, p. 55.
72. Colquhoun, quoted in Robinson, *Women of Botany Bay*, p. 54.
73. Robinson, *Women of Botany Bay*, pp. 54, 55, 56.
74. Robinson, *Women of Botany Bay*, p. 56.
75. Robinson, *Women of Botany Bay*, p. 77.
76. Rudé, *Criminal and victim*, pp. 63–4.
77. H. Mayhew, *London labour and the London poor: A cyclopaedia of the condition and earnings of those that will work, those that cannot work, and those that will not work, comprising prostitutes, thieves, swindlers, beggars*, volume 4 (London 1862), p. 23.
78. Schedvin and Schedvin, 'Nomadic tribes', pp. 263–4.
79. Jones, *Crime, protest, community*, p. 13.
80. For some examples of this rich literature, see M. Anderson, 'Urban migration in nineteenth-century Lancashire: Some insights into two competing hypotheses', in M. Drake (ed.), *Historical demography: Problems and projects* (Milton Keynes 1974); D. E. Baines, 'The labour supply and the labour market, 1860–1914', in R. Floud and D. McCloskey (eds), *The economic history of Britain since 1700*, volume 2 (Cambridge 1981); S. H. Cousens, 'The regional variation in emigration from Ireland between 1821 and 1841', *Transactions of the Institute of British Geographers* 37 (December 1965); Erickson, 'Emigration from the British Isles'; J. Mokyr and C. Ó Gráda, 'Emigration and poverty in prefamine Ireland', *Explorations in Economic History* 19 (1982); S. Nicholas and P. Shergold, 'Intercounty labour mobility during the industrial revolution: Evidence from Australian transportation records', *Oxford Economic Papers* 39 (1987); S. Nicholas and P. Shergold, 'Human capital and the pre-famine Irish emigration to England', *Explorations in Economic History* 24 (1987).
81. S. Alexander, *Women's work in nineteenth-century London: A study of the years 1820–50* (London 1983), p. 64.
82. 'The gold snuff-box', *Punch* 1 (July 1841), p. 183.
83. C. Dickens, *The Adventures of Oliver Twist* (Oxford 1978), first published in magazine form in 1837, dramatis personae.
84. Rudé, *Criminal and victim*, p. 40.
85. Rudé, *Criminal and victim*, p. 26.
86. Rudé, *Criminal and victim*, p. 35.
87. Rudé, *Criminal and victim*, p. 63.
88. Emsley, *Crime and society*, p. 44.

89. T. Curtis and J. A. Sharpe, 'Crime in Tudor and Stuart England', *History Today* 38 (1988), p. 27.
90. Rudé, *Criminal and victim*, pp. 123–6.
91. Beattie, 'Criminality of women', pp. 102–3.
92. Beattie, 'Criminality of women', p. 107.
93. D. Philips, *Crime and authority*, p. 287.
94. Jones, *Crime, protest, community*, p. 13.
95. Beattie, 'Criminality of women', pp. 101–7; Emsley, *Crime and society*, p. 41; V. A. C. Gatrell and T. B. Hadden, 'Criminal statistics and their interpretation', in E. A.Wrigley (ed.), *Nineteenth-century society: Essays in the use of quantitative methods for the study of social data* (Cambridge 1972); Jones, *Crime, protest, community*, p. 3; Radzinowicz and Hood, *English criminal law*, pp. 64–73.
96. Gatrell and Hadden, 'Criminal statistics', p. 382.
97. B. J. Davey, *Lawless and immoral: Policing a country town 1838–1857* (Leicester 1983), p. x.
98. Philips, *Crime and authority*, p. 287; Rudé, *Criminal and victim*, p. 126.
99. P. J. Byrne, 'Women and the Criminal Law: Sydney 1810–1821', *Push from the Bush* 21 (1985), pp. 2–19.
100. Payne, 'Statistical study', pp. 62–3; D. Beddoe, *Welsh convict women: A study of women transported from Wales to Australia, 1787–1852* (Wales 1979), pp. 151–2; W. Ullathorne, *The horrors of transportation: Briefly unfolded to the people* (Dublin 1838), p. 12.

4   ECONOMIC ACCOUTREMENTS

1. F. Bacon, 'Of plantations', *Essays* (London 1909), p. 95. This was also applicable to the settling of Tasmania; see M. Tipping, *Convicts unbound: The story of the 'Calcutta' convicts and their settlement in Australia* (Victoria 1988).
2. H. Mayhew and J. Binny, *The criminal prisons of London and scenes of prison life* (London 1862), p. 96.
3. M. D. Hill, quoted in V. Bailey, 'Introduction', in V. Bailey (ed.), *Policing and punishment in nineteenth-century Britain* (London 1981), p. 11.
4. A. Griffiths, *Memorials of Millbank and chapters in prison history* (London 1884), p. 258.
5. *The Times*, quoted in G. Nadel, *Australia's colonial culture: Ideas, men and institutions in mid-nineteenth century Eastern Australia* (Cambridge, Massachusetts 1957), p. 26.
6. For examples of convict behaviour and employer attitudes see A. Atkinson, 'Four patterns of convict protest', *Labour History* 37 (1979); S. Macintyre, *Winners and losers: The pursuit of social justice in Australian history* (Sydney 1988), chapter 1; M. Sullivan, 'Ann McNally: Convict servant', in M. Lake and F. Kelly (eds) *Double time: women in Victoria—150 years* (Melbourne 1985).
7. P. Cunningham (ed.), D. S. Macmillan, *Two years in New South Wales: Comprising sketches of the actual state of society in that colony; of its peculiar*

advantages to emigrants; of its topography, natural history, &c. &c. (1827; reproduction Sydney 1966), p. 303.

8. J. Mudie (ed.), W. Stone, *The felonry of New South Wales; Being a faithful picture of the real romance of life in Botany Bay with anecdotes of Botany Bay society and a plan of Sydney* (1837 reproduction Sydney 1965), pp. 186–8.

9. Griffiths, *Memorials of Millbank*, p. 244.

10. Griffiths, *Memorials of Millbank*, p. 263.

11. Macquarie to Castlereagh, 8 March 1810, *Historical Records of Australia* (hereafter *HRA*) VII, p. 221.

12. A chronicler, quoted by Griffiths, *Memorials of Millbank*, p. 251.

13. Government and general orders, 3 July 1799, *HRA* II, p. 586.

14. 'Report from the select committee on transportation, together with minutes of evidence, appendix and index', *PP*, 1837 (518) XIX, p.38 (IUP *Crime and Punishment—Transportation* 2).

15. SC on transportation', p. 148.

16. Quoted in M. Dixson, *The real matilda: Women and identity in Australia, 1788–1975* (Victoria 1976), p. 125.

17. Government and general orders, 3 July 1799, *HRA* II, p. 586.

18. 'SC on transportation', p. 96.

19. 'SC on transportation', p. 196.

20. 'SC on transportation', p. 102.

21. 'SC on transportation', pp. 103, 38.

22. Bigge, quoted in A. Summers, *Damned whores and God's police: The colonization of women in Australia* (Melbourne 1976), p. 275.

23. Nineteenth-century remark, quoted in P. Robinson, *The hatch and brood of time: A study of the first generation of native-born white Australians, 1788–1828*, volume 1 (Oxford 1985), p. 5.

24. Chesterton, quoted in D. Beddoe, *Welsh convict women: A study of women transported from Wales to Australia, 1787-1852* (Wales 1979), pp. 73–4.

25. King, quoted in Robinson, *Hatch and brood*, p. 43. Also see B. Earnshaw, 'The colonial children', *Push from the Bush* 9 (1980), p. 37.

26. Griffiths, *Memorials of Millbank*, pp. 245–6.

27. Griffiths, *Memorials of Millbank*, p. 254.

28. Lang, quoted in A. W. Baker, *Death is a good solution: The convict experience in early Australia* (St Lucia 1984), p. 19.

29. W. Ullathorne, *The Catholic mission in Australia* (Liverpool 1837), p. 12.

30. N. G. Butlin, 'Contours of the Australian economy, 1788–1860', *Australian Economic History Review* 26 (1986), pp. 96–125.

31. E. Eagar, *Letters to the Rt. Hon. Robert Peel, M.P. ... on the advantages of New South Wales and Van Diemen's Land* (London 1824), p. 21.

32. Robson suggested that a 'cautious estimate' would put the number of women transported by 1825 who would eventually marry at 60 per cent. In 1828, 42 per cent of women transported prior to 1826 had married. By comparison, 42 per cent of Irish women aged between seventeen and thirty-five had married at the time of the 1841 census, as had 58 per cent of individuals in England aged between twenty and forty years. In this light, contrary to other claims, colonial figures seem high. An official marriage rate, it should also be remembered, was

just that: a measurement of a legally institutionalised arrangement. It was not a measurement of the permanency of all relationships. Marriage rates do not describe the frequency with which families formed, nor the structure through which reproduction was effected, nor how this changes over time. As Alan Atkinson has noted, the fact that many couples cohabited without the sanction of law makes the marriage rate nearly meaningless as an indicator of the social structure of the convict population. L. L. Robson, *The convict settlers of Australia: An enquiry into the origin and character of the convicts transported to New South Wales and Van Diemen's Land, 1787–1852* (Melbourne 1965), p. 275; 'Report of the commissioners appointed to take the census of Ireland for the year 1841', *PP*, 1843 (504) XXIV (IUP *Population* 2), pp. 438–9; English figures for 1851 from M.Sturma, 'Eye of the beholder: The stereotype of women convicts, 1788–1852', *Labour History* 34 (1978), p. 8; A. Atkinson, 'Marriage and distance in the convict colonies, 1838', *Push from the Bush* 16 (1983), p. 61; K. Alford, *Production or reproduction? An economic history of women in Australia, 1788–1850* (Oxford 1984), pp. 21–6; Atkinson, 'The moral basis of marriage', *Push from the Bush* 2 (1978); M. Aveling, 'She only married to be free; Or, Cleopatra vindicated', *Push from the Bush* 2 (1978), p. 118; Summers, *Damned whores*, pp. 275–6; S. Wilson, 'Language and ritual in marriage', *Push from the Bush* 2 (1978), p. 92.

33. Butlin, 'Contours of the Australian economy'; N. G. Butlin, J. Ginswick and P. Statham, 'Colonial statistics before 1850', *Australian National University Source Papers in Economic History* 12 (1986), p. 18; G. Greenwood, *Australia; A social and political history* (Sydney 1978), p. 46.

34. See Governor Brisbane on the Engineers Department. Brisbane to Horton, 16 June 1825, *HRA* XI, p. 653.

35. Macquarie to Earl Bathurst, 22 February 1820, *HRA* X, p. 217.

36. Griffiths, *Memorials of Millbank*, p. 260.

37. Griffiths, *Memorials of Millbank*, pp. 261–2.

38. Cunningham, *Two years in New South Wales*, p. 279.

39. King to Hobart, 1 March 1804, *HRA* IV, p. 483; Hunter to Portland, 20 June 1798, *HRA* II, p. 24.

40. Grenville to Phillip, 17 June 1790, *HRA* I, p. 120.

41. *The journal and letters of Lt. Ralph Clark, 1787–1792*, (ed. P. G. Fidlon and R. J. Ryan, reproduction Sydney 1981), p. xvii. Clark is discussed further in Chapter Eight.

42. King to Hobart, 1 March 1804, *HRA* IV, p. 471.

43. Mudie, *Felonry of New South Wales*, p. 188.

44. Mudie, *Felonry of New South Wales*, p. 187.

45. Mudie, *Felonry of New South Wales*, p. 186.

46. Mudie, *Felonry of New South Wales*, p. 187.

47. Mudie, *Felonry of New South Wales*, p. 186.

48. Mudie, *Felonry of New South Wales*, p. 186.

49. Mudie, *Felonry of New South Wales*, p. 188.

50. Mudie, *Felonry of New South Wales*, p. 188.

51. This tension is explored in D. Meredith, 'Full circle? Contemporary views on transportation', in S. Nicholas (ed.), *Convict Workers: Reinterpreting*

Australia's past (Melbourne 1988). Shaw dates this turnaround in colonial prosperity from 1815; A. G. L. Shaw, *Convicts and the colonies: A study of penal transportation from Great Britain and Ireland to Australia and other parts of the British Empire* (Melbourne 1981), p. 140.

52. Prison authorities, quoted in H. Mayhew and J. Binny, *Criminal prisons*, p. 176.
53. Ellenborough, quoted in L. Radzinowicz and R. Hood, *A history of English criminal law and its administration from 1750* (London 1986), p. 474.
54. Whately, quoted in Baker, *Death is a good solution*, p. xii; C. Dickens, 'A Letter to the Marquis of Normanby, Secretary of State for the Home Office' (3 July 1840; MS 6809 MLNL).
55. Smith, quoted in Radzinowicz and Hood, *English criminal law*, p. 475.
56. Dickens proposed to rectify this state of affairs by writing 'a strong and vivid description', circulating it 'in some very cheap and easy form', with the modest ambition that 'I would have it on the pillow of every prisoner in England.' But he had, to an extent, already been beaten to it. Balanced against hopeful letters home and glowing images of the southern continent were less pleasant letters, personal experiences of losing family, frightening tales circulated in pamphlet forms or as novels, and depressing broadsides that advocated fear of this punishment, such as 'The London Convict Maid' reproduced in the front of this book and 'The Female Transport'; see G. C. Ingleton (ed.), *True patriots all: or news from early Australia, as told in a collection of broadsides* (Sydney 1952). There were numerous convict narratives: Anonymous, *The surprising adventures and unparalleled sufferings of Jane Turner, A female convict, who made her escape from New South Wales* (Doncaster 1850); B. Reilly, *A true history of Bernard Reilly, a returned convict. Who was transported in the year 1821, and has lately returned from exile with an account of his sufferings, &c. &c. Written by Himself* (Ballinamore c.1839); J. Slater, *A description of Sydney, Parramatta, Newcastle, &c., settlements in New South Wales, with some account of the manners and employment of the convicts, in a letter from John Slater, to his Wife in Nottingham, Published for the benefit of his wife and four children* (Nottingham 1819). Bishop William Ullathorne had expounded on *The horrors of transportation: Briefly unfolded to the people* (Dublin 1838). The Ferguson Collection at the Mitchell Library in Sydney, Australia holds many others, the following also reproduced in Ingleton, *True patriots all*: 'H.W.D.' wrote a broadside entitled *State of Convicts, In New South Wales, 1835*; the Reverend Richard Johnson wrote a *Dreadful Narrative of Lamentable Sufferings on board Convict Ships*; 'Humanitas' wrote *Botany Bay INHUMANITY Exposed!!!*—declaring that transportation was 'WORSE THAN DEATH!!!'; William Ashton published *A Lecture on the Evils of Emigration and Transportation*; Edward Lilburn wrote *A Complete Exposure of the Convict System. Its horrors, hardships, and severities, including an account of The Dreadful Sufferings of the Unhappy Captives*; and Frank the Poet (Francis MacNamara) wrote *A convict's tour to hell*.
57. *The Australian* (7 April 1848), quoted in M. de Lepervanche, 'Australian immigrants, 1788–1940: Desired and unwanted', in E. L. Wheelwright and K. Buckley (eds), *Essays in the political economy of Australian capitalism*, volume 1 (Sydney 1979), p. 79.

58. C. M. H. Clark, 'The origins of the convicts transported to Eastern Australia, 1787–1852', *Historical Studies: Australia and New Zealand* 7 (1956), p. 314.

59. R. W. Fogel, Nobel Prize lecture 'Economic growth, population theory, and physiology: The bearing of long-term processes on the making of economic policy', *National Bureau of Economic Research Working Paper* 4638 (1994), also to be reprinted in the *American Economic Review*. There was also a misunderstanding about the nature of work, which gave rise to claims about laziness. Because work was seasonal and casual, this necessarily meant workers had long periods not working. C. Emsley, 'The criminal past: Crime in nineteenth-century Britain', *History Today* 38 (1988), p.45.

60. S. Nicholas, 'The care and feeding of convicts', in Nicholas (ed.), *Convict workers*.

61. Clark, 'Origins', pp. 131, 314.

62. M. B. Schedvin and C. B. Schedvin, 'The nomadic tribes of urban Britain: A prelude to Botany Bay', *Historical Studies: Australia and New Zealand* 18 (1978), pp. 263–4.

63. J. B. Hirst, *Convict society and its enemies: A history of early New South Wales* (Sydney 1983), p. 32.

64. Nicholas (ed.), *Convict workers*.

65. M. Roe, 'Colonial society in embryo', *Historical Studies: Australia and New Zealand* 7 (1956), p. 158.

66. B. H. Fletcher, *Ralph Darling: A governor maligned* (Melbourne 1984), p. 119.

67. J. Williams, 'Irish female convicts and Tasmania', *Labour History* 44 (1983), pp. 5, 12.

68. Interestingly, Portia Robinson falls between two positions, having demonstrated the economic contributions of convict women, but persisting with claims that the women arrived unskilled. P. Robinson, *The women of Botany Bay: A reinterpretation of the role of women in the origins of Australian society* (Macquarie 1988), pp. 6, 235–6.

69. Robinson, *Hatch and brood*, p. 73; Robinson, *Women of Botany Bay*, p. 3. Also see J. Waldersee, *Catholic society in New South Wales, 1788–1860* (Sydney 1974), pp. 58–9.

70. S. Nicholas and P. Shergold, 'Convicts as migrants', in Nicholas (ed.), *Convict workers*, p. 60. Feminist scholars have reached similar conclusions about the lack of opportunities for women to work in the colonial economy; see K. Alford, *Production or reproduction? An economic history of women in Australia 1788–1850* (Oxford 1984).

71. Robson, *Convict settlers*, p. 142.

72. K. Macnab and R. Ward, 'The nature and nurture of the first generation of native-born Australians', *Historical Studies: Australia and New Zealand* 10 (1962), p. 290.

73. Schedvin and Schedvin, 'Nomadic tribes', p. 257.

74. Schedvin and Schedvin, 'Nomadic tribes', p. 264.

75. Schedvin and Schedvin, 'Nomadic tribes', pp. 261–2, 264.

76. Robinson, *Hatch and brood*.

77. D. Beddoe, *Welsh convict women: A study of women transported from Wales to Australia, 1787-1852* (Wales 1979), p. 144.
78. Confusingly, Portia Robinson noted this in addition to her earlier, less favourable remarks. Robinson, *Women of Botany Bay*, p. 23.
79. Robinson, *Women of Botany Bay*, p. 8.
80. Hirst, *Convict society*, p. 57.
81. For an example, see Robinson, *Women of Botany Bay*.
82. Nicholas and Shergold, 'Convicts as migrants', p. 52.
83. Meredith, 'Full circle', p. 14.
84. Catherine Finn, *Lady Rowena* 1826.
85. V. A. C. Gatrell and T. B. Hadden, 'Criminal statistics and their interpretation', in E. A. Wrigley (ed.), *Nineteenth-century society: Essays in the use of quantitative methods for the study of social data* (Cambridge 1972), p. 384; S. Magarey, 'The invention of juvenile delinquency in early nineteenth-century England', *Labour History* 34 (1978), p. 16.
86. Shaw, *Convicts and the colonies*, p. 141.
87. S. Nicholas, 'Unshackling the past', in Nicholas (ed.), *Convict workers*, p. 8.
88. C. Erickson, 'Emigration from the British Isles to the U.S.A. in 1831', *Population Studies* 35 (1981), p. 103.
89. A. S. Kussmaul, 'The ambiguous mobility of farm servants', *Economic History Review* 34 (1981), p. 230; T. McBride, *The domestic revolution: The modernisation of household service in England and France, 1820-1920* (London 1976), p. 34.
90. See references given in Chapter Three, note 100.
91. Erickson, 'Emigration from the British Isles', p. 197.
92. This approach has developed from current empirical medical research into the study of human growth (auxology) by, for example, P. B. Eveleth and J. M. Tanner, *Worldwide variation in human growth* (1976) and J. M. Tanner, *Growth of adolescence* (Oxford 1962). A rich historical literature has evolved. Examples include R. Floud, K. Wachter and A. S. Gregory, *Height, health and history: nutritional status in the United Kingdom* (Cambridge 1990); R. Fogel *et al.*, 'Secular changes in American and British stature and nutrition', *Journal of Interdisciplinary History* 14 (1983); J. Komlos, 'The secular trend in the biological standard of living in the UK, 1730–1860', *Economic History Review* 46 (1993); S. Nicholas and R. H. Steckel, 'Heights and living standards of English workers during the early years of industrialisation, 1770–1815', *Journal of Economic History* 51 (1991); S. Nicholas and D. Oxley, 'The living standards of women during the industrial revolution, 1795–1820', *Economic History Review* 46 (1993).
93. For an interesting article on this topic, see I. Brand and M. Staniforth, 'Care and control: Female convict transportation voyages to Van Diemen's Land, 1818–1853', *The Great Circle* 16 (1994).
94. Brand and Staniforth, 'Care and control', p. 36.
95. Nicholas and Shergold, 'Convicts as migrants', p. 47.
96. Excluding shipwrecks, Charles Bateson records a lower mortality rate—at 59 deaths for female convict ships to NSW, 1826–1840—than I have detected. C. Bateson, *The convict ships, 1787-1868* (Glasgow 1959), pp. 385–91.

97. J. McDonald and R. Schlomowitz, 'Mortality on convict voyages to Australia, 1788–1868', *Social Science History* 13 (1989).

98. 'Papers relating to the loss of the convict ship *Amphitrite*', *PP*, 1834 (427) XLVII.

99. Ingleton (ed.), *True patriots all*, pp. 158–9.

100. This finding was also made for convict voyages more generally. See McDonald and Schlomowitz, 'Mortality on convict voyages'.

101. I would like to thank Mark Staniforth for searching his database on the surgeon-superintendents' reports for details on the convict women who are the subject of this book. Also see M. Staniforth, 'Dangerous voyages? Aspects of the emigrant experience on the voyage to Australia, 1837–1839', unpublished MA thesis, University of Sydney, 1993.

102. Appendix to the report of the committee on immigration. Despatch relating to immigration', *PP*, 1840 (612) XXXIII, p. 25 (IUP *Colonies—Australia* 6).

103. H. Tinker, *A new system of slavery: The export of Indian labour overseas, 1830–1920* (London 1974), pp. 161–3.

104. McDonald and Schlomowitz, 'Mortality on convict voyages'; H. S. Klein, *The middle passage: Comparative studies in the Atlantic slave trade* (Princeton 1978), p. 232; H. S. Klein and S. L. Engerman, 'A note on mortality in the French slave trade in the eighteenth century', in H. A. Gemery and J. S. Hogendorn (eds), *The uncommon market: Essays in the economic history of the Atlantic slave trade* (New York 1979), p. 264.

105. The comment on rations comes from Peter Cunningham, quoted in Shaw, *Convicts and the colonies*, p. 115. Also see Nicholas, 'Care and feeding'.

106. Clark, 'Origins', p. 314.

107. Mokyr and Ó Gráda, 'Emigration and poverty', p. 375.

108. H. J. Graff, 'Literacy, jobs and industrialization: The nineteenth century', in H. J. Graff (ed.), *Literacy and social development in the West* (Cambridge 1981), p. 241.

109. W. A. Armstrong, 'The use of information about occupations', in Wrigley (ed.), *Nineteenth-century society*, pp. 191–310.

110. H. M. Boot, 'Wages of factory workers during the industrial revolution', paper presented to Australian Historical Association Conference (Australian National University 1992). For information on the modernising impact of domestic service see D. A. Kent, 'Ubiquitous but invisible: Female domestic servants in mid-eighteenth century London', *History Workshop* 28 (1989), and McBride, *Domestic revolution*.

111. Graff, 'Literacy, jobs and industrialization', pp. 233; W. B. Stephens, *Education, literacy and society, 1830–70: The geography of diversity in provincial England* (Manchester 1987), p. 29.

112. Kent, 'Ubiquitous but invisible', p. 122.

113. Beddoe, *Welsh convict women*, pp. 16, 37; Summers, *Damned whores*, p. 268.

114. *Irish convict records: Lists 1828–48* (MS 4869 MLNLA).

115. Some examples can be found in P. Clarke and D. Spender, *Life lines: Australian women's letters and diaries, 1788 to 1840* (Sydney 1992).

116. Summers, *Damned whores*, pp. 275–6.

117. Prison matron, quoted in Beddoe, *Welsh convict women*, pp. 82–3; O. Keese, *The broad arrow: Being the story of Maida Gwynnham, a 'Lifer' in Van*

Diemen's Land (London 1859). A variant of this theme can be found in S. Richardson, *Pamela, or virtue rewarded* (London 1740).

5 IRELAND'S DISTANT SHORES

1. The Scottish exceptions were Kirkcudbright, Morays, Nairn, Orkney and Sutherland.
2. The British Isles are taken here to incorporate England, Ireland, Scotland and Wales. Population ratio calculated from W. E. Vaughan and A. J. Fitzpatrick (eds), *A new history of Ireland: Irish historical statistics population, 1821–1971* (Dublin 1978).
3. K. Corcoran and S. Nicholas, 'Statistical appendix', in S. Nicholas (ed.), *Convict workers: Reinterpreting Australia's past* (Melbourne 1988), p. 204.
4. J. F. H. Moore, *The convicts of Van Diemen's Land, 1840–1853* (Hobart 1976), p. 41; L. L. Robson, *The convict settlers of Australia: An enquiry into the origin and character of the convicts transported to New South Wales and Van Diemen's Land, 1787-1852* (Melbourne 1965), p. 89.
5. For example, Irish men have been blamed for the development of an Australian misogyny; M. Dixson, *The real Matilda: Women and identity in Australia, 1788–1975* (Victoria 1976).
6. D. Dickson, 'Aspects of the rise and decline of the Irish cotton industry', in L. M. Cullen and T. C. Smout (eds), *Comparative aspects of Scottish and Irish economic and social history, 1600–1900* (Edinburgh undated circa 1982), pp. 101, 107; H. D. Gribbon, 'The Irish Linen Board, 1711–1828', in Cullen and Smout (eds), *Comparative aspects*, pp. 82–3; P. Stolar, 'Why Ireland starved: A critical review of the econometric results', *Irish Economic and Social History* 11 (1984), p. 103. Several enlightening books on Ireland have been published since *Convict Maids* was written. C. Ó Gráda, *Ireland: A new economic history, 1780–1845* (Oxford 1994); J. O'Connor, *The workhouses of Ireland: The fate of Ireland's poor* (Dublin 1995); C. Póirtéir (ed.), *The great Irish famine* (Cork 1995). Another interesting book, although dealing with a later period, is J. Bourke, *Husbandry to Housewifery: Women, economic change, and housework in Ireland, 1890–1914* (Oxford 1993).
7. L. Kennedy, 'Why one million starved: An open verdict', *Irish Economic and Social History* 11 (1984), p. 102–6; C.Ó Gráda, 'Post-famine adjustment: Essays in nineteenth-century Irish economic history', *Irish Economic and Social History* 1 (1974), p. 66; Solar, 'Why Ireland starved', p. 113.
8. J. Mokyr, *Why Ireland starved: A quantitative and analytical history of the Irish economy, 1800–1850* (London 1985), p. 145; R. F. Foster, *Modern Ireland, 1600–1972* (London 1988), p. 318–21.
9. There is some controversy over Ireland's demographic path. See, for example, F. J. Carney, 'Pre-famine Irish population: The evidence from the Trinity College Estates', *Irish Economic and Social History* 2 (1975), pp. 36–7; S. A. Royle, 'Irish famine relief in the early nineteenth century: The 1822 famine on the Aran Islands', *Irish Economic and Social History* 11 (1984), p. 57; J. Schellekens, 'The role of marital fertility in Irish population history, 1750–1840', *Economic History Review* 46 (1993).

10. Mokyr, *Why Ireland starved*, chapter 2; S. Nicholas and R. Steckel, 'Tall but poor: Nutrition, health, and living standards in pre-famine Ireland', *National Bureau of Economic Research Working Paper Series on Historical Factors in Long Run Growth*, 39 (1992).

11. S. Nicholas and D. Oxley, 'Living standards of women during the industrial revolution', *Economic History Review* 46 (1993).

12. Foster, *Modern Ireland*, p. 322–3; C. Ó Gráda, 'Some aspects of nineteenth-century Irish emigration', in Cullen and Smout (eds), *Comparative aspects*, p. 71.

13. E. L. Almquist, 'Mayo and beyond: Land, domestic industry and rural transformation in the Irish West', *Irish Economic and Social History* 5 (1978), pp. 71–2; W. H. Crawford, 'The evolution of the linen trade in Ulster before industrialization', *Irish Economic and Social History* 15 (1988), pp. 32–53.

14. K. O'Neill quoted in P. Solar, 'Book review of K. O'Neill, *Family and farm in pre-famine Ireland*', *Irish Economic and Social History* 13 (1986), p. 156.

15. Dickson, 'Aspects of the rise', p. 110.

16. Crawford, 'Evolution of the linen trade', pp. 33, 52; Foster, *Modern Ireland*, p. 321.

17. L. M. Cullen and T. C. Smout, 'Economic growth in Scotland and Ireland', and R. B. Weir, 'The patent still distillers and the role of competition', in Cullen and Smout (eds), *Comparative aspects*, pp. 16, 122–4; Dickson, 'Aspects of the rise', p. 111; Foster, *Modern Ireland*.

18. B. Collins, 'Aspects of Irish immigration into two Scottish towns', *Irish Economic and Social History* 6 (1979); S. H. Cousens, 'The regional variation in emigration from Ireland between 1821 and 1841', *Transactions of the Institute of British Geographers* 37 (1965); C. Erickson, 'Emigration from the British Isles to the U.S.A. in 1831', *Population Studies* 35 (1981); R. Gillespie, 'Migration and opportunity: A comment', *Irish Economic and Social History* 13 (1986); R. Haines, 'Indigent misfits or shrewd operators? Government-assisted emigrants from the United Kingdom to Australia, 1821–1860', *Population Studies* 48 (1994); R. E. Kennedy Jr, *The Irish: Emigration, marriage and fertility* (Berkeley 1973); J. Mokyr and C. Ó Gráda, 'Emigration and poverty in pre-famine Ireland', *Explorations in Economic History* 19 (1982); S. Nicholas and P. Shergold, 'Human capital and the pre-famine Irish emigration to England', *Explorations in Economic History* 24 (1987); Ó Gráda, 'Some aspects'.

19. For a discussion of population estimates see Mokyr, *Why Ireland starved*, pp. 261–77. E. M. Crawford (ed.), *Famine: The Irish experience, 900–1900* (Edinburgh 1989). For a recent overview of this period see C. Kinealy, *This great calamity: The Irish famine 1845–52* (Dublin 1994).

20. Cousens, 'Regional variation in emigration'; C. Ó Gráda, 'Post-famine adjustment: Essays in nineteenth-century Irish economic history', *Irish Economic and Social History* 1 (1974), p. 65.

21. Bridget Gibbons and Mary Anne Gibbons, *Elizabeth 4* 1828.

22. Brenda Collins identified this pattern of Irish family migration, and the role of economic factors in determining movement. Collins, 'Aspects of Irish immigration', p. 72.

23. John West quoted in J. Williams, 'Irish female convicts and Tasmania', *Labour History* 44 (1983), pp. 9–10.

24. Calculated from ages in the Irish census. 'Report of the commissioners appointed to take the census of Ireland for the year 1841', *PP*, 1843 (504) XXIV, pp. 488–9 (IUP *Population* 2).

25. Report of the commissioners … census of Ireland', pp. 438–9.

26. W. A. Armstrong, 'The use of information about occupation', in E. A. Wrigley (ed.), *Nineteenth-century society: Essays in the use of quantitative methods for the study of social data* (Cambridge 1972), pp. 191–310. Categorisation of Irish working women into skill categories has been taken from S. Nicholas and P. Shergold, 'Convicts as workers', in Nicholas (ed.), *Convict workers*, p. 73.

27. 'Report of the commissioners … census of Ireland', p. 440.

28. 'Great Britain census 1841. Report from the commissioners', *PP*, 1843 (496) XXII, pp. 14–6 (IUP *Population* 3).

29. For a discussion see Mokyr and Ó Gráda, 'Emigration and poverty'; Nicholas and Shergold, 'Human capital', p. 159.

30. Thomas Carlyle, quoted in Nicholas and Shergold, 'Human capital', p. 159.

31. F. Engels, *The condition of the working class in England* (Oxford 1971), p. 107. To a large extent, Irish migrants were unpopular with Engels and others, who worried that the Irish would steal jobs from English workers, cramp available housing, and reduce the wages of casual and unskilled work. They were, in short, perceived as a threat, albeit an unskilled one: as industrial 'shock troops'. A contrary argument has been put by Williamson. He argues that the overall number of Irish migrants was inadequate to depress wages, that labour markets were not regionally segmented creating areas of Irish domination, that the demand for unskilled labour in the English economy was sufficiently elastic to absorb the influx of Irish, and that the Irish were not crucial to British industrialisation as others claimed. Alternatively, it might be argued that Irish immigrations were simply too small to matter much, given a high pre-existing level of surplus labour already acting to depress wages. Far from being a sponge with unlimited powers to absorb labour, the English economy suffered seasonal swings in demand, which also varied with the trade cycle. But again the assumption is made that Irish were untrained workers. Williamson, 'The impact of the Irish on British labour markets during the industrial revolution', *Journal of Economic History* 46 (1986).

32. Captain Hutchinson Hothersall Browne, immigration agent 1851–58, quoted in P. Hamilton, '"Tipperarifying the moral atmosphere": Irish Catholic immigration and the state, 1840–1860', in Sydney Labour History Group, *What rough beast? The state and social order in Australian history* (Sydney 1982), p. 26.

33. This conclusion was reached in spite of Mokyr and Ó Gráda's own occupational comparison with the 1841 Irish census which the authors accepted 'could be seen as consistent with a "human capital drain"': 'Emigration and poverty', pp. 377–8.

34. E. Chadwick, *Report on the sanitary condition of the labouring population of Gt. Britain* (Edinburgh 1842), p. 199.

35. Irish workers formed a significant element feeding Lancashire's textile industry. M. Anderson, 'Urban migration in nineteenth-century Lancashire: Some insights into two competing hypotheses', in M. Drake (ed.), *Historical demography: Problems and projects* (Milton Keynes 1974), pp. 131–44.
36. Ricardo, quoted in Nicholas and Shergold, 'Human capital', pp. 158–9.
37. Foster, *Modern Ireland*, pp. 322, 371–2; Almquist, 'Mayo and beyond', p. 517.

6   ENGLAND'S CASTAWAYS

1. The figure of 2946 women transported from England includes 2258 women born in England plus the 486 Irish women who had migrated across the Irish Sea. In addition, 57 Welsh, 50 Scots, 66 women from a wide variety of places near and beyond the United Kingdom, and 29 women whose birthplace is unknown, had all come to live and work in England before committing their felonies.
2. Half the display belonged to Britain, the other half to the rest of the world. T. Richards, *The commodity culture of Victorian England: Advertising and spectacle, 1851–1914* (Stanford 1990), p. 18.
3. One of the great debates in economic history is over the impact of industrialisation on women. Protagonists have been divided into pessimists who argue that women's position in the society and economy deteriorated, and optimists who believed that women were liberated. The literature is too lengthy to cite here, but two key texts have been, for the pessimists, A. Clark, *Working life of women in the seventeenth century* (London 1919) and for the optimists, I. Pinchbeck, *Women workers in the industrial revolution, 1750–1880* (London 1930). For recent contributions to this debate, see S. Horrell and J. Humphries, 'Old questions, new data and alternative perspectives: Families' living standards in the British industrial revolution', *Journal of Economic History* 52 (1992); S. Horrell and J. Humphries, '"The exploitation of little children": Child labour and the family economy in the industrial revolution', *Explorations in Economic History* (forthcoming); S. Nicholas and D. Oxley, 'Living standards of women during the industrial revolution', *Economic History Review* 46 (1993); S. Nicholas and D. Oxley, 'The industrial revolution and the genesis of the male breadwinner', in G. D. Snooks (ed.), *Was the industrial revolution necessary?* (London 1994). Overviews can be found in K. Honeyman and J. Goodman, 'Women's work, gender conflict, and labour markets in Europe, 1500–1900', *Economic History Review* 44 (1991) and J. Thomas, 'Women and capitalism: Oppression or Emancipation? A review article', *Comparative Studies in Society and History* 30 (1988).
4. B. Ehrenreich and D. English, *For her own good: 150 years of the experts' advice to women* (London 1979), p. 7; C. C. Harris, *The family and industrial society* (London 1985), chapter 6; P. Hudson and W. R. Lee (eds), *Women's work and the family economy in historical perspective* (Manchester 1990).
5. J. W. Scott and L. A. Tilly, 'Women's work and the family in nineteenth-century Europe', *Comparative Studies in Society and History* 17 (1975), pp. 43–4.
6. J. C. Holley, 'The two family economies of industrialism: Factory workers in Victorian Scotland', *Journal of Family History* 6 (1981); H. Land, 'The family

wage', *Feminist Review* 6 (1980), pp. 56–62; W. Seccombe, 'Patriarchy stabilized: The construction of the male breadwinner wage norm in nineteenth-century Britain', *Social History* 2 (1986).

7. Z. Eisenstein, 'Constructing a theory of capitalist patriarchy and socialist feminism', *The Insurgent Sociologist* 7 (1977); M. L. McDougall, 'Working-class women during the industrial revolution, 1780–1914', in R. Bridenthal and C. Koonz (eds), *Becoming visible: Women in European history* (Boston 1977). See, for example, P. E. Malcolmson, *English laundresses: A social history, 1850–1930* (Urbana 1986).

8. S. Alexander, A. Davin and E. Hostettler, 'Labouring women: A reply to Eric Hobsbawm', *History Workshop* 8 (1979); J. Humphries, '"… The most free from objection …" The sexual division of labor and women's work in nineteenth-century England', *Journal of Economic History* 47 (1987); E. Jordan, 'The exclusion of women from industry in nineteenth-century Britain', *Comparative Studies in Society and History* 31 (1989); E. Richards, 'Women in the British economy since about 1700: An interpretation', *History* 59 (1974).

9. K. D. M. Snell, 'Agricultural seasonal unemployment, the standard of living, and women's work in the South and East, 1690–1860', *Economic History Review* 34 (1981), p. 413.

10. Susan Partridge, *Harmony* 1827.

11. M. Roberts, 'Sickles and scythes: Women's work and men's work at harvest time', *History Workshop* 7 (1979), pp. 22–3; K. D. M. Snell, 'Agricultural seasonal unemployment, the standard of living, and women's work in the South and East, 1690–1860', *Economic History Review* 34 (1981), pp. 419–20.

12. This trend continued throughout the century. E. J. T. Collins, 'Harvest technology and labour supply in Britain, 1790–1870', *Economic History Review* 22 (1969), p. 470; Roberts, 'Sickles and scythes', p. 13; Snell, 'Agricultural seasonal unemployment', p. 433. For an overview, see D. Bythell, 'Women in the work force', in P. K. O'Brien and R. Quinault (eds), *The industrial revolution and British society* (Cambridge 1993).

13. S. Alexander, *Women's work in nineteenth-century London: A study of the years 1820–50* (London 1983), p. 26; Clark, *Working life*; S. O. Rose, 'Gender antagonism and class conflict: Exclusionary strategies of male trade-unionists in nineteenth-century Britain', *Social History* 13 (1988); K. D. M. Snell, *Annals of the labouring poor, social change and agrarian England, 1660–1900* (Cambridge 1985), pp. 275–6. For an alternative analysis, see J. Humphries, 'Protective legislation, the capitalist state, and working-class men: The case of the 1842 Mines Regulation Act', *Feminist Review* 7 (1981).

14. Alexander, *Women's work*, p. 39.

15. For a more detailed discussion of this process, see L. Bennett, 'The construction of skill: Craft unions, women workers and the conciliation and arbitration system', *Law in Context* 2 (1984).

16. Alexander, *Women's work*, p. 26.

17. Ann Stewart, *Henry Wellesley* 1836; Ann Yellop, *Louisa* 1827; Mary Bates, *Princess Royal* 1829.

18. B. Smith, *A cargo of women: Susannah Watson and the convicts of the 'Princess Royal'* (Sydney 1988), pp. 40–1, 50, 67.

19. Frances Nolan, *Forth* 1830; Elizabeth Wilkinson, *Mary Anne 5* 1839.
20. Alexander, *Women's work*, p. 40.
21. Alexander, *Women's work*, pp. 34–5.
22. Alexander, *Women's work*, pp. 13, 26, 30, 48.
23. N. McKendrick, 'Home demand and economic growth: A new view of the role of women and children in the industrial revolution', in N. McKendrick (ed.), *Historical perspectives: Studies in English thought and society* (London 1974).
24. Alexander, *Women's work*, p. 9; Alexander, Davin and Hostettler, 'Labouring women', p. 179; McKendrick, 'Home demand', p. 184; Scott and Tilly, 'Women's work', p. 44.
25. According to John Burns writing on 'The unemployed' for the journal *Nineteenth Century*, quoted in Malcolmson, *English laundresses*, p. 22.
26. M. A. Crowther, *The workhouse system, 1834–1929: The history of an English social institution* (London 1981), p. 251.
27. Scott and Tilly, 'Women's work', p. 54.
28. The level of skill necessary to perform this occupation has been clearly demonstrated by Malcolmson, *English laundresses*.
29. Alexander, *Women's work*, p. 39.
30. T. McBride, *The domestic revolution: The modernisation of household service in England and France, 1820–1920* (London 1976), p. 9.
31. Hume, quoted in D. A. Kent, 'Ubiquitous but invisible: Female domestic servants in mid-eighteenth century London', *History Workshop* 28 (1989), p. 117.
32. McBride, *Domestic revolution*, p. 35.
33. Hecht, quoted in Kent, 'Ubiquitous but invisible', p. 112.
34. McBride, *Domestic revolution*, p. 20.
35. Kent, 'Ubiquitous but invisible', p. 114.
36. Kent, 'Ubiquitous but invisible', p. 111; McBride, *Domestic revolution*, p. 34.
37. McBride, *Domestic revolution*, p. 18.
38. W. Neff, quoted in F. L. Jones, 'Occupational statistics revisited: The female labour force in early British and Australian Censuses', *Australian Economic History Review* 27.2 (1987), p. 60.
39. Scott and Tilly, 'Women's work', p. 40.
40. A. S. Kussmaul, 'The ambiguous mobility of farm servants', *Economic History Review* 34 (1981), p. 234; J. Rendall, *The origins of modern feminism: Women in Britain, France and the United States, 1780–1860* (London 1985), p. 53.
41. Kussmaul, 'Ambiguous mobility', p. 234.
42. Anonymous, *The servant girl in London, showing the dangers to which young country girls are exposed on their arrival in town with advice to them, to their parents, to their masters, and to their mistresses, respectfully dedicated to all Heads of Families & Benevolent Societies* (London 1840), quoted in F. Barret-Ducrocoq, *Love in the time of Victoria: Sexuality and desire among working-class men and women in nineteenth-century London* (New York 1992), p. 72.
43. P. Robinson, *The hatch and brood of time: A study of the first generation of native-born white Australians, 1788–1828*, volume 1 (Oxford 1985), p. 73.
44. See McBride, *Domestic revolution*, chapter 6.

45. McBride, *Domestic revolution*, p. 11. For a contrary view that sees domestic service as a feudal remnant, see M. I. Thomis and J. Grimmett, *Women in protest 1800-1850* (London 1982), p. 24; E. Higgs, 'Domestic service and household production', in A. V. John (ed.), *Unequal opportunities: Women's employment in England, 1800–1918* (Oxford 1986).

46. McBride, *Domestic revolution*, p. 34.

47. Kussmaul, 'Ambiguous mobility', p. 222; Kent, 'Ubiquitous but invisible', p. 112.

48. Kent, 'Ubiquitous but invisible', pp. 112–18.

49. Alexander, *Women's work*, pp. 22–5.

50. Thomis and Grimmett, *Women in protest*, p. 18; McKendrick, 'Home demand', p. 189.

51. See D. Kent and N. Townsend, 'Deborah Oxley's "Female convicts": An accurate view of working-class women?', *Labour History* 65 (1993). In reply, see D. Oxley, 'Exercising agency', *Labour History* 65 (1993).

52. Thomis and Grimmett, *Women in protest*, p. 21; McKendrick, 'Home demand', pp. 155, 185.

53. Quoted in M. Lake, 'Socialism and manhood: The case of William Lane', *Labour History* 50 (1986), p. 55.

54. Thomis and Grimmett, *Women in protest*, p. 18.

55. Nicholas and Oxley, 'Living standards'; Nicholas and Oxley, 'Industrial revolution'; J. Humphries, ' "Bread and a penny's worth of treacle": Excess female mortality in England in the 1840s', *Cambridge Journal of Economics* 15 (1991).

56. Great Britain census 1841. Report from the commissioners', *PP*, 1843 (496) XXII (IUP *Population* 3), pp. 84–7.

57. H. Mayhew and J. Binny, *The criminal prisons of London and scenes of prison life* (London 1862), pp. 362, 384. For an example of what historians have said, see M. B. Schedvin and C. B. Schedvin, 'The nomadic tribes of urban Britain: A prelude to Botany Bay', *Historical Studies: Australia and New Zealand* 18 (1978).

58. Mayhew and Binny, *Criminal prisons*, pp. 90, 358.

59. Also see S. Nicholas and P. Shergold, 'Internal migration in England, 1817–1839', *Journal of Historical Geography* 13 (1987); S. Nicholas and P. Shergold, 'Intercounty labour mobility during the industrial revolution: Evidence from Australian transportation records', *Oxford Economic Papers* 39 (1987).

60. Kussmaul, 'Ambiguous mobility', p. 225.

61. McBride, *Domestic revolution*, pp. 35, 37.

62. Kent, 'Ubiquitous but invisible', p. 111.

63. Kent, 'Ubiquitous but invisible', p. 120.

64. Kent, 'Ubiquitous but invisible', p. 121.

65. Kent, 'Ubiquitous but invisible', p. 120.

66. Schedvin and Schedvin, 'Nomadic tribes', p. 275.

67. M. Sanderson, 'Literacy and social mobility in the industrial revolution in England', *Past and Present* 64 (1974), p. 98.

68. R. S. Schofield, 'Dimensions of illiteracy, 1750–1850', *Explorations in Economic History* 10 (1973), p. 440.

69. 'Report from the select committee on education of the poorer classes', *PP*, 1837–38 (589) VII, p. 42 (IUP *Education—Poorer Classes* 6).
70. Symons quoted in D. Beddoe, *Welsh convict women: A study of women transported from Wales to Australia, 1787-1852* (Wales 1979), p. 76; Mayhew and Binny, *Criminal prisons*, p. 390.
71. Jones, 'Occupational statistics'; Land, 'Family wage', pp. 60–1.
72. This is based on the fact that women canvassed in the census represented only 40 per cent of the number of men counted. 'Great Britain census 1841. Part I England and Wales, occupational abstract', *PP*, 1844 (587) XXVII, p. 45 (IUP *Population* 5).
73. Alexander, *Women's work*, p. 11.
74. K. Corcoran and S. Nicholas, 'Statistical appendix', in S. Nicholas (ed.), *Convict workers: Reinterpreting Australia's past* (Melbourne 1988), p. 214.
75. McBride, *Domestic revolution*.
76. Kent, 'Ubiquitous but invisible', pp. 111–28. Some women would have had no choice.
77. 'GB census 1841. Occupational abstract', p. 51.
78. McBride, *Domestic revolution*, p. 22.
79. McBride, *Domestic revolution*, pp. 22–5.
80. Laslett, Lichfield and Ardleigh, quoted in Kent, 'Ubiquitous but invisible', p. 127.
81. Mayhew and Binny, *Criminal prisons*, p. 384.

7   COLONIAL REQUIREMENTS

1. Repeating some of the references from earlier chapters, see M. Roe, 'Colonial society in embryo', *Historical Studies: Australia and New Zealand*, 7 (1956), p. 158; B. Fletcher, *Ralph Darling: A governor maligned* (Melbourne 1984), p. 119; S. Nicholas and P. Shergold, 'Convicts as migrants', in Stephen Nicholas (ed.), *Convict workers: Reinterpreting Australia's past* (Melbourne 1988), p. 60; J. Waldersee, *Catholic society in New South Wales, 1788–1860* (Sydney 1974), pp. 58–9; J. Williams, 'Irish female convicts and Tasmania', *Labour History* 44, (1983), pp. 5, 12.
2. K. M. Dallas, 'Transportation and colonial income', *Historical Studies: Australia and New Zealand* 3 (1949), p. 299.
3. C. Erickson, 'Emigration from the British Isles to the U.S.A. in 1831', *Population Studies* 35 (1981), p. 181.
4. A. J. Hammerton, '"Without natural protectors": Female immigration to Australia, 1832–36', *Historical Studies: Australia and New Zealand* 16 (1975), p. 539.
5. 'New South Wales final report of the committee of the Legislative Council on emigration, and minutes of evidence, 18 May 1835. Enclosure in No. 1— Copy of a despatch from Governor Richard Bourke to Lord Glenelg, 14 October 1835. Correspondence between the Secretary of State and Governors of the Australian colonies', *PP*, 1837 (358) XLIII, p. 10 (IUP *Colonies—Australia* 5).
6. 'NSW final report on emigration', p. 10.

7. 'General return of emigration for 1839. Report from the agent-general for emigration with correspondence', *PP*, 1840 (113) XXXIII, p.48 (IUP *Colonies— Australia* 6).

8. It was not until the late 1860s that colonial governments gained control over this vital section of policy. However, after colonial authority was asserted there was no apparent change in either the types of female migrants that were targeted, or the ones that came.

9. 'NSW final report on emigration', pp. 10–15.

10. Nineteenth-century remark, quoted in P. Hamilton, '"Tipperarifying the moral atmosphere": Irish Catholic immigration and the state, 1840–1860', in Sydney Labour History Group, *What rough beast? The state and social order in Australian history* (Sydney, 1982), p. 15. See R. Haines, 'Indigent misfits or shrewd operators? Government-assisted emigrants from the United Kingdom to Australia, 1831–1860', *Population Studies* 48 (1994); R. Haines, 'Government-assisted emigration from the United Kingdom to Australia, 1831–1860: Promotion, recruitment and the labouring poor', unpublished PhD thesis, Flinders University of South Australia, 1993.

11. Cunningham, quoted in Hammerton, '"Without natural protectors"', p. 540.

12. Hammerton, '"Without natural protectors"', p. 539.

13. There were also 904 children under the age of 14 years. Alan Atkinson, 'Free settlers before 1851', in J. Jupp (ed.), *The Australian people* (Sydney 1988), p. 41.

14. 'NSW final report on emigration', p. 10.

15. 'NSW final report on emigration', pp. 11, 13.

16. 'NSW final report on emigration', p. 11.

17. 'NSW final report on emigration', p. 11.

18. 'NSW final report on emigration', p. 12.

19. Hamilton, '"Tipperarifying the moral atmosphere"', pp. 19–28.

20. K. Alford, 'Convict and immigrant women before 1851', in Jupp, *The Australian people*, p. 43.

21. The same needs evident in New South Wales were to emerge in Van Diemen's Land. J. Gothard, '"Radically unsound and mischievous": Female migration to Tasmania, 1856–1863', *Australian Historical Studies* 23 (1989), pp. 386–7; J. Gothard, 'A compromise with conscience: The reception of female immigrant domestic servants in Eastern Australia, 1860–1890', *Labour History* 62 (1992).

22. 'General information for intending emigrants and others', *Colonial Secretary*, Special Bundle 4/861.2, AONSW.

23. 'NSW final report on emigration', p. 11.

24. See A. Summers, *Damned whores and God's police: The colonization of women in Australia* (Melbourne 1976).

25. Calculated from C. Bateson, *The convict ships, 1787–1868* (Glasgow 1959). Also see A. G. L. Shaw, *Convicts and the colonies: A study of penal transportation from Great Britain and Ireland to Australia and other parts of the British Empire* (Melbourne 1981), Appendix pp. 361–8.

26. Calculated from Shaw, *Convicts and the colonies*, pp. 366–7.

27. K. Alford, *Production or reproduction? An economic history of women in Australia, 1788–1850* (Oxford 1984), p. 15.

28. For a study of the complexity of these relations later in the century, see A. McGrath, '"Black velvet": Aboriginal women and their relations with white men in the Northern Territory, 1910–40', in K. Daniels (ed.), *So much hard work: Women and prostitution in Australian History* (Sydney 1984), pp. 233–97.

29. Alford, *Production or reproduction?*, p. 23; M. Dixson, *The real Matilda: Women and identity in Australia, 1788–1975* (Victoria 1976), pp. 140–1.

30. 'NSW final report on emigration', p. 11.

31. J. B. Hirst, *Convict society and its enemies: A history of early New South Wales* (Sydney 1983), p. 79; R. B. Madgwick, *Immigration into Eastern Australia, 1788–1851* (Sydney 1969), p. 229; M. Sturma, 'Eye of the beholder: The stereotype of women convicts, 1788–1852', *Labour History* 34 (1978), p. 7.

32. 'Report from the select committee on transportation, together with minutes of evidence, appendix and index' (Molesworth Report), *PP*, 1838 (669) XXII, p. ix (IUP *Crime and Punishment—Transportation* 3).

33. Katrina Alford has also pointed to the near axiomatic belief held at the time that the sex imbalance was responsible for an excessively high crime rate, and the irony that 'the presence or absence of women was blamed for what was generally a male pastime'. Alford, *Production or reproduction?*, pp. 21–2; R. Hughes, *The fatal shore: A history of the transportation of convicts to Australia, 1787–1868* (London 1987), pp. 264–72, 320, 429, 516, 529-32, 536–8, 545, 593.

34. Alford, *Production or reproduction?*, p. 21.

35. Hirst, *Convict society*, p. 79; Summers, *Damned whores*, p. 268.

36. Gothard, 'Radically unsound and mischievous', p. 387.

37. N. G. Butlin, J. Ginswick and P. Statham, 'Colonial statistics before 1850', *ANU Source Papers in Economic History* 12 (1986), p. 18.

38. *Assisted (bounty) immigrants*, 1828–37, AO reel no. 1286, Archives Authority of New South Wales.

39. C. Erickson, 'Emigration from the British Isles', p. 185.

40. R. Teale, *Colonial Eve: Sources on women in Australia 1788–1914* (Melbourne 1978), p. 39.

41. Since this book was written, I have undertaken collaborative work on this topic. A sample of 9820 women arriving free in 1841 confirms the findings made here. See D. Oxley and E. Richards, 'Convicts and free immigrant women compared: 1841—a turning point?', in E. Richards (ed.), *Visible Women* (Canberra, forthcoming).

42. Madgwick, *Immigration into Eastern Australia*, pp. 228–9.

43. R. J. Shultz, 'Immigration into Eastern Australia, 1788–1851', *Historical Studies: Australia and New Zealand* 14 (1970), p. 274.

44. Madgwick, *Immigration into Eastern Australia*, p. 149.

45. Shultz, 'Immigration into Eastern Australia', pp. 275–6.

46. Madgwick, *Immigration into Eastern Australia*, p. 229.

47. Hammerton, '"Without natural protectors"', pp. 539–66; A. J. Hammerton, *Emigrant gentlewomen: Genteel poverty and female emigration, 1830–1914* (London 1979); Teale, *Colonial Eve*, p. 39.

48. C. Durston, '"Unhallowed wedlocks": the regulation of marriage during the English revolution', *The Historical Journal* 31 (1988), pp. 45–9; Sturma, 'Eye of the beholder', p. 7.

49. S. Wilson, 'Language and ritual in marriage', *Push from the Bush* 2 (1978), p. 92.

50. B. M. Penglase, 'An enquiry into literacy in early-nineteenth-century New South Wales', *Push from the Bush* 16 (1983).

51. Shultz's figures were used for immigrant age distribution, but not for literacy. This is because his sample of bounty immigrants covers the years from 1837 to 1850, a slightly later period. There was a general rise in literacy levels over this period, which makes the comparison problematic. Certainly the migrants in his sample appear more literate than those in Penglase's study. Shultz, 'Immigration into Eastern Australia'; Penglase, 'An enquiry into literacy'.

52. 'Letter from Mr Elliot, in answer to the report of the agent for emigrants at Sydney. Enclosure in No. 9—Lord John Russell to Sir G. Gipps, 22 February 1840. Report from the agent-general for emigration with correspondence', *PP*, 1840 (113) XXXIII, pp. 25, 27, 33, 35 (IUP *Colonies—Australia* 6). Work is currently being undertaken at Flinders University by Robin Haines and Eric Richards, History Department, and by members of the Department of Economic History at the University of New South Wales.

53. Possibly, then, there was some exaggeration by immigrants about the usefulness and appropriateness of their skills (if so, this makes the convicts look even better!). Erikson also believes that many so-called farm labourers had sought work outside agriculture before emigrating. This would appear, however, to extend their range of skills rather than to diminish it. Erickson, 'Emigration from the British Isles', pp.185–6.

54. M. Perrott, *A tolerable good success: Economic opportunities for women in New South Wales, 1788–1830* (Sydney 1983), pp. 51–4. But Alford argues that employment opportunities were diminishing: *Production or reproduction?*, p. 151.

55. 'NSW final report on emigration', p. 22.

56. 'NSW final report on emigration', pp. 22–3.

57. 'Return showing the average wages of mechanics and others, in the town of Sydney, for the six months ended 30th June 1836, and the number required in addition to those already employed, obtained from returns transmitted by the first police magistrate to the Colonial Secretary's Office, 28 February 1836. Enclosure 1 in No. 11—Copy of a despatch from Governor Sir Richard Bourke to Lord Glenelg, 2 January 1837. Correspondence between the Secretary of State and Governors of the Australian colonies', *PP*, 1837 (358) XLIII, p. 75 (IUP *Colonies—Australia* 5).

58. 'Return of wages', p. 76.

59. 'Return of wages', p. 77.

60. 'Return of wages', pp. 76–7.

61. 'Regulations for the assignment of male convict servants', *New South Wales Government Gazette*, 13 May 1835, pp. 287–94.

62. H. Weatherburn, 'The female factory', in Mackinolty and Radi (eds), *In pursuit of justice: Australian women and the law, 1788–1979* (Sydney 1979), p. 5; A. Salt, *These outcast women: The Parramatta female factory, 1821–*

1848 (Sydney 1984); B. Smith, *A cargo of women: Susannah Watson and the convicts of the 'Princess Royal'* (Sydney 1988), pp. 52–9.

63. P. Robinson, *The hatch and brood of time: A study of the first generation of native-born white Australians, 1788–1828*, volume 1 (Oxford 1985), p. 79.

64. *New South Wales Government Gazette* 13, 30 May 1832, p. 111.

65. Salt, *Outcast women*, p. 102; Smith, *Cargo of women*, p. 54.

66. B. H. Fletcher, *Ralph Darling: A governor maligned* (Melbourne 1984), p. 117.

67. 'Return relative to the employment of convicts in New South Wales 1826–28', *PP*, 1831–32 (161) XXXII, pp. 4–5; Robinson, *Hatch and brood*, p. 79.

68. Hammerton, '"Without natural protectors"', pp. 539–66.

69. Governor Arthur to Hay, 10 September 1832, quoted in Hammerton, '"Without natural protectors"', pp. 544–5.

70. Lang, quoted in G. C. Ingleton (ed.), *True patriots all: or news from early Australia, as told in a collection of broadsides* (Sydney 1952), pp. 270–1.

71. 'Report from the select committee on transportation, together with minutes of evidence, appendix and index', *PP*, 1837 (518) XIX, p. 230 (IUP *Crime and Punishment—Transportation* 2). Also see Hamilton, '"Tipperarifying the moral atmosphere"', p. 26.

72. Contemporary Australian claim, quoted in C. Kinealy, *This great calamity: The Irish famine, 1845–52* (Dublin 1994), p. 323.

73. Poor Law commissioners, quoted in Kinealy, *Great calamity*, pp. 324–5.

74. Bourke, quoted in Alford, 'Convict and immigrant women', p. 44.

75. Hamilton, '"Tipperarifying the moral atmosphere"', pp. 13–9.

76. Children aged between fourteen and eighteen years, imported under orphan migration schemes, experienced the same short shrift. The *Argus* described them as 'coarse, useless creatures' with 'squat stunted figures, thick waists and clumsy ankles'. They were young and untrained, but not untrainable as claimed by employers unwilling to invest effort in skilling young workers: Hamilton, '"Tipperarifying the moral atmosphere"', pp. 22–3. No doubt had a 'factory' existed where these young workers could have been returned and replaced, as it did for convict women, it would have been much used.

77. Governor Denison, quoted in Hamilton, '"Tipperarifying the moral atmosphere"', p. 27.

78. Molesworth Report, p. 95.

79. Hammerton, '"Without natural protectors"', p. 548; Appendix.

80. Hamilton, '"Tipperarifying the moral atmosphere"', p. 20.

8   MISCONCEPTIONS

1. Some examples can be found in P. Clarke and D. Spender (eds), *Life lines: Australian women's letters and diaries, 1788–1840* (Sydney 1992). Given that we have evidence of much letter writing between New South Wales and the United Kingdom, it would seem possible that a repository at the British end may yet be found.

2. H. S. Payne, 'A statistical study of female convicts in Tasmania, 1843–53', *Tasmanian Historical Research Association Papers and Proceedings* 9 (1961), p. 56; L. L. Robson, 'The origin of the women convicts sent to Australia, 1787–1852', *Historical Studies: Australia and New Zealand* 11 (1963), p. 43.

3. *The journal of Arthur Bowes Smyth: Surgeon, 'Lady Penrhyn', 1787–1789* (ed. P. G. Fidlon and R. J. Ryan, reproduction Sydney 1979), p. 55.
4. R. Clark, quoted in A. Summers, *Damned whores and God's police: The colonization of women in Australia* (Melbourne 1994), p. 313. This quotation differs from Summers' earlier attribution, 'No, no—surely not! My God—not more of those damned whores! Never have I known worse women!', on p. 267 of the original 1976 edition of her book. Hereafter, page references are to the 1976 edition.
5. Darling, quoted in B. H. Fletcher, *Ralph Darling: A governor maligned* (Melbourne 1984), p. 116.
6. Macquarie to Castlereagh, 8 March 1810, *HRA* VII, p. 221; Government and general orders, 3 July 1799, *HRA* II, p. 586; Hunter, quoted in P. Robinson, *The hatch and brood of time: A study of the first generation of native-born white Australians, 1788–1828*, volume 1 (Oxford 1985), p. 65.
7. MacQueen, quoted in Summers, *Damned whores*, p. 272; Ullathorne, quoted in M. Dixson, *The real Matilda: Women and identity in Australia, 1788–1975* (Victoria 1976), p. 125.
8. Osborne, quoted in Dixson, *The real Matilda*, p. 125.
9. 'Report from the select committee on transportation, together with minutes of evidence, appendix and index', *PP*, 1837 (518) XIX, p. 38 (IUP *Crime and Punishment—Transportation* 2).
10. 'SC on transportation', p. 96.
11. 'SC on transportation', p. 196
12. 'SC on transportation', p. 148.
13. 'Report from the select committee on transportation, together with minutes of evidence, appendix and index' (Molesworth Report), *PP*, 1838 (669) XXII, p. ix (IUP *Crime and Punishment—Transportation* 3).
14. W. Ullathorne, *The horrors of transportation: Briefly unfolded to the people* (Dublin 1838), p. 12.
15. Quoted in Ullathorne, *Horrors*, p. 8.
16. Quoted in Ullathorne, *Horrors*, pp. 17–18.
17. 'SC on transportation', p. 148.
18. Ullathorne, *Horrors*, pp. 8–9.
19. *New South Wales Government Gazette* 13, 30 May 1832, p. 111.
20. P. Hamilton, '"Tipperarifying the moral atmosphere"': Irish Catholic immigration and the state, 1840–1860', in Sydney Labour History Group, *What rough beast? The state and social order in Australian history* (Sydney 1982), p. 21.
21. 'SC on transportation', p. 148.
22. 'SC on transportation', p. 196.
23. S. Macintyre, *Winners and losers: The pursuit of social justice in Australian history* (Sydney 1985), pp. 4–5.
24. M. Aveling, 'Gender in early New South Wales', *Push from the Bush* 24 (1987), p. 37.
25. *The journal and letters of Lt. Ralph Clark 1787–1792*, (ed. P. G. Fidlon and R. J. Ryan, reproduction, Sydney 1981), pp. 61–2.
26. Clark, quoted in D. Beddoe, *Welsh convict women: A study of women transported from Wales to Australia, 1787–1852* (Wales 1979), p. 96.

27. Fidlon and Ryan, 'Introduction', in Bowes Smyth, *Journal*, p. xvii.
28. Bowes Smyth, *Journal*, pp. 47–8.
29. Bowes Smyth, *Journal*, p. 48.
30. Fidlon and Ryan, *Journal*, p. v.
31. Bowes Smyth, *Journal*, p. 48.
32. Bowes Smyth, *Journal*, pp. 48–9.
33. Bowes Smyth, *Journal*, p. 70.
34. 'SC on transportation', p. 38.
35. H. Mayhew and J. Binny, *The criminal prisons of London and scenes of prison life* (London 1862), p. 462.
36. Mayhew and Binny, *Criminal prisons*, p. 454.
37. Mayhew and Binny, *Criminal prisons*, p. 269.
38 Anonymous, 'Criminal women', *Cornhill Magazine* 14 (1866). A Mrs Owen is recorded as receiving payment for this article in the magazine's accounts. *Wellesley index to Victorian periodicals*, volume 1 (London 1966), p. 342.
39. Anonymous, 'Criminal women', p. 153.
40. J. J. Gurney, quoted in R. P. Dobash, R. E. Dobash and S. Gutteridge, *The imprisonment of women* (Oxford 1986), pp. 43–4.
41. A. Griffiths, *Memorials of Millbank and chapters in prison history* (London 1884), p. 198.
42. Anonymous,'Criminal women', pp. 152–3.
43. Griffiths, *Memorials of Millbank*, p. 202.
44. Griffiths, *Memorials of Millbank*, p. 202.
45. P. Linebaugh, 'The Ordinary of Newgate and his account', in J. S. Cockburn (ed.), *Crime in England, 1550–1800* (London 1977), p. 252.
46. Quoted in Dobash *et al.*, *The imprisonment of women*, p. 42.
47. Mayhew and Binny, *Criminal prisons*, p. 271.
48. Mayhew and Binny, *Criminal prisons*, pp. 271–3.
49. Mayhew and Binny, *Criminal prisons*, pp. 466, 470.
50. Mayhew and Binny, *Criminal prisons*, p. 465.
51. Griffiths, *Memorials of Millbank*, p. 202.
52. Griffiths, *Memorials of Millbank*, p. 202.
53. Griffiths, *Memorials of Millbank*, p. 203.
54. Griffiths, *Memorials of Millbank*, p. 204.
55. Griffiths, *Memorials of Millbank*, p. 206.
56. Griffiths, *Memorials of Millbank*, p. 208.
57. Griffiths, *Memorials of Millbank*, p. 205.
58. Griffiths, *Memorials of Millbank*, p. 215.
59. Griffiths, *Memorials of Millbank*, pp. 217, 219, 222.
60. Griffiths, *Memorials of Millbank*, p. 208.
61. Griffiths, *Memorials of Millbank*, p. 214.
62. Griffiths, *Memorials of Millbank*, pp. 215, 207.
63. Griffiths, *Memorials of Millbank*, pp. 258, 246, 223.
64. F. W. Robinson, *Female life in prison, by a prison matron* (London 1862), pp. 11–12, 14–16.

65. 'Report from the select committee on secondary punishments; together with the minutes of evidence, an appendix, and index', *PP*, 1831–32 (547) VII, pp. 116–27 (IUP *Crime and Punishment—Transportation* 1).

66. Surgeon on the *Earl of Liverpool*, the wife of General Darling, Reverend Dr Lang, quoted by Elizabeth Fry in evidence, 'SC on secondary punishments', pp. 116–27.

67. 'SC on secondary punishments', p. 11.

68. Griffiths, *Memorials of Millbank*, p. 204.

69. D. Philips, 'Moral entrepreneurs and the construction of a "criminal class" in England, c. 1800–1840', paper presented to the Australian Historical Association Conference (University of Sydney 1988).

70. H. Mayhew, *London labour and the London poor: A cyclopaedia of the condition and earnings of those that will work, those that cannot work, and those that will not work, comprising prostitutes, thieves, swindlers, beggars* (London 1862); E. P. Thompson and E. Yeo (eds), *The unknown Mayhew: Selections from the 'Morning Chronicle', 1849–50* (London 1973).

71. Fielding, quoted in S. Garton, *Out of luck: Australians and social welfare, 1788–1988* (Sydney 1990), p. 8.

72. Young and Schwartz, quoted in Garton, *Out of luck*, pp. 7, 11.

73. Garton, *Out of luck*, p. 11.

74. Carpenter, quoted in Beddoe, *Welsh convict women*, p. 75.

75. Garton, *Out of luck*, p. 12.

76. Quoted in C. M. H. Clark, 'The origins of the convicts transported to Eastern Australia, 1787-1852', *Historical Studies: Australia and New Zealand* 7 (1956), p. 135.

77. Darwin, quoted in S. J. Gould, *The mismeasure of man* (New York 1981), title page.

78. C. Emsley, 'The criminal past: Crime in nineteenth-century Britain', *History Today* 38 (April 1988), p. 45.

79. See, for example, S. Pollard, *The genesis of modern management: A study of the industrial revolution in Great Britain* (London 1965).

80. V. A. C. Gatrell and T. B. Hadden, 'Criminal statistics and their interpretation', in E. A. Wrigley (ed.), *Nineteenth-century society: Essays in the use of quantitative methods for the study of social data* (Cambridge 1972), pp. 381–2; Mayhew and Binny, *Criminal prisons*, pp. 84–7.

81. Beddoe, *Welsh convict women*, p. 75.

82. Quoted in A. W. Baker, *Death is a good solution: The convict experience in early Australia* (St Lucia 1984), pp. 16–17.

83. Manning Clark picked up this last theme; Clark, 'Origins', pp. 315–16.

84. R. Billington, 'The dominant values of Victorian feminism', in E. M. Sigsworth (ed.), *In search of Victorian values: Aspects of nineteenth-century thought and society* (Manchester 1988); D. Gorham, *The Victorian girl and the feminine ideal* (London 1982).

85. Robinson, *Hatch and brood*, p. 73.

86. C. Durston, '"Unhallowed wedlocks": The regulation of marriage during the English revolution', *Historical Journal* 31 (1988), pp. 45–9.

87. The Leeds *Mercury*, quoted in J. Humphries, '"... The most free from objection ..." The sexual division of labor and women's work in nineteenth-century England', *Journal of Economic History* 47 (1987), p. 939.
88. Redgrave, quoted in Mayhew and Binny, *Criminal prisons*, p. 461.
89. Beddoe, *Welsh convict women*, p. 15.
90. Mayhew and Binny, *Criminal prisons*, p. 462.
91. P. Robinson, *The women of Botany Bay: A reinterpretation of the role of women in the origins of Australian society* (Macquarie 1988), p. 5.
92. Hay, quoted in A. Shubert, 'Private initiative in law enforcement: Associations for the prosecution of felons, 1744–1856', in V. Bailey (ed.), *Policing and punishment in nineteenth-century Britain* (London 1981), p. 37.
93. Emsley, 'Criminal past', p. 42.
94. K. Hollingsworth, *The Newgate novel, 1830–1847: Bulwer, Ainsworth, Dickens, and Thackeray* (Detroit 1963), p. 14.
95. J. M. Beattie, 'Crime and society in eighteenth-century England', paper presented to the Law History Theory Conference (La Trobe University, May 1988), p. 3; J. M. Beattie, *Crime and the courts in England, 1660–1800* (Princeton 1986), pp. 153-4.
96. Clark, 'Origins', p. 318.
97. 'S.C. on transportation', p. 290.
98. Their emphasis; Mayhew and Binny, *Criminal prisons*, pp. 88–9, 395–6.
99. P. Colquhoun, *A treatise on the police of the Metropolis: Containing a detail of the various crimes and misdemeanours by which public and private property and security are, at present, injured and endangered: and suggesting remedies for their prevention* (London 1805); P. Cunningham, ed. D. S. Macmillan, *Two years in New South Wales: Comprising sketches of the actual state of society in that colony; of its peculiar advantages to emigrants; of its topography, natural history, &c. &c.* (reproduction Sydney 1966).
100. L. L. Robson, *The convict settlers of Australia: An enquiry into the origin and character of the convicts transported to New South Wales and Van Diemen's Land, 1787–1852* (Melbourne 1965), p. 150.
101. Clark, 'Origins'; Robson, *Convict settlers*; A. G. L. Shaw, *Convicts and the colonies: A study of penal transportation from Great Britain and Ireland to Australia and other parts of the British Empire* (Melbourne 1981); M. B. Schedvin and C. B. Schedvin, 'The nomadic tribes of urban Britain: A prelude to Botany Bay', *Historical Studies: Australia and New Zealand* 18 (1978).
102. G. A. Wood, 'Convicts', *Royal Australian Historical Society Journal and Proceedings* 8 (1922).
103. Payne, 'Statistical survey'.
104. Mayhew and Binny, *Criminal prisons*, p. 88.
105. Clark, 'Origins', p. 133.
106. Shaw, *Convicts and the colonies*, p. 165.
107. Quoted in Mayhew and Binny, *Criminal prisons*, p. 84.
108. Clark, 'Origins', p. 314.
109. Mayhew and Binny, *Criminal prisons*, p. 385.

110. Clark, 'Origins', p. 314; W. K. Hancock, Australia (Melbourne 1966), pp. 24–5.
111. Mayhew and Binny, *Criminal prisons*, pp. 84–7.
112. Shaw, Convicts and the colonies, p. 160.
113. Robson, *Convict settlers*, p. 154.
114. Mayhew and Binny, *Criminal prisons*, p. 385.
115. Schedvin and Schedvin, 'Nomadic tribes', p. 275.
116. Mayhew and Binny, *Criminal prisons*, p. 384.
117. J. B. Hirst, *Convict society and its enemies: A history of early New South Wales* (Sydney 1983), p. 32.
118. Robson, 'Origins of women convicts', p. 53.
119. Robson, 'Origins of women convicts', p. 53.
120. Mayhew, quoted in Robson, 'Origins of women convicts', p. 46.
121. Robson, 'Origins of women convicts', p. 53.
122. Hughes observed this: R. Hughes, *The fatal shore: A history of the transportation of convicts to Australia, 1787–1868* (London 1987), p. 244.
123. A. Behn, *The Rover (The Banished Cavaliers)*, first published 1677 (Stratford 1986), p. 38.
124. S. Alexander, *Women's work in nineteenth-century London: A study of the years 1820–50* (London 1983); E. Hostettler, 'Women's work in the nineteenth-century countryside', *Society for the Study of Labour History* 33 (1976); K. D. M. Snell, *Annals of the labouring poor* (Cambridge 1985).
125. Alexander, *Women's work*, pp. 33–49. Also see L. Davidoff and C. Hall, *Family fortunes: Men and women of the English middle class, 1780–1850* (London 1987).
126. Snell, *Annals*, p. 270.
127. L. Bennett, 'The construction of skill: Craft unions, women workers and the conciliation and arbitration system', *Law in Context* 2 (1984), p. 119. A good overview of this literature can be found in R. Frances, *The politics of work: Gender and labour in Victoria, 1880–1939* (Melbourne 1993), introduction.
128. J. B. Hirst, 'Convicts and crime', *Overland* 113 (1988), pp. 82–3. Also see R. Fitzgerald, 'Ruffians or gentlemen?', *Sydney Morning Herald*, 3 December 1988, p. 87; P. Robinson, 'Getting a nation's record straight?', *Age*, 21 January, p. 14.
129. *Classification of Occupations, 1950* (HMSO 1951); W. A. Armstrong, 'The use of information about occupation', in Wrigley (ed.), *Nineteenth-century society*, p. 209.
130. Hamilton, '"Tipperarifying the moral atmosphere"', p. 20.
131. For a lively debate on this topic, see F. L. Jones, 'Occupational statistics revisited: The female labour force in early British and Australian censuses', *Australian Economic History Review* 27 (1987); D. Deacon, 'Political arithmetic: The nineteenth-century Australian census and the construction of the dependent woman', *Signs* 11 (1985); K. Alford, 'Colonial women's employment as seen by nineteenth-century statisticians and twentieth-century economic historians', *Labour History* 51 (1986); A. M. Endres, 'A twentieth-century economic historian on colonial women's employment: Comment on Alford', *Labour History* 52 (1987); K. Alford, 'On polemics and patriarchy: A rejoinder', *Labour History* 52 (1987).

132. Katrina Alford is one of the few economic historians to have explicitly recognised the significance of this role to the long-term growth of the colony. 'Within marriage, the principal function of women was reproduction. Although in theory a non-economic function, it was obviously of considerable economic value in providing a principal source of labour, along with immigration. And since population growth was conducive to economic development, women's reproductive functions were influential in the process of economic growth': K. Alford, *Production or reproduction? An economic history of women in Australia, 1788–1850* (Oxford 1984), pp. 54–5. For current efforts to rectify this see M. Waring, *Counting for nothing: What men value and what women are worth* (Wellington 1988).

133. R. B. Madgwick, *Immigration into Eastern Australia, 1788–1851* (Sydney 1969), p. 229.

134. S. Nicholas and P. Shergold, 'Convicts as migrants', in S. Nicholas (ed.), *Convict workers: Reinterpreting Australia's past* (Melbourne 1988), pp. 52, 60.

135. Nicholas and Shergold, 'Convicts as migrants', *Convict Workers*, p. 52.

136. For example, Alford, *Production or reproduction*; B. Kingston, *My wife, my daughter and poor Mary Ann* (Melbourne 1975); M. Perrott, *A tolerable good success: Economic opportunities for women in New South Wales, 1788–1830* (Sydney 1983); Robinson, *Hatch and brood*; Robinson, *Women of Botany Bay*.

137. B. Dyster, *Servant and master: Building and running the grand houses of Sydney, 1788–1850* (Sydney 1989).

138. M. Roe, 'Colonial society in embryo', *Historical Studies: Australia and New Zealand* 7 (1956), p. 158.

139. K. Daniels, 'Introduction', in K. Daniels (ed.), *So much hard work: Women and prostitution in Australian history* (Sydney 1984), p. 1.

140. Allen and Golder, quoted in Daniels, 'Introduction', p. 12.

9   BRITAIN'S LOSS, AUSTRALIA'S GAIN?

1. G. Rudé, *Criminal and victim: Crime and society in early nineteenth-century England* (Oxford 1985), p. 25.

2. P. Robinson, *The women of Botany Bay: A reinterpretation of the role of women in the origins of Australian society* (Macquarie 1988), p. 3.

3. P. Robinson, 'The first forty years', in J. Mackinolty and H. Radi (eds), *In pursuit of justice: Australian women and the law, 1788–1979* (Sydney 1979), p. 10.

4. B. Kingston, *The world moves slowly* (Cornell 1977), p. 8.

5. Beard, quoted in K. M. Dallas, 'Transportation and colonial income', *Historical Studies: Australia and New Zealand* 3 (1949), p. 299.

6. Dallas, 'Transportation and colonial income', p. 299.

7. Governor Darling, quoted in B. H. Fletcher, *Ralph Darling: A governor maligned* (Melbourne 1984), p. 116.

8. S. Nicholas and P. Shergold, 'Convicts as workers', in S. Nicholas (ed.), *Convict workers: Reinterpreting Australia's past* (Melbourne 1988).

9. S. Thomas, Master's thesis nearing completion, Economic History, University of Melbourne.

10. This case is cited by M. Perrott, *A tolerable good success: Economic opportunities for women in New South Wales, 1788–1830* (Sydney 1983), p. 53.
11. N. G. Butlin, J. Ginswick and P. Statham, 'Colonial statistics before 1850', *Australian National University Source Papers in Economic History* 12 (1986), p. 18.
12. 'Fatal accident', *Goulburn Herald and Chronicle,* 6 July 1867.

Bibliography of Works Cited

OFFICIAL PUBLICATIONS

An Act for punishment of rogues, vagabonds and sturdy beggars, 39 Elizabeth. c. 4 (1597)

An Act for the further preventing of robbery, burglary, and other felonies, and for the more effectual transportation of felons, etc., 4 George. 1, c. 11 (1717)

An Act to authorise, for a limited time, the punishment by hard labour of offenders who, for certain crimes, are or shall become liable to be transported to any of His Majesty's colonies and plantations 16 George. 3, c. 43 (1776)

An Act to explain and amend the laws relating to transportation, imprisonment, and other punishment, of certain offenders 19 George. 3, c. 74 (1779)

An Act for the effectual transportation of felons and other offenders, etc., 24 George. 3, session 2, c. 56 (1784)

An Act for the transportation of offenders from Great Britain 5 George. 4, c. 84 (1824)

'Appendix to the report of the committee on immigration. Despatch relating to immigration', *PP*, 1840 (612) XXXIII (IUP *Colonies—Australia* 6)

Assisted (bounty) immigrants, 1828–37, reel no. 1286, AONSW

Central criminal court (Old Bailey) sessions papers, 1835/36–1836/37 FM4/5851 reel no. 41; 1836/37-1837/38 FM4/5852 reel no. 42

Classification of Occupations, 1950 (HMSO 1951)

Convict indents of transported prisoners 4/4003–4019, and *convict indents of transported Irish prisoners* 4/7076–7078, also reproduced as *Convict indents 1788–1842*, F614–744, Genealogical research kit stage 1, both at the AONSW

Criminal registers, Australian Joint Copying Project, HO26, 27

'General information for intending emigrants and others', Colonial Secretary, Special Bundle 4/861.2, AONSW

'General return of emigration for 1839. Report from the agent-general for emigration with correspondence', *PP*, 1840 (113) XXXIII (IUP *Colonies—Australia* 6)

'Great Britain census 1841. Part I England and Wales, occupational abstract', *PP*, 1844 (587) XXVII (IUP *Population* 5)

'Great Britain census 1841. Report from the commissioners', *PP*, 1843 (496) XXII (IUP *Population* 3)

Historical Records of Australia, I, II, IV, VII, X, XI

Irish convict records: Lists 1828-48, (MS 4869 MLNL)

'Letter from Mr Elliot, in answer to the report of the agent for emigrants a: Sydney. Enclosure in No. 9—Lord John Russell to Sir G. Gipps, 22 February 1840. Report from the agent-general for emigration with correspondence', *PP*, 1840 (113) XXXIII (IUP *Colonies—Australia* 6)

'New South Wales final report of the committee of the Legislative Council on emigration, and minutes of evidence, 18 May 1835. Enclosure in No.1—Copy of a despatch from Governor Richard Bourke to Lord Glenelg, 14 October 1835. Correspondence between the Secretary of State and Governors of the Australian colonies', *PP*, 1837 (358) XLIII (IUP *Colonies—Australia* 5)

New South Wales Government Gazette, 1832, 1836

'Papers relating to the loss of the convict ship *Amphitrite*', *PP*, 1834 (427) XLVII

'Regulations for the assignment of male convict servants', *New South Wales Government Gazette*, 13 May 1835

'Report of the commissioners appointed to take the census of Ireland for the year 1841', *PP*, 1843 (504) XXIV (IUP *Population* 2)

'Report from the select committee on education of the poorer classes', *PP*, 1837–38 (589) VII (IUP *Education—Poorer Classes* 6)

'Report from the select committee on secondary punishments; together with the minutes of evidence, an appendix, and index, *PP*, 1831-2 (547) VII (IUP *Crime and Punishment—Transportation* 1)

'Report from the select committee on transportation, together with minutes of evidence, appendix and index', *PP*, 1837 (518) XIX (IUP *Crime and Punishment—Transportation* 2)

'Report from the select committee on transportation, together with minutes of evidence, appendix and index' (Molesworth Report), *PP*, 1838 (669) XXII (IUP *Crime and Punishment—Transportation* 3)

Report on the sanitary condition of the labouring population of Gt. Britain 1842 by Edwin Chadwick, edited by M. W. Flinn (Edinburgh 1842)

'Return relative to the employment of convicts in New South Wales 1826-28', *PP*, 1831–32 (161) Vol. XXXII

'Return showing the average wages of mechanics and others, in the town of Sydney, for the six months ended 30th June 1836, and the number required in addition to those already employed, obtained from returns transmitted by the first police magistrate to the Colonial Secretary's Office, 28 February 1836. Enclosure 1 in No. 11—Copy of a despatch from Governor Sir Richard Bourke to Lord Glenelg, 2 January 1837. Correspondence between the Secretary of State and Governors of the Australian colonies', *PP*, 1837 (358) XLIII (IUP *Colonies—Australia* 5)

Transportation accounts, Australian joint copying project, Reel FM4/2283

OTHER PRIMARY SOURCES

Anonymous, 'Criminal women', *Cornhill Magazine* 14 (1866)

Anonymous, *The surprising adventures and unparalleled sufferings of Jane Turner; A female convict, who made her escape from New South Wales* (Doncaster 1850)

'Australia ... Domestic servants', *Original poster*, c. 1883, document 93, AONSW

'Australia. Government emigration', Original poster, c. 1884, document 102, AONSW

Bacon, F., 'Of plantations', *Essays* (reprinted London 1909)

Bowes Smyth, A., *The journal of Arthur Bowes Smyth: Surgeon, 'Lady Penrhyn', 1787–1789*, reproduction edited by P. G. Fidlon and R. J. Ryan (Sydney 1979)

Clark, R., *The journal and letters of Lt. Ralph Clark 1787–1792*, reproduction edited by P. G. Fidlon and R. J. Ryan (Sydney 1981)

Colquhoun, P., *A treatise on the police of the Metropolis: Containing a detail of the various crimes and misdemeanours by which public and private property and security are, at present, injured and endangered: and suggesting remedies for their prevention* (London 1805)

Cunningham, P., *Two years in New South Wales: Comprising sketches of the actual state of society in that colony; of its peculiar advantages to emigrants; of its topography, natural history, &c. &c.*, reproduction edited by D. S. Macmillan, first published 1827 (Sydney 1966)

Daniels, K., and M. Murnane (eds), *Uphill all the way: A documentary history of women in Australia* (St Lucia 1980)

Dickens, C., 'A Letter to the Marquis of Normanby, Secretary of State for the Home Office' (3 July 1840; MS 6809 MLNL)

Dickens, C., *The Adventures of Oliver Twist* (Oxford 1978), first published in magazine form in 1837

Eagar, E., *Letters to the Rt. Hon. Robert Peel, M.P. ... on the advantages of New South Wales and Van Diemen's Land* (London 1824)

Eldershaw, P. R., *Guide to the public records of Tasmania. Section three: Convict department record group* (Hobart 1965)

'Fatal accident', *Goulburn Herald and Chronicle*, 6 July 1867

'Female emigration to Australia', Original poster, 1834, ref. D356/17: CY1118, f. 535, Mitchell

'Female emigration to New South Wales', Original poster, 1836, ref. D356/17: CY1118, f. 534, Mitchell

'The gold snuff-box', *Punch* 1, July 1841

Index to photographic descriptions book, volume 3, 3/6040, AONSW

Ingleton, G. C. (ed.), *True patriots all: or news from early Australia,—as told in a collection of broadsides* (Sydney 1952)

'The London convict maid', ref. D366/15 no. 10: CY1118 f. 1376, Mitchell

Mayhew, H., *London labour and the London poor: A cyclopaedia of the condition and earnings of those that will work, those that cannot work, and those that will not work, comprising prostitutes, thieves, swindlers, beggars*, volume 4 (London 1862)

Mayhew, H., and J. Binny, *The criminal prisons of London and scenes of prison life* (London 1862)

Mudie, J., *The felonry of New South Wales; Being a faithful picture of the real romance of life in Botany Bay with anecdotes of Botany Bay society and a plan of Sydney*, reproduction edited by W. Stone, first published 1837 (Sydney 1965)

'Notice to young women', 1833, ref. D356/17: CY1118, f. 529, Mitchell

Keese, O., *The broad arrow: Being the story of Maida Gwynnham, a 'Lifer' in Van Diemen's Land* (London 1859)

Reilly, B., *A true history of Bernard Reilly, a returned convict. Who was transported in the year 1821, and has lately returned from exile with an account of his sufferings, &c. &c. Written by Himself* (Ballinamore c. 1839)

Richardson, S., *Pamela, or virtue rewarded* (London 1740)

Robinson, F. W., *Female life in prison by a prison matron* (London 1862)

Slater, J., *A description of Sydney, Parramatta, Newcastle, &c., settlements in New South Wales, with some account of the manners and employment of the convicts, in a letter from John Slater, to his Wife in Nottingham, Published for the benefit of his wife and four children* (Nottingham 1819)

Sydney Gazette and New South Wales Advertiser, 1838

Ullathorne, W., *The Catholic mission in Australia* (Liverpool 1837)

Ullathorne, W., *The Horrors of transportation: Briefly unfolded to the people* (Dublin 1838)

SECONDARY SOURCES

Alexander, S., *Women's work in nineteenth-century London: A study of the years 1820–50* (London 1983)

Alexander, S., A. Davin and E. Hostettler, 'Labouring women: A reply to Eric Hobsbawm', *History Workshop* 8 (1979)

Alford, K., *Production or reproduction? An economic history of women in Australia, 1788–1850* (Oxford 1984)

Alford, K., 'Colonial women's employment as seen by nineteenth-century statisticians and twentieth-century economic historians', *Labour History* 51 (1986)

Alford, K., 'On polemics and patriarchy: A rejoinder', *Labour History* 52 (1987)

Alford, K., 'Convict and immigrant women before 1851', in J. Jupp (ed.), *The Australian people* (Sydney 1988)

Alford, K., 'Book review of G. D. Snooks, *Portrait of the family within the total economy*', *Labour History* 67 (1994)

Almquist, E. L., 'Mayo and beyond: Land, domestic industry and rural transformation in the Irish West', *Irish Economic and Social History* 5 (1978)

Amos, K., *The Fenians in Australia 1865–1880* (Sydney 1988)

Anderson, M., 'Urban migration in nineteenth-century Lancashire: Some insights into two competing hypotheses', in M. Drake (ed.), *Historical demography: Problems and projects* (Milton Keynes 1974)

Armstrong, W. A., 'The use of information about occupation', in E. A. Wrigley (ed.), *Nineteenth-century society: Essays in the use of quantitative methods for the study of social data* (Cambridge 1972)

Atkinson, A., 'The moral basis of marriage', *Push from the Bush* 2 (1978)

Atkinson, A., 'Four patterns of convict protest', *Labour History* 37 (1979)

Atkinson, A., 'Marriage and distance in the convict colonies, 1838', *Push from the Bush* 16 (1983)

Atkinson, A., *Camden: Farm and village life in early New South Wales* (Oxford 1988)

Atkinson, A., 'Free settlers before 1851', in J. Jupp (ed.), *The Australian people* (Sydney 1988)

Attwood, B., *The making of the Aborigines* (Sydney 1989)

Aveling, M., 'She only married to be free: Or, Cleopatra vindicated', *Push from the Bush* 2 (1978)

Aveling, M., 'Gender in early New South Wales', *Push from the Bush* 24 (1987)

Aveling, M., 'Bending the bars: Convict women and the state', in K. Saunders and R. Evans (eds), *Gender relations in Australia: Domination and negotiation* (Sydney 1992)

Bailey, V., 'Introduction' and 'The Metropolitan police, the Home Office and the threat of outcast London', in V. Bailey (ed.), *Policing and punishment in nineteenth-century Britain* (London 1981)

Baines, D. E., 'The labour supply and the labour market, 1860–1914', in R. Floud and D. McCloskey (eds), *The economic history of Britain since 1700*, volume 2 (Cambridge 1981)

Baker, A. W., *Death is a good solution: The convict experience in early Australia* (St Lucia 1984)

Barret-Ducrocoq, F., *Love in the time of Victoria: Sexuality and desire among working-class men and women in nineteenth-century London* (New York 1992)

Bateson, C., *The convict ships, 1787–1868* (Glasgow 1959)

Beattie, J. M., 'The criminality of women in eighteenth-century England', *Journal of Social History* 8 (1975)

Beattie, J. M., 'Crime and the courts in Surrey, 1736–1753', in J. S. Cockburn (ed.), *Crime in England, 1550–1800* (London 1977)

Beattie, J. M., *Crime and the courts in England 1660–1800* (Princeton 1986)

Beddoe, D., *Welsh convict women: A study of women transported from Wales to Australia, 1787–1852* (Wales 1979)

Behn, A., *The Rover (The Banished Cavaliers)*, first published 1677 (Stratford 1986)

Bennett, L., 'The construction of skill: Craft unions, women workers and the conciliation and arbitration system', *Law in Context* 2 (1984)

Billington, R., 'The dominant values of Victorian feminism', in E. M. Sigsworth (ed.), *In search of Victorian values: Aspects of nineteenth-century thought and society* (Manchester 1988)

Bishop K., and I. Gray, 'HTAA National Conference—Hobart 1989', *The History Teacher* 27 (1989)

Bourke, J., *Husbandry to housewifery: Women, economic change, and housework in Ireland, 1890–1914* (Oxford 1993)

Brand, I., and M. Staniforth, 'Care and control: Female convict transportation voyages to Van Diemen's Land, 1818–1853', *The Great Circle* 16 (1994)

Butlin, N. G., 'Contours of the Australian economy 1788–1860', *Australian Economic History Review* 26 (1986)

Butlin, N. G., *Economics and the dreamtime: A hypothetical history* (Cambridge 1993)

Butlin, N. G., J. Ginswick and P. Statham, 'Colonial statistics before 1850', *Australian National University Source Papers in Economic History* 12 (1986)

Byrne, P. J., 'Women and the criminal law: Sydney, 1810–1821', *Push from the Bush* 21 (1985)

Byrne, P. J., *Criminal law and colonial subject: New South Wales, 1810–1830* (Melbourne 1993)

Bythell, D., 'Women in the work force', in P. K. O'Brien and R. Quinault (eds), *The industrial revolution and British society* (Cambridge 1993)

Carney, F. J., 'Pre-famine Irish population: The evidence from the Trinity College Estates', *Irish Economic and Social History* 2 (1975)

Clark, A., *Working life of women in the seventeenth century* (London 1919)

Clark, C. M. H., 'The origins of the convicts transported to Eastern Australia, 1787–1852', *Historical Studies: Australia and New Zealand* 7 (1956)

Clark, C. M. H., *A history of Australia* (Melbourne 1962)

Clarke, P., and D. Spender, *Life lines: Australian women's letters and diaries, 1788 to 1840* (Sydney 1992)

Cockburn, J. S. (ed.), *Crime and the courts in Surrey, 1550–1800* (London 1977)

Coghlan, T. A., *Labour and industry in Australia: From the first settlement in 1788 to the establishment of the commonwealth in 1901*, volume 1, first published 1918 (Melbourne 1969)

Collins, B., 'Aspects of Irish immigration into two Scottish towns', *Irish Economic and Social History* 6 (1979)

Collins, E. J. T., 'Harvest technology and labour supply in Britain, 1790–1870', *Economic History Review* 22 (1969)

Corcoran, K., and S. Nicholas, 'Statistical appendix', in S. Nicholas (ed.), *Convict workers: Reinterpreting Australia's past* (Melbourne 1988)

Cousens, S. H., 'The regional variation in emigration from Ireland between 1821 and 1841', *Transactions of the Institute of British Geographers* 37 (December 1965)

Crawford, E. M. (ed.), *Famine: The Irish experience, 900–1900* (Edinburgh 1989)

Crawford, R. M. *'A bit of a rebel'. The life and work of George Arnold Wood* (Sydney 1975)

Crawford, W. H., 'The evolution of the linen trade in Ulster before industrialization', *Irish Economic and Social History* 15 (1988)

Crowther, M. A., *The workhouse system, 1834–1929: The history of an English social institution* (London 1981)

Cullen, L. M., and T. C. Smout, 'Economic growth in Scotland and Ireland', in L. M. Cullen and T. C. Smout (eds), *Comparative aspects of Scottish and Irish economic and social history, 1600–1900* (Edinburgh, undated circa 1982)

Curtis, T., and J. A. Sharpe, 'Crime in Tudor and Stuart England', *History Today* 38 (1988)

Dallas, K. M., 'Transportation and colonial income', *Historical Studies: Australia and New Zealand* 3 (1949)

Daniels, K. (ed.), *So much hard work: Women and prostitution in Australian history* (Sydney 1984)

Daniels, K., 'Prostitution in Tasmania during the transition from penal settlement to "civilized" society', in K. Daniels (ed.), *So much hard work: Women and prostitution in Australian history* (Sydney 1984)

Davey, B. J., *Lawless and immoral: Policing a country town, 1838–1857* (Leicester 1983)

Davidoff, L., and C. Hall, *Family fortunes: Men and women of the English middle class, 1780–1850* (London 1987)

Deacon, D., 'Political arithmetic: The nineteenth-century Australian census and the construction of the dependent woman', *Signs* 11 (1985)

Dickson, D., 'Aspects of the rise and decline of the irish cotton industry', in L. M. Cullen T. C. Smout (eds), *Comparative aspects of Scottish and Irish economic and social history, 1600–1900* (Edinburgh, undated circa 1982)

Dixson, M., *The real Matilda: Women and identity in Australia, 1788–1975* (Victoria 1976; rev. edn 1994)

Dobash, R. P., R. E. Dobash and S. Gutteridge, *The imprisonment of women* (Oxford 1986)

Durston, C., '"Unhallowed wedlocks": the regulation of marriage during the English revolution', *The Historical Journal* 31 (1988)

Dyster, B., 'Employment and assignment', in S. Nicholas (ed.), *Convict workers: Reinterpreting Australia's past* (Melbourne 1988)

Dyster, B., *Servant and master: Building and running the grand houses of Sydney, 1788–1850* (Sydney 1989)

Dyster, B., 'Convicts', *Labour History* 67 (1994)

Earnshaw, B., 'The colonial children', *Push from the Bush* 9 (1980)

Ehrenreich, B., and D. English, *For her own good: 150 years of the experts' advice to women* (London 1979)

Eisenstein, Z., 'Constructing a theory of capitalist patriarchy and socialist feminism', *The Insurgent Sociologist* 7 (1977)

Ekirch, A. R., *Bound for America: The transportation of British convicts to the colonies, 1718–1775* (Oxford 1987)

Emsley, C., *Crime and society in England, 1750–1900* (London 1987)

Emsley, C., 'The criminal past: Crime in nineteenth-century Britain', *History Today* 38 (1988)

Endres, A. M., 'A twentieth-century economic historian on colonial women's employment: Comment on Alford', *Labour History* 52 (1987)

Engels, F., *The condition of the working class in England* (Oxford 1971)

Erickson, C. 'Emigration from the British Isles to the U.S.A. in 1831', *Population Studies* 35 (1981)

Eveleth, P. B., and J. M. Tanner, *Worldwide variation in human growth* (1976)

Fine, B., and E. Leopold, 'Consumerism and the Industrial Revolution', *Social History* 15 (1990)

Fitzgerald, R., 'Ruffians or gentlemen?', *Sydney Morning Herald*, 3 December 1988

Fitzpatrick, B., *British imperialism and Australia, 1788–1833* (London 1939)

Fletcher, B., *Ralph Darling: A governor maligned* (Melbourne 1984)

Floud, R., K. Wachter and A. S. Gregory, *Height, health and history: nutritional status in the United Kingdom* (Cambridge 1990)

Fogel, R., S. Engerman, R. Floud, R. Steckel, J. Trussell, K. Wachter, R. Murgo, K. Sokoloff and G. Villaflor, 'Secular changes in American and British stature and nutrition', *Journal of Interdisciplinary History*, 14 (1983)

Foster, R. F., *Modern Ireland 1600–1972* (London 1988)

Frances, R., *The politics of work: Gender and labour in Victoria, 1880–1939* (Melbourne 1993)

Frost, A., *Convicts and empire: A naval question, 1776–1811* (Oxford 1980)

Garton, S., *Out of luck: Australians and social welfare 1788–1988* (Sydney 1990)

Garton, S., 'The convict origins debate: Historians and the problem of the "criminal class"', *Australian New Zealand Journal of Criminology* 24.2 (1991)

Gatrell, V. A. C., and T. B. Hadden, 'Criminal statistics and their interpretation', in E. A. Wrigley (ed.), *Nineteenth-century society: Essays in the use of quantitative methods for the study of social data* (Cambridge 1972)

Gillen, M., 'The Botany Bay decision, 1786—convicts, not empire', *English Historical Review* 97 (1982)

Gillespie, R., 'Migration and opportunity: A comment', *Irish Economic and Social History* 13 (1986)

Gorham, D., *The Victorian girl and the feminine ideal* (London 1982)

Gothard, J., '"Radically unsound and mischievous": Female migration to Tasmania, 1856–1863', *Australian Historical Studies* 23 (1989)

Gothard, J., 'A compromise with conscience: The reception of female immigrant domestic servants in Eastern Australia, 1860–1890', *Labour History* 62 (1992)

Gould, S. J., *The mismeasure of man* (New York 1981)

Gould-Davis, E., *The first sex* (London 1973)

Graff, H. J., 'Literacy, jobs and industrialization: The nineteenth century', in H. J. Graff (ed.), *Literacy and social development in the west: A reader* (Cambridge 1981)

Greenwood, G., *Australia: A social and political history* (Sydney 1978)

Gribbon, H. D., 'The Irish Linen Board, 1711–1828', in L. M. Cullen and T. C. Smout (eds), *Comparative aspects of Scottish and Irish economic and social history 1600–1900* (Edinburgh, undated circa 1982)

Griffiths, A., *Memorials of Millbank and chapters in prison history* (London 1884)

Haines, R., 'Indigent misfits or shrewd operators? Government-assisted emigrants from the United Kingdom to Australia, 1821–1860', *Population Studies* 48 (1994)

Hamilton, P., '"Tipperarifying the moral atmosphere": Irish Catholic immigration and the state 1840–1860', in Sydney Labour History Group, *What rough beast? The state and social order in Australian history* (Sydney 1982)

Hammerton, A. J., '"Without natural protectors": Female immigration to Australia, 1832–36', *Historical Studies: Australia and New Zealand* 16 (1975)

Hammerton, A. J., *Emigrant Gentlewomen: Genteel poverty and female emigration, 1830–1914* (London 1979)

Hammond, J. L., and B. Hammond, *The town labourer, 1760–1832: The new civilization*, second impression (London 1917)

Hammond, J. L., and B. Hammond, *The village labourer, 1760–1832: A study in the government of England before the Reform Bill*, new edition (London 1913)

Hancock, W. K., *Australia* (Melbourne 1966)

Harris, C. C., *The Family and Industrial Society* (London 1985)

Hartwell, R. M., *The economic development of Van Diemen's Land, 1820–1850* (Melbourne 1954)

Hay, D., P. Linebaugh and E. P. Thompson, *Albion's fatal tree: Crime and society in eighteenth-century England* (London 1975)

Henriques, U. R. Q., 'Bastardy and the New Poor Law', *Past and Present* 37 (July 1967)

Higgs, E., 'Domestic service and household production', in A. V. John (ed.), *Unequal opportunities: Women's employment in England, 1800–1918* (Oxford 1986)

Hirst, J. B., *Convict society and its enemies: A history of early New South Wales* (Sydney 1983)

Hirst, J. B., 'Convicts and crime', *Overland* 113 (1988)

Holley, J. C., 'The two family economies of industrialism: Factory workers in Victorian Scotland', *Journal of Family History* 6 (1981)

Hollingsworth, K., *The Newgate novel, 1830–1847: Bulwer, Ainsworth, Dickens, and Thackeray* (Detroit 1963)

Honeyman, K., and J. Goodman, 'Women's work, gender conflict, and labour markets in Europe, 1500–1900', *Economic History Review* 44 (1991)

Horrell, S., and J. Humphries, 'Old questions, new data and alternative perspectives: Families' living standards in the British industrial revolution', *Journal of Economic History* 52 (1992)

Horrell, S., and J. Humphries, '"The exploitation of little children": Child labour and the family economy in the industrial revolution', *Explorations in Economic History* (forthcoming)

Hostettler, E., 'Women's work in the nineteenth-century countryside', *Society for the Study of Labour History* 33 (1976)

Howard, J., 'Why are there not more women law-breakers?', *The Australian*, 5 June 1985

Hudson, P., and W. R. Lee (eds), *Women's work and the family economy in historical perspective* (Manchester 1990)

Huggins, J., 'Experiences of a Queensland Aboriginal domestic servant: Agnes Williams talks to Jackie Huggins', *Labour History* 61 (1991)

Hughes, R., *The fatal shore: A history of the transportation of convicts to Australia, 1787–1868* (London 1987)

Humphries, J., 'Protective legislation, the capitalist state, and working-class men: The case of the 1842 Mines Regulation Act', *Feminist Review* 7 (1981)

Humphries, J., '"… The most free from objection …": The sexual division of labor and women's work in nineteenth-century England', *Journal of Economic History* 47 (1987)

Humphries, J., '"Bread and a pennyworth of treacle": Excess female mortality in England in the 1840s', *Cambridge Journal of Economics* 15 (1991)

Jones, D., *Crime, protest, community and police in nineteenth-century Britain* (London 1982)

Jones, F. L., 'Occupational statistics revisited: The female labour force in early British and Australian censuses' *Australian Economic History Review* 27 (1987)

Jordan, E., 'The exclusion of women from industry in nineteenth-century Britain', *Comparative Studies in Society and History*, 31 (1989)

Kennedy, L., 'Why one million starved: An open verdict', *Irish Economic and Social History* 11 (1984)

Kennedy, R. E. Jr, *The Irish: Emigration, marriage and fertility* (Berkeley 1973)

Kent, D., and N. Townsend, 'Deborah Oxley's "female convicts": An accurate view of working-class women?', *Labour History* 65 (1993)

Kent, D. A. 'Ubiquitous but invisible: Female domestic servants in mid-eighteenth century London', *History Workshop* 28 (1989)

Kinealy, C., *This great calamity: The Irish famine, 1845–52* (Dublin 1994)

Kingston, B., *My wife, my daughter and poor Mary Ann: Women and work in Australia* (Melbourne 1975)

Kingston, B., *The world moves slowly* (Cornell 1977)

Klein, H. S., *The middle passage: Comparative studies in the Atlantic slave trade* (Princeton 1978)

Klein, H. S., and S. L. Engerman, 'A note on mortality in the French slave trade in the eighteenth century', in H. A. Gemery and J. S. Hogendorn (eds), *The uncommon market: Essays in the economic history of the Atlantic slave trade* (New York 1979)

Komlos, J., 'The secular trend in the biological standard of living in the UK, 1730–1860', *Economic History Review*, 46 (1993)

Kussmaul, A. S., 'The ambiguous mobility of farm servants', *Economic History Review* 34 (1981)

Lake, M., '"Socialism and manhood": The case of William Lane', *Labour History* 50 (1986)

Lake, M., 'Convict women as objects of male vision: An historiographical review', *Bulletin of the Centre for Tasmanian Historical Studies* 2 (1988)

Land, H., 'The family wage', *Feminist Review* 6 (1980)

Lepervanche, M. de, 'Australian immigrants, 1788–1940: Desired and unwanted', in E. L. Wheelwright and K. Buckley (eds), *Essays in the political economy of Australian capitalism*, volume 1 (Sydney 1979)

Lewis, F. D., 'The cost of convict transportation from Britain to Australia, 1796–1810', *Economic History Review* 41 (1988)

Linebaugh, P., 'The Ordinary of Newgate and his account', in J. S. Cockburn (ed.), *Crime in England, 1550-1800* (London 1977)

Macintyre, S., *Winners and losers: The pursuit of social justice in Australian history* (Sydney 1985)

Macnab, K., and R. Ward, 'The nature and nurture of the first generation of native-born Australians', *Historical Studies: Australia and New Zealand* 10 (1962)

Madgwick, R. B., *Immigration into Eastern Australia, 1788–1851* (Sydney 1969)

Magarey, S., 'The invention of juvenile delinquency in early nineteenth-century England', *Labour History* 34 (1978)

Malcolmson, P. E., *English laundresses: A social history, 1850–1930* (Urbana 1986)

Martin, G. (ed.), *The founding of Australia* (Hale and Iremonger 1978)

McBride, T., *The domestic revolution: The modernisation of household service in England and France, 1820–1920* (London 1976)

McDonald, J., and R. Schlomowitz, 'Mortality on convict voyages to Australia, 1788–1868', *Social Science History*, 13 (1989)

McDougall, M. L., 'Working-class women during the industrial revolution, 1780–1914', in R. Bridenthal and C. Koonz (eds), *Becoming visible: Women in European History* (Boston 1977)

McGrath, A., '"Black velvet": Aboriginal women and their relations with white men in the Northern Territory, 1910–40', in K. Daniels (ed.), *So much hard work: Women and prostitution in Australian history* (Sydney 1984)

McGrath, A., *Born in the cattle* (Sydney 1987)

McKendrick, N., 'Home demand and economic growth: A new view of the role of women and children in the industrial revolution', in N. McKendrick (ed.), *Historical perspectives: Studies in English thought and society* (London 1974)

McQueen, H., *A new Britannia: An argument concerning the social origins of Australian radicalism and nationalism* (Victoria 1980)

McQuilton, J., 'Women convicts', in J. C. R. Camm and J. McQuilton (eds), *Australians: A historical atlas* (Canberra 1988)

Meredith, D., 'Full circle? Contemporary views on transportation', in S. Nicholas (ed.), *Convict Workers: Reinterpreting Australia's past* (Melbourne 1988)

Mitchell, B. R., and P. Deane, *Abstract of British Historical Statistics* (Cambridge 1992)

Mokyr, J., *Why Ireland starved: A quantitative and analytical history of the Irish economy, 1800–1850* (London 1985)

Mokyr, J., and C. Ó Gráda, 'Emigration and poverty in pre-famine Ireland', *Explorations in Economic History* 19 (1982)

Moore, J. F. H., *The convicts of Van Diemen's Land, 1840–1853* (Hobart 1976)

Nadel, G., *Australia's colonial culture: Ideas, men and institutions in mid-nineteenth century Eastern Australia* (Cambridge, Massachusetts 1957)

Needham, A., *The women transported on the 1790 'Neptune'* (Sydney 1988)

Nicholas, S., 'Unshackling the past', and 'The care and feeding of convicts', in S. Nicholas (ed.), *Convict workers: Reinterpreting Australia's past* (Melbourne 1988)

Nicholas, S., 'Understanding Convict Workers', *Australian Economic History Review* 31.2 (1991)

Nicholas, S., and D. Oxley, 'The living standards of women during the industrial revolution, 1795–1820', *Economic History Review*, 46 (1993)

Nicholas, S., and D. Oxley, 'The industrial revolution and the genesis of the male breadwinner', in G. D. Snooks (ed.), *Was the industrial revolution necessary?* (London 1994)

Nicholas, S., and D. Oxley, 'Convict economies', in R. Jackson (ed.), *The Cambridge economic history of Australia*, volume 1 (forthcoming)

Nicholas, S., and P. Shergold, 'Human capital and the pre-famine Irish emigration to England', *Explorations in Economic History* 24 (1987)

Nicholas, S., and P. Shergold, 'Intercounty labour mobility during the industrial revolution: Evidence from Australian transportation records', *Oxford Economic Papers* 39 (1987)

Nicholas, S., and P. Shergold, 'Internal migration in England, 1817–1839', *Journal of Historical Geography* 13 (1987)

Nicholas, S., and P. Shergold, 'Convicts as migrants', in S. Nicholas (ed.), *Convict workers: Reinterpreting Australia's past* (Melbourne 1988)

Nicholas, S., and P. Shergold, 'Convicts as workers', in S. Nicholas (ed.), *Convict workers: Reinterpreting Australia's past* (Melbourne 1988)

Nicholas, S., and R. H. Steckel, 'Heights and living standards of English workers during the early years of industrialisation, 1770–1815', *Journal of Economic History*, 51 (1991)

O'Connor, J., *The workhouses of Ireland: The fate of Ireland's poor* (Dublin 1995)

O'Farrell, P., *The Irish in Australia* (Sydney 1987)

Ó Gráda, C., 'Post-famine adjustment: Essays in nineteenth-century Irish economic history', *Irish Economic and Social History* 1 (1974)

Ó Gráda, C., 'Some aspects of nineteenth-century Irish emigration', in L. M. Cullen and T. C. Smout (eds), *Comparative aspects of Scottish and Irish economic and social history, 1600–1900* (Edinburgh undated c. 1982)

Ó Gráda, C., *Ireland: A new economic history, 1780–1845* (Oxford 1994)

Oldham, W., *Britain's convicts to the colonies* (Sydney 1990)

Oxley, D., 'Who were the female convicts?', *Journal of the Australian Population Association* 4 (1987)

Oxley, D., 'History and mythology: Researching female convicts', *Locality* 3 (1989)

Oxley, D., 'Women transported: gendered images and realities', *Australian New Zealand Journal of Criminology* 24 (1991)

Oxley, D., 'Female convicts', in S. Nicholas (ed.), *Convict workers: reinterpreting Australia's past* (Melbourne 1988). Reprinted in G. Whitlock and G. Reekie (eds), *Uncertain beginnings* (St Lucia 1993)

Oxley, D., 'Exercising agency', *Labour History* 65 (1993)

Oxley, D., 'Packing her (economic) bags: Convict women workers', *Historical Studies: Australia and New Zealand* 102 (1994)

Oxley, D., and Richards, E., 'Convicts and free immigrant women compared: 1841—a turning point?', in E. Richards (ed.), *Visible Women* (Canberra, forthcoming)

Payne, H. S., 'A statistical study of female convicts in Tasmania, 1843–53', *Tasmanian Historical Research Association Papers and Proceedings* 9 (1961)

Peacock, A. J., 'Village radicalism in East Anglia 1800–50', in J. P. D. Dunbabin (ed.), *Rural discontent in nineteenth-century Britain* (New York 1974)

Penglase, B. M., 'An enquiry into literacy in early nineteenth-century New South Wales', *Push from the Bush* 16 (1983)

Perrott, M., *A tolerable good success: Economic opportunities for women in New South Wales, 1788–1830* (Sydney 1983)

Philips, D., *Crime and authority in Victorian England: The Black Country, 1835–1860* (London 1977)

Philips, D., 'Crime, law and punishment in the industrial revolution', in P. O'Brien and R. Quinault (eds), *The industrial revolution and British society* (Cambridge 1993)

Pinchbeck, I., *Women workers in the industrial revolution, 1750–1880* (London 1930)

Póirtéir, C. (ed.), *The great Irish famine* (Cork 1995)

Pollard, S., *The genesis of modern management: A study of the industrial revolution in Great Britain* (London 1965)

Radzinowicz, L., and R. Hood, *A history of English criminal law and its administration from 1750: The emergence of penal policy*, volume 5 (London 1986)

Rayner, T., *Historical survey of the female factory historic site, Cascades* (Tasmania 1981)

Reiger, K., *The disenchantment of the home* (Melbourne 1986)

Rendall, J., *The origins of modern feminism: Women in Britain, France and the United States, 1780–1860* (London 1985)

Reynolds, H., *The other side of the frontier* (Ringwood 1982)

Reynolds, H., *Frontier* (Sydney 1987)

Reynolds, H., *With the white people* (Ringwood, 1990)

Reynolds, H., *Law of the land* (Ringwood 1992)

Richards, E., 'Women in the British economy since about 1700: An interpretation', *History* 59 (1974)

Richards, T., *The commodity culture of Victorian England: Advertising and spectacle, 1851–1914* (Stanford 1990)

Richardson, R., *Death, dissection, and the destitute* (London 1987)

Roberts, M., 'Sickles and scythes: Women's work and men's work at harvest time', *History Workshop* 7 (1979)

Robinson, P., 'The first forty years', in J. Mackinolty and H. Radi (eds), *In pursuit of justice: Australian women and the law, 1788–1979* (Sydney 1979)

Robinson, P., *The hatch and brood of time: A study of the first generation of native-born white Australians, 1788-1828*, volume 1 (Oxford 1985)

Robinson, P., *The women of Botany Bay: A reinterpretation of the role of women in the origins of Australian society* (Macquarie 1988)

Robinson, P., 'Getting a nation's record straight?', *Age*, 21 January 1989)

Robson, L. L., 'The origin of the women convicts sent to Australia, 1787–1852', *Historical Studies, Australia and New Zealand* 11 (1963)

Robson, L. L., *The convict settlers of Australia: An enquiry into the origin and character of the convicts transported to New South Wales and Van Diemen's Land, 1787–1852* (Melbourne 1965)

Roe, M., 'Colonial society in embryo', *Historical Studies: Australia and New Zealand* 7 (1956)

Rose, S. O., 'Gender antagonism and class conflict: Exclusionary strategies of male trade-unionists in nineteenth-century Britain', *Social History* 13 (1988)

Royle, S. A., 'Irish famine relief in the early nineteenth century: The 1822 famine on the Aran Islands', *Irish Economic and Social History* 11 (1984)

Rudé, G., *Protest and punishment: The story of the social and political protesters transported to Australia, 1788–1868* (Melbourne 1978)

Rudé, G., *Criminal and victim: Crime and society in early nineteenth-century England* (Oxford 1985)

Ryan, L., *The Aboriginal Tasmanians* (Brisbane 1989)

Ryan, L., 'The governed: Convict women in Tasmania, 1803–1853', *Bulletin of the Centre for Tasmanian Historical Studies* 3 (1990–91)

Salt, A., *These outcast women: The Parramatta female factory, 1821–1848* (Sydney 1984)

Sanderson, M., 'Literacy and social mobility in the industrial revolution in England', *Past and Present* 64 (1974)

Schedvin, M. B., and C. B. Schedvin, 'The nomadic tribes of urban Britain: A prelude to Botany Bay', *Historical Studies* 18 (1978)

Schellekens, J., 'The role of marital fertility in Irish population history, 1750–1840', *Economic History Review* 46 (1993)

Schofield, R. S., 'Dimensions of illiteracy, 1750–1850', *Explorations in Economic History* 10 (1973)

Scott, J. W., and L. A. Tilly, 'Women's work and the family in nineteenth-century Europe', *Comparative Studies in Society and History* 17 (1975)

Seccombe, W., 'Patriarchy stabilized: The construction of the male breadwinner wage norm in nineteenth-century Britain', *Social History* 2 (1986)

Shann, E., *An economic history of Australia*, first published 1930 (Cambridge 1948)

Shaw, A. G. L., *Convicts and the colonies: A study of penal transportation from Great Britain and Ireland to Australia and other parts of the British Empire* (Melbourne 1981)

Shubert, A., 'Private initiative in law enforcement: Associations for the prosecution of felons, 1744–1856', in V. Bailey (ed.), *Policing and punishment in nineteenth-century Britain* (London 1981)

Shultz, R. J., 'Immigration into Eastern Australia, 1788–1851', *Historical Studies: Australia and New Zealand* 14 (1970)

Smith, B., *A cargo of women: Susannah Watson and the convicts of the 'Princess Royal'* (Sydney 1988)

Smith, F. B., 'The fatal subject', *Scripsi* 4 (1987)

Snell, K. D. M., 'Agricultural seasonal employment, the standard of living and women's work in the South and East, 1690–1810', *Economic History Review*, 34 (1981)

Snell, K. D. M., *Annals of the labouring poor, social change and agrarian England, 1660–1900* (Cambridge 1985)

Snooks, G., *Portrait of the family within the total economy: A study in longrun dynamics, Australia, 1788–1990* (Cambridge 1994)

Solar, P., 'Why Ireland starved: A critical review of the econometric results', *Irish Economic and Social History* 11 (1984)

Solar, P., 'Book review of K. O'Neill, *Family and farm in pre-famine Ireland*', *Irish Economic and Social History* 13 (1986)

Stephens, W. B., *Education, literacy and society, 1830-70: The geography of diversity in provincial England* (Manchester 1987)

Sturma, M., 'Eye of the beholder: The stereotype of women convicts, 1788–1852', *Labour History* 34 (1978)

Sturma, M., *Vice in a vicious society: Crime and convicts in mid-nineteenth-century New South Wales* (St Lucia 1983)

Sullivan, M., 'Ann McNally: Convict servant', in M. Lake and F. Kelly (eds), *Double time: women in Victoria—150 years* (Melbourne 1985)

Summers, A., *Damned whores and God's police: The colonization of women in Australia* (Melbourne 1976; revised edition 1994)

Sweeney, C., *Transported: In place of death. Convicts in Australia* (Melbourne 1981)

Swift, R., 'Urban policing in early Victorian England, 1835–86: A reappraisal', *History* 73 (1988)

Tanner, J. M., *Growth of adolescence* (Oxford 1962)

Tardiff, P., *Notorious strumpets and dangerous girls: Convict women in Van Diemen's Land, 1803–1829* (North Ryde 1990)

Teale, R., *Colonial Eve: Sources on women in Australia, 1788–1914* (Melbourne 1978)

Tipping, M., *Convicts unbound: The story of the 'Calcutta' convicts and their settlement in Australia* (Victoria 1988)

Thomas, J., 'Women and capitalism: Oppression or emancipation? A review article', *Comparative Studies in Society and History* 30 (1988)

Thomis, M. I., and J. Grimmett, *Women in protest, 1800–1850* (London 1982)

Thompson, E. P., *Whigs and hunters: The origins of the Black Act* (London 1975)

Thompson, E. P., and E. Yeo (eds), *The unknown Mayhew: Selections from the 'Morning Chronicle', 1849–50* (London 1973)

Tinker, H., *A new system of slavery: The export of Indian labour overseas, 1830–1920* (London 1974)

Tobias, J. J., *Crime and industrial society in the nineteenth century* (London 1967)

Tobias, J. J., *Crime and police in England, 1700–1900* (Dublin 1979)

Vaughan, W. E., and A. J. Fitzpatrick (eds), *A new history of Ireland: Irish historical statistics population, 1821–1971* (Dublin 1978)

Waldersee, J., *Catholic society in New South Wales, 1788–1860* (Sydney 1974)

Waring, M., *Counting for nothing: What men value and what women are worth* (Wellington 1988)

Weatherburn, H., 'The female factory', in J. Mackinolty and H. Radi (eds), *In pursuit of justice: Australian women and the law, 1788-1979* (Sydney 1979)

Webb, S., and B. Webb, *The history of trade unionism*, new edition (London 1911)

Weir, R. B., 'The patent still distillers and the role of competition', in L. M. Cullen and T. C. Smout (eds), *Comparative aspects of Scottish and Irish economic and social history, 1600–1900* (Edinburgh, undated circa 1982)

Wellesley index to Victorian periodicals, volume 1 (London 1966)

Williams, J., 'Irish female convicts and Tasmania', *Labour History* 44 (1983)

Williams, J., *Ordered to the Island: Irish convicts and Van Diemen's Land* (Sydney 1994)

Williamson, G., 'The impact of the Irish on British labour markets during the industrial revolution', *Journal of Economic History* 46 (1986)

Wilson, S. 'Language and ritual in marriage', *Push from the Bush* 2 (1978)

Wood, 'Convicts', *Royal Australian Historical Society Journal and Proceedings* 8 (1922)

UNPUBLISHED WORKS

Beattie, J. M., 'Crime and society in eighteenth-century England': paper presented to the Law History Theory Conference (La Trobe University 1988)

Belcher, M. J., 'The child in New South Wales society: 1820–1837', unpublished PhD thesis, University of New England, 1982

Boot, H. M., 'Wages of factory workers during the industrial revolution', paper presented to Australian Historical Association Conference (Australian National University 1992)

Fogel, R. W., Nobel Prize lecture, 'Economic growth, population theory, and physiology: The bearing of long-term processes on the making of economic policy', *National Bureau of Economic Research Working Paper* 4638 (1994), also to be reprinted in the *American Economic Review*

Haines, R., 'Government-assisted emigration from the United Kingdom to Australia, 1831–1860: Promotion, recruitment and the labouring poor', unpublished PhD thesis, Flinders University of South Australia, 1993

Nicholas, S., and D. Oxley, 'Understanding Convict Workers', *Flinders University Working Papers in Economic History* 43 (1990)

Nicholas, S., and D. Oxley, '"For better or for worse": The genesis of the male breadwinner', *UNSW School of Economics Discussion Paper* 92/15 (1992); also printed as *ANU Working Papers in Economic History* 168 (1992)

Nicholas, S., and R. Steckel, 'Tall but poor: Nutrition, health, and living standards in pre-famine Ireland', *National Bureau of Economic Research Working Paper Series on Historical Factors in Long Run Growth*, 39 (1992)

Oxley, D., 'Convict maids', unpublished PhD thesis, University of New South Wales, 1991

Oxley, D., 'Feminism and economic history', *ANU Working Papers in Economic History* 156 (1991)

Oxley, D., 'Selected for exile? Profiles of convict women transported to New South Wales, 1826–40', *UNSW School of Economics Discussion Paper* 94/32 (1994)

Philips, D., 'Moral entrepreneurs and the construction of a "criminal class" in England, c. 1800–1840', paper presented to the Australian Historical Association Conference (University of Sydney 1988)

Staniforth, M., 'Dangerous voyages? Aspects of the emigrant experience on the voyage to Australia, 1837–1839', unpublished MA thesis, University of Sydney, 1993

Index

age, 109–11, 124, 235, 238
  England, 166–7
  immigrants, 175, 184–5
  Ireland, 134–5, 145
  prisoners, 110–11
age–heaping, *see* numeracy
agency, 8, 11, 225, 241–2
Aldous, James, 59
Alexander, Sally, 164, 226
Alford, Katrina, 11, 230, 240
Allen, Elizabeth (Bett), 84
Allen, Judith, 231
Anderson, M., 201
Andrews, Ann, 49–50
antithetical values, 40, 203, 215–21, 225–6, 232
apprenticeships, *see* education
Armstrong, W. A., 121
  see also skill classification
Arthur, *Governor* George, 19–20, 26, 201, 221
assignment, 11, 194, 201
assisted immigrants, 172–82, 196, 241
  see also age; character; convicts;
    Emigration Committee; immigration;
    literacy; numeracy; occupations; skill
Associations for the Prosecution of Felons, 39, 51
Atkinson, Alan, 11
Atkinson, Hannah, 53, 58
Atkinson, Rachel, 52, 58
Australian population (white), 102, 124, 180–1, 182–3, 240
  see also colonial labour supply; currency
    children; sex im/balance
Aveling (now Quartly), Marian, 11, 204, 240

Bacon, Francis, 98
bad behaviour
  British workers, 217–19
  convict women, 80–1, 100–1, 194–6, 198, 199–206, 224, 232

criminal women, 206–13, 218–19
  worse than men, 100, 108, 199, 207–8, 223
  see also character; colonial employers;
    contemporary social critics;
    prostitution
baggage (luggage), 18, 33, 98, 109, 171, 237–8
  see also economic assets
Barnett, Susan, 239
Barr, Catherine, 144
Barrath, Mary, 151
Bateman, James, 49
Bates, Mary, 151
Baxter, A. M., 239
Beattie, John, 51, 95
Beckett, Ernest W., 81
Beddoe, Deirdre, 9, 10, 31, 49
Beggs, Thomas, 64
Behn, Aphra, 226
Belcher, Michael, 11
benefit of clergy, 35–7, 44, 45, 58
Bigge, *Commissioner* John Thomas, 26, 101, 102, 182
Binny, John, 9, 78–82, 99, 169, 206–7, 219, 221–3
black and white relations, 1, 181, 182
  see also invasion
Blackwood, Eliza, 59
Blaxland, John, 172
bloody code, 28, 36, 38
Bourke, *Governor* Richard, 195
Bovil, *Sir* William, 50
Bowes Smyth, Arthur, 199, 204–5
Bowman, Esther, 158
Boyle, Betty, 46
Brackingbury, Betsey, 51
Branham, Mary, 204
Breton, *Lieutenant-Colonel* Henry, 200, 201, 202, 216
British hierarchy, 4, 12
British laws, 18, 36, 37, 38, 39
British legal system, 34–9, 71, 79

see also crime; transportation
British workers, 106
  see also age; bad behaviour; convicts;
    literacy; numeracy; occupations; skill
Brooks, Elizabeth, 239
Bryant, Rachel, 17, 29
  crime, 44
  economic assets, 110, 112, 115, 117,
    123, 158
Bunker, E., 239
Burnett (alias Buchanan), Euphemia, 71
Buttledoor, Hannah, 17, 28, 29, 126, 231,
    242
  crime, 43, 49
  economic assets, 110, 115
Byrne, Paula Jayne, 11

Campbell, *Lord Chief Justice*, 78
capital statutes, 34, 36, 38
Carlyle, Thomas, 141
Carmichael, *Reverend* Henry, 189
Carpenter, Mary, 214
Casey, Charles, 59
causes of crime, 47, 48, 51, 53, 60, 76, 79,
    86, 95–6, 125, 242
  alcohol, 50–1, 79, 101
  criminal class, 40, 72, 76, 78–94
  declining welfare, 82
  genetic, 39, 80–1
  low wages, 10, 213, 215
  lower-class failings, 82
  parental neglect, 83, 108, 233
  poverty, 4, 40, 56, 66, 77, 79, 82–6, 88,
    89, 93, 125, 221
  prosperity, 77–8, 82, 87–8, 89, 93–4
  unchastity, 206–7, 219
  urbanisation, 81, 82
  see also criminal class; criminality;
    London Season
census, problems, 137, 139–40, 161, 163–4
Central Criminal Court, *see* Old Bailey
Chadwick, Edwin, 213
  see also moral entrepreneurs
character, 84, 86, 225, 234
  bad, 6, 100, 106, 208, 219, 224
  good, 103, 105
  immigrants, 173, 175, 179, 180–2, 194–6,
    202
  see also bad behaviour
Chesterston, George Laval, 101
childcare, *see* household sector
Clark, Betsey-Alicia, 204
Clark, John, 19, 242
Clark, Lieutenant Ralph, 103, 199, 204
Clark, Manning, 4–8, 65, 67, 75, 76, 106
  literacy, 115
  influences, 221–3, 233

classes redefined, 213, 214–15
climate, 104–5
Coffee, Ellen, 59
cohabitation, 6, 9, 217
  see also prostitution; working-class
    values
colonial economic development
  expectations, 96, 98–101
  future research, 240–1
  living standards, 179, 182, 238
  success, 102–5
  whole story, 1–2, 180, 231, 241
  women's contributions, 10–11, 12–13,
    83, 103, 108, 233–4
  women's colonial occupations, 194, 230
  women's perceived failure to contribute,
    13–14, 100–1, 105–8, 171, 198, 233,
    237–41
  women's economic worth, 108–9,
    226–31, 232–43
  see also colonial society; currency
    children; household sector; marriage
colonial employers
  complaints, 99, 195, 199–201, 232
  unreliable, 202–3, 206
  see also colonial labour demand;
    colonial labour relations
colonial freedom, 52, 104
colonial gender relations, 203–6
colonial labour allocation, 109, 193–4, 239
colonial labour demand, 105, 171, 172,
    173, 175, 189–93, 240
  domestic servants, 154, 173–82, 197, 213
  immigrants, 171, 172, 173
  see also assisted immigrants
colonial labour relations, 100, 200–3, 232,
    241
  see also crime; Female Factory
colonial labour supply, 97–101, 104, 109,
    127, 129, 182–3, 240
  unencumbered workers, 126, 185
  see also assisted immigrants; Australian
    population; immigration
colonial society, 7–8, 11, 12, 13, 234
colonisation, 8, 28, 31, 59, 129
  appropriation of resources, 102
  method, 98, 104
  women's part, 231, 238
  see also black and white relations;
    invasion
Colquhoun, Patrick, 64, 213, 221, 232
  London criminals, 77–8, 82, 87, 88
  casual poor, 85
  see also moral entrepreneurs
Coltman, Elizabeth, 17–21, 26–9, 32–3, 34,
    64, 97, 98, 142, 198, 231, 232, 242–3
  crime, 41, 43, 47, 49, 71

Coltman, Elizabeth, *contd*
  economic assets, 109, 110, 115, 117–18,
    123
  in England, 147, 151, 158, 160, 169
Committee for Promoting the Emigration
    of Single Women (and Widows), 175
Committee of Emigrant Mechanics, 189
Condon, Mary, 54, 153
conjugal status, 125–6, 235–7
  England, 166–7
  immigrants, 185
  Ireland, 134–5
Constance (surname unknown), 52, 58
contamination, *see* criminality
contemporary social critics
  biased sources, 198, 222, 224–6, 233
  British, 206–11, 211–13
  colonial, 199–206
  positive, 212–13
  undue influence, 221–6
  see also antithetical values; bad
    behaviour; Binny, John; Colquhoun,
    Patrick; Griffiths, Arthur; Mayhew,
    Henry; moral entrepreneurs
control of labour supply, 152–4, 227–8
convict indents, 5, 94, 109
  contents, 21, 73, 112
  examples, 18, 22–5
  methodology, 4, 5, 26, 28–9, 31–3
  musters, 20
  nature, 18–29
  sample, 31–2
  validity, 21, 26–7
convict mothers
  bad, 10, 101, 107–8, 226, 233
  good, 103, 108, 233
  Britain, 124–7
  see also currency children;
    transportation
convict musters, *see* convict indents
convict parents, 107, 108
convict stain, 4, 7–8, 108–9, 198
convict workers
  bad, 96–101, 106–7
  good, 102–5
  see also criminal class
Convict Workers, 13, 27, 106, 107, 229
conviction rates, *see* post convictions;
    prior convictions; sentencing
convicts
  and English workers, 158–69, 236
  and free immigrants, 182–97, 237, 238
  and Irish emigrant workers, 141–4
  and Irish workers, 136–41, 236
  and prisoners, 110–11, 162, 167–8, 236
convicts as victims, 4, 8
  see also village Hampdens

Cosgrove, *Matron* at Millbank, 209
courts, 88, 93, 104
  see also Old Bailey
Cowper, *Reverend* William, 182
crime
  colonial definitions, 96, 200–1
  economic indicators, 94, 95
  employment related, 53–5, 59, 69–70,
    74–5, 76, 218–19
  England and Ireland, 65–72
  London, 77–94
  London transportees, 87–94, 158, 234
  opportunistic, 54–5, 69–70, 74–5, 234
  redefined, 36, 40, 53, 75, 213, 215, 221
  rural/urban, 64–5, 73–7, 134–5
criminal class, 40, 47, 51, 77–82, 232–3
  Australian historians, 5–6, 11–12, 13,
    83–7, 221–6
  British historians, 94–5, 213
  casual and deserving poor, 78, 79, 82,
    83–6, 213–16
  convicts, 40–1
  defined, 5–6, 39–41, 51, 88, 222–3
  divisions, 60, 62, 64–5, 72
  gender, 216–20
  lacking work and social values, 65, 88,
    97, 98–101, 106–8, 223, 233–4
  London, 78–94
  occupation, 6, 86, 222
  parental neglect, 83, 99, 106, 107–8, 232
  politics of, 213–21
  prostitution, 5–7, 11, 13, 39, 78, 206–7,
    223–4, 232
  repeat offenders, 41, 56, 234
  vagabonds, 77, 82, 83, 87–8, 90, 112,
    159, 222–3, 234–5
  workers, 97, 98–101
  see also antithetical values; causes of
    crime; moral entrepreneurs
criminal offences, 41–7
  breaking and entering, 43, 45, 57–8, 68,
    73, 92
  forgery, 46, 84
  highway robbery, 44, 84, 220
  infanticide, 42, 52–53
  maiming beasts, 46, 74
  man robbery, 44, 53, 73, 225
  murder, 42, 44, 52, 63, 70
  person robbery, 68
  pickpocketing, 43, 45, 57–8, 68, 70, 73,
    75, 225
  pledging, 43, 70, 92
  poaching, 75
  poisoning, 42, 52
  property crime, 68
  receiving, 43, 45, 47, 57–8, 68, 73
  robbery, 43–4, 47, 57, 68, 70, 72

robbery with violence, 42–3, 44, 57–8
shoplifting, 43, 45, 57, 68, 70, 73, 92
stealing, 43, 47, 57–8, 68, 70, 72, 73,
   74–5, 225
trespass, 75
vagrancy, 45–6, 57–8, 67–8, 82
violent crime, 41–3, 51, 68, 85–6
criminality, 39, 80–1, 82, 236
   see also causes of crime; criminal class
Cunningham, Hannah, 59
Cunningham, Peter, 21, 99, 103, 173, 221
currency children, 8, 10, 102, 103, 107,
   108, 124, 181, 233
   see also convict mothers; convict parents
Curtis, Timothy, 94
customary rights, *see* crime

Dallas, K. M., 238
damned whores, *see* prostitution; sexual
   terminology
Daniels, Kay, 11, 230–1
Darling, *Governor* Ralph (NSW), 199
Darwin, Charles, 215
Davey, B. J., 95
Davies, May, 54
Defoe, Daniel, 9
Dennahy, Mary, 52–3
deskilling, 150–2
Desmond, Abby, 158
detection, 54, 213
Dickens, Charles, 91, 104–5, 221, 232
Dickson, Alice, 54
diet, 106, 113, 114–15
Dixson, Miriam, 8
domestic industry (putting out), 130, 147,
   236
domestic servants
   and the middle class, 154, 217–18, 238
   and prostitution, 217–18, 228
   over–represented, 139–41, 145, 164–9,
      187–9, 196–7, 235–6, 238
   sexual harassment and abuse, 10, 53,
      84, 126, 154–5, 217–18, 241
   see also occupational categories;
      prostitution
Downer, Augusta, 158
Dundas, Jane, 239
Dundas, *Lord*, 117

economic assets, 1, 109, 235, 242
   see also age; convict mothers; health;
      internal migration; literacy; numeracy;
      occupations; skill
economic transition, 130–4, 147–58,
   215–16, 220, 227, 235
education, 79, 80, 123, 157
   formal, 122, 124, 142, 150–1, 226–8, 240

informal, 116, 124, 153–5, 226–9, 240
Elizabeth (no surname), 52, 58
Ellenborough, *Lord*, 104
Emigration Committee, 172, 173, 181
employment contracts, 121, 160
Emsley, Clive, 75, 94, 215
Enclosure, 4, 65, 130, 148
Engels, Friedrich, 6, 141, 155–6
England, 146–69, 235–6
   agricultural revolution, 147-9, 154,
      156–7
   declining living standards, 52–3, 112,
      157
   industrial revolution, 147–58
   position of women, 147–58
   regional differences, 167

Fahy, Margaret, 46
family production, *see* household sector
Farr, *Dr* William, 164
felonies and misdemeanours, 34, 37
Female Factory (Parramatta), 10–11, 110,
   193, 194, 201–2, 242
femininity
   and masculinity, 155–6
   essence of, 154, 217, 225–6
   loss of, 207–8, 216–19, 232
   see also heterosexual employment
Fielding, Henry, 64, 214
Finn, Catherine, 109–10, 131
First Fleet, 199, 204
first generation, *see* currency children
Fisher, Elizabeth, 160
Fitzgerald, Catherine, 183, 243
Fletcher, Brian, 194
Forbes, Francis, 172
   see also Emigration Committee
foreigners, 97, 136
Forster, Edward, 175, 184
   see also Committee for Promoting the
      Emigration of Single Women
Foster, Catherine, 160
Fry, Elizabeth, 209, 212
   see also Society for the Reformation of
      Female Prisoners

Garton, Stephen, 214
Gatrell, V. A. C., 95
gendered values, 203–6, 232
Gibbons, Bridget, 135, 137
Gibbons, Mary Anne, 135, 137
God's police, 180, 194
Golder, Hilary, 231
good women, 180–2
Greenwood, William, 243
Grenville, *Lord*, 103
Griffiths, Arthur, 99, 103, 207–11, 213

Grimes, Catherine, 142–4
Grivell, Eliza, 151
Guerry, M., 79
Gurney, Joseph John, 207
Guthrie, James, 208

Hadden, T. B., 95
Hague, Mary, 239
Hancock, Keith, 222
Harrington, Catherine, 52–3
Hart, Lydia, 158
Hay, Douglas, 219
health, 112–15
    see also height; shipboard mortality
height, 112–13, 157–8
heterosexual employment, 218
    see also sexual division of labour
Hirst, John, 11, 65, 223, 234
historical records
    Admiralty, 18
    court records, 19, 27, 31, 94
    Home Office, 18, 19
    hulk lists, 18, 19
    paucity of working-class accounts, 198,
        212
    see also convict indents
Hobart, *Lord*, 103
Hogan, J. F., 66
homosexuality, *see* sex im/balance
Hostettler, Eve, 226
household sector, 2, 3, 240–1
    and paid employment, 149, 153–4
    childcare, 2, 126, 235
    family production, 148, 235
    homemaking, 124, 180, 182, 230, 242
    reproduction, 2, 11, 148–9, 182, 184,
        230, 235
    undervalued, 226, 229–30
    see also education; marriage
Howells, Maria, 160
Hughes, Robert, 5, 76
Hugo, Victor, 63
human capital, *see* economic assets
Humphries, Caroline (alias Catherine), 17,
    28, 29, 231, 242
    crime, 43, 49, 54, 71
    economic assets, 110, 115, 123
Hunter, *Governor* John (NSW), 103, 199
Hunter, Thomas, 242
Hyde Park Barracks, 193

illegitimate children, 9, 52–3, 181
immigration, 13, 85, 102
    coerced, 114
    from Ireland, 134, 142
    pauper, 99, 173, 195
    to Australia, 170–97

to the US, 111, 172
    see also assisted immigrants; assisted
        immigration schemes; colonial labour
        demand; convicts; diet; Irish emigrant
        convicts
immorality, *see* bad behaviour; sexual
    terminology
intermittent employment, 75, 84, 86, 136,
    156, 215, 242
    see also seasonal shifts; unemployment
internal migration, 242
    and employment, 75, 90, 112, 155,
        159–60, 235
    brain–drain, 144, 236
    dangers, 75–6, 97, 136, 161
    England, 158–61
    Ireland, 134–9, 141–4
    see also criminal class; transportation
invasion, 1, 38, 231, 243
    see also colonisation
Ireland, 128–45, 235–6
    economy, 130–4
    international competition, 131–2
    over-representation, 129–30
    regional variations, 131–5
    size of population, 129
    Union with Great Britain, 133, 235
    see also Irish emigrant convicts
Irish emigrant convicts, 70, 129, 135,
    141–4, 159
    see also internal migration; literacy;
        numeracy; skill
Irish Famine, 66, 132, 134

Jack, from Lancashire, 155
Jackson, Randle, 64
Jardine, Anna, 49
Jeggings, Maria, 44
Jeggings, Sara, 44
Jones, David, 95
Jones, Gwenlliam, 158
journeying, 17, 97, 241–2
juveniles, 52, 56, 110–11

Kennedy, Bridget, 134
Kiernan, T. J., 67
King, *Governor* P. G. (NSW), 101, 103
King, Warder, 210
Kingston, Beverley, 230, 234, 240
Kussmaul, Anne, 112

labour aristocrats, 86
Lake, Marilyn, 11, 240
Lanarch, John, 203
Lang, *Reverend* Dr John Dunmore, 101,
    172, 195
language, 203, 216, 232

Linebaugh, Peter, 208
literacy, 27, 107, 115, 116, 123, 235–6, 242
  as skill, 228
  England, 159, 161–2
  immigrants, 185–6
  Ireland, 137
  Irish convict emigrants, 142–3
  paupers, 161–2
  prisoners, 162
  work habits, 116
London Season, 87–90
  see also crime
lower orders, 12, 14, 83, 86, 99, 107, 109, 234
  see also causes of crime; criminal class
Ludlow, Sarah, 239

Macarthur, James, 100, 200, 202
MacCluskey, Mary, 183, 243
Macnab, Ken, 10, 107
Macpherson, William, 189
  see also Committee of Emigrant Mechanics
Macquarie, Governor Lachlan (NSW), 26, 100, 101, 102, 103, 199
MacQueen, Thomas Potter, 172, 199
Madgwick, R. B., 184, 229–30
Magarey, Susan, 56
magistrates (NSW), 200, 202
  see also colonial labour relations
Malmesbury, Earl of, 221
Marjoribanks, Alexander, 66, 67
marriage, 101, 102, 107, 241
  convict wives, 101, 102, 107, 124–6, 226, 233
  immigration, 175, 179–82, 185
  see also conjugal status; convict mothers; sex im/balance; working-class values
Marsden, Samuel, 9, 201, 218
Marshall, John, 175, 195–6
Mayhew, Henry, 40, 64, 162, 169, 221, 232
  criminal class and historians, 105–6, 221–4
  criminal women, 208–9
  London, 78–82, 88
  neglected source, 221–2
  prostitution, 9–10, 206–7, 219
  redeeming workers, 213–16
  transportation, 99
  see also moral entrepreneurs
McBride, Theresa, 112
McCarthy, Honora, 46
McCarthy, Mary, 49–50, 210
McCave, Henry, 46
McKey, Elizabeth, 239
McLeay, *Colonial Secretary* Alexander, 172

McQueen, Humphrey, 7
menstruation, 205
middle-class values, 203–6, 211, 217–20, 232
Miles, William Augustus, 213
  see also moral entrepreneurs
mobility, *see* internal migration
Molesworth, *Sir* William, 200
  see also Select Committee on Transportation
Molton, Susannah (alias Lavinia), 53, 58
Moore, James, 64, 71, 97
moral entrepreneurs, 77, 213, 232
  see also contemporary social critics
moral judgements, 63–7, 82, 233–4
  and economic categories, 78–6, 226, 230
  and servants, 166
  see also bad behaviour; character; colonial employers; gendered values; middle-class values; working-class values
Morris (alias Burke alias Morrison), Mary
Mudd, Ann, 208
Mudie, James, 99, 100–1, 103–4, 199–200, 202–3, 206, 219
Murnane, Mary, 11

Napoleonic Wars, 130–2, 135, 149
Needham, Anne, 31
Newman, Julia St Clair, 210–11
Nicholas, Stephen, 229–30
Nichols, Elizabeth, 239
Nichols, Ellen, 239
Nihil, *Governor* of Millbank, 211
Nolan, Frances, 151
nomadic tribes, *see* internal migration
non–market sector, *see* household sector
numeracy, 115–16, 123, 235–6, 242
  age-heaping, 27, 115
  immigrants, 186
  Ireland, 136–7
  Irish convict emigrants, 143

O'Farrell, Patrick, 66
occupational categories
  allworkers, 121, 127, 139, 154, 160, 228
  bakers, 191
  bootmakers, 151, 193
  charring, 90
  children's maids, 191
  cooks, 10, 121, 159, 188–91, 228
  dairymaids, 118, 160, 173, 188–91
  dealers, 121
  domestic servants, 90, 118, 121, 139, 154–5, 156, 160, 165–9, 173–80, 188–91
  dressmakers, 90, 121, 151, 159, 166, 188–91, 227

occupational categories, *contd*
  factory work, 155, 156, 160, 166
  farm servants, 139–40, 160, 166; 173,
    188–91
  hat binders, 10
  house servants, 10
  housekeepers, 159, 189–91
  housemaids, 118, 121, 141
  kitchenmaids, 118, 121, 141, 189–91,
    228
  laundryworkers, 118, 121, 141, 149,
    166–7, 188–91, 227
  manufacturers and crafts, 117–8, 121,
    151, 155, 166–9, 188, 227
  midwives, 121, 188
  millinery, 166, 188, 227
  needlewomen, 90, 166, 188–91
  nursemaids, 118, 188–91, 228
  outworkers, 149, 156
  schoolmistresses, 121, 188
  servants, 118, 121
  shoemakers, 151
  textile producers, 121, 140–1, 155,
    166–9, 188, 191
  thorough servants, 191
  washerwomen, 118, 121, 149, 153–4,
    166–7, 189
  see also crime; internal migration;
    occupations; skill classification
occupations, 116–21, 236–7
  colonial, 189–93, 227, 239, 242
  dishonourable trades, 151–2
  England, 163–8
  immigrants, 173–80, 187–93
  Ireland, 137–41
  multiskilled, 117, 118, 121, 123, 236
  prisoners, 167–8
  specificity, 117–18
  see also skill
Old Bailey (Central Criminal Court), 47,
  49–50, 53, 59, 83, 87, 93
Osborne, Alick, 199
Owen, E., 207–8
Oxley, Sara, 45, 55

paradox, 11–13, 102–9
  see also colonial economic development
Partridge, Susan, 149
pawnbrokers and shops, 47–8, 59, 70, 74,
  92, 152
Payne, H. S., 4–5, 96, 222
Peel, *Sir* Robert, 38, 40, 64
Peel's Bobbies (Peelers), 39, 87
penitentiary, 38, 211
Perrott, Monica, 10, 240
Philips, David, 95
Phillip, *Governor* Arthur (NSW), 103, 182

pious perjury, 50
Piso, *Magistrate*, 63
police forces, 39, 51, 79, 213
  see also Peel's Bobbies
political prisoners, 3, 36, 64, 66, 169, 234
poor (casual and undeserving), *see* classes
  redefined; criminal class
Portland, Duke of, 103
post convictions, 96
poverty, 12, 60, 75–6, 83–6, 89, 105, 215,
  236
  England, 152–3
  Ireland, 134–5
  see also causes of crime; prostitution
prior convictions, 41–5, 56–8, 70–1, 75, 84,
  93, 224
Prison Discipline Society, 111
prisoners, *see* age; literacy; numeracy;
  occupations; skill
prisons, 80–1, 105
  Brixton, 208
  Cold Bath Fields, 81, 101
  House of Correction, 84
  Millbank, 104, 206, 208–11
  Newgate, 207, 208, 209–10
  see also criminality
Pritchard, Hannah, 239
prosecution rates, 76, 78, 87
prostitution, 6–7, 8–10, 76, 85, 94, 124,
  155, 217–19, 223–6
  and criminality, 206–7
  and poverty, 153
  and rude and unfeminine labours,
    218–19
  bad women, 7, 217, 231
  colonial demand, 8–9, 60, 241
  convict women, 6–7, 9–10, 101, 206
  double standard, 217–18
  only identity, 7, 198, 226, 230–1
  robbing clients, 44, 47, 53, 92
  see also bad behaviour; Binny, John;
    criminal class; Mayhew, Henry; sex
    im/balance; sexual terminology;
    transportation

Racey, Sarah, 158
Raine, Elizabeth, 242
Redgrave, Samuel, 218
reform, 11, 12, 83, 108, 212–13
regional differences, 115, 116, 121, 123,
  130, 186
religion, 79, 97, 134, 143–4
  lack of, 101, 107, 232
reproduction, *see* household sector
Revlet, Mary, 53, 54
Ricardo, David, 144
Riley, Mary Ann, 59

Robinson, Frederick William, 211–12
Robinson, Portia, 11–13, 31, 67, 230, 234, 240
  contemporary views, 9–10, 218, 219
  London, 83–6
Robson, Lloyd, 4–8, 66, 67, 107, 221–4, 233
Roe, Michael, 11, 230, 234
Rose (alias Rowles), Caroline, 44
Royal Commission on the Constabulary, 216, 222
Rudé, George, 48, 49, 58, 77, 94, 232
Russell, John, 38
Ryan, Lyndall, 11, 240

Salt, Annette, 10, 240
Schedvin, M. B. and C. B., 66, 87–8, 107–8, 222–3
Schwartz, R. B., 214
Scott, Elizabeth, 59
season shifts, 88–90, 96, 141
Select Committee on Secondary Punishments, 212
Select Committee on the Education of the Poorer Classes in England and Wales, 161
Select Committee on Transportation, 19, 100, 196, 199–200, 221; Molesworth report, 4, 27, 181
selection
  basis, 60, 63, 97, 109
  possible factors, 60, 168, 236–7, 240
  see also sentencing
sentencing, 55–60, 75, 76
  capital sentences, 63, 64, 220
  commuted, 37, 39, 45
  rates, 87, 88–9
  regional variations, 71–2
  variability by crime, 55–60
sex im/balance, 107, 175, 180–2, 229, 238
  and evil, 181–2
  among immigrants, 183
  see also black and white relations; marriage
sexual division of labour, 148–58, 165
  see also bad behaviour; heterosexual employment
sexual terminology, 100, 203, 212, 217–20, 232
  and immigrants, 195
  damned whores, 6, 8, 194–5, 199–200, 202, 204, 206, 217–20, 223–6
Shannahan (then Greenwood), Margaret, 29, 30f., 32, 54, 64, 130, 242–3
  crime, 44, 71
  economic assets, 110, 115, 118, 123
Sharpe, J. A., 94

Shaw, A. G. L., 4–7, 66, 221–3, 233
Sheppard, Sophia, 158
Shergold, Peter, 229–30
shipboard mortality, 17, 113–15
ships (convict)
  Amphitrite, 113–14
  Andromeda, 54
  Calcutta, 31
  Caroline, 29, 54
  City of Edinburgh, 46
  Competitor, 17, 28, 31, 44, 98, 142, 151, 158
  Diana, 151
  Elizabeth, 20
  Fanny, 114
  Friendship, 204
  Lady Juliana, 103
  Lady Penrhyn, 199, 204
  Neptune, 31
  Neva, 114
  Numa, 44
  Palambam, 134
  Planter, 144
  Princess Charlotte, 54
  Princess Royal, 31
  Pyramus, 20
  Recovery, 21, 99
  Roslin Castle, 45, 51
  Sovereign, 151
  Whitby, 46
  see also shipboard mortality
ships (immigrant)
  Marianne, 172
  Red Rover, 183, 194, 243
  Princess Royal, 195
  David Scott, 195
shipwreck, 113–14
Silk, Ann, 239
skill, 121–4, 235–6
  and age, 123
  and literacy, 122–3
  England, 159, 163–4
  historiography, 105–9, 226–30, 233
  immigrants, 187–9
  Ireland, 138
  Irish convict emigrants, 143
  stock of skills, defined, 117
skill classification, 121, 127, 164, 228
Smith, Babette, 11, 31, 151, 240
Smith, Bernard, 63
Smith, Charles Neville, 59
Smith, Julia, 46
Smith, *Reverend* Sydney, 105, 219
Snell, K. D. M., 226
social control, 76, 79, 81, 134
Society for the Reformation of Female Prisoners, 209, 212

Stanford, Dinah, 158
Steel, Ann Maria, 44
Stephen, *Judge* Alfred, 81
Steward, *Commander*, 242
Stewart (alias Curtis), Ann, 151
stolen goods, 47–51, 54, 59
    alcohol, 50–1
    clothes, 49, 54–5, 69, 70, 71, 72, 74, 86,
        92
    fabric, 49, 69, 70, 74, 92
    food and animals, 49, 69, 70, 74–5, 92
    handkerchief, 92, 93
    household items, 49, 69, 70, 74, 92
    jewellery, 47–8, 69, 70, 74, 75, 92, 93
    money, 48, 69, 70, 72, 74, 92, (in
        London) 82, 93
    value of, 49–50, 92
    watches, 92, 93
Stuart, Factory Inspector for Scotland, 142
Sturma, Michael, 8, 11, 218
Sullivan, Martin, 11
Summers, Anne, 8, 60
surgeon-superintendents, 19–20, 113, 114,
    242
    see also Bowes Smyth, Arthur;
        Cunningham, Peter
Surman, Elizabeth, 85–6
Symons, Jelinger C., 50, 64, 162, 218–19
Symons, *Subcommissioner*, 218

Tasmania, *see* Van Diemen's Land
Thomas, Elizabeth, 59
Thomas, Susan, 240
Tipping, Marjorie, 31
Tobias, J. J., 64
transportation, 37–8, 39, 98–9, 101
    and enforced prostitution, 8–9, 241
    and family separation, 111, 125–6, 185,
        241
    as beneficence, 45–6, 58, 136
    as desirable, 104–5
    as imperialism, 98, 104
    as international migration, 3
    return from, 34, 55, 62
    to America, 37–8, 98–9
    see also British laws

Ullathorne, *Father, Bishop* William, 66, 67,
    100, 199, 200, 201
unemployment, 4, 12, 75, 83, 85, 89, 96,
    125, 242
    England, 148–58
    Ireland, 134
    see also intermittent employment
urbanisation, 81, 82
    see also causes of crime; crime

vagrancy, *see* crime; poor
Van Diemen's Land
    and New South Wales, 67, 129, 134
    convict ship to, 17
    duration of transportation to, 38
    Female Factory, 194
    historiography on, 5, 10, 11, 13, 96, 107,
        114
    immigration, 175, 179, 182, 195
    numbers to, 31
    prostitutes to, 6
    see also Arthur, *Governor* George
    victims, 51–5, 69, 70, 234
        anonymous, 51, 61, 92
        benefactors, 84
        children, 46, 86
        clients, 53, 62, 92
        employers, 53–4, 59, 69, 70, 92
        houses, 69, 70
        infants, 52–3
        lodging keepers, 50, 62, 69, 70, 84, 92
        masters and mistresses, 53–4, 58, 59, 62,
            69, 70, 74, 92
        miscellaneous properties, 53
        persons, 53, 69
        relatives, 53–4
        shop or shopkeepers, 59, 62, 69
        streets, 70
        see also prostitution
village Hampdens, 3, 6, 67, 222

wages
    colonial wages, 173, 175, 179, 189–90
    eroded, 152
    high, 86
    independent wage, 148, 155
    low, 4, 10, 53, 79, 84, 125, 215
    wage profile, 122
Wakefield, Edward Gibbon, 64
Wakefield, Harriet, 17
    crime, 29, 44
    economic assets, 110, 115, 123
Ward, Russel, 10, 107
Watson, Susannah, 11
Watts, Elizabeth, 151
Weatherburn, Hilary, 10, 240
welfare, 65, 75, 82, 83, 213–14
    Female Factory, 194
    Ireland, 134–5
    Poor Law, 79, 214
West, *Reverend* John, 46
Western Australia, 31, 38
Weston, Maria, 49
Whately, *Archbishop* Richard, 104
Wilde, Oscar, 28
Wilkinson, Elizabeth, 151
Williams, Ann, 210

Williams, John, 10, 31, 67
Williams, Sarah, 239
Wilson, Ann, 52–3
Wood, George Arnold, 4, 5, 6, 65, 222, 232
Woodward, Francis J., 66
workhouses, 45, 88, 105, 153, 161–2, 167
working-class values, 9, 81, 82, 217–18,
    220–1
  see also bad behaviour; economic
    transition
Wright, S., 201

Yellop, Ann, 151
Young, Arthur, 214

Please remember that this is a library book,
and that it belongs only temporarily to each
person who uses it. Be considerate. Do
not write in this, or any, library book.

Printed in the United Kingdom
by Lightning Source UK Ltd.
2013